Principles of Organisational Behaviour: An Irish Text

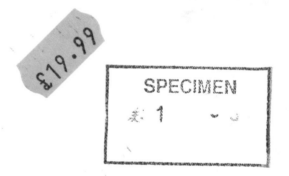

PRINCIPLES OF ORGANISATIONAL BEHAVIOUR: AN IRISH TEXT

Michael Morley, Sarah Moore,
Noreen Heraty and Patrick Gunnigle

GILL & MACMILLAN

Gill & Macmillan Ltd
Goldenbridge
Dublin 8
with associated companies throughout the world

© Michael Morley, Sarah Moore, Noreen Heraty and Patrick Gunnigle 1998
0 7171 2668 4

Index compiled by Helen Litton

Print origination by Andy Gilsenan

Printed by ColourBooks Ltd, Dublin

The paper used in this book is made from the wood pulp of managed forests.
For every tree felled, at least one tree is planted, thereby renewing natural resources.

A catalogue record is available for this book from the British Library.

Contents

Preface

There are few laws or absolutes that govern 'proper' conduct for organisational stakeholders or predict with any certainty their behaviour. Arguably we have learned, through empirical investigation, as much about those things that do not work, as we have about those things that do work. The experience of most social scientists demonstrates that there is a multiplicity of factors which shape and determine the behaviour of people at work, and consequently any investigation of behaviour in the workplace necessitates a rather broad treatment.

In this book we seek to describe and examine the complex work organisation, from a behavioural perspective. Our concern, especially, is to provide some explanations of why people behave the way they do at work. In this respect organisational behaviour as a subject can be seen to be interdisciplinary and concerned with integrating explanations, messages and lessons from the fields of psychology, social psychology, political science and sociology insofar as they relate to people at work and assist in explaining and predicting workplace interactions. Indeed, virtually all of the founding fathers of organisational behaviour such as Kurt Lewin, Elton Mayo, Rensis Likert and Victor Vroom, were researchers from older social/psychological disciplines, many of whom found new homes in schools of management and business. While these multifaceted interdisciplinary roots have given rise to concerns about the utility of organisational behaviour in some quarters, we have come a long way in this fledgling discipline. Organisational behaviour is now viewed as a serious and intellectually rigorous area of research and teaching. In this book, in an attempt to provide some answers to the 'Why' of human behaviour in the workplace, we examine individual, group and organisational processes. Sources of individual difference (personality, perception, motivation, stress and learning), group processes (communications, groups and group dynamics, and team and team dynamics) and organisational processes (leadership, culture, work design, conflict, power, politics, ethics and organisational change and development) are all dealt with in some detail. Here we have had to make hard choices. No single text could hope to adequately engage all aspects of this multidisciplinary subject. We have chosen on the basis that the areas covered are those most likely to be relevant to the potential readership of this book.

Limerick
March 1998

CHAPTER 1

Organisational Behaviour in Perspective

LEARNING OBJECTIVES
- To introduce and define the concept of organisational behaviour.
- To highlight the interdisciplinary nature of the field.
- To describe dominant methodologies in organisational behaviour.
- To examine the changing nature of organisations and their environments.

INTRODUCTION

Historically, the precursor of modern 'organisation' consisted of the medieval guild structure, a simple tripartite structure between the apprentice, the journeyman and the master based upon a system of task-oriented status structures in which obedience to a wide range of technical rules was required (Offe, 1976; Hardy and Clegg, 1996). The emergence of industrial society brought with it a new order dominated by complex institutional arrangements not easily understood by reference to the largely agrarian society from which they had sprung. We now live in an organisational/institutional world from which we can rarely escape (Huczynski and Buchanan, 1991; Furnham, 1997). Large-scale organisations have revolutionised the economic, technical, political, social and cultural fabric of our society, and whether as internal/direct or external/indirect stakeholder, they play an important role in all our lives. Purposeful large-scale organisation has become one of the most important resources of the developed world and one which most developing regions eagerly embrace. This complexity has given rise to a body of knowledge on theories of industrial/business management and corporate governance and control which can be intellectually stimulating and practically relevant. There are many ways one can conceptualise the elements of organisational design. To understand this complexity and to analyse organisations from different perspectives is an important area of knowledge (Dawson, 1996; Kotter *et al*, 1979). Achieving it, on the other hand, is a difficult task because both the way in which the phenomenon of organising is characterised and the theoretical and the methodological equipment thought most appropriate to its analysis have undergone significant changes in recent years (Reed, 1992).

DEFINING ORGANISATIONAL BEHAVIOUR

The field of organisational behaviour is a relatively new field that has evolved from the older disciplines of psychology, sociology, political science and from some of the early work on management (see Figure 1.1). Psychologists concern themselves with studying and attempting to understand individual behaviour in a variety of settings. Of significance here has been research on learning/behaviour modification, personality, perception, attitudes and stress. Sociology refers to the study of human social life, groups and societies, and demonstrates the need to take a much broader view of why we are as we are and why we act as we do. Arguably sociologists have made their most significant contribution to organisational behaviour through their research on group dynamics, conflict, culture, power and communications. Political scientists have long been concerned with the study of individual and group behaviour within the political arena. Aspects of organisational behaviour particularly informed by political science include conflict, power and organisational politics. Management, referring to the body of knowledge on how to manage to achieve desired results through the efficient utilisation of human and material resources, provided the impetus for the eventual emergence of organisational behaviour through its early research on bureaucracy, classical organisational theory and job design (see Figure 1.1).

Most scholars would agree that organisational behaviour began to emerge as a mature field of study in the late 1950s and early 1960s. Of particular significance in bringing about this development was the landmark study at the Western Electric Hawthorne Plant which eventually gave rise to the Human Relations Movement. Furthermore, in rationalising the rise of the social sciences in management literature and thinking, Baritz (1960, p. 191) in a systematic examination of the relationship between research and knowledge on the one hand and society on the other argues that: '. . . management came to believe in the importance of understanding human behaviour because it became convinced that this was one sure way of improving its main weapon in the struggle for power, the profit margin'.

Perrow (1967) in his seminal critical essay on complex organisations argues that the explanation of organisational behaviour is not primarily in the formal structures of the organisation, the announcement of goals and purposes or in the output of goods and services. Rather, he suggests, it is that submerged part of the iceberg, or the myriad of subterranean processes of informal groups, conflicts between groups, recruitment policies, dependencies upon outside groups and constituencies, the striving for prestige, community values, the local community power structure, and legal institutions. For the purposes of this book organisational behaviour is defined as *'the study of individual group and organisational processes as a means of explaining and predicting behaviour in the workplace'*. Figure 1.2 outlines the processes examined and provides a schema of the book.

2

Figure 1.1: The emergence of organisational behaviour

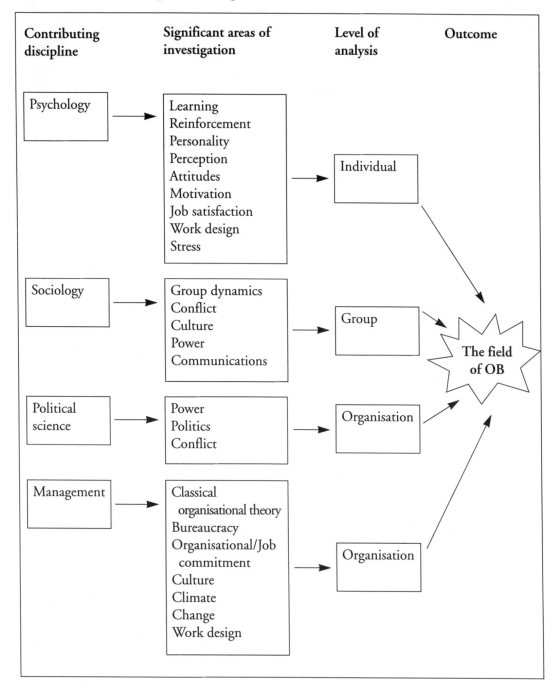

Figure 1.2: The nature of organisational behaviour

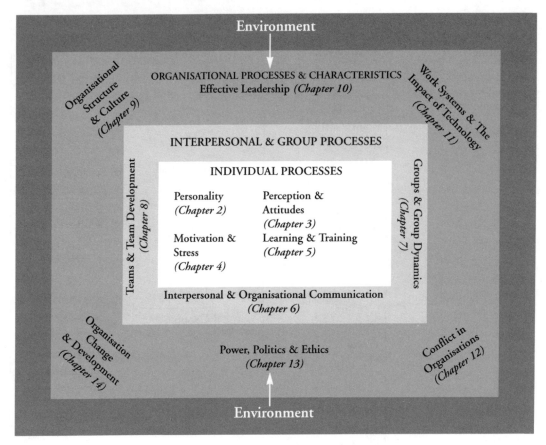

The study of organisational behaviour must be framed in the organisational context as a work arena. An organisation may simply be defined as a collection of persons working within a particular structural configuration to achieve group and/or individual objectives. The model outlines the key determinants of behaviour in organisations examined in this text and is consistent with the broad sweep of the extant literature in identifying the core elements of what constitutes the subject area of organisational behaviour. Key questions arising include: What causes employees to behave the way they do? To what extent is employee behaviour predictable? What are the determinants of personality and what is the relevance of personality research for organisations? How significant are perception and attitudes in governing employee behaviour? What motivates the workforce and why do some employees perform better than others? What is the reality of organisational stress? What is the value of investment in individual learning and can organisations learn? How do organisations develop a communication-rich environment? What is the rational for the renewed emphasis on group/team dynamics in organisations? Is there one best way of structuring for organisational effectiveness? Does culture matter? What is the most potent way of leading? How do managerial choices concerning work systems design affect worker satisfaction and performance? Is all organisational conflict dysfunctional? What makes organisations political arenas? Must organisations be socially responsible? Can change be managed in organisations?

Arguably therefore, in explaining the nature of organisational behaviour, it may not be possible to separate the situational context of the organisation from the nature of the individual: rather they interact in complex ways. Only through the development of an awareness of these issues and their interconnectedness can one build knowledge in the field that is organisational behaviour.

STUDYING WORKPLACE BEHAVIOUR: FROM POSITIVISM TO NATURALISM

Like any of the behavioural sciences, organisational behaviour requires the utilisation of rigorous methodologies to better understand human behaviour in the workplace. There is no consensus about the best way to understand and describe social interaction at organisational level. The researcher must select from competing and conflicting views that, in turn, will likely give direction to all aspects of the enquiry. Gill and Johnson (1991) highlight that most researchers experience at least some tension between a view that highlights the supremacy of enquiry modelled on physical science on the one hand, and the necessity to contextualise and individualise the investigation on the other. This selection of paradigmatic choice is therefore the starting point. Broadly speaking, the researcher can take a *positivist* or a *naturalist* route. In this way organisational behaviour researchers can be seen to be eclectic with differing philosophical approaches giving rise to different research methods, depending upon the precise area of investigation.

Positivism assumes that there is an objective reality that is measurable and thus a preference for quantitative approaches to data collection is preferred. This is so as there is a widespread tendency to view quantitative survey and experimental research as suited to the confirmation or rejection of theoretical propositions and hypotheses (McNeill, 1990). Positivism assumes that the world is knowable in objective terms – that there is an objective reality that can be discovered and explained by laws, theories etc. Making these discoveries entails a marked preference for quantitative data collection methods.

Positivist researchers believe that there is a single reality that can be segmented and broken down into quantifiable units or variables that can be independently studied, and for which causal relationships can be identified. In this way it is believed that the various aspects of behaviour in the workplace can be described and linked to particular causes. Once the causal relationship is known, it is believed that predictions can be made about the situations in which certain behaviours recur. In this way positivism assumes that for every action there is a corresponding cause. As a result this approach takes its logic from the model of the physical sciences and applies this logic to the social world. Tiernan (1996, p. 135) summarises well the central tenets of this approach:

> The positivist approach assumes that social research is similar in nature to that of the natural and physical sciences, namely, that knowledge can be viewed in an objective way and that such an objective reality can be developed and explained by causal theories and laws using quantitative analysis. As a consequence, in operational terms, positivism assumes that social phenomena like those of the natural and physical sciences can be broken down into quantifiable variables, studied independently and that theories and laws that predict future observations through causal analysis and hypothesis testing can be developed. The logic of the physical and natural sciences is, therefore, imposed on the social sciences. The tendency is to reduce human action to the status of automatic responses achieved by external stimuli, ignoring the subjective dimension of human action, namely, the internal logic and interpretative processes by which such action is created.

Among the most prominent positivist research methods are *laboratory experiments, field experiments* and, to a lesser extent, *quantitative surveys*.

Laboratory experiments involve the researcher in testing the effects of one or more independent variables on one or more dependent variables through the utilisation of both control and experimental groups which are randomly selected. Here the independent variable refers to that variable which has been identified as the possible cause of the phenomena under investigation and the dependent variable is one that is thought to be causally linked to the independent variable, and is therefore expected to change. Thus, in what is essentially an artificial environment that is dedicated to preserving controlled conditions, the researcher manipulates an independent variable and deduces that any changes in the dependent variable are as a result of that manipulation. In experiments of this nature, the researcher trades off realism/naturalism for precision and control. Associated advantages with this research method include the high level of control maintained by the researcher, and the possibility of isolating only those variables under investigation and therefore eliminating 'experimental error'. Disadvantages include its artificial nature and so its possible irrelevance to the real world (what naturalists describe as 'naïve realism'), the potential emergence of the 'hawthorne effect' whereby participants alter their behaviour when they know they are under investigation, and issues associated with deception and ethics in social research.

Field experiments involve the researcher sampling and investigating behaviour in natural situations rather than attempting to replicate behaviour in a laboratory. Here, the researcher similarly utilises both control and experimental groups. While the natural setting is less controlled it clearly is more realistic than any laboratory-generated scenario and hence the field experiment typically provides the most generalisable findings.

Quantitative surveys are designed to collect data that allow the researcher to describe and/or analyse the world as it is and lie in the middle of the positivism/naturalism continuum. Here the researcher typically defines an area of research and then designs a set of questions that will elicit the attitudes, beliefs and experiences of the respondents as they relate to the research under investigation. Typically, a sample of respondents is selected to represent a larger group. Respondents are then surveyed and the researcher makes inferences from their responses about the larger population. Among the key phases associated with quantitative survey design are: choosing the topic to be studied; developing core research hypotheses; isolation of the population to be surveyed; preparation of the research questionnaire; conducting a pilot test; selecting a representative sample from the population; collecting the data; processing and analysing the results. Particular advantages associated with survey designs include their ability to be highly specific in terms of research objective, the high level of anonymity afforded to respondents, the possibility of targeting large numbers of people to be studied and the subsequent generalisability of results to the wider population under investigation, and the possibility of comparison of results with other populations. Among the disadvantages are the limited scope for response, particularly where the questionnaire is highly structured, and the potential problem of lack of validity as the method uncovers what people say they are doing when they are filling the questionnaire rather than what they are actually doing.

In recent times, there has been considerable interest in alternative ways of understanding organisations. A growing number of researchers have become suspicious of the orthodox view that organisations can best be understood by using a positivistic perspective. The growing critique of positivism and the search for alternative epistemological and methodological foundations for the social sciences has led many researchers to veer towards the qualitative method of analysis. To this group, according to Gill and Johnson (1991), the positivist approach, with its search for an objective reality and universally applicable rules, has failed to capture and illuminate the substance, inter-relatedness and totality of organisational life. The more subjective approach, described as naturalism, has parted company with the natural physical science methodology, and borrows from a number of sources, such as anthropology, sociology and psychology, in an attempt to find more meaningful ways of investigating and understanding the reality of organisational life. This more qualitative approach to research is depicted as placing an emphasis on the discovery of the novel and the unfamiliar which its more unstructured approach to data gathering is deemed to facilitate.

Naturalists argue that in contrast to physical objects and animals, human beings attach meaning to surrounding events and, from these interpretations, select courses of meaningful action which they can reflect upon and monitor (Gill and Johnson, 1991). Such subjective processes, it is argued, are the sources of human behaviour explanations. Therefore, humans, unlike physical objects, can become aware of predictions made about their behaviour and can alter their behaviour, thereby negating or moderating the prediction. The aim of the naturalist approach is to understand how people make sense of their worlds, with human behaviour seen as purposive and meaningful rather than externally determined.

Thus, naturalistic researchers assume that objective knowledge is not available and stress the subjective experience of individuals. The naturalistic researcher believes that there are multiple realities, subjectively constructed within each social setting, available only by considering the whole organisation. These socially constructed realities shift and change and thus cannot be predicted before an inquiry, or completely controlled during research. To the naturalist the only way to understand an organisation is to become immersed in its world and inquire into whole systems, searching for changes, patterns and inter-relationships.

According to Diesing (1972), the natural approach 'includes the belief that human systems tend to develop a characteristic wholeness. They are not simply a loose collection of variables; they have a unity that manifests itself in nearly every part.'

Similarly Tiernan (1996, p. 128) adds that:

In contrast to the deductive research methodology of the positivist approach, naturalism favours a more inductive approach. The essence of the inductive approach is that in order to understand social phenomena, such as an organisation, the researcher has to become immersed in its world and inquire into whole systems searching for patterns and explanations. Induction, therefore, begins with an observation of the empirical setting and then proceeds to construct theories about observed phenomena.

From this perspective it emerges that everything is interwoven, and it is not necessary to distinguish between cause and effect. The over-riding goal of the research is to provide a contextually bound picture of what is going on and to illuminate as much as possible how the organisation has constructed itself.

In order to understand whole systems and whole organisations, naturalistic inquirers favour qualitative research methods such as *participant observation, in-depth open-ended/semi-structured interviewing,* and *documentary evidence.* These are the methods that allow the researcher to interact with the field site as collaboratively and intimately as possible. The purpose is to collect what Geertz (1970) has termed 'thick descriptions' of the way people create and sustain a social experience.

Participant observation, originally associated with the early work of the Chicago school of sociology, involves the researcher playing a dual role, namely that of participant in everyday organisational activities and that of observer and recorder of the specific processes and interactions which are being investigated. Here the researcher does not attempt to manipulate aspects of the research environment, but rather he/she records as much information as possible about the situation, its characteristics and processes. While categories of behaviour may be selected for observation and recording methods devised, typically, participant observation is unstructured with the researcher being prepared to collect all data which might prove relevant to the inquiry. As a research tool it is primarily descriptive, often focusing on intra-group and inter-group interactions within organisations. Advantages associated with this form of enquiry include its ability to reflect the reality of organisational life as it is occurring, and its capacity to provide direct information through watching what people do and recording what they say, rather than asking about attitudes and feelings. Among the potential disadvantages are the possibility of the researcher being less than objective as a result of being acculturated into the environment to the detriment of his/her research independence, and the potential for loss of control. Typically, it also requires considerable time commitments from the researcher.

The interview, typically described as a conversation with a purpose, is one of the most common methods of inquiry in organisational behaviour research. Interviews differ in terms of the extent to which they are structured. Semi-structured interviewing implies a questioning process which has been generically organised by the researcher before the interview takes place. Conversely, open-ended or unstructured interviewing implies that no predetermined structure has been prepared by the interviewer other than a reflection on what overarching areas the research is examining. Arguably therefore it is closer to the 'true conversation' than are more structured interviews. Particular advantages include its flexibility and adaptability and its potential to deliver new or additional information through non-verbal cues. Disadvantages include the potential for interviewer bias, its time-consuming nature and the lack of anonymity for respondents.

Documentary evidence in organisational behaviour research refers primarily to written documents such as books, company magazines, papers, newsletters, memos, minutes of meetings and noticeboard displays. It may also refer to video material. Thus, it involves an analysis of materials that have been produced by individuals or organisations, not the researcher. This technique requires that the researcher do an in-depth content analysis of the documents in an attempt to make valid inferences from the data contained in the documents. In order that content analysis be executed effectively, the researcher must have a clear research question, make decisions about what sampling strategy to use when collecting documents, define the recording unit (typically the frequency with which a particular word occurs in the various documents being content analysed) and construct categories for analysis. Advantages associated with this research method include its unobtrusive nature and its potential for the provision of longitudinal data at relatively low cost. Common disadvantages include the possibility of bias or distortion as documents used are typically written for purposes other than that of the research. The establishment of causal relationships is also problematic.

THE NEW ENVIRONMENT OF ORGANISATION

The revolution of change occurring in organisations which has been well documented in the extant literature over the past twenty years supports the claim that an appreciation of organisational behaviour, and of the methods available for understanding it, has never been more important. The major source of this revolution, according to Block (1992), is the growing realisation that tight controls, greater work pressure, more clearly defined jobs, and tighter supervision have, in recent years, run their course in terms of their ability to give organisations productivity gains. Buchanan and McCalman (1989) note that the strategic imperative of the 1990s has heightened the argument for a more comprehensive approach to organisational design and work structuring, and set it within a new macro context defined by developments in labour and product markets, trading conditions and manufacturing technology.

The need for flexibility

In recent years we have witnessed the emergence of a debate on different ways of engaging and utilising labour in both the personnel management and the economics literature (Atkinson, 1984; Briggs, 1991). It would appear that shifts in employment structure and the changing economic environment, coupled with changing individual priorities, have led to a greater variation in the forms of employment, with a trend away from traditional employment arrangements to more 'atypical' employment forms, atypical employment being defined as any form of employment which deviates from the full-time permanent format. Accompanying these changes, there have been significant changes in work patterns. Largely due to the recession of the 1980s, the composition of the workforce has changed. Curson (1986) highlights a number of important international trends:

- Reduction in the size of the workforce in some countries has led to an examination of how to make best use of those employed.
- Though currently falling in Ireland, unemployment with unions and employees more concerned and prepared to consider different ways of working in order to retain jobs.
- Change in company philosophy, with an increased concentration on the core activities and skills and a willingness to let others provide periphery services in order to

be more flexible and meet demands, with commitment to employing permanent staff.
- Increased competition from abroad, which has led many to look at the work patterns of their foreign competitors.
- More flexibility in response to demand.

Overall, therefore, there would appear to be three core needs: to reduce unit costs, to respond quickly to environmental changes, and to meet the demands of the 'new' knowledge workforce.

The 'new' workforce

One could argue that there has been a general increase in employee expectations over the years. This is particularly true in the Irish context with the existence of a large, young, well-educated workforce (Gunnigle and Morley, 1993). Better-educated employees can offer employers more; however, they also expect more. Increasingly, many of the most progressive, entrepreneurial and talented people are no longer willing to commit their working lives in a typical pattern to one employer (Brewster *et al.*, 1994). This has had, and continues to have, its influence on management style, contributing to a decline in autocratic management. Recent contributions such as Vaill (1982), Perry (1984), Moss-Kanter (1983) and Quinn-Mills (1991) consequently highlight the need to empower employees in an attempt to make the organisation more effective. Such empowerment is necessary in order to develop a highly skilled, flexible, co-ordinated, motivated, committed, productive workforce and a leaner, flatter, more responsive organisation. Lawler (1986), commenting on the difference between the 'new' organisation and more traditional ones suggests that: 'almost no aspect of the organisation is left untouched. The nature of jobs, the structure, the reward system, the personnel management system are all changed in significant ways'.

He is therefore advocating an integrative approach to the structuring of work and the management of the human factor. Inherent in the concept of a 'new workforce' is the notion that a basic reassessment of the value of an individual's worth to the organisation has taken place, with many of the core assumptions of the traditional model being both challenged and rejected. In this respect, Mooney (1989) suggests that it is important to distinguish between 'system' and 'value' changes within an organisation. A system change simply encompasses changed methodology; value changes, he suggests, run deeper. The change from the control (traditional) model to the commitment (new) model is said to be of the second order. Clearly, while system changes are a central focus in the 'new' organisation, they are driven by and maintained by a value change in relation to a revised understanding of workplace relations. The concept therefore of the new organisation represents a change in the underlying value system of an organisation. The worth and value placed on the commitment of the workforce, and the effort made by organisations to solicit this, provides a key conceptual difference between a control and a commitment ethos. The traditional notion of an individual as simply an extension of the machine has given way to a belief that employees feel that work is important and want to contribute to it (see Mooney, 1989).

The total quality management environment

The increased emphasis on quality has led many organisations to adopt a total quality management approach in an attempt to provide for full customer satisfaction at economical costs, and achieve competitive advantage over rivals. Quality has become a crucial hinge for business success or failure in today's quality performance-oriented markets, a fact that has been emphasised in the literature (Collard, 1989; Harrison, 1992). Feigenbaum (1983) stated:

> essential to the development of zero defects in the products and services provided by an organisation is a recognised quality system. This is an agreed company wide and plant wide work structure documented in effective, integrated, technical and managerial procedures, for the guiding co-ordinated actions of the workforce, the machines, and the information of the company and plant, in the best and most practical ways to assure customer quality satisfaction and economical costs of quality.

Therefore, TQM needs to be viewed as a two-part process involving:

- The harnessing of people's commitment in the organisation towards achieving the goal of complete customer satisfaction.
- The development of systems and procedures which allow for continuous improvement.

This distinction is vital. New technology, new systems, and new concepts may of themselves produce some improvement in effectiveness, but it may only be short run unless sufficient attention is given to the harnessing of people's commitment. World standards of organisational effectiveness are not achievable without fully developed and committed people at all levels in the organisation.

The empowerment environment

Employee empowerment is a central feature of the new organisation scenario, but conditions must be right for empowerment to thrive. In many organisations, empowerment has become a buzz word, and although often used, the term is often not understood. Where does empowerment begin? What must organisations be like in order for empowerment to occur? Dobbs (1993) suggests that there is often agreement about the way an empowered employee should behave, but much less so on which conditions are necessary for fostering enough empowerment to change a traditionally hierarchical organisation into a more participative one. He highlights four necessary conditions to encourage empowerment: participation; innovation; access to information; and accountability. These factors combined produce an organisational feeling and tone that can have a dramatic, positive effect on employees.

A number of key triggers of empowerment can be identified in the literature. Salamon (1982) cites the 1960s and the 1970s and the concomitant rise in employee aspirations as the key factor. Others include the issue of industrial alienation (Fox, 1974), the necessity to eliminate poor quality and productivity levels (Lawler, 1986), and the necessity to improve levels of trust between the parties to the labour process (Harrison, 1992).

Conversely, a number of arguments against greater employee involvement have gained prominence over the years. They include the likelihood of a negative impact on unions and union power, principally because forms of involvement such as joint consultation are in effect duplicate channels of representation. Another criticism is that constant and close relationships between management and employees could lead to a situation where the actions of the two become indivisible. It is suggested that if management and unions have parallel views of success, their relationship may become too 'cosy'. There is the perception that in such circumstances, it is the union that sacrifices most in terms of risk, but fares worst in the exchange of benefits.

The question of equity in terms of benefits that accrue to management due to involvement initiatives and the rewards offered to unions for their role as facilitators remains a contentious issue. Marchington (1982) maintains that people give their co-operation to management in terms of involvement at a very 'calculative level', principally because there is too much evidence of it being used in a manipulative way and not really contributing to a better work environment or a better power balance in the employment relationship. Consequently, if workplaces continue to stifle enterprise, innovation and entrepreneurship through an unwillingness to engage in 'real' empowerment initiatives, individuals will continue to go elsewhere to engage in activities that provide them with the stimulus to innovate, where they demonstrate far more skill than most employers encourage them to show at work.

Competitive cultures

Recent literature highlights the importance of a facilitative culture as a prerequisite to the introduction of other changes (Purcell, 1991; Hardscombe and Norman, 1989). As a pattern of shared attitudes, beliefs, assumptions and expectations, it encompasses the norms and core values of an organisation and manifests itself in the form of organisational climate. The existence and development of a strong culture is essential for two reasons:

- The fit of culture and strategy.
- The increased commitment by employees to the organisation.

In order for a competitive strategy such as flexibility and quality to be successful, it requires an appropriate culture. An organisation's strategy will dictate a set of critical tasks or objectives that must be accomplished through a congruence between systems and culture.

Buchanan and McCalman (1989), conducting research at Digital in Ayr, found the concept of organisation culture a slippery one, relatively difficult to define in theory and difficult to identify in practice. Williams *et al.* (1989) highlight six key characteristics of culture.

Culture is:

- learnt;
- both an input and an output;
- partly unconscious;
- historically based;
- commonly held rather than shared;
- heterogeneous.

Culture assumes significance usually because the strategy of the organisation, the type of people in power and its structure and systems reflect the dominant managerial ideology or culture. Furthermore, such managerial ideologies may be more important than environmental factors in guiding organisational response. Managerial ideology, in recent years, has focused on the core characteristics associated with the 'best run', 'achievement-oriented', 'excellent' organisations. Core dimensions include:

1. an action focus;
2. high customer awareness;
3. entrepreneurship;
4. autonomy.

Therefore by implication, it is being suggested that a model that assumes low employee commitment simply cannot match the standards of excellence set by world-class manufacturers. The overall lesson that emerges from this analysis of best practice, according to Clutterbuck (1985), is that success is characterised by doing 'a lot of fairly simple and obvious things well', after all there is relatively little that is revolutionary in the view that individuals give their best when they are treated as caring, responsible individuals.

The key concern lies with bringing about cultural change, usually for strategic reasons. Cultural change does not occur in a vacuum, but is often linked to organisational effectiveness via strategic planning. In planning cultural change, organisations need to consider not only how to change the culture of the organisation, but also how to link the change with organisational goals and effectiveness. Cultural change may therefore be driven by business demands. This is clearly significant because business priorities and responses are now changing at a rate much faster than previously, with the result that cultural realignment may become the norm rather than the exception. While recognising that the problems of conversion to a new mode of thinking and behaving are significantly smoothed where the pre-existing culture of the organisation is one that is generally receptive to such ideas, value shifts are never easily won (Buchanan and McCalman, 1989).

SUMMARY OF KEY PROPOSITIONS

- The field of organisational behaviour is a relatively new field that has evolved from the older disciplines of psychology, sociology, political science and from some of the early work on management.
- Organisational behaviour is defined as the study of individual group and organisational processes as a means of explaining and predicting behaviour in the workplace.
- Most researchers experience at least some tension between a view that highlights the supremacy of inquiry modelled on physical science on the one hand, and the necessity to contextualise and individualise the investigation on the other.
- The new organisation environment necessitates an examination of issues associated with flexibility, the new knowledge workforce, total quality management, empowerment and organisational culture.

DISCUSSION QUESTIONS

1. What reasons can you think about for the importance of organisational behaviour?
2. We all belong to many different organisations in our lives. Fellow members within each organisation will have a set of expectations of us depending on what role/roles we play. Identify four key organisations to which you belong and identify the various roles you play.
3. Most researchers tend to view themselves as either 'positivists' or 'naturalists'. Reflect again on each of these approaches. What appeals to you most about each perspective and why?

CHAPTER 2

Personality

LEARNING OBJECTIVES

- To define personality.
- To identify the main sources of personality difference.
- To understand the interdependence of influence between inherited characteristics and those that are learned.
- To critically evaluate attempts to assess and 'measure' personality.

INTRODUCTION

Box 2.1

UN journal tips Robinson for human rights job

Stephen Collins
Political correspondent

As the campaign to make President Robinson the next High Commissioner for Human Rights gets into full swing, an internal United Nations journal has tipped her as the front runner for the job.

The *IPS Daily Journal* which is written for internal UN consumption, said the consensus among diplomats was that a woman should be selected for the job although there was a preference for the developing world.

'But the front runner so far would likely be from Europe – Irish President Mary Robinson, who enjoys some popularity in the developing world, as well as key support in the United States', said the journal.

It added that there was support at the UN for a courageous individual to take up the post rather than a traditional diplomat like Jose Ayala Lasso from Ecuador who has stepped down from the post.

Assessing President Robinson's chances, one UN diplomat told the journal: 'Most of all she has guts. What is most important for the post is that the commissioner has guts and can face up to challenges, not just to be a diplomat and achieve nothing.'

Amnesty International's General Secretary, Pierre Sané, made similar comments. 'While quiet diplomacy is at times necessary in discussing sensitive issues, dialogue is not an end in itself and must lead to change. The new high commissioner should be a person who is prepared to challenge governments publicly where necessary.'

Within the Department of Foreign Affairs a special team is co-ordinating President Robinson's campaign. Department Secretary Paddy McKernan and Political Director Richard Townsend have been joined by former Irish Ambassador to the UN, Mahon Hayes, who has been brought back from retirement.

While there is no strict time-frame, it is expected that the Secretary General's choice will be made by the summer and the General Assembly's decision by September.

Source: Sunday Tribune, 6 April 1997

Most people intuitively feel that personality characteristics have an impact on the ways in which people behave at work. In the excerpt above, variables that related to Mary Robinson's personality were highlighted as important considerations for her suitability in the role of High Commissioner. References to her characteristics ('she has guts') and her likely behaviour ('[she] can face up to challenges') imply that her personality has a significant impact on people's assessment of her suitability for the job. This is no different in the case of Mary Robinson than it is for any of us. We are often judged on what people see as our traits or the stable psychological characteristics that give rise to our unique personality and patterns of behaviour.

Personality is a commonly used concept in everyday language. We refer to people's personalities in much the same way as we refer to their behaviour, their attitudes and their predispositions. This chapter identifies the importance of understanding dimensions of personality in organisational settings. The distinctions between different personalities in the workplace can have a significant impact on the types of behaviours that manifest themselves. Understanding personality is a key requirement for understanding behaviour in organisations. And while there are many other factors which affect people's behaviour, personality generally has a consistent, stable effect which sometimes outweighs the influences that come from elsewhere.

DEFINING PERSONALITY

It is not easy to define personality. People in organisations often attribute behaviour to personality characteristics, when in fact the behaviour is being influenced by other factors within the system (e.g. Pomice, 1995). Problems can all too easily be attributed to personality 'flaws', personality clashes or personality conflicts when in fact there may be structural problems that need to be addressed, or other organisational processes causing difficulties (Thomas, 1976). Rose (1975) demonstrates that much of the early literature from the human relations school 'over attribute' events to people's personalities without recognising the influences of external factors like group dynamics, power and politics, authority structures, and other constraints or behavioural ingredients in the workplace.

This is not to underestimate the powerful influence that personality can have on behavioural patterns and interactions at work. However, as with all key concepts in organisational behaviour, an examination of the influence of personality variables must be undertaken in conjunction with the consideration of a wide range of other factors. It is inevitably simplistic to suggest, for example, that someone has a 'personality flaw' even in situations where an individual is seen to behave in ways that seem unacceptable or inexplicable. Students of organisational behaviour should recognise that there are interdependent influences on behaviour, and that personality is only one of a variety of different influences.

So what is personality? There are many definitions of personality; some are very different from others. Traditional personality theorists say that personality is a stable set of psychological characteristics which can provide generalised predictions about a person's behaviour. They emphasise people's traits and explore personality as a unitary concept. More recently, however, cognitive/information-processing theorists have proposed that personality may not be as stable a set of characteristics as the traditional theorists suggest. Since the 1960s, cognitive models of behaviour have become more predominant. These cognitive models view people as complex and sophisticated (though error-prone) information processors (Pervin, 1990).

Cognitive theories have now been incorporated into views on motivation, group dynamics, conflict and conflict management, and other important organisational behaviour concepts. But the basis for this approach originated with the personality theorists. The cognitive approach sees personality as flexible and often context-specific. Pervin (1990) provides a framework which outlines the differences between traditional and cognitive approaches to personality:

Essentially the traditional theorists imply that we may have little or no control over the kinds of people that we are and the sorts of personalities that we have. We are, according to traditional theorists, products of our genetic inheritance and our life experiences. Cognitive theorists do not ignore these influences either, but they suggest that people do have a choice about the types of personality types that they have. In a sense, cognitive theory is more optimistic that individuals can (at least to some extent) control their own destinies, behavioural patterns and responses to the situations they encounter.

Table 2.1: Traditional and cognitive approaches to personality

Traditional personality theory sees personality as:	Cognitive theory sees personality as:
Stable and consistent.	Flexible and at least somewhat choice-based.
Able to provide generalised predictions about individual behaviour.	Able to provide predictions about behaviour that are situation-specific.
Largely structured and stable.	Largely a process characterised by development and fluidity.
Based on dispositions, needs and traits.	Based on belief systems, inferential strategies and cognitive competencies.
Based on the self as a unitary concept.	Based on the self as composed of a diverse set of possibilities and potential.

SOURCES OF PERSONALITY DIFFERENCE AND THE NATURE/NURTURE DEBATE

There are some broad key reasons why individual personalities differ in some significant ways. This section outlines some of the main sources of personality difference and explores the ways in which these sources might affect people's personality.

Genetic inheritance

For centuries, philosophers and theorists have debated about whether individuals inherit their characteristics or whether they are acquired through learning. This question has given rise to the long-standing nature/nurture debate, with theorists, philosophers and psychologists adopting various positions on the issue. There are some extreme arguments in the context of this debate. For example, some theorists have suggested that we are born without any psychological characteristics and that it is only our experiences in life that determine the kinds of characteristics that we develop. Others say that our genetic blueprint can determine a vast amount of personal characteristics, including our intelligence, our levels of aggression, our conservatism, our creativity, our rationality and so on. Most psychologists recognise that genetic inheritance plays at least some role in helping to determine our characteristics.

Studies have shown, for example, that there is some evidence to suggest that there are certain personality dimensions that may be influenced at least in some way by the genetic patterns and codes that we inherit from our biological parents. Gottesman (1963) has addressed the nature/nurture debate by proposing the concept of the 'reaction range'. The reaction range suggests that people inherit a range of potential characteristics, and that experiences dictate which of these characteristics are activated by the environment or acquired experientially through the learning process.

Sex and inheritance

One of the most important set of features determined by people's genetic coding are their sexual characteristics. Sexual characteristics (which are inherited) have a strong effect on sexual identity or gender (which are learned as a result of the way that society interacts with individuals according to their sex). Anthropologists have demonstrated that people in all societies and communities are socialised differently according to whether they are male or female, and that this socialisation process (also known as gendering) can have at least some impact on the personality characteristics they develop. Sexual characteristics and sexual identity demonstrate in sharp focus the interdependence of influence between what people inherit and what they learn.

Family experiences

An individual's family is usually the first social group to which he/she comes into contact. Parents act as strong role models, giving their children normative examples of how adults behave. They selectively reward various behaviours and provide strong guidance to their children which can affect various aspects of their personalities.

Theory on dysfunctional families in which there is a serious and ongoing problem (for example alcoholism, abuse or illness) shows that early family experiences can 'create' certain types of personality characteristics among individuals (see Table 2.2).

This framework is based on work carried out with so-called dysfunctional families. While it is inevitably an oversimplification of the kinds of dynamics associated with family influences, it demonstrates the powerful effects to which family roles and patterns of behaviour can give rise. Whatever the patterns of behaviour that individuals learn when they are young, it seems that their family can have a fundamental and intense impact on the characteristics that they bring with them into adult life.

Families provide important early experiences for individuals which can help to shape personalities. The question then arises, how is it that members of the same family can demonstrate such different psychological characteristics? It seems also that different experiences based on family size, birth order, gender and so on can have a significant impact on the way in which each individual personality type emerges.

Culture

Each culture has its own established and approved patterns of behaviours that are learned by members of that culture. Cultural norms can specify ranges of tolerable behaviour and impose serious restrictions on unacceptable or intolerable behaviour. Irish cultural norms are explored in some detail in Chapter 3.

Table 2.2: Family roles and personality characteristics

	Visible behaviours	Inner feelings	Potential problems as adults	Potential positive attributes as adults
The Hero	Always does what is right. Over-achiever. Over-responsible. Always seeks approval.	Inadequacy. Confusion. Guilt. Fear. Low self-esteem.	Addicted to work. Driven by a need to control and manipulate. Afraid of failure. Can't say no.	Competent. Organised. Responsible. Reliable. Effective. Good at follow-through. Committed to achieving goals.
The Scapegoat	Defiant. Looks for negative attention. Makes trouble.	Hurt and abandonment. Anger and bitterness.	Aggressive. Belligerent. Hostile.	Courage. Works well under pressure. Realistic. Risk taker. Assertive.
The Lost Child	Withdrawn. Introverted. Quiet. Solitary.	Feels unimportant and unwanted. Lonely. Defeated.	Indecisive. Avoidant. Unassertive. Self-doubt.	Independent. Talent. Creative. Imaginative. Resourceful.
The Mascot	Attention-seeking. Hyperactive. Short attention span. Facetious.	Feels under pressure to 'be funny'. Feels worry, stress and anxiety.	Compulsive clown. Impulsive. Insensitive.	Quick-witted. Good sense of humour. Independent. Helpful.

Source: Wegscheider-Cruise, 1987, p. 43

Life experiences

People who come from the same culture, the same family and even those who have identical genetic codes (identical twins), are exposed to a different series of life experiences. Some researchers (e.g. Dunn and Plomin, 1990) suggest that experiences outside the family can have an even stronger effect on personality development than those inside the family. It seems that the 'non-shared environment' of family members is an important factor in the attempt to understand the diversity of influences on personality development

So personality develops as a result of a complex aggregation and interaction between an individual's genetic inheritance, their family membership, their cultural groups and their life experiences. The sources of personality difference are impossible to isolate, and efforts to do so have led to excessive simplification of the causes of personality difference. The most important aspect of the sources of personality difference is the interdependence of influence of each of these factors upon the others.

PERSONALITY AND BEHAVIOUR

Trait theories of personality suggest that behaviour is linked to personality in predictable and clear ways. That is, if an individual has a certain attribute or set of attributes, the trait theorists say that these characteristics are likely to determine their behaviour. There are five key personality dimensions which have been found to be linked to patterns of behaviour in individuals.

Introversion/extroversion

In the 1960s, Hans Eysenck proposed that personality could be understood mainly by examining whether people were introverted or extroverted.

This personality dimension refers to the extent to which different people are either shy and retiring, or outgoing and sociable. Steers and Mowday (1977) define the introversion/extroversion dimension as follows: 'introverts tend to focus their energies inwards and have a greater sensitivity to abstract feelings, whereas extroverts direct more of their attention towards other people, objects and events'.

Generally then, introverts tend to look inwards to their own thoughts, feelings and ideas and extroverts tend to look outwards to other people's actions and reactions. As a result, the trait theorists have suggested that introverts and extroverts demonstrate different kinds of behaviour patterns in the workplace:

Introverts
- Usually prefer to work in quieter places with less activity going on around them.
- Tend to be very clear about their own feelings and thoughts.
- Tend to be analytical (looking at different angles of a given problem).
- Tend to spend time thinking and reflecting about issues and ideas at work.

Thus introverts are seen to be good at:

- Working on jobs that require reflection.
- Concentrating on difficult or time-consuming tasks.
- Being sensitive to their own positions and feelings towards work.
- One-to-one encounters, especially when sorting out a problem.
- Working alone on projects without the help of others.

Introverts are seen to be less good at:

- Dealing with large groups of people.
- Speaking their thoughts and articulating their ideas.
- 'Networking' (developing important links with other people at work).
- Having to interact with a wide range of different people on an ongoing basis.

Extroverts

- Usually prefer to work with groups of people rather than on their own.
- Are vigilant about other people's actions and reactions at work.
- Prefer to operate close to the centre of the action at work.
- Appreciate attention and approval from others.
- Prefer to spend more time working with others than working alone.

Extroverts are seen to be good at:

- Dealing with large groups of people.
- Creating a friendly, open atmosphere at work.
- Putting other people at their ease.
- Talking to and interacting with a wide range of different people.

Extroverts are seen to be less good at:

- Working alone on deadlines.
- Reflecting on the key issues of the task at hand.
- Preparing carefully for meetings or key events.
- Thinking before acting.
- Concentrating on one task at a time.

Locus of control

Rotter (1966, 1982) has built on work by others in the area of learned helplessness in order to establish another personality dimension, that of 'locus of control'. This dimension (for which Rotter has developed a questionnaire-based measure) is based on social learning theory, which suggests that our experiences cause us to develop relatively stable personality traits which we bring to all situations in life.

Locus of control represents a generalised expectancy concerning the determinants of rewards and punishments in one's life. (Pervin, 1990, p. 38)

Essentially this is a personality dimension which refers to the extent to which people feel in control of what goes on around them. Rotter proposes that all individuals can be defined as having either an 'internal locus of control' (that is, people who believe that their own behaviour and actions will have a direct impact on what happens to them) or an 'external locus of control' (that is, people who believe that events in their lives are determined by more powerful people than themselves, or by chance or fate).

Locus of control is, then, a concept which refers to how 'in control' people feel. 'Internals' feel that they are masters of their own destiny and are in control of what goes on around them. 'Externals' feel that they don't have much impact on what happens to them and that events in their lives will happen independently of their actions or influence.

Locus of control and behaviour

People with an internal locus of control will tend to:

- make more decisions by themselves;
- be more politically and socially active because they believe this activity can help to change or to shape different events;
- investigate their situations more actively;
- be more likely to attempt to influence others and to take control of situations.

People with an external locus of control will tend to:

- be less likely to demonstrate any of the above tendencies;
- prefer other people to direct their activities;
- like other people to make decisions on their behalf.

Rotter's research originated from observations he made with his colleague Jerry Phares (1976), of a single individual. Their observations revealed that many of the problems encountered in one case were based on the individual's perceived control over his/her environment. Based on the hypothesis that locus of control was an important dimension which affects behaviour, these researchers carried out years of research before coming up with their first established measure of locus of control. This measure attempted to identify how individuals perceive the relationship between their own actions and the consequences of those actions. Rotter's main hypothesis centred around the principle that individuals learn from their life experiences whether to believe that rewards and punishments depend on their own actions or on variables external to themselves. Nowicki and Strickland (1981) later developed a test which builds on the locus of control concept. Table 2.3 shows a typical series of items contained in a locus of control questionnaire.

Table 2.3: Typical questions to establish locus of control

- Do you believe that some people are born lucky?
- Do you believe that if someone studies hard they can pass any subject?
- Do you believe that many of the unhappy things that happen to people are due partly to bad luck?
- Do you believe that people's misfortunes result from the mistakes they make?
- Do you believe that the average citizen can have an influence on government decisions?
- Do you feel that you have a lot of choice in deciding your friends?
- Do you feel that people can get their own way if they just keep trying?

The personality dimension of locus of control has been supported as a valid dimension in several different studies. However, methods of establishing the locus of control on individuals (including the sample questionnaire outlined above) have been exposed to some criticism. Any questionnaire-based method of uncovering personality dimensions is vulnerable to problems of validity and reliability. These problems will be discussed in more detail in the next section.

Self-esteem

This personality characteristic simply refers to the assessment that people make of themselves in their everyday lives. Coopersmith (1967) has shown how self-esteem is an extremely important psychological characteristic which can have significant influence on behaviour, both in childhood and in adult life.

Individuals with high levels of self-esteem see themselves in a good light, have confidence in their abilities and don't spend too much time worrying about what other people think of them. People with low self-esteem have less confidence in their abilities, look for affirmation and approval from others and are more critical of themselves and their behaviour.

Trait theorists suggest that self-esteem is a relatively constant personality variable. However, any measures used to establish levels of self-esteem show that, while there are general ranges within which individuals usually score, self-esteem can vary quite significantly over time, and even from day to day (Gleitman, 1991).

Studies have shown that people with high self-esteem are more likely to:

- take more risks in choosing their jobs;
- be more assertive, more independent and more creative;
- develop effective interpersonal relationships;
- be less easily influenced by the opinions of others;
- set challenging goals for themselves at work.

People with low self-esteem are more likely to:

- be more dependent on and swayed by the opinions of others;
- take fewer risks in all work-related activities;
- set fewer and easier goals for themselves.

What affects people's self-esteem?

Like the other personality dimensions outlined in this section, early experience seems to play a central role in the development of high or low levels of self-esteem. *Reflected appraisal* (the assumptions that children make about themselves by studying the reactions of people close to them), *degree of acceptance* (the amount of affection, warmth and approval that children receive in the early years of their lives), *clarity of boundaries* (the extent to which parents establish and clarify guidelines of behaviour) and early experiences of *democratic practices* (the extent to which children are encouraged to take part in the identification and negotiation of boundaries and rules of behaviour) all appear to play a part in the development of levels of esteem. People who receive positive appraisals, high degrees of acceptance, clear rules of behaviour and who have experience of democratic practices may develop higher levels of self-esteem, which in turn can affect their behaviour in adult life (Coopersmith, 1967).

Authoritarianism

Important research carried out by Aronoff and Wilson (1985) identifies a collection of behavioural tendencies which together can be referred to as the 'authoritarian' personality. These researchers propose, however, that personality is not a fixed and stable series of characteristics, but that it is a social process. Through interaction with others, people develop positions and reactions on various issues and responses to various events. That personality is a social process, is a perspective that represents a more recent development in the theory of personality. Nevertheless, as Hosking and Morley (1991) argue, the research that has proposed an authoritarian personality type, is still strongly trait-orientated in its perspective on personality and personality development. The argument made is that some people are more prone to becoming authoritarian than others.

Aronoff and Wilson's research suggests that people with an authoritarian personality demonstrate the following tendencies:

- Authoritarians are extremely sensitive to status, formal authority and official rule. When operating in organisational settings, their common responses are submission (towards those perceived to be of a higher status) and aggression (towards those perceived to be of a lower status within the system).
- Authoritarians are highly sensitive to any information that might reveal the nature of other people's status, because this information will help them to determine how

to behave towards that person (aggressive/submissive). The research also shows that authoritarian personalities are driven by a deep fear of failure, causing them to avoid tasks that are difficult, complex or ambiguous. They depend on the authority of their rank within their organisation when engaged in attempts to influence others, and as a result, much prefer to work in highly structured organisations where there are clear lines of authority and divisions of activity and responsibility.

Theorists have suggested that the authoritarian personality is highly linked to the 'bureaucratic personality' (e.g. Allinson, 1990). The authoritarian has been found to be least comfortable and least able to cope at the early stages of a new task, and especially at times when change is being planned or is under way.

While, as mentioned earlier, it is wise to avoid constantly attributing organisational problems to personality defects, it would be impossible to deny that examples of dysfunctional behaviour can often be observed in organisational settings. Dixon (1976) has argued that the authoritarian personality can give rise to problematic patterns of behaviour within organisational settings. Because authoritarian personalities are also good at reaching the top in more traditional organisational settings, their patterns can become reinforced and more intense as time goes by, because these patterns are somehow rewarded and give rise to positive outcomes for the individuals who demonstrate them (Hosking and Morley, 1991).

Problems with trait theories of personality

The research which gave rise to the personality dimensions of introversion/extroversion, locus of control and self-esteem, all largely assume that personalities are stable sets of characteristics which can determine people's behaviour and tendencies over the course of their lives. However, as Mischel (1968) points out, there is evidence to suggest that people behave much less consistently than many of the trait theories would suggest.

Individual personality traits (whether inherited or learned) may play a role in determining people's behaviours, but other situational influences are also important to consider. At work, group influence (e.g. Milgram, 1963; Haney and Zimbardo, 1977), organisational structures (e.g. Allinson, 1990) and power relationships can all influence the ways in which people are likely to behave and even suggest that personality is a flexible concept which adjusts in each individual according to the situations that they encounter.

Most people can identify times when they have felt introverted and other times when they have been extroverted. Some situations may provide people with a sense of control over their lives, whereas other may cause them to feel out of control. And, as mentioned earlier, people's levels of self-esteem may change from day to day. In assessing personality, it is important to keep in mind that while people may have certain tendencies or dimensions which affect their behaviour, situational variables are also very powerful and may provide evidence that personality traits are not as constant or as apparent as traditional trait theorists might suggest.

Merits of the trait theory of personality

Other studies have shown that people do demonstrate sometimes remarkable consistency of behaviour over time (Block, 1977). Longitudinal studies show high levels of correlation between personality characteristics over ten- to twelve-year periods (e.g. Costa and McCrae, 1980). Similarly, while there is strong evidence to suggest that people's personalities seem to change quite radically from one situation to another, there are other studies which show that cross-situational consistency in certain personality characteristics is also possible to establish (e.g. Epstein, 1983).

The debate between trait and situational theories of personality simply shows how the concept of personality may be subject to a multiplicity of influences and how difficult it is to isolate causal variables. Indeed, the scientific basis for exploring personality dimensions and their causes is not robust and is often accused of being able to provide only the flimsiest evidence that findings are valid or reliable. The next section outlines the pitfalls associated with attempting to measure personality.

ASSESSING PERSONALITY

Not only is the concept of personality difficult to define, but even when a definition has been accepted and articulated, there are fundamental difficulties associated with measuring or assessing individual personalities.

Attempts to develop structured personality tests have traditionally been attacked by conventional scientists for being inadequate in a number of ways. However, access to information about the sources of individual difference is already very limited. One way of attempting to discover the way in which individuals differ and the reasons why they do is by asking people questions about their beliefs, values, feelings and likely behaviour. Established personality tests which address such questions to the individuals being tested, can at least be evaluated for their consistency and their predictive validity. In the workplace, common personality tests like the 16PF and the Myers Briggs type indicator are used to help make decisions about recruitment, selection and promotion. However the extent to which such tests provide valid information about individuals and their personalities is still subject to considerable dispute.

Predictive validity

Personality tests are generally developed in order to predict how people will behave. However, the uniqueness and complexity of human nature has so far confounded all of the best attempts of psychologists to provide any complete predictive framework for behaviour. Usually situations and people are so complex that even when certain personality dimensions or situational variables are isolated successfully, their ability to tell us anything about real life situations are quite limited. It has regularly been suggested that commonsense methodologies for finding out about individuals' personalities are generally as effective (and sometimes more effective) than elaborate questionnaires that have been developed over long periods of time using large samples.

The Barnum effect

Some personality tests have been bestowed high levels of validity even when this is not the case. The following extract explaining the 'Barnum effect', shows how this can sometimes happen:

Box 2.2: There's one born every minute!

An early demonstration of the Barnum effect was performed by Bertrand Forer who asked the students of one of his classes to take a personality test (Forer, 1949). This test made them list the hobbies, personal characteristics, secret hopes and ambitions of the person they would like to be. Forer promised that within a week he would give them a brief description of their personality based on the results of the test. True to his word, he gave each subject what appeared to be a personalised interpretation: a typed personality sketch with the student's own name written on the top. The subjects were assured that their privacy would be strictly respected.

After reading the sketches, the students were asked to rate the effectiveness of the test in describing their personality using a scale from 0 ('poor') to 5 ('perfect'). They evidently thought that the test had done a good job, for their average rating was 4.3. There was only one thing wrong. Unbeknown to the subjects, Forer had given each of them the identical personality sketch.

Source: Gleitman, 1991

The 'self-report' problem

Many classic personality tests require individuals to answer a series of questions about themselves. From this data, the assessors then infer, through a variety of patterns and clues, what type of personality the individual possesses. This methodology is implicitly trait-orientated, often failing to recognise that individuals may change and develop over time, or even from moment to moment. Questionnaires and personality measures that do produce identical scores over time can be assumed to be more valid than those that don't, and may support the case for the trait approach. But there are other problems with self-report questioning which cause difficulties for effective personality assessment:

The 'Give them what they want' syndrome. There is evidence to suggest that respondents to personality questionnaires often respond in a way that they think they are supposed to. This is especially the case if personality tests are being used as a mechanism for selecting people for jobs or promotion

The 'I'd like to be, so I'll say I am' syndrome. Even if there are no positive or negative outcomes to be gained from various responses to a personality assessment, people often have built-in tendencies to answer in a particular way. We often are vulnerable to ego defence mechanisms which prevent us from recognising the truth about ourselves in a variety of settings. This tendency can cause people to give inaccurate responses to personality tests.

The self-awareness principle. Individuals are sometimes notoriously inaccurate or subjective about their own characteristics and about how they portray themselves to other people. If people are not self-aware, it is not always likely that they will be able to provide effective and accurate responses to questions about themselves.

The 'construct validity' problem. The construct validity of any measure refers to the extent to which the measure actually does test the variables that it sets out to test. For the reasons laid out above, it is difficult to establish the construct validity of personality tests. Instead of measuring personality as they set out to do, they may measure other variables such as an individual's mood, their dispositions, their aspirations, their illusions about themselves or their own assumptions of acceptability.

For these reasons, personality tests are prone to a variety of inaccuracies and pitfalls, particularly in relation to construct validity, predictive validity and generalisability.

SUMMARY OF KEY PROPOSITIONS

- This chapter explored the concept of personality and looked at some of the ways in which personality can affect individual behaviour at work.
- Definitions of personality vary considerably. For example, trait theorists define personality as a stable set of psychological characteristics associated with each individual. On the other hand, cognitive theorists see personality as characteristics which are flexible and adjustable according to the different cognitive assessments people make about the world around them.
- Personality can be seen to be shaped at least to some degree by a variety of identifiable sources. Common sources of personality difference include genetic inheritance, early family experience, cultural influences and life experiences. The importance and significance of each of these sources in still unclear, but it is clear that there is a high degree of interdependence of influences between the variables outlined.
- Personality has been found to influence behaviour in a variety of ways. Trait approaches identify different personality types that can be seen to exert significant influence on the ways in which people behave at work. Introversion/extroversion is a dimension which can determine the extent to which individuals are inward-looking and private or outward-looking and sociable; locus of control is a dimension

which can have an effect on the levels of control an individual perceives that he/she has over events in the workplace; self-esteem, or an individual's evaluation of himself/herself, can have an impact on such patterns as job choices and goal setting; and authoritarianism is a personality dimension that determines the levels of status orientation that individuals demonstrate at work.

- Finally, this chapter addressed the issue of personality assessment, showing how difficult it often is to develop and measure people's personalities. With any personality test, problems of predictive and construct validity are likely to arise, making personality measurement and assessment a difficult assignment for organisational psychologists.

DISCUSSION QUESTIONS

1. Differentiate between trait theories and cognitive theories of personality. Which, in your view, is a more accurate perspective?
2. Have a nature/nurture debate in class – one side should propose that people inherit their personalities and the other that people learn or acquire their personalities through life experiences. Which side found it easier to assert their position? Why?
3. Develop a list of positive and negative behaviours that might occur in the workplace. See if you can identify personality traits that might have produced the behaviours you have identified. Are there other factors that might have given rise to these behaviours?
4. Why is it so difficult to measure or to assess people's personalities? Discuss the principles of construct and predictive validity as they relate to personality assessments.

CHAPTER 3

Perception and Perceptual Processes

LEARNING OBJECTIVES
- To define perception, describe the perceptual process and understand the role that individual perception plays in the workplace.
- To explain the reasons why people are selective in the ways in which they perceive their environment.
- To demonstrate how the context in which people receive information can have a significant influence on the ways in which they understand and deal with this information.
- To identify common distortions in perception that can prevent people from making an accurate assessment of their work environments.
- To understand some of the key cultural influences that can affect the ways in which people perceive their environments.

INTRODUCTION
How people perceive their environment is a fundamentally important consideration for understanding behaviour at work. People react to and interact with their work environments based on the perceptions that they develop. Processes of perception, and the ways in which they develop, can help to explain how individuals make sense of the information they receive.

Research and experience show us that people rarely receive information passively. We receive information in active and sometimes individually unique ways. Events, issues, changes, people, groups and activities are seldom interpreted in the same ways by different people. This chapter will deal with the following issues relating to perception at work: the process of perception, the development of common perceptual errors and biases, the ways in which information is organised and interpreted, and the functions of attitudes. Such an exploration should help to clarify why perceptual and attitudinal processes are fundamental to our understanding of organisational behaviour.

PERCEPTION AND PERCEPTUAL INFLUENCERS

It is nearly impossible for people to avoid biases in perception and attitudes (Plous, 1993). Everything we see and all the information we receive is *processed* by us. Our own perceptual and attitudinal systems have a fundamental effect on the events that occur around us. Box 3.1 displays an advertisement that appeared in the *Sunday Tribune* on behalf of an Irish organisation for lone parents. It shows, quite simply, that identical images can be perceived in different ways according to the ways in which that information is presented and the kinds of criteria that we use to evaluate it.

Our attitudes and our perceptions can influence all aspects of the decisions that we make both inside and outside the workplace.

Box 3.1: Spot the difference

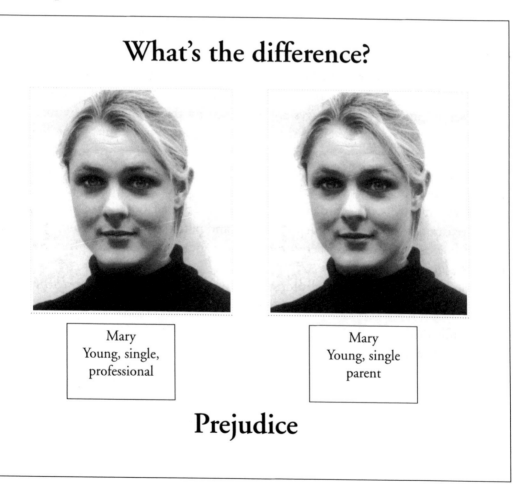

Source: Sunday Tribune newspaper, 2 February 1997

INDIVIDUAL DIFFERENCES AND PERCEPTION

People behave in accordance with the way they perceive information (Stranks, 1994). Definitions of perception focus on the idea that perception is a *process,* not a static or passive concept. People *receive* information from the outside world through the sensory channels of sight, hearing, touch, taste and smell, but they *perceive* information differently according to their attitudes, values, expectations, motives and contexts.

Sensing information from the environment is not an automatic given. Just because something is 'out there' doesn't mean that we will notice it or interpret it in an objective manner. Our perceptual processes influence not just how we see things, but also what we see and what we don't see. And even once we have noticed something in our environment, individual perceptions will interpret that information in different ways.

Perception can be defined as:

> The psychological process through which people receive, organise and interpret information from their environment. (Atkinson, *et al.,* 1993)

A lot of research has been carried out by psychologists to determine how the perceptual process works (e.g. Osherson *et al.,* 1990; Rock, 1983; Posner, 1989). Much of this work focuses on how visual images are processed by the brain and the visual system. This work has provided perceptual theorists with a good 'bottom up' grounding in key aspects of visual perception. For the purposes of understanding organisational behaviour, it is not necessary to investigate this type of visual research in too much detail. It is enough for us to know that our brains allow us to process information in such a way that we can normally differentiate objects from each other (i.e. figure ground perception), we can perceive distance, depth, colour, and patterns in the environment around us. But how do we use these perceptual skills to organise more complex perceptions about the environment?

To understand the perceptual process in any situation, it is important to focus on the three key factors that influence perceptions:

1. The individual.
2. The perceived.
3. The context or setting.

Figure 3.1: Factors that influence perception

Individual (The perceiver)	Object (What is perceived)	Context (The setting in which perception takes place)
• Expectations • Motives	• Contrast • Intensity • Motion • Repetition	• Physical factors • Social factors • Organisational factors

1. The individual

It is impossible to understand why someone perceives his/her environment in a particular way unless we have considered certain factors relating to that individual. Individual expectations, motivations, emotions, values and attitudes are characteristics which influence the perceptual process and which must be considered when attempting to understand perception.

Individual expectations

A person's expectations are important considerations when attempting to understand why that person perceives things in the ways that they do. Research as far back as the 1950s shows us that our expectations influence our perceptions in very powerful ways (Bruner and Minturn, 1955). Look at the picture in Figure 3.2.

Figure 3.2: Expected and unexpected stimuli

You will probably notice after a while that the queen of hearts is black: but until you have really studied the picture, it can be difficult to see why it is a different or unusual image. Existing expectations can make people unobservant. Often the stronger our expectations are, the less likely we are to notice any variations that emerge. This is an important perceptual tendency to consider when coming to grips with behaviour at work. People often see only what they expect to see.

Individual motives

Individual motives can have a powerful effect on the way in which people interpret the environment around them. People don't just see what they *expect* to see, they often perceive things in the ways that they *want* to see them. At work, people often misinterpret negative messages (like a poor performance appraisal or unfavourable signals in market trends) because they don't want to receive pessimistic or threatening information from their environment. Individuals are notoriously effective at screening out information which is unpalatable, difficult to face, or in some way tells them things that they don't want to hear.

Reactions to unexpected/unwanted stimuli

Research has demonstrated that people can react in a variety of ways when they are exposed to information in their environment that is unexpected or in some way surprising to them (Bruner and Postman, 1949). Using the black 3 of hearts as a stimulus, Bruner and Postman found that it took people more than four times longer to recognise that anything was strange or different about this image. Their research led them to identify four types of reactions to unexpected stimuli. These were termed dominance, compromise, disruption and recognition (see also Plous, 1993)

Dominance reaction to unexpected stimuli

When we fail to recognise the nature of unexpected stimuli, our normal expectations are said to dominate the unexpected stimulus and prevent us from seeing anything different. Subjects who did not spot the black 3 of hearts and who claimed to have seen a red 3 of hearts or a black 3 of clubs reacted to the stimulus by having their normal expectations dominate their experience and their perceptions, thus preventing them from identifying the different nature of the image.

Compromise reaction to unexpected stimuli

When we recognise that a stimulus is unexpected, but fail accurately to identify the reasons why, it may be because our perceptual system is attempting to compromise for the unexpected stimulus. Some people who are exposed to a black 3 of hearts report that it appears 'greyish' or purple in colour. This is a perceptual error that draws attention to the unexpected nature of the stimulus in some way though failing to identify the manner in which the stimulus is different.

Disruption reaction to unexpected stimuli

Disruption in our perceptions occurs when we fail to detect even the recognisable aspects of an object. For example, some people on seeing a black 3 of hearts, may even fail to recognise that it is a playing card and become quite confused as to the nature of the object. While this type of reaction is relatively rare, it can happen to people when they are under pressure to react, or if they are being bombarded with a series of different stimuli in rapid succession.

Recognition reaction to an unexpected stimulus

Recognition occurs when individuals are accurate in their diagnosis of the nature of an unexpected stimulus. On seeing a black 3 of hearts, a recognition reaction would be to say 'This card should be red.'

Individuals expect and want to see things in a certain way. At work for example, we *expect* normal activities to be carried out in a particular sequence and we may *want* to believe that people respect us or that we are good at what we do. But our expectation and our motives can prevent us from being objective in our analysis of the real situation.

Box 3.2: Some good advice for decision-makers

Before making an important judgement or decision, it often pays to pause and ask a few key questions:

- Am I motivated to see things a certain way?
- What expectations did I bring to the situation?
- Would I see things differently without these expectations and motives?
- Have I consulted with others who don't share my expectations and motives?

By asking such questions, decision-makers can expose many of the cognitive and motivational factors that lead to *biases in perception*.

Source: Plous, 1993, p. 21

2. The perceived

It is not just our own motives and expectations that affect the way in which we perceive our environment, or objects in that environment – the perceptual process depends centrally on the nature of what we are perceiving. There are some basic principles of object perception that can affect people's ability to notice and perceive events or objects in their environment.

Principles of object perception

Contrast: You have seen earlier that perceptual theory says that people do not always spot the unexpected. On the other hand, it is also true that people are more likely to notice things that stand out from their environment. A bright red desk in a dingy room will mean that our attention is most likely to be drawn to the desk. People who look or act differently in contrast to others will often cause our attention and perceptions to be drawn towards them.

Intensity: Intensity of an image or a sound is likely to have a significant effect on the extent to which people are likely to become aware of that image or sound. For example, very loud or very low noises tend to attract attention more effectively than those of a moderate intensity.

Motion: Moving objects tend to attract more perceptual attention than those that are still or motionless. We are more likely to notice someone moving through the workplace or an object flying through the air. Our perceptions tend to be drawn towards objects or people in motion.

Repetition: Information that is repeated over and over again can be more likely to be learned and recognised than information which only gets a single airing. However, our perceptions can screen out repeated information as if it is just background noise. A supervisor who continually reminds people to wear their hard hats or to keep their workplaces tidy may end up being ignored because of the repetitive nature of the message that they are sending.

In asking the question, 'Why do people see things in different ways?', it is important then to consider not only what the expectations and needs of individual perceivers are, but also the nature of the objects, events or people that they perceive. This can help to explain why some events at work receive extreme reactions and others go almost completely unnoticed.

3. The context

A third factor which affects the ways in which we perceive our environment is the context or setting within which our perceptions occur. People do not perceive information in isolation; they interpret new information in the light of the context within which they receive that material.

The physical, social and organisational setting in which we receive information can have an enormous effect on the ways in which we interpret and understand this information. When trying to understand meaning in someone's behaviour, we normally pay attention to certain contextual factors associated with that behaviour. If we see someone shouting, we look around to find out what they're shouting at. If we see someone crying, we search for further contextual information to help clarify the reasons why. All behaviours that we see at work are usually interpreted within a complex contextual framework which we use to take into account important aspects of the environment when attempting to understand what's going on around us.

THE PROCESS OF PERCEPTION

Perception is a process and, as such, it involves a series of steps or stages. Of course, in reality it is difficult to see where one stage in the perceptual process begins and another one ends; but for the purposes of analysing perception, it is important to break the process down into its different stages in order to reach a more effective understanding of how perception works and how people come to make sense of what goes on around them. Figure 3.3 outlines the key stages in and sequence of the perception process and shows how perceiving and reacting to events in our environment is not automatic – it depends on the unfolding of a sequence of stages outlined below.

Figure 3.3: Stages in the perception process

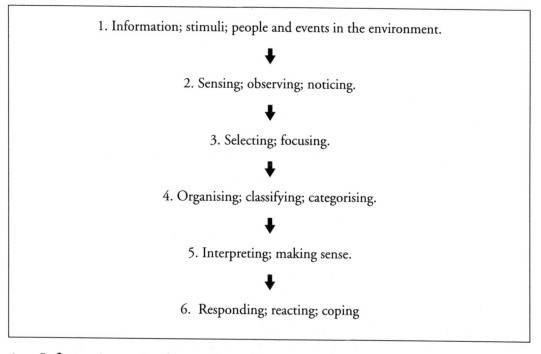

1. Information; stimuli; people and events in the environment.

2. Sensing; observing; noticing.

3. Selecting; focusing.

4. Organising; classifying; categorising.

5. Interpreting; making sense.

6. Responding; reacting; coping

1.   Information; stimuli; people and events in the environment

There are many more elements in our environment than we are ever likely to be aware of at any one point in time. This is an important principle of perception. People at work exist in environments which are complex and multi-dimensional. What they notice or become aware of depends on the individual factors, object features and contextual characteristics outlined in the last section. It is worth remembering that, at work, it is not guaranteed that everyone will be aware of issues or information that may seem obvious to you.

2.   Sensing; observing; noticing

People can't notice everything that goes on around them. If they did, they would be bombarded with information, overloaded with data from the outside world and more than likely unable to function effectively. From the time they are born, individuals learn to filter out information from the environment that is not relevant or not important in their attempts to cope with their world. This filtering mechanism is what determines the fact that people notice some aspects of our environment and do not sense other aspects. Our filtering system is sometimes over-efficient in that it can filter out important information that might help us to operate better in various situations.

3. Selecting; focusing

One of the most important characteristics of an organisational leader is his/her ability to 'read the signs', that is to be on the look-out for signals that say the market is changing, or that various opportunities are becoming available, and not to filter out important information about the environment that might affect the organisation and its future (Kakabadse, 1997). This relates very centrally to the process of selective perception at work.

Some people deliberately develop their perceptual abilities by constantly being on the look-out for signals or signs that need to be considered for example when organisational survival or success is at stake. Indeed, research into the strategic management of organisations demonstrates that a 'careful assessment of the environment' is necessary if organisations are to manage their strategic development successfully (Pettigrew and Whipp, 1991). The ability of people in organisations to 'select' and focus on the important aspects of the environment is crucial in determining subsequent action and behaviour, and central to the concept of perception and the perceptual process.

Just as we cannot *notice* everything in the environment, we also cannot *focus on* everything. Our ability to organise, categorise and classify information can make it easier to focus on issues in a structured and coherent way.

4. Organising; classifying; categorising

In order to make sense of the environment, people develop coding systems to help them to categorise the information that they receive. Typical coding systems used by individuals are *schemas* and *scripts*. A schema is a mental framework which encompasses memories, ideas, concepts and programmes for action which are relevant to a particular object, event or person in the environment.

People have schemas (Rumelhart, 1984; Weick, 1983) for various aspects of their environment. They even develop schemas for themselves, (called self-schemas) which help to organise and control information they receive relating to themselves as individuals. Schemas can be complex or simple, but their function is generally to help people to organise information about certain (usually important) aspects of their lives and their environments.

Scripts are another way in which individuals organise, manage and classify the complex information that they receive. Scripts are knowledge frameworks that describe the appropriate sequence of events in a given situation (Schermerhorn, *et al.*, 1994). Individuals at work tend to develop scripts for activities such as performance appraisals, interviews, meetings, lunch breaks, conversations with different people within the organisational setting, and so on.

Generally, scripts and schemas make it easier for people to manage the diverse range of information that they face every day. Scripts and schemas tend to define people's expectations about what they think they will see or hear at work. Keep in mind that expectations can in turn have an effect on the aspects of the environment that we pay attention to and those that we ignore. So scripts and schemas provide a structure around which information is organised; if new information does not fit into our existing schemas, we may react in the ways outlined earlier in this chapter (i.e. dominance, compromise, disruption or recognition).

Box 3.3: A classic example of two different organisational scripts

In the 1960s, Douglas McGregor suggested that there were two different and opposing views relating to people's behaviour at work. These views have come to be known as Theory X and Theory Y and are classic examples of the kinds of schema that different people at work can have. These schema guide behaviour in sometimes very powerful ways (McGregor, 1960).

The Theory X 'schema'

- People generally dislike work and therefore need to be coerced into working effectively.
- Most people dislike taking on responsibility.
- People generally prefer to carry out tasks that have been clearly defined by others.
- Most people lack creativity and are resistant to change.

The Theory Y 'schema'

- Work is as natural to individuals as play or rest.
- People who are committed to goals can achieve them through their own self-direction without the need for coercion or supervision.
- Most people actively seek out responsibility and like to be in control of their own actions.
- People are naturally creative and can solve problems without having to be told what to do.

You can see that if someone used Theory X as their guiding schema, their behaviour is likely to be very different than if they were guided by Theory Y. Schemas guided by Theory X would be more likely to result in supervisory behaviour which involved control and coercion of others, threats and punishment, and generally discouraged people from making their own decisions or solving their own problems. Schemas guided by Theory Y would be more likely to result in behaviour which involved encouraging people to direct and motivate themselves, and to take responsibility for their own actions.

5. Interpreting; making sense

Perception is the psychological process through which we attempt to make sense of our environment; sense-making often requires that we ask the question 'Why?'

In organisational settings, particularly those in which there are many people doing many different things, behaviour and events can often be bewildering to us. Psychologists tell us that when people do not understand or cannot make sense of what's going on, they experience 'psychological discomfort' (Festinger, 1957) and are motivated to identify reasons and logic in the behaviour of others. The concept of attribution is a way of attempting to explain the rules that people use to explain their own behaviour and the behaviour of others (Kelley, 1973).

Attribution theory originates from the work of Heider (1958) and since then has come to be recognised as an important aspect of perceptual theory. Attributions are interpretations of the causes of behaviour. People make attributions about their own and others' behaviour. The types of attributions that people make (i.e. the ways in which they explain their own and others' behaviour) have a proven influence on subsequent behaviours and interactions. Based on a series of investigations, Kelley (1967) showed that there are three basic information cues which people attend to when trying to establish the causes of people's behaviour:

1. Consistency (that is, the extent to which a particular action is consistent with an individual's pattern of behaviour over time).
2. Consensus (that is, the extent to which a particular individual action mirrors the actions of others).
3. Distinctiveness (that is, the extent to which a particular action is similar to or different from various other activities in which the individual is involved).

If you see someone you know behaving aggressively, you may try to attribute causes to that person's behaviour by implicitly addressing the following questions:

1. Has this person behaved aggressively in similar situations in the past?
   Yes = high consistency.
   No = low consistency.

2. Do other people behave aggressively in similar situations?
   Yes = high consensus.
   No = low consensus.

3. Does this person behave aggressively in different situations?
   Yes = low distinctiveness.
   No = high distinctiveness.

Our answers to these questions will affect the ways in which we explain the individual's behaviour. In situations where we perceive high consistency, low consensus and low distinctiveness, we tend to assume that the individual's behaviour is a result of their own personal characteristics. The way we explain the behaviour is then to say that 'He/she is just an aggressive person.' In situations where we perceive low consistency, high consensus and high distinctiveness, we tend to assume that the individual's aggressive behaviour occurred as a result of situational factors. We are more likely to assume that the person behaved aggressively 'because he/she was driven to it'.

6. Responding; reacting; coping

How people identify, focus on, organise and make sense of information affects very strongly the ways in which they are likely to behave. Perceptual processes play a central role in the ways in which people respond, react to and cope with their organisational environments. An enhanced understanding of the process of perception can help to shed important light on the complex network of behaviours in organisations.

COMMON PERCEPTUAL DISTORTIONS

As with any psychological process, perception is vulnerable to a variety of errors. We have seen that people do not process information accurately or objectively. Perception is a subjective process, vulnerable to all sorts of inaccuracies, distortions and errors. Understanding perception requires a focus on the common distortions that people display in their attempts to make sense of the environment around them.

Box 3.4: Common perceptual distortions

- Stereotyping.
- Projection.
- Halo effect.
- The fundamental attribution error.

Stereotyping

Because of the enormous amount of information that our brains have to process every day of our lives, people have a natural capacity to categorise, arrange and pigeonhole the information that they encounter as they interact with their world. This is an important capacity. We need to know how to recognise the differences between various aspects of our environment. For example, it is important for us to have an ability to make a quick assessment of dangerous versus safe situations, of helpful and unhelpful people at work, or of difficult or easy tasks. As we process information from the outside world, we tend to label it according to these kinds of concepts. We see some work situations as boring or interesting; worthwhile or useless; challenging or effortless; and so on.

Similarly, we label people using categories like friendly/unfriendly, similar or different from us, attractive/unattractive, honest/dishonest, and so on. But how do we decide on these labels? What information do we use to decide whether we think someone is honest or dishonest, clever or stupid? Research has shown that the kinds of information we use in the assigning of labels to others can be notoriously irrelevant. People develop stereotypes about other people in often very inaccurate ways.

Stereotypes – a definition

> A stereotype is a pre-established expectation about an individual or a group. Stereotypes allow those who hold them to reduce uncertainty about what people or groups are likely to want, to believe or to do. (Rumelhart, 1984)

Stereotypes are like social schemas, which help people to make sense of other people and decide how they will develop their relationships and interactions with others. But stereotypes, while useful in helping people to manage diverse information can also be damaging, and cause people to make mistakes in their assessment and evaluations of others.

Cultural stereotypes may be extremely inaccurate and yet can be widely held by various groups. *Gender stereotypes* can influence and differentiate people's behaviour, depending on whether they are interacting with men or women. *Age stereotypes* can cause people to discriminate against people who are young or old in work situations; and *socioeconomic stereotypes* can cause people to make inaccurate and even damaging assumptions and attributions about people according to background information about where they live, and even their dialects or accents.

Box 3.5: An example of how gender stereotypes can influence behaviour

Results of a recent Irish study investigating husband and wife perceptions of their marital roles in the purchase of several consumer products demonstrates important differences in gender perceptions.

The first objective of the research was to examine the level of agreement between husbands and wives on the relative influence of each spouse in the decision-making process for each purchase. The relationship between husband and wife was analysed both across families and within families. A high level of consensus at both levels of analysis was found.

A second objective was to identify which spouse had stronger influence on the consumer decision processes for the six products/services chosen for the study. It was found that the husband had the stronger influence on the car, television and lawnmower purchases. The wife's influence was stronger for the three-piece suite and the washing machine purchase. A very high level of joint decision-making was found for the mortgage choice.

Source: Mohan, 1995

Projection

Projection is a perceptual process that occurs when we assume that other people think or are likely to act like us. Quite simply, it is when we project our own thoughts and feelings onto someone else, and assume that our thoughts and feelings belong to others. Egocentricity is related to projection. That is, the less able someone is to see things from perspectives other than their own, the more likely they are to assume that other people are reacting, thinking or feeling in the same ways as they are. At work, it is easy to assume that people are motivated by the same things that we are, that they get annoyed by the same irritants, that they are driven by the same ambitions. Discovering that this is often not the case can be disorientating or at least surprising. It is possible to avoid excessive projection by endeavouring to see things from different perspectives and by exploring different viewpoints with others at work.

Halo effect

The halo effect occurs when a single characteristic associated with an individual is used to generate an overall impression or assessment of that person. In this way, someone who appears warm or honest may be assumed to have a whole range of positive attributes which may not necessarily be the case in reality. The halo effect is so called because one characteristic serves to create a saintly or inherently good overall impression of an individual.

The opposite of the halo effect (sometimes called the trident effect) is also possible where one negative characteristic can overshadow and dominate any positive attributes of an individual. Obviously in organisational settings, unfair or inaccurate evaluations of people can have serious implications. An awareness of the tendency to pay attention to one characteristic at the expense of another is important to recognise.

The 'fundamental' attribution error

We have already seen that attribution is a crucial stage in the perceptual process; evidence suggests that it is a stage in which people are particularly prone to error. 'The fundamental attribution error' finding proposed by Ross (1977) suggests that people are more likely to explain other people's behaviour by considering only internal/dispositional characteristics (such as the individual's personality, attitudes, motivations and so on) and to explain their own behaviour by considering external variables (like circumstances, environmental influences, pressures from other people and other contextual factors). For example, on witnessing a car crash, the attribution error theory suggests that people are more likely to attribute the event to the internal characteristics of the driver, using explanations like: 'He must be a very careless person', 'He wasn't looking where he was going', 'He is not a good driver.' On the other hand, on being involved in a crash where they themselves were the drivers, explanations are more likely to involve external attributions like 'It was very dark', 'The other car was going too fast', or 'There was a very dangerous bend in the road.'

Why do people make skewed or distorted attributions leading to notoriously subjective accounts of events and occurrences? It's because of the perceptual process and (at least some researchers argue) the fundamental attribution error. The fundamental attribution error can be made as a way of defending people's self-esteem, by developing accounts which allow them to continue to think highly of themselves and protecting themselves from unpalatable truths about their own tendencies and behaviours. This of course relates to what was discussed in the first section of this chapter: people *expect*, and *want* to see things in a certain way – and will explain things to themselves in order to support these expectations and motivations.

However, recent investigators into the perceptual aspects of behaviour suggest that the fundamental attribution error may not be 'fundamental' in all cultures and that it is arguably a *culturally influenced inaccuracy*. Smith and Harris Bond (1993) point out that the fundamental attribution error is much less likely to be found in collectivist cultures than in individualist cultures (see the discussion on individualism in the next section). Hofstede (1983) found that Ireland ranks moderately to strongly individualistic as a culture, so it can be argued that people in the Irish cultural setting are less likely to make the fundamental attribution error than people from highly individualistic cultures such as the USA, Australia or Britain, but more likely to make it than people from highly collectivist cultures such as Asia, South America and China.

STOP AND DISCUSS

How can knowledge of common perceptual distortions help to prevent errors and problems in organisational settings?

Use the following typical work scenarios to explore this question:

- A selection interview.
- A performance appraisal.
- A team briefing/meeting.
- Training a new employee.

CULTURAL VALUES AND PERCEPTION

People see things in different ways depending on their cultural contexts. Chapter 9 explores the concept of organisational culture in more depth and demonstrates the different dimensions of culture that can affect organisational behaviour. Perception, or the way people select, organise and interpret information in the outside world, is often loaded with culturally defined influences which can sometimes make interaction between cultures difficult and bewildering.

Nations tend to share a broadly common history and heritage and are exposed to similar values and beliefs and social rules. And while there is an increasing awareness that diversity exists and needs to be valued in any culture, a common set of value systems, beliefs and norms tends to permeate any one cultural setting. These value systems can provide a filter or lens through which members of that culture process and perceive information. Cultural differences in perception can help to explain many of the differences and misunderstandings that can emerge between individuals and groups from different cultures.

Hofstede (1983, 1991) refers to culture as 'the collective programming of the mind which distinguishes the members of one group from another', explaining that the programmes that we have in our minds affect the way in which we process any new information that we receive.

Using four main dimensions of culture, Hofstede has classified a wide variety of different countries according to their cultural values. The four values he identifies are as follows.

Power distance

Power distance refers to the extent to which people in a particular culture recognise and respect status differences between individuals. The type of question asked to establish the extent of power distance is: 'How frequently in your experience, does the following problem occur: employees being afraid to express their disagreement with their managers?'

Uncertainty avoidance

Uncertainty avoidance refers to the extent to which people in a particular culture can or cannot tolerate uncertainty. Hofstede also found variations across cultures in uncertainty avoidance. While it is a general psychological principle that people do not like uncertainty, it seems that some cultures are much more likely to tolerate high levels of uncertainty in the environment than others. The type of question asked to establish uncertainty avoidance in this study was: '[Do you agree that] company rules should not be broken, even if it's in the company's best interest?' and 'How long do you think you will continue working for this company?' High uncertainty avoidance was assumed to exist if people tended to stick to established rules and avoid changes (like leaving one organisation for another).

Individualism

Individualism refers to the extent to which people in a particular culture pursue individual, autonomously selected goals in contrast to collectivist, group-orientated goals. Some cultures have been found to hold individualist values whereby competition, independent action and self-reliant activity is highly valued. Other cultures have more collectivist values which focus on the development and reward of group activity (e.g. family involvement, consensus building at work and so on) and values.

Masculinity/femininity

The masculinity/femininity dimension refers to the extent to which work values like high earnings, status, recognition and achievement are seen as important (this defines so-called 'masculine' cultural values) as opposed to values such as good working relationships, co-operative work atmospheres and interpersonal harmony (this defines so-called 'feminine' cultural values).

Since Hofstede defined these cultural value dimensions in the early 1980s, there have been some criticisms of the validity and clarity of his definitions of culture and its characteristics. However, the large samples that he used in his research (117,000 individuals from a total of fifty-three different countries) and the statistical rigour of his analysis gives us one of the most comprehensive studies to date of the differences between cultures and their values. While some may disagree with aspects of the measures used in the study, differences and contrasts found in the research demonstrate that it is possible to show that different countries tend to espouse and believe in very different kinds of values.

What does this add to our knowledge of perception and the perceptual process? As mentioned at the beginning of this section, people see things in different ways according to their cultural values. Nationalities may strongly influence the perceptual process, and even though in Europe, national barriers may be breaking down, evidence suggests that people still see themselves as having strong cultural identities. Being 'Irish', 'French', 'British', 'Italian' or whatever, is just as important to individuals now as it has ever been (Moore and Punnett, 1994).

Irish cultural values as defined by the Hofstede framework

According to Hofstede's framework, Irish people score very low on the dimensions of power distance and uncertainty avoidance, very high on the dimension of individualism, and particularly high on the 'masculinity' dimension.

This may give us some important clues as to how Irish people are likely to interpret and process information both within and outside their work settings. Our priorities, values and beliefs and the rules of behaviour that we think are important may indeed give rise to some cultural stereotypes and may challenge others. The rankings in Table 3.1 are based on the average responses of samples from the countries mentioned. Not all members of a culture share the same values and ideas. Average scores can at best give us a roughly representative picture of the cultural dimensions under review.

Table 3.1: Rankings of national cultures using Hofstede's classification

Country	Power distance	Uncertainty avoidance	Individualism	Masculinity
Africa (East)	22	36	34	39
Africa (West)	10	34	40	30
Arab region	7	27	26	23
Argentina	35	12	22	20
Australia	41	37	2	16
Austria	53	24	18	2
Belgium	20	5	8	22
Brazil	14	21	26	27
Canada	39	41	4	24
Chile	24	12	38	26
Colombia	17	20	49	11
Costa Rica	43	12	46	48
Denmark	51	51	9	50
El Salvador	18	5	42	40
Ecuador	8	28	52	13
Finland	46	31	17	47
France	15	12	10	35
Germany	43	29	15	9

Britain	43	47	3	9
Greece	27	1	30	18
Guatemala	3	3	53	43
Hong Kong	15	49	37	18
Indonesia	8	41	47	30
India	10	45	21	20
Iran	29	31	24	35
Ireland	**49**	47	**12**	7
Israel	52	19	19	29
Italy	34	23	7	4
Jamaica	37	52	25	7
Japan	33	7	22	1
Korea	27	16	44	41
Malaysia	1	46	36	25
Mexico	6	18	32	6
Netherlands	40	35	4	51
Norway	47	38	13	52
New Zealand	50	40	6	17
Pakistan	32	24	47	25
Panama	2	12	51	34
Peru	22	9	45	37
Philippines	3	44	31	11
Portugal	24	2	34	45
Singapore	13	53	40	28
South Africa	35	39	16	13
Spain	31	12	20	37
Sweden	47	49	10	53
Switzerland	45	33	14	4
Taiwan	29	26	43	32
Thailand	22	30	40	44
Turkey	18	16	28	32
United States	38	43	1	15
Uruguay	26	4	29	42

Adapted from Hofstede, 1983

According to Hofstede's research, then, Irish cultural values are more likely to be represented by:

- Relatively low amounts of respect and deference between those in 'superior' and 'subordinate' positions (for example, people surveyed were generally not afraid of or nervous about talking to their bosses).
- Relatively low emphasis on planning and stability as a way of dealing with life's uncertainty (revealing a 'Take it as it comes' attitude to changes in life and work).
- Relatively high levels of importance attached to individual as opposed to collective achievement.
- Particularly high levels of importance attached to achievement, recognition and respect in working life.

While it can be convincingly argued that this profile provides an inevitably broad and sweeping generalisation of the values that Irish people hold, it is important to recognise that cultural factors do play an important part in influencing people's perceptions. In current organisational contexts, where global issues now affect a growing number of businesses, it is worthwhile keeping this in mind.

Although on the one hand, people seem to be retaining a strong sense of their national cultural identities, on the other, circumstances dictate that more and more of us will need to communicate effectively with people from a wide range of different cultural backgrounds. It is increasingly important for organisational members to understand some of the central reasons why people can perceive information differently due to the cultural influences to which they are exposed.

ATTITUDES AND PERCEPTION

Attitudes relate to an important concept that is also strongly connected with the perceptual process. People at work develop attitudes about a wide variety of issues, events and people in their environment. Attitudes are developed through perception. The link between attitudes and perception is, in both theoretical and practical senses, not always clear; and the differences between these two concepts not always easy to define. Certainly the two concepts are inextricably linked. For example, it might be argued that perceptual biases like stereotypes and halo effects contribute in powerful ways to the network of attitudes that individuals develop.

The importance of attitudes in the workplace

People develop attitudes at work which can affect and influence their behaviour. Students and researchers into organisational behaviour need, therefore, to consider how attitudes develop, what their functions are and how they affect behaviour. However, as with most concepts in organisational behaviour, such questions are not straightforward, or easy to answer.

51

Also, if a purely managerialist perspective is adopted, then the rights of people to develop their own attitudes, no matter how negative, are rarely considered, and the ethical or moral constraints associated with changing or manipulating people's attitudes have received little attention in management literature. However, regardless of the perspective taken, there are some theoretical foundations about attitudes that can be considered in objective ways, and which can also help to enhance an understanding of the behaviour of people and groups within organisational settings.

It is important in addressing the question of how attitudes influence behaviour to recognise that attitudes are *neither necessary nor sufficient determinants of behaviour*. In other words, just because you have, say, a negative attitude towards someone else at work, does not necessarily mean that you will behave negatively towards them. Similarly, there may be times that even when you do have a positive attitude towards someone, that circumstances and influences may cause you to behave negatively towards them.

Attitudes do not dictate or determine the kinds of behaviours that people engage in at work. Rather they are *facilitative* or *probabilistic* causes of behaviour in the sense that they make it *more likely*, depending on a range of other variables, that someone will behave in a certain way towards others or in reaction to various events at work.

Attitudes – a definition

Attitudes can be defined simply as: A person's relatively enduring disposition toward people, objects, events or activities (Bird and Fisher, 1986). These dispositions are evaluative, in that they are usually positive or negative in orientation, they are acquired or developed over time and they are not immutable; although, depending on the functions that they serve for the individual, some may be more fixed and difficult to change than others.

Functions of attitudes

Psychologists have developed a useful perspective on attitudes that help to understand the function that they serve for the individual, rather than focusing – as much of the management literature does – on how attitudes affect the organisations within which they are developed. Attitudes serve functions for individuals. One of the first things that people often notice as newcomers to organisations, is the variety of opinions and attitudes that people have about the same things. Often, the first information that people will volunteer to newcomers is their own predispositions about various issues, activities and people at work. Psychologists have long argued that the reason why attitudes are so prevalent and often so obvious at work is that they help people to make more sense of their world, to develop a stronger sense of their own identities, to protect their own egos from negative information about themselves, or to gain more effective knowledge about what's going on around them (Katz, 1960).

Knowledge function

Attitudes can give meaning to our experience in the same ways that the perceptual processes help us to organise and categorise the world.

Utilitarian function

Developing certain attitudes can help us to get the most out of our social situations.

Self-expressive function

Attitudes can help us to develop a stronger sense of the kinds of people that we are. People are more likely to develop a coherent and somewhat consistent framework of attitudes which allow them and others to define the kinds of people that they are.

Ego defensive function

We often develop attitudes simply to avoid potentially unpleasant information about ourselves and to project to ourselves a positive self-image. This might mean, for example, developing negative attitudes towards people who react badly towards us in the workplace as a way of explaining their behaviour in a way that does not threaten our own image of ourselves.

Being aware of attitudes, and more particularly knowing that people develop attitudes in order to fulfil some important psychological function, is important, especially if we are attempting to uncover the attitudes that people have or to change existing attitudes in an organisational setting.

SUMMARY OF KEY PROPOSITIONS

- This chapter has explored some of the central aspects of the process and determinants of perception.
- Perception is a psychological process through which people receive, organise and interpret information from their environment.
- Three major factors influence the ways in which people perceive the world around them: the individuals themselves (and his/her expectations and motives for seeing things in a particular way); the characteristics of object/person/event being perceived (including such features as contrast, motion, novelty, intensity and repetitiveness); and the context within which the perceptions are being formed (including physical, social and organisational aspects of the setting).
- People can react to unexpected or unwanted stimuli in a number of ways. Their expectations can completely dominate or distort the information that they receive, or they can cause people to fail to recognise important aspects of their environment.
- The perceptual process involves a series of stages, starting with sensing or observing stimuli in the environment, and then selecting aspects of the stimuli, organising the information into manageable categories, making sense of the information and then

responding in some way. The perceptual process is complex and involved and can give rise to distortions at any of the key stages.

- Common perceptual distortions include people's tendency to stereotype others, to assume that others see things in the same ways that they do (projection), to use a single characteristic to create an overall impression of another person (halo effect), and to attribute internal causes to other people's behaviour (the fundamental attribution error).
- Differences in cultural values can give rise to different ways of perceiving events, issues and people in the environment. Irish people may be more likely to perceive things differently than people from other cultural backgrounds.

DISCUSSION QUESTIONS

1. People often have to deal with unexpected or surprising events at work. Have you experienced situations in which the information you have received has been totally different from what you expected or what you wanted to hear? How did you react? Can you think of workplace examples of the different reactions to unexpected information that have been outlined above (i.e. dominance, compromise, disruption and recognition)?

2. Imagine that you have an important message to send to all employees in a large organisational setting (for example, new regulations for safety procedures; the introduction of a product or the arrival of a new employee). What techniques would you use to make sure that everyone in the organisation was aware of the message that you wanted to get across? Discuss this in the light of what you now know about perception and the factors that influence it.

3. Write your own simple self-schema.

   Instructions: Write down six to eight key words that define who you are as an individual. This list is an example of a self-schema. It represents a simple framework of information you probably use in some implicit way to organise new or complex information about yourself and allows you to classify your perceptions in a structured and predefined manner.

4. The study outlined (on page 45) briefly showed how gender stereotypes can guide or direct people's personal lives and choices. Do gender stereotypes exist at work? Are there strong gender stereotypes among organisations in Ireland? If so, how do you think they affect people's behaviour at work?

5. What do *you* think of Hofstede's cultural dimensions? Does the 'Irish profile' outlined on page 51 make sense to you? How can our understanding of culture and its influence on perception be enhanced by recognising the concept of subcultures both within countries and within organisations? Think about how cultural dimensions outlined by Hofstede might affect people's perceptions of various situations in work.

CHAPTER 4

Motivation and Stress

LEARNING OBJECTIVES
- To define motivation and identify the essential elements of the motivation process.
- To show how an understanding of the psychological effects of unemployment can help to explain the motivation to work.
- To apply broad concepts of individual behaviour to the motivation process at work.
- To critically evaluate central theories of motivation.
- To analyse issues of motivation using a variety of theoretical concepts.
- To identify key sources of stress within the workplace and common responses to the stress experience.

INTRODUCTION

This chapter provides a theoretical overview of the behavioural concepts of motivation and stress. Both these concepts are central to the treatment of organisational behaviour. Motivation – or what drives people to perform in their work settings – is a subject that has received enormous attention in the literature. From the classic 'hierarchy of needs' theory proposed by Maslow (1943) to the network of expectancies and outcomes outlined by the expectancy theorists, there have been a variety of attempts to establish how efforts at work are initiated, sustained and directed. Motivation is an important concept both from a managerial and an individual perspective. However, while motivation is important, the relationship between motivation and performance is not straightforward; motivation and job performance are not synonymous (e.g. Greenberg and Baron, 1997).

In exploring motivation, this chapter highlights a definition of motivation and outlines the key theoretical perspectives that have been adopted in relation to this concept. Stress is also a familiar experience for people at work. The experience of stress is linked to motivation in that the drive and commitment created by high levels of motivation may also contribute to higher stress levels in individuals and groups at work. This chapter also outlines the main sources of stress at work, and explores the effects of and the reactions to stress, as well as outlining some key coping strategies that individuals can use to manage stress more effectively.

Box 4.1: Approaching the theory of motivation

Behaviourist and experimental psychology has traditionally had problems trying to come to grips with the broader questions about human nature. As a result of the dominance of these two traditions in European and American psychology for most of this century, many aspects of human life remain very little researched – although with the increasing acceptance of qualitative methodologies, many of these areas have started to come into focus. This is a recent development, however, and their omission has left many gaps and distortions in accepted psychological knowledge.

Motivation is one of those areas which became distorted as a result of the emphasis on laboratory studies of overt behaviour. A typical psychology textbook of the 1960s or 1970s will have a chapter on motivation which will almost inevitably be devoted to research into psychological drives such as hunger and thirst; some discussion of neural mechanisms underlying these drives. If the authors were being really radical, they might even include Maslow's hierarchical model at the very end of the chapter.

But what about the other reasons why people do things? In fact a great deal of psychology is concerned with human motivation. But those aspects of human motivation which are to do with social or personal motives tend not to come under the same heading – they are treated under social psychology or personality theory, or something quite different. If they are all brought together as aspects of motivation though, they produce a very interesting and much fuller picture of why people do things.

Source: Hayes, 1994, p. 438

DEFINING MOTIVATION

The concept of motivation is used and referred to often in organisational contexts. From a personal perspective, most people are familiar with times when they find it difficult to be interested in or feel energetic about work that they have to do. At other times or in other contexts, people can feel focused, can be eager to start a task, maintain high levels of energy and interest while the job is under way, and derive high levels of satisfaction once it has been completed. Low or high levels of motivation have an effect on the experience and perceptions of work and can be (but not necessarily) related to performance.

Motivation is the set of processes that stimulate, guide and sustain human behaviour towards accomplishing some goal.

Stimulating behaviour

In an effort to understand what stimulates or initiates behaviour, theorists have proposed that in order for any behaviour to be initiated, that behaviour needs to be triggered by some *driving force* that influences an individual. For example, a feeling of hunger is the driving force that causes people to be motivated to search for ways of acquiring food; a need for achievement may be the driving force that motivates people to attempt to achieve challenging work-related goals; curiosity at work may be the driving force that motivates people to try out new ideas or experiment with new combinations of activities. A driving force is essentially anything that triggers a certain behaviour.

Guiding behaviour

Behaviour may be initiated by some driving force, but it is guided or directed by the decisions that the individual makes as to what are the best alternatives to select in order to achieve the goal that they are pursuing most effectively. Events in the environment may cause individuals to make a new decision or to change a course of action that they are pursuing. A change in perception about the appropriateness of a given goal or about the appropriateness of certain activity in the achievement of a goal, are the types of events that can serve to direct people's behaviour during the process of motivation.

Sustaining behaviour

Motivated behaviour varies in its overall levels of robustness. What is it that sustains behaviour towards the achievement of a certain goal? How long will someone persist in attempting to achieve a particular goal? The stronger or more robust the motivated behaviour, the more likely someone is to persist in the achievement of the relevant goals.

Key questions that relate to motivation:

- What initiates behaviour?
- What directs behaviour?
- What sustains behaviour?

These are important preliminary questions in the attempt to understand the complex and multi-faceted concept of motivation, and the theories of motivation outlined in this chapter each address at least one of these three questions.

Different individuals aim for different kinds of goals in their lives. The different goals that people set are often pursued at different levels of intensity and immediacy, depending on experienced needs at a particular point in time; so the theories of motivation do not always account for these individual differences. Theoretical frameworks of motivation have often been criticised as at least in some way inadequate in the face of the uniqueness and complexity of the human spirit.

Attempting to explain all of human motivation processes under a single framework has proved to be a daunting theoretical task. Nevertheless, different theories make different contributions to a more complete understanding of motivation. There are two major categories of motivation theory: need or content theories and process theories.

Effectance motivation

It has been proposed by psychologists that people are dispositionally motivated to deal and to interact with their environments in effective and functional ways (White, 1959). Piaget has also shown how children are driven to be effective. Learning to master the environment is an important motivator for individuals, apparently driving behaviour from a very early age.

Motivation patterns at work may also be characterised by effectance motivation. However, because different people master their environments in very different ways in their work settings, it is difficult to identify a theoretical model which describes, explains or predicts individual motivation patterns in any comprehensive way.

The basic proposition of effectance motivation is that people want to be capable members of society and so are anxious to grasp and to master the aspects of society that are valued.

Why do people work?

Some psychologists suggest that to humans (and indeed to other animals) work is as natural as rest or play. Anthropologists have also found that all societies engage in work-based, organised activity of some kind, even though the nature of these activities may vary dramatically from one culture to another.

Peter Warr's studies (1984) have outlined some of the psychological effects of unemployment which may help to clarify some of the answers to the question of why people are motivated to work.

Box 4.2: Psychological effects of unemployment

Financial anxiety

Financial pressures are an almost inevitable feature of unemployment, and studies have shown that worries about money are a strong predictor of overall anxiety levels in unemployment situations.

Loss of 'traction' or life structure

Employment seems to create a structure and direction that may not be as easy to attain in situations of unemployment. Traction is a concept which refers to the structure in people's lives that helps to direct their energies. It provides a focus and creates various landmarks in life that can help to provide people with a sense of progress and achievement. For example, people at work look forward to their weekends and their holidays. They may feel a sense of achievement on Fridays when the week is complete or at the end of any day. People who are unemployed often report a feeling that every day is the same, and that there is nothing particular to look forward to. Although of course it is possible to create one's own structures and frameworks in life, it appears that this is harder for people who are not involved in some form of paid or unpaid work.

Less decision-making

When people are unemployed, they are not answerable to an employer and are not subjected to rules and regulations that they may find stressful or unacceptable. However, while there may be more freedom in theory, generally people find that there is less to be free about. Decisions tend to be seen as less important and less significant, which may have an effect on overall levels of self-esteem and confidence

Less skill development

Organisations have the potential to provide people with an effective arena for developing their skills. Opportunities for training and development may be more available and employers may carry some or all of the costs of skill or competence enhancement. Without a job, people may find that their opportunities for skill development are not as easy to create without the backing of an organisation.

Increase in psychologically threatening activities

Looking for another job, risking rejection, having to reorganise loan payments or other financial-related worries generally give rise to an increase from psychologically threatening activities.

Loss of status

The attitudes towards unemployment that exist in society can make people feel less important and less valuable as members of that society. Even the words that our society uses to describe unemployment are charged with negative connotations; for example, the word 'redundant' (literally meaning something which no longer has a use) is commonly used to describe people who have lost their jobs. In implicit and explicit ways, 'not having a job' is often seen and described in very negative ways, leading to an overall sense of a lowering of status.

Adapted from Warr, 1984

Peter Warr's study of the psychological effects of unemployment has been generally supported by more recent studies exploring the same concept. Surveys have shown, for example, that aspects of work that are motivating include: having control over activities; using knowledge and experience; having a variety of things to do; earning money; making friends; and doing a job that people respect (Handy, 1990). If people suffer psychological ill-effects when out of work, then we can infer that they may be motivated to work in order to avoid these ill-effects or to seek out the positive outcomes that work can provide.

Thus we can argue that people work in order to:

- protect themselves from financial anxiety;
- gain a structure and momentum in their lives;

- develop their skills and knowledge;
- have an arena in which to exercise control and to make decisions;
- protect themselves from psychologically threatening activities to which they may be more vulnerable outside employment;
- enhance or maintain their perceived status in their lives and communities.

Defining work in the narrow terms of 'paid employment' can prevent an effective analysis of the issue of motivation. Many people work in non-paid situations and derive similar benefits from their work as those in paid employment. Indeed, there are arguments which suggest that no one should be labelled unemployed, and that motivation does not derive from work or even from employment, but from activity. To illustrate this point, Charles Handy proposes ways in which we can start to think more broadly about the nature of 'employment' and 'unemployment' and how these concepts may relate to motivation:

> We should stop talking and thinking about employment and employees. They are words, after all, which only entered the English language some hundred years ago. If work were defined as activity, some of which is paid for, then everyone is a worker, for nearly all of their natural life. If everyone were treated as self-employed during their active years, then by law and logic they could not be unemployed. (Handy, 1990, p. 20)

Some people argue that many of the psychological effects of unemployment are attributable to the attitudes, perceptions, labels and evaluations that society places on people who do not work in conventional, paid employment, and that the label 'unemployment' can itself be demotivating. It is worthwhile thinking of motivation in a wider sense than in the conventional context of organisational settings. People are motivated by a wide range of needs, activities and goals. Motivation manifests itself in a myriad of ways, from running companies to running marathons. A broader view of the phenomenon of motivation can help managers to understand the passion and commitment to which it sometimes gives rise – even if this is not always easy to apply or to capture in all work settings.

With this in mind, the following theories help to throw some important light on motivational structures, processes and outcomes.

NEED/CONTENT THEORIES OF MOTIVATION

Need theories of motivation focus on the question 'What initiates or stimulates behaviour?' By focusing on the different types of needs that people experience and by exploring which needs are most important at any one point in time, need theorists implicitly assume that needs are the most important determinant of individual levels of motivation. In attempting to answer the question 'What motivates people to work?', the need theorists would say that people are motivated by *needs,* particularly those that are strongest and most salient to them at a particular time.

Maslow's hierarchy of needs theory

Maslow's hierarchy of needs (1943, 1954, 1970) theory has been widely quoted in organisational behaviour texts all over the world. In fact, Maslow was a humanistic psychologist, never claiming to be an expert in organisational contexts and processes. However, organisational theorists (notably Hall and Nougaim, 1968) have traditionally borrowed strongly from the ideas promoted by him, applying them to motivation in the workplace.

Figure 4.1: Maslow's hierarchy of needs

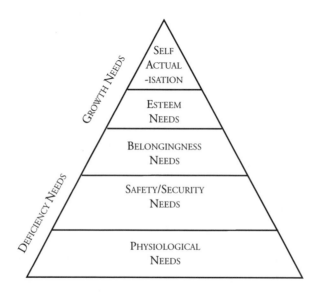

According to Maslow, needs at the lower level of the hierarchy dominate an individual's motivational drive as long as they continue to be unsatisfied. Once they are adequately satisfied, they move into a 'higher' need category, being motivated by a different set of needs. Maslow identifies a total of five different need types. He also identifies two broader categories: deficiency needs (physiological and safety needs) and growth needs (belongingness, esteem and self-actualisation needs). All of these are important needs to consider in the workplace as well as in wider contexts.

- *Physiological needs* include basic, deficiency needs for water, oxygen, rest, sexual expression and physiological tension release.
- *Safety needs* include needs for security, comfort, tranquility and freedom from fear.
- *Belongingness/social needs* include the need to belong, to love and to be loved.

- *Esteem needs* include needs for confidence, sense of worth and competence, self-esteem and respect from others.
- *Self-actualisation* refers to the need to realise one's full human potential, to achieve long-term goals in life and to become everything that one is capable of becoming.

The strongest implication emerging from the hierarchy is that unless people's basic deficiency needs are satisfied, they will not be motivated to pursue goals which relate to higher-order needs. Therefore, activities that demand organisationally popular dimensions of team work, 'empowerment', creativity, innovation, or knowledge enhancement will not be relevant or important to people who don't earn enough money to survive, or who are not sufficiently protected from danger in their workplace. According to Maslow's theory, people in low-paid work or who face hazardous or dangerous environments in the workplace will be less interested in developing social networks, achieving high status in their jobs or realising their potential in other ways.

A brief critique of Maslow

There is a certain intuitive appeal to Maslow's 'hierarchy of needs' theory. It recognises that needs motivate people in different ways and assumes that if someone experiences deficiency needs, they will not be motivated to grow or to develop until those needs have been satisfied. Furthermore, it identifies important categories of individual needs and encourages us to consider the variety of needs which at different times stimulate or initiate behaviour.

However, as a comprehensive model of motivation, it is insufficient in both descriptive and predictive terms for the following reasons:

1. There is plenty of evidence to suggest that needs are not organised in the hierarchical structure suggested in Maslow's framework. On a regular basis, people sacrifice lower-order needs in order to satisfy those at a 'higher' level on the hierarchy. For example: people who have risked their lives to save other people (thus ignoring their needs for safety in favour of say attachment or esteem needs); people who have gone on hunger strike (depriving themselves of basic survival needs in order to satisfy a higher-order need); or even someone who has stayed up all night to study for an exam (bypassing the need for sleep in order to fulfil their individual potential) all provide clear evidence the need order is not as straightforward or as linear as the hierarchy suggests.

2. An implicit assumption of Maslow's hierarchy is that need deprivation is what motivates people's behaviour. The theory is based on a 'fulfilment progression' dynamic which indicates that as soon as a need has been sufficiently satisfied, it ceases to be a motivator. There is a connotation inherent in this assertion which suggests that in any attempts to motivate people, needs should be deprived in order to sustain motivated behaviour.

Both intuitively and empirically, this implication points to a flaw in the theory. Need deprivation may motivate for a certain length of time, after which its effects may yield quite the opposite reaction. If people are continually denied an opportunity to satisfy needs that they are experiencing, this eventually leads to demotivated, apathetic and disheartened behaviour (e.g. Seligman, 1973; De Vellis *et al.*, 1978).

Alderfer's ERG theory

Alderfer (1972) proposes that there are three broad need categories: existence (roughly corresponding to Maslow's physiological and safety needs), relatedness (corresponding to Maslow's belongingness needs) and growth (corresponding to Maslow's esteem, and self-actualisation categories). Responding to the problematic 'fulfilment progression' dimension proposed by Maslow, Alderfer suggests that motivated behaviour can be activated either via 'need fulfilment, progression' or by another dynamic referred to as 'need frustration, regression'.

Fulfilment progression: once a need is satisfied in someone, he/she ceases to be motivated by that need category and moves on to another, higher order category of needs.

Frustration regression: if a need is consistently frustrated, an individual 'regresses' to being motivated by lower-order needs that are already being fulfilled to a sufficient degree.

McClelland's achievement motivation theory

Work by David McClelland (1961) which gained popularity around the same time as Maslow's theory proposes that there are three key needs which motivate people's behaviour at work. Unlike Maslow, McClelland's work was grounded more firmly within organisational settings and may relate more directly to patterns of work and how people operate within organisational structures. According to this theory, needs that people experience can be directly related to people's work preferences. The three needs that he identifies are:

1. The need for achievement.
2. The need for power.
3. The need for affiliation.

These are need categories that are learned through life experiences, and any one person will tend to be more driven by one of the three needs that are identified. McClelland's research has shown that people who are mainly driven by a need for achievement will have distinctly different work preferences than those driven by a need for power or by a need for affiliation. Table 4.1 summarises the preferences that have been found to be associated with each of the three need categories in this theory.

Table 4.1: Preferences associated with needs

Individual needs	Work preferences
Need for achievement	**People driven by a need for achievement are motivated to:** • set challenging but achievable goals; • work on goals that they have set for themselves; • receive timely and accurate feedback about their performance.
Need for power	**People driven by a need for power are motivated to:** • influence and affect the behaviour of others; • position themselves within organisational settings so that they can legitimately control situations; • receive attention and recognition through having mobilised the activity of others.
Need for affiliation	**People driven by a need for affiliation are motivated to:** • develop strong interpersonal ties at work; • work in situations where they are given the opportunity to interact with others; • receive approval from others; • spend time in social settings.

The needs identified by McClelland can be useful in helping managers to recognise the diversity of behaviours that people display at work. Recognising individual differences is an important starting point in the attempt to understand motivation, and McClelland's propositions make some progress towards this goal. People with a need for power will behave in very different ways than people with a need for achievement and affiliation.

McClelland's model provides the field of organisational behaviour with more food for thought in relation to needs and driving forces. The methodologies through which he gathered his data was also quite innovative at the time the theory was developed. He used thematic aperception tests (TATs) in order to ascertain the needs that were operating in any one individual. These were projective tests which displayed pictures to subjects, asking them to create their own story about what the picture was about.

Qualitative analyses of the responses given provided information and perspectives which McClelland believed allowed him to infer whether someone was driven by achievement, by affiliation or by power.

Another technique involved asking people to tell stories, or to finish stories that had been started by someone else. By exploring the content, language and imagery of the stories, McClelland attempted to determine the dimensions of achievement, affiliation or power motivation.

This methodology was inevitably criticised for being too subjective and not testable according to rigorous or valid measures. However, his methodologies marked an important contribution to an increasingly popular approach in organisational behaviour for exploring intangible concepts like motivation, culture and personality. Many qualitative researchers argue that the language, imagery and stories that people use contain important clues to the sorts of inner drives that direct and sustain their energies.

Furthermore, McClelland's work yielded some interesting inter-cultural observations, in particular with respect to the need for achievement. McClelland argued that the differences in achievement motivation observed in different cultures was reflected in each culture's use of literature and imagery and that language was an important source of evidence which can help to establish the intensity with which different needs are experienced in any one culture.

Herzberg's two factor theory

Frederick Herzberg provides a perspective on needs which adds another consideration to the area of needs and the motivation to which they give rise. His research suggests that there are two types of factors in the workplace. One set of factors (called satisfiers or motivators) is capable of motivating people to perform and the other set of factors (called hygiene/maintenance factors or 'dissatisfiers') only has a negative or dissatisfying impact if they are absent, but are not capable of motivating behaviour when present.

The two sets of factors his research has identified are summarised in Table 4.2.

Table 4.2: Two factor theory

Satisfiers/Motivators	Dissatisfiers/Hygiene factors
Sense of achievement.	Salary/pay.
Recognition.	Job security.
Responsibility.	Working conditions.
Nature of the work.	Level and quality of supervision.
Personal growth and advancement.	Company policy and administration.
	Interpersonal relations.

While the methods that Herzberg used to reach his conclusions were also criticised for their questionable rigour and validity, the principle that he highlights is still worth considering in work settings, though perhaps not in the rigid way that his theoretical assertions suggest. His theory has been criticised for its method boundedness; that is, similar findings have only been established using the same methods applied in the original study. The original work elicited information from respondents by requesting them to do the following:

1. 'Tell me about a time when you felt exceptionally good about your job.' Responses to this request were assumed to be the factors that people found motivating.
2. 'Tell me about a time when you felt exceptionally bad about your job.' Responses to this request were assumed to be the factors that people found demotivating or dissatisfying.

When other samples of respondents have been asked directly what motivates them at work, responses have yielded very different patterns of results. It may be that potential problems with the construct validity of Herzberg's work have led to an inaccurate or at least an overly rigid framework.

A key criticism often directed at Herzberg is his assertion that money is not a motivator. Intuitively people often respond quite fiercely to any suggestion that money is not capable of motivating people's work. Studies have shown that people, for example with high needs for achievement, rank money very highly on their list of motivators in that it can be a tangible and measurable way of gauging their progress and performance. And money itself is capable of fulfilling a wide range of needs outlined by many of the content theorists, so it cannot be so easily dismissed as incapable of motivating behaviour.

However, there is some strong evidence in applied settings that money can play a dissatisfying role and be at least less able to give rise to motivated behaviour than other factors. For example, bonus schemes or yearly percentage increases can become institutionalised in organisational settings such that they are seen as a condition of the job and only serve to create dissatisfaction if they are not received, but fail to motivate people in any directed or sustained way.

This example draws attention to a series of ideas that relate to process theories of motivation; that is, a comparison between what people expect and what they get in organisational settings is an important consideration when attempting to explain motivation at work. This comparison will be explored in more detail in the next section which deals with the process theories of motivation.

The contribution of need theories to the study of motivation

Need theories provide useful direction for the recognition and understanding that there are different types of needs, which, when experienced, will give rise to different types of motivated behaviour. However, it is far from certain that there are only five broad categories of needs. Alderfer (1972) identifies only three major need categories while Murray (1975) proposes a long list of different categories.

Indeed, it may not be as important to know exactly what needs people experience and how they can be categorised as it is to understand some of the individual processes associated with motivation. It seems that efforts to classify these experiences will almost inevitably lead to imprecise generalities or to cumbersome lists, neither of which are particularly useful in the development of sound theoretical principles.

Any need theory focuses on the identification of the nature of the needs that people experience which motivate them to behave in certain ways. As such, it can be argued that none of them go far enough in the quest to understand motivation. As the process theorists have shown, there is more to motivation than simple responses to experienced needs.

PROCESS THEORIES

There is no doubt that the content/need theories of motivation make an important contribution to the understanding of motivation at work, particularly via the identification of factors and needs that drive behaviour. Need theorists are centrally focused on the question: what drives behaviour and what initiates motivation? Need theorists broadly maintain that people experience needs and respond in a way that will satisfy whatever need they feel most intensely. The work of the process theorists proposes that people are more complex, more pragmatic and more contemplative than the need theorists suggest or at least imply.

Process theorists have collected evidence to show that before people exert energy in pursuit of any goal, they go through a decision-making process which explores the validity of the goals that they are pursuing; examines the extent to which they are likely to achieve objectives by pursuing a particular course of action; compares their situation to those of others; investigates the difference between what they put into work and what they get out, or in some way considers the benefits associated with devoting energy to a particular activity or set of activities at work. In analysing what motivates people at work, process theories focus not only on what people want from their work situations, but how they believe they can get it.

Expectancy theory

The original expectancy theory (Vroom, 1964) identifies three important expectations that individuals bring to the workplace:

1. That effort will lead to performance. (Effort – Performance Expectancy)   E ➡ P.
2. That performance will lead to a further outcome/outcomes. (Performance Outcome Expectancy) P ➡ O.
3. That each outcome is perceived to have a certain value, V. (Valence).

Vroom proposes that the strength of someone's motivation can be established by using the following formula:

Motivation = effort performance expectancy X performance outcome expectancy X valence

This means that each of the three expectations outlined are equally important in establishing or determining levels of motivation. Table 4.3 demonstrates the types of statements that can reveal the existence or strength of an individual's expectations with respect to performance, outcomes and value of outcomes.

Table 4.3: Performance expectations

	Example statements which may reveal that the expectation does exist.	Example statements which may reveal that the expectation does not exist.
Effort performance expectancy	'If I work hard, I know I'll achieve results.'	'No matter how hard I work, I never seem to be able to reach my targets.'
Performance outcome expectancy	'If I achieve results, I'll get a rise.' 'If I meet my targets this year, I'll be promoted.'	'Even if I achieve the results, I'm not at all sure that I'll get rewarded for it.' 'My boss isn't interested in promoting me no matter how good she thinks I am.'
Valence	'It's really important I get a rise this year.' 'I really hope that I'll be promoted by the end of this year.'	'I don't really care whether I get a rise or not – after tax it's not worth much to me anyway.' 'I wouldn't care if I never got promoted.'

Porter and Lawler

As a way of extending the original expectancy theory, Porter and Lawler also consider the role that abilities and role perceptions play in producing various outcomes. They also draw an explicit difference between intrinsic and extrinsic rewards, the former being rewards that are generated by the individuals themselves (e.g. a sense of achievement, personal satisfaction, a feeling of pride in work and so on) and the latter being rewards that are provided from external sources (pay, promotion, praise, recognition and so on).

Figure 4.3: Porter and Lawler's extension of the expectancy model of motivation

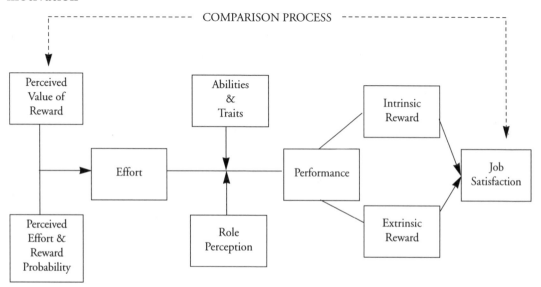

Like the original expectancy theory, Porter and Lawler also highlight that before people make a decision to exert effort, they need to value the rewards that are available and to feel if they do exert effort, that the rewards will be available to them.

Perceived value of the reward

Porter and Lawler's model highlights that before people give their effort and commitment to any activity, they ask themselves 'What's in it for me?' and that people are constantly engaged in a process of examining the value of the rewards or benefits that are associated with the effort involved.

Perceived effort – reward probability

It's not enough that people value the potential rewards associated with an activity. People must also believe that they are capable of carrying out that activity successfully or that the rewards that they are being promised are actually going to materialise on completion of the task. When perceived effort – reward probability is high, then the individual has confidence in his/her ability to carry out the tasks and that the rewards will be available once the task has been completed. When perceived effort reward probability is low, the individual does not have confidence in his/her ability to carry out the tasks, or he/she is not confident for some reason that the rewards for carrying out the tasks will be available once the required tasks are complete. Perceived effort – reward probability is a function of the individual's faith and belief in his/her own capacities and/or his/her faith in the likelihood that rewards will be administered by the organisation.

Effort

If the perceived value of the reward is high enough and the perceived effort reward probability exists at least to some degree, then the individual is likely to exert effort. However, effort does not automatically lead to performance. Most people can think of times when their most concerted efforts did not give rise to the performance or the results that they expected. Highlighted in Porter and Lawler's model is the identification of factors which intervene to facilitate or to impede the path from effort to performance.

Abilities, traits and role perception

In order for effort to translate into performance, individuals need to have appropriate abilities and traits to carry out the tasks required as well as a clear role perception and a good knowledge of the parameters of the tasks or activities they are being asked to carry out.

Intrinsic and extrinsic rewards

Effective performance is unlikely to be repeated if individuals do not receive the rewards that they expected. Porter and Lawler assert that motivation is not sustained just because a particular need is experienced or activated. Motivated activity must give rise to results and rewards. These rewards can be intrinsic (e.g. an inner sense of achievement) or extrinsic (a pay rise, a promotion or some other externally provided reward).

Overall levels of satisfaction

The combination of intrinsic and extrinsic rewards experienced or provided to individuals, leads to overall levels of satisfaction. These overall levels are compared to the individual's original expectations and if they compare favourably (that is, if rewards are the same or better than expected), then motivated behaviour is likely to continue. If the rewards compare unfavourably to original expectations (that is, if rewards are worse than originally expected) then motivated behaviour will decrease and may eventually disappear altogether.

Unlike the need theorists, expectancy theories recognise the role of conscious thought processes and assert that people's personal calculations, their expectations and their evaluations are central to a comprehensive understanding of how the process of motivation works.

Equity theory

Adams' equity theory (1963) is based on the assumption that the most important motivator for individuals is the perception that they are being treated fairly in comparison to other people in the same context. According to this theory, people's motivation to be treated fairly is so overwhelming, that they become involved in any number of 'strategies' to reduce situations of injustice or inequity.

Like the other process theories, Adams asserts that it is individuals' own conscious evaluations of their situation and their work outcomes that drives the motivation process and can explain the bases of motivation at work.

Adams' research indicated that people are constantly engaged in three main evaluative processes:

1. A comparison between their work inputs and their work outcomes.
2. A comparison between other people's work inputs and outcomes.
3. An analysis of these two comparisons.

It is the perception of equity and balance between an individual's rewards and those of others that maintains their levels of motivation. As soon as people feel (or even suspect) that they are being treated unfairly in comparison to others, their framework of motivation can change quite radically in a variety of different ways.

An individual will conclude that he/she is being treated unfairly if his/her ratio of inputs and outcomes does not match the input/outcome ratios of 'comparison others' (i.e. people to whom the individual compares himself/herself). (See Table 4.4.)

Adams states that when individuals compare their own work inputs and outcomes with those of others, they are motivated to maintain their levels of input just as long as they feel that they are being treated fairly. Someone who puts in an eight-hour day and gets paid say £48 would expect someone else who puts in four hours to get paid £24. This means that both people are getting treated equally according to their inputs. However, if their 'comparison other' gets more or less per hour than they do, a situation of perceived inequity is said to have arisen. Of course, time is not the only work input that may be considered, and money not the only outcome. People may choose from a wide range of different inputs and outcomes when they are evaluating whether or not they are being treated fairly.

Table 4.4: Adams' equity theory

Key terms associated with Adams' equity theory	
Inputs	'Anything a person perceives as an investment in the job and worthy of some return' (Ribeaux and Poppleton, 1978).
	Individuals can consider a wide range of factors to be work inputs, or valuable assets or contributions that they bring to their jobs.
	Inputs can include: time, effort, commitment, loyalty, qualifications, skills, attitudes, or competencies.
Outcomes	Any outcomes that a person receives from doing their job.
	Outcomes can include: money, respect, satisfaction, friendship, skill acquisition, status fringe benefits, bonuses and so on.
'Comparison others'	Other people with whom people compare themselves.
	People tend to compare themselves with people doing the same or similar jobs. However, they may rule out comparing people who have different qualifications, or different levels of experience.
Perceived equity	Occurs when the individual perceives that he/she is being treated fairly when compared to their comparison others.
Perceived inequity	Occurs when the individual perceives that he/she is being treated unfairly when compared to their comparison others.

There are two types of perceived inequity that people can experience:

- *Negative inequity:* when people feel that the unfair treatment affects them in negative ways (like less pay, or fewer positive work outcomes than other people in the same or similar work situations).
- *Positive inequity:* when people feel that the unfair treatment affects them in positive ways (for example they receive more positive work outcomes than their colleagues including pay, fringe benefits, skill development, interpersonal contact etc.).

When people are happy that they are being treated fairly, they are motivated to maintain the *status quo*, by maintaining their current levels of input. However, if they perceive that they are being treated unfairly, then they may respond, according to this theory, in any one of the following ways:

- changing their level of input to the job;
- changing the outcomes they receive;
- changing other people's inputs or outcomes;
- changing their perception of their or others' inputs/outcomes;
- changing their comparison others;
- leaving the work situation in which they feel unfairly treated.

1. Changing work inputs

If inequitable treatment is perceived, the individual may lower his/her inputs, by putting in less effort or time (if he/she feels they are being treated *worse* than others) or increase his/her inputs by working harder (if he/she feels they are being treated *better* than others).

2. Changing work outcomes

If people feel that their outcomes are less than other people in the same situation, they may try to increase their outcomes by appealing to their bosses, supervisors or trade unions. They may bring the inequity to public attention in some way in an effort to establish or to restore a level of equity. The example in the Discussion Questions at the end of this chapter provides an example of this effort to increase work outcomes. By organising a public demonstration, the Garda Siochana can be seen to have taken action which was the direct result of perceived inequity on the part of the organisation and its members.

There is less evidence to support the hypothesis that people will try to decrease their outcomes even in situations where they feel that they are receiving more for their inputs than others are. However, Adams' theory suggests that this is also a possible response when people feel that they are being treated better than other people to whom they compare themselves. More recent research by Miles *et al.* (1994) has demonstrated that different individuals vary in their levels of 'equity sensitivity'. Their research has identified evidence which suggests that some people are more 'benevolent' than others and as a result more likely to highlight situations of positive inequity (i.e. situations where they perceive that they are being treated or rewarded more favourably than others in their work situation).

3. Changing others' inputs/outcomes

Similar efforts may be made to redress the perceived inequity by attempting to change other people's inputs (encouraging them to increase or to decrease their inputs) or other people's outcomes.

4. Changing perceptions of own or others' inputs/outcomes

Adams argues that people's *perceptions* are what influences their behaviour most strongly. In order to redress a situation of perceived inequity, changes in perception may be just as powerful as any real changes in the environment. And because people feel uncomfortable when they perceive inequity, they may voluntarily re-evaluate the situation and become satisfied that they are not being treated unfairly in comparison to others. Some people find the experience of inequity so intolerable that failure to change the situation may cause them to reconsider their original assessments. So for example, someone who sees that they are being paid less than others doing the same work may introduce other variables into the equation for their considerations. They may look at the amount of experience others have, or other people's level of skill or qualifications, and then establish that they are not being treated unfairly once these considerations are accounted for. By changing perceptions, people can convince themselves, or become convinced that they are being treated fairly.

5. Changing comparison with others

Sometimes perceptions cannot be changed. In situations where there is obvious favouritism in an organisation, individuals may restore feelings of equity by ceasing to consider certain individuals as comparable to them. Someone who is picked out for special treatment (e.g. the boss's son/daughter) may be getting a better deal than everyone else, and one way of overcoming a personal feeling of inequity is to recognise the special circumstances surrounding a certain individual and stop using this individual as a measure of equity. Of course, legislation and other policy-based rules should prevent any individual from receiving special treatment, but in situations where it does arise a sense of inequity may be overcome via perceptual changes as well as actual ones.

6. Leaving the situation

Adams argues that if someone continues to feel unfairly treated even after efforts to redress the balance (either actually or perceptually) have been made, they will quit their jobs. It has been recognised, especially in times where alternatives are unavailable, that many people tolerate high levels of perceived inequity without ever leaving their jobs. However, it is also possible to withdraw psychologically from work and working life. Adams says that people who experience negative inequity for any length of time are likely to withdraw in some way from their jobs, even if this means simply allowing their levels of motivation on the job to decrease or to disappear.

Essentially, the equity theory highlights the importance that a feeling of fairness plays in people's motivational processes.

Recent research has shown that the equity theory appears to have more global applicability than other motivation theories which may be more culturally biased. Because many of the original theories of motivation derive from American researchers, a common allegation is that they may be limited in their applicability to the American cultural context. Equity theory has shown higher levels of applicability in a variety of cultural settings including Europe and China (Shenkar and von Glinow, 1994).

Generally, research evidence is particularly supportive of the theory in situations of underpayment or other forms of negative inequity (Crosier and Dalton, 1989). It seems that the concept of fairness is an important one in a wide variety of cultural and organisational settings. Anecdotal evidence abounds in the Irish context as much as anywhere. Examples of intense reactions to inequitable situations are everywhere. 'It's not fair' is a commonly used phrase in situations where people are demotivated or where they are attempting to make efforts to establish and maintain fair treatment for themselves and for others with whom they identify. Theory and evidence frequently suggests that organisational fairness pervades the psyche of organisational members and the groups that represent them.

Goal setting and motivation

People can be motivated by the needs that drive them, the cognitive processes that help them to calculate 'what's in it for them' but also by goals and targets which can help them to direct, to measure and to assess their performance in tangible and often effective ways.

Setting goals at work has been found in some settings to be an effective way of unlocking motivational processes in individuals and groups. To motivate people, Latham and Locke (1979), among others, have found that setting goals elicits higher performance levels than in the absence of goals. However, goal setting is not a simple management technique which necessarily increases effort and performance in any linear or automatic way. Combined with effective and equitable reward systems, developed in a participative context and accompanied by accurate and timely feedback on the levels of achievement, organisations can benefit by setting challenging but achievable goals and targets for their employees.

Table 4.5 outlines how some goals can motivate performance in a positive way and how others can be demotivating.

Table 4.5: Goals and performance

Goals can motivate people to perform when they are:	Goals can be demotivating when they are:
• specific and clear;	• non-specific and ambiguous;
• challenging but achievable;	• impossible to achieve or too easy to achieve;
	• (excessively difficult goals eventually become ignored or cause high levels of stress with low levels of performance; excessively easy goals set a ceiling on performance);
• flexible when the task is novel or ambiguous to give people time to explore the parameters of the new activities involved;	• inflexible in times of change, uncertainty, crisis or novelty;
• agreed on by those required to achieve the goals;	• imposed without consultation or communication;
• monitored and reviewed so that people can be provided with effective feedback on their performance towards the attainment of the goals.	• rarely reviewed, or only mentioned when people are not achieving them.

Goal-setting theory is another helpful perspective on motivation which can be useful in enhancing our understanding of some of the triggers and directors of motivation and sustained behaviour at work.

STRESS AT WORK

Motivation is an important concept for understanding organisational behaviour. Motivation is a driving force that energises, directs, sustains, animates and stimulates people at work. As such, motivated behaviour is generally seen as positive and desirable. However, a closely associated concept is the well-known and common experience of stress. Stress in the workplace may not always be damaging, but it has the potential to inflict damage on the individual and create negative results for the organisation.

Definition of stress

Three definitions of stress:
1. A perceived imbalance between demand and response capacity, under conditions where failure to meet demand has important consequences (McGrath, 1970).

2. A general feeling of pressure, anxiety and tension.

3. A fight or flight capacity to any threatening situation.

These different definitions each tell us something important about stress and what it means. Firstly, people who experience stress at work often report that it arises due to a feeling that they won't be able to meet their goals, or carry out the tasks that are required of them. If people feel that their future work lives will be affected by their current inability to carry out a task, the experience of stress is likely to arise. There are many reasons why people may feel unable to carry out the tasks required of them at work. Being overloaded with work, being unsure about appropriate steps to take, not having enough information, or feeling that skills and abilities are inadequate for the tasks at hand are all possible reasons why someone might feel that there is an imbalance between the demands being made upon them and their capacity to respond effectively to those demands.

Secondly, almost everyone is familiar with the 'general feeling of pressure, anxiety and tension' that accompanies the experience of stress. Most people find stress an unpleasant or uncomfortable experience and are motivated to decrease the levels that they feel, or to eliminate the source of the stress.

Thirdly, stress can be defined as a fight or flight response capacity to a threatening situation. In the face of threat, people's bodies become ready for fight or flight. Heart rate increases, blood pumps around the body faster than usual, palms start to sweat and adrenaline is released into the systems. This creates extra energy in individuals which, on the one hand can help them to concentrate and focus on the problem they are facing or the threat that is challenging them, but on the other hand, often the energy they create cannot be released fully in normal work situations. This extra energy can create the feeling of tension referred to above.

Sources of work stress

How do people become excessively stressed at work? Cary Cooper *et al.* (1988) provides a useful framework for identifying various sources of pressure at work, showing that there is a variety of potential sources of stress to which individuals may be vulnerable at different times in their working lives (Figure 4.4).

Figure 4.4: Identifying sources of pressure at work

SOURCES OF WORK STRESS
• Workload   • Job conditions   • Role conflict and ambiguity
• Career development   • Interpersonal relationships in the organisation
• Conflict between demands at work and demands outside work

The various categories of stress sources show how different the experience of stress may be for different people. While one person may be stressed because of the clashing demands between their home and work responsibilities, someone else may experience stress because of a bad relationship with their boss. Moderate levels of stress may actually help people to perform, but as stress levels increase (perhaps aided by an increase in the number different sources of work stress) people's performance becomes significantly more likely to suffer. As well as the potential problems associated with poor work performance, organisations are increasingly being seen as having a moral and even legal responsibility to ensure that individuals are not exposed to levels of stress that may have an adverse effect on their health.

Responding to stress

People can respond to stress in various ways. Eysenck (1996) shows how different types of responses can be categorised into different coping classifications (Table 4.6).

Table 4.6: Stress coping classifications

Task focused coping	Emotional coping	Avoidance coping
Establish priorities.	Vent frustrations by expressing anger, irritation or anxiety.	Put the problem out of one's mind.
Come to terms with the nature and parameters of the problem.	Blame oneself for being too emotional about the situation.	Take time away from the source of the stress.
Spend time thinking about the stressful event and working out strategies for coping with future, similar events.	Re-enact a stressful situation in an emotionally expressive way.	Engage in behaviour that temporarily relieves the symptoms of stress (e.g. drinking, smoking or eating).

Some coping mechanisms are effective in that they help the individual to overcome or to deal with stress in a positive way. Others are less effective in that they may not remove the source of the stress or may cause the individual to create more harmful situations for themselves (e.g. in the case of excessive drinking in order to avoid stressful situations).

In the quest for high levels of motivation at work, managers should be mindful that pressures to perform and to achieve can create high stress levels which may be damaging to the individual and to his/her organisation.

SUMMARY OF KEY PROPOSITIONS

- This chapter explored the concepts of motivation and stress at work. The study of motivation aims to address three key questions: What initiates behaviour? What directs behaviour? What sustains behaviour?

- An exploration of the psychological effects of unemployment may provide some important insights into why people are motivated to work. In general terms, people are motivated to be protected from excessive financial anxiety, to have a structure in their lives, to develop skills and knowledge, to make decisions and to enhance or maintain their perceived status in their lives.

- The content theories of motivation focus on the needs that people experience and how these needs might drive or initiate behaviour. Maslow's hierarchy of needs, Alderfer's ERG theory, McClelland's achievement motivation theory and Herzberg's two factor theory all attempt to explain, from a variety of perspectives, the role that needs play in motivating people's behaviour. Need theories are useful, but do not provide a comprehensive base for understanding motivation at work.

- Process theories are based on the assumption that individuals and groups think consciously about the effort that they expend at work and its relative utility in reaching valued goals. Expectancy theories and equity theories focus on how people consider or weigh up various factors which contribute to their decisions to engage in effort at work

- Goal setting is another method for understanding what motivates people in the workplace. Goals can be an important motivator, but only when they satisfy essential criteria. Goals should be clear, specific, agreed upon, flexible in certain situations, and people should be given timely and accurate feedback about their levels of goal attainment.

- Finally, stress is an important experience to understand in the workplace. There is a variety of sources of stress and people can make attempts to cope with stress through task orientation, emotional expression or avoidance.

DISCUSSION QUESTIONS

Gardai insist that they are underpaid

by John Mooney

Despite having legitimate reasons to protest, rank and file gardai who marched on the Dail to demand better pay received little public or political support.

The march, the first garda demonstration in the history of the state, was aimed at raising awareness on low pay but was greeted with much public cynicism.

Unlike the nursing unions who received widespread public support when they threatened to strike, gardai get little sympathy because people believe they are well paid.

However, members of An Garda Siochana disagree, claiming that they are among the worst paid police force in Europe. Such is the level of resentment among younger members of the force, particularly those working in Dublin, that most regret ever joining.

According to Tony Hand of the Garda Representative Association, the public's perception of a policeman's job is far removed from reality.

'An increasing number of gardai are being assaulted in the line of duty. Gardai have to deal with drug addicts, armed robbers and syringe attackers. Our members receive no recognition from the government for the dangers that they face.'

At least one garda has been infected with Hepatitis B. Hundreds of officers who have been attacked with syringes have undergone medical tests to see if they are infected.

The waiting period inevitably causes distress to their families. Another problem associated with syringe or armed attacks is the fact that gardai are traditionally slow to seek professional counselling.

The national secretary of the Garda Federation, Chris Finnegan, added that gardai have to foot the medical expenses incurred in such attacks.

The basic pay for a garda is £10,044 per annum, rising to a maximum of £18,970 over a 12-year period. However, they also receive allowance payments which average around £30 per week.

In Britain, graduates of the Metropolitan police training college start their careers on a wage of £14,916. This eventually rises to a maximum of £23,607.

Gardai are resentful that customs officers are better paid. A customs officer with one year's service earns £13,143 and this rises to a maximum of £20,436.

Customs personnel also receive danger money for high-risk work. Officers seconded to the Criminal Assets Bureau received a tax-free allowance of £6,500 for their secondment. Gardai attached to the Bureau received no financial supplement.

Although the rival GRA and Garda Federation agree that something needs to be done to improve garda pay and working conditions, the two organisations have not joined forces to campaign on the matter.

The GRA is pressing ahead with its publicity campaign to highlight the issue. The federation is waiting to see what the Strategic Management Initiative Report recommends on garda pay.

Source: Sunday Business Post, 6 April 1997

1. Discuss the case of the Garda Siochana in the light of your knowledge of the theory of motivation and the sources of work stress.

Reynolds 'won't pay all trial costs'

by Andy Pollack

On his return to Ireland yesterday, Mr Albert Reynolds said that he had no intention of paying all the costs of his libel case against the *Sunday Times*. 'I'll not be railroaded into paying the costs, having won a substantial part of the case, which is that the *Sunday Times* libelled me', he said at Dublin Airport. 'They can't get away from that fact – the jury brought that verdict, they can't change that verdict. I believe it's immoral and unjust that the person who wins a libel case is being asked to pay for the total cost. I've no intention of doing that.'

He said that the cost of the case would not ruin him financially. 'I've always paid my bills and I'll pay my bills in the future. It won't put me out of business.'

Mr Reynolds said that he was 'delighted to come back holding my head high with what I wanted to get'. His name, reputation and integrity were 'everything' to him, and that is why he had gone to London to fight the case.

Irish Times, 22 November 1996

2. How would Maslow's hierarchy of needs explain Albert Reynolds' motivation to take a case against the *Sunday Times*? What role do you think has money played in the dynamics of his levels of motivation and satisfaction with the outcome of the case?

3. Compare three different need theories of motivation. In what ways are they similar and how do they differ in their approaches to motivation at work.

CHAPTER 5

Learning and Training in Organisations

LEARNING OBJECTIVES
- To define learning and training.
- To differentiate between various theories of learning.
- To understand the key principles of learning in organisations.
- To describe the learning organisation paradigm.

INTRODUCTION

As indicated by the structure of this book, behaviour in organisations is largely governed by individual, group and organisational processes. However, learning as a concept bridges all three strata since learning can occur at all levels and through a variety of systems. It is pertinent, therefore, that some attention is given to how and why individuals learn, and how the organisation as a system can facilitate continuous learning. Indeed, in recent times, we have witnessed a consistent organisational focus on the importance of the individual's contribution to successful functioning which has led to a situation whereby employees are increasingly being viewed as critical competitive resources which, if developed effectively, are seen to contribute significantly to the attainment of strategic business goals.

Box 5.1: Government commitment to learning and training

The long-awaited White Paper on human resource development was published in May, 1997 and details the government's commitment to raising the profile of learning and training in Ireland. It highlights the promotion of a learning society as one of the key platforms of the White Paper and stresses the need for a strategic approach to the development of human resources, at both the organisational and national level.

> To meet the competitive challenge requires more than just an additional investment in education or training. It requires business and the individual worker and the training and education institutions to embrace new, better approaches, to quality management and to human resource development.

Within its strategy to develop Ireland's human resources, the White Paper identifies a number of key policy objectives that are concerned with enterprise training, small enterprise training, management training and development, developing young people's skills, and so forth. Objective seven is concerned with lifelong learning and training:

> To encourage individuals to keep their skills and knowledge up to date, the government has decided that fees of up to £1,000 per year paid by individuals towards the cost of approved training and development courses leading to a qualification that achieves recognised certification, can be deductible from income liable to tax at the standard rate.

Source: White Paper on Human Resource Development, Department of Enterprise and Employment, May 1997

The debate for many years, and from an organisational behaviour perspective, focused on various measures to improve employee motivation and morale, as a means of increasing productivity and effectiveness. More recently, however, the focus has shifted to developing an environment that enables employees to learn and develop and thereby heighten productivity. In empowerment and total quality cultures, for example, individuals are expected to accept greater responsibility at their level of operations and to follow a path of continuous improvement. At the core of such cultures lies the recognition that employees have far more to offer than just performing work in a functional manner (Garavan *et al.*, 1995). The last two decades have witnessed considerable change and it is increasingly recognised that the future cannot merely be an extrapolation of past practices. In particular, Barrow and Loughlin (1992) postulate that modern organisations require that employees:

- have the ability to learn new skills and adapt to changing circumstances;
- can conceptualise the contribution of their role to organisational effectiveness;
- are capable of working in flatter structures and without supervision;
- have the ability to manage the interface between customers and the organisation;
- possess capabilities such as problem-solving, creative thinking and innovativeness.

Indeed, as highlighted in Chapter 1, the new environment of organisation has resulted in the emergence of the term 'knowledge employees' to describe the requirements of future workforces whereby individuals' capacity to learn, and their involvement in a process of self-development, can significantly enhance participation and innovation. Learning to learn, therefore, and self-development are viewed as necessarily facilitated in organisations, if the contribution of the workforce is to be maximised. In this chapter we explore the dimension of learning, both from the individual and organisation perspective. In particular, we identify the range of critical learning theories that have informed our understanding of the individual's learning process. Furthermore, we focus on key learning criteria and the notion of learning transfer as it applies to training. Finally, we outline current thinking on the learning organisation paradigm in an effort to locate individual learning within the organisation system, and conclude with a review of recent data on the scope of training and development practices in Ireland.

DEFINING LEARNING

Any discussion on learning as a concept must necessarily be prefaced by an attempt to define the concept itself. Learning, by its very nature, is difficult to define since there is no complete agreement on the parameters of learning, or where learning crosses over into other behavioural determinants. Finding a conclusive definition of learning is therefore difficult, and perhaps counterproductive. Indeed, Hatch (1997) and Leavitt and March (1988) indicate that organisations learn in a variety of ways that can often be explained by other organisational processes. For instance, they learn through direct experience when they engage in trial and error decision-making, and indirectly from the experience of other organisations through imitation (explained by institutional theory). Furthermore, organisations communicate their learning through stories, symbols, and behavioural norms and expectations; thus learning can also be bound up with cultural processes.

A narrow definition might suggest that learning is broadly consistent with education and so all learning takes place at school, or within a formal learning environment. Learning therefore is viewed as a deliberate activity that occurs within identified parameters. This definition is unacceptable in the context of organisation behaviour, however, since it does not take cognisance of the range of learning opportunities that is presented to individuals on their employment in an organisational setting.

A more acceptable definition of learning might be that it is a process through which individuals assimilate new knowledge and skills that result in relatively permanent behaviour changes. Learning can thus be conscious or unconscious, formal or informal and requires some element of practice and experience. McGehee (1958, p. 2) describes learning thus:

> You have seen people in the process of learning, you have seen people who behave in a particular way as a result of learning and some of you have 'learned' at some time in your life. In other words, we infer that learning has taken place if an individual behaves, reacts, responds as a result of experience in a manner different from the way he formally behaved.

It is important to differentiate learning from training. In its most basic sense, training refers to the acquisition of knowledge, skills and abilities required to perform effectively in a given role. Learning, however, is broader in that it is not limited to an organisational role, but learning is a necessary occurrence in any training intervention. Garavan et al. (1995) differentiate between learning and training along a number of key characteristics (see Table 5.1).

Table 5.1: Learning and training compared

Comparison Factor	Learning	Training
Focus of activity	On values, attitudes, innovation and outcome accomplishment.	On knowledge, skills, ability and job performance.
Clarity of objectives	May be vague and difficult to identify.	Can be specified clearly.
Time scale	Continuous.	Short term.
Values which underpin activity	Assumes continuous change. Emphasises breakthrough.	Assumes relative stability. Emphasises improvement.
Nature of learning process	Instructional or organic.	Structured or mechanistic.
Content of activity	Learning how to learn, values, attitudes relevant to work.	Knowledge, skills and attitudes relevant to specific job, basic competencies.
Methods used	Informal learning methods, learner-initiated methods.	Demonstration, practice, feedback.
Outcomes of process	Individuals learn how to learn and create own solutions.	Skilled performance or tasks which make up job.
Learning strategy used	Inductive strategies.	Didactic tutor-centred.
Nature of process	Inside out, seeks to do for self.	Outside in, done by others.
Role of professional trainer	To facilitate and guide.	To instruct, demonstrate and guide.
Document trainer philosophy	Existentialism: self-managed process.	Instrumentalism: Transferring knowledge using formal methods and measuring results.
Type of need emphasised	Individual and organisational needs.	Organisational needs.
Process of evaluation	Continuous evaluation.	Evaluation against specific job performance standards.
Link with organisational mission and strategies	Directly aligned with organisation's vision and requirements for success.	Not necessarily linked to organisation's mission and goals.
Payback to organisation	Immediate and ongoing.	Almost immediately in terms of skilled performance.

Source: Garavan *et al.* (1995)

Learning is thus concerned with changes in an individual's behaviour that endure over time. A fundamental feature of learning, therefore, is that it is acquired. Garavan *et al.,* (1995) postulate that the acquisition of new knowledge and learning is dependent on three main factors:

- the innate qualities of the learner (i.e. intelligence, personality);
- the skills of the teacher (i.e. as applied in tuition, instruction, etc.);
- the conditions in which learning takes place (i.e. the learning environment).

In terms of organisational behaviour, learning refers to the assimilation of new knowledge that leads employees to behave in a new or different way. Learning, however, does not exist within a vacuum and so organisations must make some attempt to facilitate individual learning if employees' full potential is to be harnessed in pursuit of greater organisational efficiency. This brings us to another concept that requires some attempt at definition, namely the learning organisation. The literature on the learning organisation as a distinct concept is relatively new; and again, while there is no agreement on what exactly constitutes a learning organisation, it is generally described as a participative learning system which places an emphasis on information exchange and being open to enquiry and self-criticism. As such it describes an organisation that facilitates continuous development and consciously transforms itself.

A distinction can be made between two types of learning: namely single loop learning and double loop learning. Single loop learning is said to occur where actions lead to consequences – if the consequences are not those desired, then the actions are changed and the process continues. Single loop learning is useful for routine, repetitive issues and is useful for getting the job done. Argyris (1992) uses an electrical engineering analogy to demonstrate single loop learning – a thermostat is programmed to detect states of 'too hot' or 'too cold', and to correct the situation by turning the heat on or off. Thus whenever an error is detected and corrected without questioning or altering the underlying values of the system, the learning is single loop. Double loop learning, on the other hand, occurs where mismatches are corrected by first examining and altering the underlying systems and then changing the actions. Returning to the thermostat analogy, if the thermostat asked itself such questions as why was it set at 68 degrees, or why was it programmed as it was, then it would be a double loop learner. In an organisational context, double loop learning is required for complex, non-programmable issues, where a number of variables can be said to influence the learning situation. Argyris and Schon (1978) differentiate single and double loop learning as shown in Table 5.2.

Table 5.2: Single and double loop learning

Features of single loop learning	Features of double loop learning
Goals designed unilaterally based on local information and reinforcing behaviour:	Individuals, groups and departments are open with data:
Individual/organisational objectives to be winners:	Interests and understandings move beyond functional and hierarchical boundaries:
Information is a power resource and kept 'close to one's chest'; little sharing of information:	Decisions through partnership, not imposition:
Emphasis on rationality and objectiveness on the surface – even if it is clearly inappropriate:	Norms and values open to change: Communality in values and perceptions an objective:
Conflict not confronted but smoothed over or postponed:	Shared ownership and commitment:
Attractive in that it is familiar, measurable, and reflects functional activities:	Policies and strategies seen as open and complex:

Source: Adapted from Argyris and Schon, 1978

Having defined learning, it now becomes pertinent to explore some of the key learning theories that have informed our understanding of the learning process.

THEORIES OF LEARNING

The dimensions of individual learning have been the focus of considerable research and experimentation over time. Garavan *et al.* (1995) suggest that the roots of learning theory may be traced back to Plato and Aristotle, and the notion of the 'trained mind', whereby training is seen to require extensive self-discipline and control. They proposed that the exercise of mental faculties (e.g. reason, memory, will-power, etc.) was crucial to the development of the individual and ultimately of the community at large. However, it is in the last two centuries that some of the most important research into learning has occurred and this research now informs our current understanding of the process of learning. Luthans (1992) indicates that the purpose of a theory is to better explain the phenomenon under investigation and so a true theory can be universally applied and allow one to predict outcomes with reliability and validity. In this way, a perfected theory of learning would be able to explain all aspects of learning (how, why and when), have universal application (i.e. to children, college students, managers and workers), and predict and control learning situations (Luthans, 1992, p. 208). To date, however, no such theory on learning exists for, while there is some broad agreement on many of the principles of learning, considerable divergence remains as to the theory underpinning such principles. Thus, a considerable number of theories on learning have been proposed, the more instructive of which are discussed here under the classification of behaviourist theories, cognitive theories and experiential theories.

BEHAVIOURIST THEORIES

The behaviourist school of psychology is perhaps the most dominant in terms of learning research and suggests that learning is a function of experience and that ideas that are experienced together tend to be associated with each other. The behaviourist approach to learning can be further subdivided into classical conditioning and operant conditioning.

Classical conditioning

Classical conditioning was derived from the scientific experiments of Ivan Pavlov (1849–1936) and probably represents the most famous study ever completed in the behavioural sciences. Pavlov attributed learning to the association between a stimulus and response (S-R) and sought to test this using dogs in a laboratory experiment. When Pavlov presented dogs with a piece of meat they automatically salivated – this salivating represented an unconditioned or reflexive response to the smell of the meat. Thus the meat in this case was an unconditioned stimulus, i.e. nothing was done to it to make the dogs salivate. When Pavlov rang a bell, however, nothing happened. Then Pavlov started to ring a bell each time he gave the dogs a piece of meat until such time as the dogs began to salivate each time the bell was rung, regardless of whether there was meat present or not. This is known as classical conditioning – the dogs were conditioned to believe there was meat on the way as soon as they heard the bell, and so they started to salivate. In this experiment the saliva produced represents a conditioned response to a conditioned stimulus, i.e. the bell. So, making no assumptions about the thinking or feeling processes that might be implied in this experiment, Pavlov merely described or predicted overt behaviour, and demonstrated the connection between stimuli and responses in learning. Classical conditioning thus suggested that, in order to change human behaviour, some form of further conditioning is required.

Operant conditioning

Following in the behaviourist tradition, Skinner (1904–90) mainly focused on the concept of reinforcement of behaviour and on how associations are formed between a stimulus and response. He suggested that classical conditioning was limited since it only explained reflexive or involuntary responses, and, since human behaviour is so complex, learning must be a function of more conscious behaviour. Using rats in his experiments, Skinner designed a particular type of box that had a lever inside. When this lever was pressed, it released food into the box. Over time, the rats learned that, the more the lever was pressed, the more food they received. Since the rats were hungry each time they were put into the box, it is not surprising that they spent a considerable amount of time pressing the lever. This experiment demonstrated the link between a stimulus and response whereby, when the rats behaved in a certain way (pressing the lever) they were rewarded (received food) and this behaviour was reinforced through the continual rewarding with food whenever the lever was pressed. A central feature, therefore, of operant conditioning is what happens as a consequence of a particular behavioural response.

Garavan *et al.* (1995) suggest that the work of these behavioural scientists is significant, not only for its direct contribution to training practice, but also because the reaction to their ideas in theoretical circles provoked the emergence of other learning theories. Some of the key concepts arising from this work include:

- *The law of readiness* – the circumstances under which a learner tends to be satisfied or annoyed, to welcome or reject.
- *The law of exercise* – the strengthening of a particular response through repeated practice.
- *The law of effect* – strengthening or weakening of a particular response on the basis of subsequent reward or punishment.

While behavioural theorists have added considerably to our understanding of how people learn, their work did not prove acceptable to other researchers in the field of learning as related to human behaviour. It is argued that human behaviour is particularly complex and that learning and behaviour are not necessarily synonymous. For example, even though learning may have taken place (e.g. an individual knows that driving fast in foggy conditions can be extremely hazardous) this individual may choose not to apply this learning (e.g. may still be unwilling to drive slowly). So, while learning and behaviour are undoubtedly inter-related, they are not necessarily one and the same thing.

Luthans (1992) illustrates the differences between classical and operant conditioning as follows:

Box 5.2: Classical versus operant conditioning

Classical conditioning		
	[S] Stimulus	[R] Response
The individual . . .	is stuck by a pin	flinches
	is tapped below the kneecap	flexes lower leg
	is shocked by an electrical current	jumps/screams
	is surprised by a loud sound	jumps/screams
Operant conditioning		
	[R] Response	[S] Stimulus
The individual . . .	works	is paid
	talks to others	meets more people
	enters a restaurant	obtains food
	enters a library	finds a book
	works hard	receives praise and a promotion

Source: Luthans, 1992

COGNITIVE THEORIES

In organisation behaviour, the cognitive approach is often used as a valued means of explaining motivation in the organisation (see Chapter 4 for detailed treatise on motivation theories and processes). The cognitive approach to learning primarily sets out to describe the person as a knowing being rather than a simple or complex mechanism. The early advocates of cognitivism, such as Wertheimer (1889–1943) and Koeheler (1887–1967), were particularly interested in the subject of perception, i.e. in how human beings and animals 'see' their world, and from their experiments they demonstrated that learning is a matter of assembling one's world into meaningful patterns, rather than just making connections between separate elements. This view of perception was encapsulated in the statement that 'the whole is greater than the sum of its parts' and so the focus of cognitivists is on the structure and processes of human competence, i.e. the role that memory, intuition, perception and information processing have on learning. Garavan *et al.* (1995) identify three particular aspects of learning associated with cognitive thought:

1. A person develops a map of the world and extends this map through experience.
2. New facts may be taken in which call for extending (assimilation) or revising (accommodation) this map.
3. Reflective or accumulated data can lead to insights about patterns and relationships (an holistic view of learning).

Thus, while the behaviourist theories view learning in terms of a stimulus and a response whereby behaviour can be determined by reinforcement (via rewards), the cognitive approach suggests that learning is about how the environment is perceived by the individual and that learning can be stored away until it is required (latent learning – i.e. a student attends lectures, tutorials, reads notes and materials and assimilates information that will be used later (hopefully) to pass an exam).

Insight also plays a role in the cognitive approach to learning, in terms of how an individual perceives his/her environment. Specifically, three stages are involved:

1. The individual understands the situation and identifies a problem to be solved.
2. He/she thinks about the problem and the context within which it occurs.
3. He/she experiences a sudden flash of inspiration where a solution suddenly becomes evident.

Insight thus represents the dawning of understanding, whereby a person grasps the essentials of a problem, can formulate a solution, and then apply the learning from this experience on a future occasion, while acknowledging the learning situation. Its principal relevance is to situations of a complex, problem-solving nature.

SOCIAL LEARNING THEORY

Social learning theory seeks to combine both the behaviourist and cognitive approaches to learning. Bandura (1986), most noted for his work on social learning, argues that learning must be more than conditioning and that, while reinforcement has a considerable influence on an individual's behaviour, 'most of the behaviours that people display are learned either deliberately or inadvertently through the influence of example' (Bandura, 1986, p. 5). In practice, this suggests that individuals observe each other on a continuous basis and, where they perceive a positive consequence of certain behaviour, they will tend to emulate that behaviour and thereby achieve the positive outcomes associated with it. In a work situation, for example, a new employee may adopt an approach to a difficult supervisor that seems to work for more established workers and thereby hope to achieve the same positive result.

Before we complete this section on learning theories it is necessary to address the notion of behaviour modification. At the core of behaviour modification lies an attempt to control individual behaviour through the systematic reinforcement of behaviours that are deemed to be desirable. This reinforcement refers to the process through which certain consequences serve to strengthen a particular behaviour. There are three types of reinforcement that are relevant in an organisational behaviour context.

Positive reinforcement

This is used to increase the frequency of desirable behaviour, whereby positive consequences are applied in order that a particular type of behaviour be encouraged and so increase the frequency with which it may occur again. For example, an employee that performs above expectation in his/her job is praised/given a bonus/promoted to encourage him/her to continue to work well. In other words, an employer accentuates the positive behaviour in order to eliminate the likelihood of any negative behaviour occurring.

Negative reinforcement

This is also used to increase the frequency of desirable behaviour. In this situation, however, a particularly undesirable consequence is withdrawn in order to increase the frequency with which desired behaviour occurs. Luthans (1992) refers to this as a form of social blackmail. An organisational example of this type of reinforcement might be where a threat of punishment or disciplinary action is withdrawn as soon as an employee behaves in a manner that is desirable by the organisation. Thus an individual will behave in a particular manner to avoid being punished.

Punishment

This is used to decrease the frequency of undesirable behaviour. Here, a useful example might be an organisation's disciplinary procedure which seeks to eliminate undesirable behaviour (such as unauthorised absences) through the imposition of sanctions.

In most organisations, the two key reinforcement mechanisms are feedback on performance (to encourage/discourage good/bad behaviour) and money (to reward desirable behaviour).

THE APPLICATION OF LEARNING THEORY

From a training and development perspective learning may be summarily described as a complex process of acquiring knowledge, understanding, skills and values in order to be able to adapt to the environment in which we live (Garavan *et al.*, 1995). Such adaptation generally involves some recognisable change in behaviour, though this is not always the case. Having established that all training involves some form of learning, and since effective training is dependent upon the extent to which the knowledge gained results in improved performance, it becomes pertinent to explore some of the principles underpinning effective learning, through employee development at the organisational level.

Learning to learn is essentially concerned with improving the ability to learn. According to Law (1986), learning skills can be described as ways of organising and co-ordinating learning activities, so that changes in behaviour or disposition are retained, while Revans (1982) identified four cardinal conditions of successful learning:

1. The subjects are motivated to learn of their own volition and not solely at the will of others.
2. They may identify themselves with others who may not only share their needs, but who may also satisfy some of these needs.
3. They can try out any new learning in actions of their own design.
4. Within a reasonable lapse of time, they can attain first-hand knowledge of the results of their trials.

Gunnigle *et al.* (1997) suggest that these factors have important implications for the design and delivery of training programmes and postulate that the choice of training approach and method must take cognisance of the following principles:

- *Motivation to learn.* The employee must want to learn and thus, in order to be committed to the process, must perceive that the learning event will result in the achievement of certain desired goals.
- *Involvement of the learner.* The training/learning should be seen as an active, rather than a passive process. Pont (1991) suggests that adults learn more effectively when they are actively involved in the learning process.
- *Reinforcement and feedback.* Employees should be given an opportunity to practise what they have learned and be provided with continuous feedback on their performance. This facilitates continuous improvement, and employees can engage in goal-setting to heighten the learning process. In tandem with this, the training event must allow employees sufficient time both to absorb the material and practise/test new knowledge and skills.
- *Meaningfulness of the material.* The nature of the training/learning intervention must be seen to be relevant to the employee's work. Wexley and Latham (1991) suggest that, to increase meaningfulness, trainees should be provided with an overview of the material to be learned; the material should be presented using examples, concepts and terms familiar to the learner; material is sequenced in a logical manner; and finally complex intellectual skills are composed of simpler skills and the attainment of these subordinated skills is essential before the complex skills can be acquired.

Employees are not homogenous but rather represent a diverse group of individuals that happen to be working in the same organisation. As such, each individual brings a unique set of experiences and expectations to the learning event that can shape the level of learning that takes place and the degree to which the learning becomes a significant aspect of subsequent behaviour. Rogers (1969) argues that the focus of learning is best directed at the experiences of the learner, rather than at the actions of the trainer. Thus the aim of educators and trainers should be to facilitate, rather than direct, the learning of others. Garavan *et al.* (1995) summarise a number of principles underpinning Rogers' work:

- People have a natural tendency and potential for learning.
- Significant learning takes place when the subject matter is perceived as relevant by the learner.
- Learning which involves change in oneself is threatening and may be resisted.
- Learning which appears threatening can be acquired, and exploited, when external threats are minimised.
- Much significant learning is acquired by 'doing'.
- Learning is facilitated when the learner participates responsibly in the learning process.
- Self-initiated learning, involving the whole person (emotionally and intellectually), is the most lasting and pervasive form of learning.
- Independence, creativity and self-reliance are all facilitated when self-criticism and self-evaluation are encouraged (rather than external forms of evaluation).
- Learning about the process of learning is essential to enable individuals to cope with change.
- The task of the facilitator is to provide an environment in which individuals can set their own learning goals.

Kolb (1984), whose work has been particularly influential in management development, developed the experiential learning cycle which, as a starting point, has a concrete experience of some kind. Following this, the learner/trainee makes observations and reflects on these, and begins to formulate abstract concepts. These concepts are then tested in a new situation, which provides a fresh experience and thus the cycle beings again. Boydell (1976) cautions that experience of and for itself is not the same as learning. Learning (the acquisition and application of knowledge and skills) occurs subsequent to the experience being reflected on and assessed by the learner.

As indicated earlier, individuals are not homogenous. A number of pertinent factors determining individual differences have been identified by Buckley and Caple (1990) which include the employee's age (affects attitudes, motivations and interests), his/her levels of intelligence and ability (affects preferences for structured versus unstructured learning events), his/her background and emotional disposition (can result in predetermined perceptions of the value of training), his/her learning style and preference, and finally his/her trainability or motivation to learn (affects aptitude for improved performance and expectations of training outcomes). An understanding of learning styles is particularly important, since the training method chosen by an organisation must take cognisance of particular learning preferences that individual employees might express. For example, some individuals may learn more effectively in a structured training environment using concrete examples, whereas others might prefer a more informal conceptual framework. Mumford (1989) suggests that a failure to take account of different learning styles can have seriously negative implications for the training process, while Garavan *et al.* (1995) quoting Arment (1990) indicate that:

1. By the time we reach adulthood, each of us has developed our own method of learning, reflected in a unique and well-established learning style.
2. Trainers also have well-established learning styles and preferences.
3. The more compatible the style of learning with the approach to training adopted, the more likely it is that a positive learning experience will occur.

Transfer of learning

The term 'learning transfer' refers to the extent to which skills and abilities acquired during a training session are applied to the actual work situation or to the learning of a new, but related, skill. Reid *et al.* (1992) distinguish between two types of positive learning transfer: vertical and lateral. Vertical transfer occurs where one subject area acts as a basis for another, i.e a foundation course in general business forms the basis upon which students/learners can progress to greater specialism/diversification where students can apply the general principles learned at foundation level. In training terms this involves the acquisition of additional knowledge/skills that build upon existing skills and abilities. Lateral transfer occurs where the same type of stimulus requires the same response. In this respect, training simulates a particular type of task and allows the learner an opportunity to practise in a 'safe' environment. Reid *et al.* use the example of training simulations that are used to train aircraft pilots. Buckley and Caple (1990) indicate that positive transfer will have taken place if the trainee is able to apply on the job what has been learned in training with relative ease (lateral), or is able to learn a new task more quickly as a result of earlier training on another task (vertical).

Gunnigle *et al.* (1997a) suggest that, in some circumstances, negative transfer occurs and this may be as a result of past learning experiences that contradict present practice, or perhaps the learning experience creates inhibitions which impede the acquisition of new skills. To illustrate the former, they use the analogy of a driver who learns to drive on one side of the road and who might find it difficult to drive on the opposite side while abroad – this is particularly so in cases where the driver is distracted or stressed. The particular choice of training method, style of trainer, or indeed the training situation might, individually or combined, serve to inhibit the learning process and this results in negative learning transfer.

As indicated earlier, reinforcement plays a key role in encouraging/discouraging particular behaviours, and feedback and money were identified as two particular organisational tools in behaviour modification. Latham and Crandall (1991) identify pay and promotion policies as key organisational variables that influence the level of training transfer because they affect training outcome expectations. Bandura (1986) suggests that trainees may believe that they are capable of performing a specific behaviour but may choose not to do so because they believe it will have little or no effect on their status in the organisation. This highlights the necessity that employee development practices take cognisance of the key learning principles discussed here and that they create environments that facilitate continuous learning – in other words, they move towards developing into learning organisations.

The learning organisation paradigm

Heraty and Morley (1995) argue that, in recent years, the notion of the learning organisation has been raised to the status of an orthodoxy; but despite the growing prescriptive, burgeoning literature, the transition to this new organisation scenario is one that is not well researched and may well be under threat due to poor conceptualisation and a lack of systematic empirical evidence. Indeed, it is plausible to argue that the learning organisation debate is taking on the guise of post-industrial futurology. The problem for most organisations lies in what is described as 'transition management' (Perry, 1984; Buchanan and McCalman, 1989). While it is comparatively straightforward to identify the work and organisation design features that one wishes to implement, it is much more difficult to determine how to take an organisation and its members through the actual transition. This is a high-risk venture, one that involves the creation and communication of a number of different vision sets dedicated to the changing of all aspects of the organisation system. It is a venture that involves the changing of what has been 'a way of life'.

Traditionally, competitiveness was gained through either financial efficiency, marketing capability or technological innovation. However, heightened global competition and rapid technological development is leading to the realisation that the primary source of competitive advantage in the future is sharply focused on creating new knowledge which is disseminated through the company and which, in turn, leads to continuous innovation (West, 1994). This view is shared by both Senge (1990) and Stata (1989) who suggest that the ability of an organisation to learn faster than its competitors may yet become the only sustainable competitive advantage. According to Daft (1995), the learning component of competitive advantage refers to the ability to advance financial, marketing and technological capabilities to a higher level by disengaging employees from traditional notions of efficiency and engaging them in active problem-solving that helps the organisation change. The increasing impact of new information and production technologies also demands new skills and puts a premium on individual and organisational learning (Iles, 1994). Furthermore, the move towards organisational delayering, employee empowerment and the adoption of some elements of the flexible firm model requires a culture of continuous development and competency upgrading. Hence, the more learning capability is increased, the more adaptable and successful the organisation can become. Many organisations are therefore turning towards the paradigm of the learning organisation in order to facilitate this development. What then is this paradigm?

The concept of the learning organisation denotes an organisation which facilitates the learning of all its members and continuously transforms itself (Pedler *et al.*, 1989). It is a place where:

> . . . people continually expand their capacity to create the results they truly desire, where new and expansive patterns of thinking are nurtured, where collective aspirations are set free, and where people are continually learning how to learn together. (Senge, 1990)

West (1994) indicates that the learning organisation concept is embedded in the notion that innovative organisations should be designed as participative learning systems which place an emphasis on information exchange and are open to enquiry and self-criticism, while Pedler *et al.* (1989) propose that a learning organisation is one which:

- has a climate in which individuals are encouraged to learn and to develop to their full potential;
- extends its learning culture to include customers, suppliers and other significant stakeholders;
- makes human resource development strategy central to its business policy so that the process of individual and organisational learning becomes a major business activity.

Hodgetts *et al.* (1994) similarly indicate that learning organisations are characterised by a strong commitment to generating and transferring new knowledge and utilise the external environment as a source of learning.

Calvert *et al.* (1994) maintain that learning organisations use learning as a means of attaining their goals and create structures and procedures that facilitate and support continuous learning and development. There is an attempt made to link individual and organisational performance which is often reflected in the reward choices made by the organisation. However, the process of becoming a learning organisation is not easily realised since it requires fundamental changes to how individuals think and interact and involves a comprehensive evaluation of deeply held assumptions and values. As with any change process, the move towards adopting the learning mantle is often perceived with suspicion and mistrust by those that are averse to changing all that has traditionally been stable and consistent, and moving towards a situation where they are required to take responsibility for their continuous development and competency improvement.

Box 5.3: The challenge for Irish firms

A strategic perspective on the opportunities available to the firm and the means to achieve them, together with new attitudes to worker/management relationships and to training, are required. The successful enterprise must be seen as a *learning organisation* where people at all levels are supported in achieving and renewing the knowledge and skills necessary to meet the commercial objectives of the firm and the needs of individuals to attain satisfaction in the jobs for which they have responsibility. Closer links with the education and training sectors are also essential to underpin the capacity of firms for innovation across the full range of business activities and to ensure that the education and training sectors are responsive to the needs of the firm. The aim must be to benchmark training performance, at both national level and at the level of the individual firm, against the best practice available internationally.

Source: White Paper on Human Resource Development, Department of Enterprise and Employment, May 1997, p. 112

McGill *et al.* (1992) suggest that the essential characteristics of the learning organisation become visible when one compares the traditional 'adaptive' organisation with the 'generative' organisation. They perceive the adaptive organisation as one that focuses on incremental improvements to existing products, markets, services or technologies, often within the context of its pre-existing track record of success. As such it is termed 'learning disadvantaged' since incremental change becomes the basis for a predictable future strategy that can be discriminated and copied; and the danger, therefore, is that as the competitive environment changes, adaptive organisations are blind to the need to examine the way that they define and resolve problems. The generative organisation, on the other hand, emphasises continuous experimentation and feedback in an ongoing examination of the very way the organisation goes about defining and solving problems. They suggest that, in the generative organisation, the ability to learn is not measured by what individuals know (the product of learning) but rather how individuals learn (the process of learning). Using this typology, McGill *et al.* contrasted adaptive and generative organisations along a range of critical variables in order to demonstrate how management practices must change in order to have a learning organisation (see Table 5.3).

Table 5.3: Characteristics of types of learning organisations

	Adaptive	Generative
Strategic characteristics		
Core competence	Better sameness	Meaningful difference
Source of strength	Stability	Change
Output	Market share	Market creation
Organisational perspective	Compartmentalisation.	Systematic
Developmental dynamic	Change	Transformation
Structural characteristics		
Structure	Bureaucratic	Network
Control systems	Formal rules	Values, self-control
Power bases	Hierarchical position	Knowledge
Integrating mechanisms	Hierarchy	Teams
Networks	Disconnected	Strong
Communications flow	Hierarchical	Lateral
Human resource practices		
Performance appraisal reward basis	Stability.	Flexibility
Focus of rewards	Distribution of scarcity	Determination of synergy
Status symbols	Rank and title	Making a difference
Mobility patterns	Within division/function	Across divisions/functions
Mentoring	Not rewarded	Integral part of performance
Culture	Market	Clan
Manager's behaviours		
Perspective	Controlling	Openness
Problem-solving orientation.	Narrow	Systemic thinking
Response style	Conforming	Creative
Personal control	Blame and acceptance	Efficacious
Commitment	Ethnocentric	Empathic

Source: McGill *et al.,* 1992

Pearn and Honey (1997) similarly argue that, in order to sustain competitiveness, organisations must necessarily adopt the generative route to learning and advocate a systems approach to workforce management as a means of generating creativity and innovation. This approach is illustrated in Pearn's systems thinking poem (Box 5.4).

Box 5.4: Systems thinking poem

Systems thinking

Did you know there are two kinds of learning?
Don't be confused, it's an issue that's burning.
One is called adaptive and is the norm.
The other's generative and takes you by storm.

When adaptive, you work with the accepted,
The familiar, the known and the respected.
When generative, you experiment, test and create.
It helps you challenge, and to innovate.

Adaptive learning is slow and incremental.
Generative is fast, and is fundamental.
So break the mould, go in and be bold.
It's systems thinking that leads to gold.

Systems thinking, systems thinking.
Look for the structure and for the linking.
between events and what action portrays,
Find causal loops, reveal the delays.

Forget symptoms, look for the causes,
Check for relationships, reflect in the pauses.
Then search for the mental models to bust,
Like it or not, systems thinking's a must.

Source: Pearn and Honey, 1997

Burgoyne (1988) suggests that learning organisations are works in progress, both conceptually and in practical terms, and maintains that no organisation that has been investigated has yet reached the higher stages of the learning organisation. The concept of the learning organisation is difficult to implement since, by its nature, it represents a longitudinal, continuous process. Indeed it is plausible to suggest that since the goalposts keep moving, and since each intervention may divert an organisation down a different route, it may represent a process that can never be fully mastered. In this respect, Calvert *et al.* (1994) indicate that while many organisations are attempting to apply some or all of the learning organisation principles, breakthrough experiences are few and far between. Garavan *et al.* (1995) propose that the driving force for managing the movement towards a learning organisation must reside at the top of the organisation. However, by its very nature, a learning organisation cannot be constructed by a management directive. Instead, it must be pursued by effectively influencing, persuading and communicating across all organisational levels. It means:

- attending to the requirements of all members and groups, and building a sense of cohesion and group purpose and support;
- identifying and satisfying individual motivational and developmental needs;
- harnessing the efforts of all members to meet the desired goal.

It therefore requires the establishment of a clear vision of what needs to be achieved and the adoption of appropriate strategies to enable this.

Heraty and Morley (1995) suggest that the premise of most of the available literature on the learning organisation is, perhaps, overtly prescriptive and the concept itself may be difficult to comprehend since, by its definition, organisations never reach the stage at which they can be said to have fulfilled the criteria required to become a learning organisation. Notwithstanding this, the principles upon which the concept is founded represent a set of ideals to which most organisations would aspire, namely: the creation of an organisation climate that facilitates continuous development; a system that rewards continuous improvement; and a structural design that promotes ongoing learning.

Pedler *et al.* (1989) have identified a number of characteristics pertinent to a learning organisation, and these can be briefly summarised as follows:

- A learning approach to strategy whereby strategies and policies take cognisance of learning capabilities.
- Participative policy-making to engender commitment to shared goals.
- Promotion of information technology as a source of empowerment.
- Formative accounting and control organised around the creation of small business units.
- Internal exchange that recognises internal customers and acts accordingly.
- Reward flexibility that reflects individual needs, wants and contribution.
- Enabling structures that encourage flexibility, participation and motivation.
- Boundary scanning that allows the organisation to learn from its environment.
- Inter-company learning through information exchange and joint investment.
- Learning climate that facilitates learning and encourages experimentation.
- Promotion of self-development.

Garavan *et al.* (1995) indicate that an organisation cannot become a continuous learning system surreptitiously, and call for the establishment of a clear vision of what needs to be achieved and the adoption of appropriate strategies to enable this. They suggest that these strategies may be devised by examining various aspects of training and development in the current organisation in terms of the 'vision', for example:

1. *Positioning:* how congruent is the training function with the current goals of the organisation? How is it perceived by organisational stakeholders? How should it be perceived in order to ensure the success of the vision?
2. *Power:* what is the power base of the training function? What influences and resources does it have? What status issues may arise and how can these be best managed?
3. *Processes:* what are the internal systems which co-ordinate training and development activity? What are its current communication flows (internal/external)? How are these likely to support or hinder the vision?
4. *People:* what is the current store of organisational knowledge, skills and expertise? How do they relate to the vision? What are the attitudinal motivational factors which shape the culture of the organisation? What are the likely sources of resistance? What is the best approach to motivating and encouraging the acceptance of the vision?
5. *Product:* what are the current training and development products/services? What are the delivery mechanisms employed? How effectively does the training function contribute to business goals and objectives? How will it need to change in order to resource, support and encourage the vision? What will the training and development function 'look like' in the learning organisation?
6. *Plans:* what are the strategies which will encourage learning and transformation? What is the most appropriate and effective starting point? What are the support structures which must be put into place? At what speed should progress be paced? What will the role of the training function be?

LEARNING AND TRAINING IN IRISH ORGANISATIONS

It was noted earlier that training is a function of learning; that is, that learning is a necessary prerequisite for effective training and for the successful application of new knowledge and skills to the workplace. While the White Paper on human resource development (1997) provides evidence that, at an overall level, Irish business does not invest sufficiently to upgrade the skills of workers and managers, data from the most recent Cranfield University of Limerick Study (CUL) survey (see Gunnigle *et al.* (1997b) for detailed treatise) suggests that a considerable number of those organisations surveyed are focusing greater attention on the competency upgrading of their workforces. In this final section of this chapter we briefly explore the types of training methodologies that are currently being employed in Irish organisations in an effort to determine the current nature of organisational learning.

A critical aspect of any learning intervention must necessarily involve some analysis of the current level of learning in order to determine whether knowledge or skill gaps are apparent. In organisational terms this is most often referred to as a training needs analysis which can be viewed as a systematic process of determining and ordering training goals, measuring training needs and deciding on priorities for training action. Gunnigle *et al.* (1997a) argue that a needs analysis is a central component of the training process as it ensures that training and development occurs only where there is a valid need for it. Many organisations invest considerable resources in training but often fail to examine how effectively training can meet the business objectives.

In an attempt to determine whether an underlying strategic imperative governs employee development activities, respondents to the CUL survey were asked whether they systematically analysed employee training needs. A total of 75 per cent of respondents suggest that they do. This represents an increase of almost 6 per cent since 1992. However, one in four respondents still fail to carry out a systematic training needs analysis and in such circumstances it is difficult to envisage how employee development can make a strategic contribution to effective organisational functioning. Larger organisations are substantially more likely to analyse their training needs than are their smaller counterparts (82 per cent as against 68.5 per cent respectively). Understandably while time and resource constraints will impact more adversely on the smaller organisation in their training needs analysis effort, the necessity for such an analysis remains critical, regardless of size, and indeed arguably could be more critical in smaller concerns. Sector also emerges as a critical determinant of the likelihood of a training needs analysis taking place. Almost 20 per cent more private sector organisations analyse training needs. It is interesting that almost 40 per cent of public sector organisations do not consider it necessary to conduct training needs analysis as a basis for effective training. This is again consistent with results from 1992 which revealed a broadly similar pattern. When compared with their foreign-owned counterparts, indigenous Irish organisations appear far less likely to conduct a systematic training needs analysis. This seems to follow through from the 1992 findings which revealed that while 62 per cent of Irish-owned organisations conducted training needs analysis, some 73 per cent of UK-owned and 85 per cent of US-owned organisations systematically analysed training requirements.

A number of methods of identifying training/learning requirements are available to organisations. Table 5.4 details the main findings of the 1995 CUL survey, using 1992 as a comparator. Overall, we find stability in the results. The methodologies employed appear twofold, i.e. highly formalised mechanisms (analysis of projected plans, training audits and performance appraisal) and less structured, more informal arrangements such as line management requests and employee requests, both types being relatively frequently drawn upon. Predictably, a greater proportion of respondents continue to rely on line management requests and/or the performance appraisal system to identify training needs. However, while there has been an increase in the use of training audits and analysis of projected plans since 1992, indicating perhaps some moves towards greater formality in this area, these methods remain largely under-utilised, thus militating against the strategic integration and functioning of employee development.

Table 5.4: Methods for determining training needs

	Always		Often		Sometimes		Never		N	
	1995	1992	1995	1992	1995	1992	1995	1992	1995	1992
Analysis projected plans	29	24	31	23	35	27	5	13	178	119
Training audits	22	21	30	28	34	28	15	16	173	115
Line management requests	31	28	44	55	24	17	0.5	0.7	189	145
Performance appraisal	37	35	28	38	29	22	5	6	187	149
Employee requests	15	9	42	48	42	40	1	4	184	141

Source: Gunnigle *et al.*, 1997a

Delivery of training/organisational learning methodologies

The choice of training delivery method available to organisations is considerable and thus organisations, when deciding on the most appropriate method to use, must take cognisance of the principles of learning, the needs of the employees to be trained and the logistics of training that affect every organisation. All training delivery methods have their own particular strengths and can be modified to suit the organisation's requirements. The most important criteria in determining the choice of training delivery method is the extent to which it meets the particular objectives that have been established through the training needs analysis.

Respondents to the CUL survey were asked to identify their choice of training delivery method and to indicate whether their use of such method(s) had changed over the previous three years (see Table 5.5).

Table 5.5: Changing use of training delivery methods

	Increased	Same	Decreased	Not used
Internal training staff	48.7	33.0	4.2	7.3
Line managers	34.9	41.8	3.4	8.8
External providers	54.8	31.4	5.7	3.1
On-the-job training	45.2	48.3	0.4	0.4
Internal courses	54.4	32.2	3.4	2.7
External courses	41.4	39.5	6.5	3.8
Coaching	23.8	32.2	1.5	27.2
Computer-based packages	44.1	24.1	0.8	20.7
Open learning	25.3	16.9	3.4	37.9
Mentoring	16.9	16.5	—	51.3

Source: Gunnigle *et al.*, 1997a

It is evident that the responding organisations use a variety of delivery mechanisms in their training activities. Interestingly, it would appear that organisations are reluctant to rely solely on one training delivery strategy and appear to strike a balance between formal and informal delivery mechanisms in an effort to maximise efficiency returns. This is evident in the reported increased usage of internal and external formal training programmes (54.4 per cent and 54.8 per cent respectively) and so training is delivered through a combination of external and internal service providers. On-the-job training retains its popularity and, while on-the-job training strategies were traditionally perceived as ineffective since they were usually unplanned, unsystematic, informal and difficult to evaluate, the advantages of on-the-job training delivery are recognised in terms of providing a natural learning environment and thereby facilitating the transfer of knowledge to the job situation. The least popular training delivery mechanisms, among respondents, include mentoring and coaching. This may be due to the large commitment of time, and hence resources, required for coaching and mentoring, yet such delivery methods have consistently been lauded for their critical contribution to strategic employee development and their capacity to provide cognitive-rich learning (see, for example, Wexley and Latham, 1991).

Evaluation of training/learning transfer

While the importance of training and development has been consistently highlighted, it is of limited value to the organisation unless the learning acquired can be transferred back to the job context. Buckley and Caple (1990) describe evaluation as the process of attempting to assess the total value of training. It further ensures that control is maintained over the training process and allows for assessment of the outcomes, methods and overall impact of any training and development programme. Gunnigle *et al.* (1997a) caution that a lack of training evaluation can result in inappropriate training which is wasteful of both financial and human resources. The difficulty for most organisations lies in identifying a set of measurable criteria that can facilitate the effective evaluation of employee development interventions. Participants to the survey were asked to indicate whether they evaluate the effectiveness of their training activities. The results are presented in Table 5.6, and 1992 data is included for comparative purposes.

Table 5.6: Monitor the effectiveness of training

	1995	1992
Monitor effectiveness	74.3	71.9
Don't monitor effectiveness	20.7	21.9
Don't know	3.1	2.2

Source: Gunnigle *et al.*, 1997

It would appear that almost three-quarters of those surveyed evaluate their training and development activities (74.3 per cent), which is broadly consistent with results obtained in 1992. However, some 20.7 per cent of respondents still fail to evaluate the effectiveness of their training. In a time of scarce resources and pressures of 'bottom-line added value' the requirement for some evaluative process is increasingly evident if training is to continue to be considered a critical organisational activity.

A variety of techniques are employed by responding organisations to evaluate the effectiveness of their training output (see Table 5.7).

The findings indicate that responding organisations tend to place a large emphasis on informal mechanisms of evaluation, and are less likely to use more structured mechanisms such as formal evaluation or tests. Informal feedback from both line managers and trainees emerge as the most frequent evaluation mechanisms utilised, which is similar to that found in 1992. However, the use of more structured and valid evaluation criteria which quantifiably measure learning and learning transfer, such as tests and formal evaluation some months after training, remains negligible in many organisations or, where utilised, is evidently on an *ad hoc* basis.

Table 5.7: Methods of evaluating training

How often are the following methods used?	Always	Often	Sometimes	Never
Tests	2.3	5.4	14.6	28.7
Formal evaluation immediately after training	30.3	14.6	15.3	5.7
Formal evaluation some months later	3.8	10.7	27.6	13.8
Informal feedback from line managers	29.1	34.9	10.0	1.5
Informal feedback from trainees	33.0	28.4	12.3	1.1
Other	4.6	–	–	–

Source: Gunnigle *et al.*, 1997a

Longer-term developmental activities

The extant literature suggests that organisations can facilitate the long-term development of their human capital by providing a range of structures and systems that offer appropriate support and opportunities. Such supports might include:

- self-assessment tools such as career planning workshops;
- individual counselling services;
- information on the workings of the internal labour market;
- assessment of future potential through succession planning, testing, etc.;
- development programmes such as mentoring systems and/or job rotation.

In an attempt to gauge the extent to which organisations are concerned with the long-term strategic development of its employees, respondents to the CUL survey were asked to indicate the type(s) of developmental strategies they employed in their organisation (see Table 5.8).

Table 5.8: Use of longer-term developmental strategies

Development strategy utilised	1995	1992
Formal career plans	23.0	15.8
Assessment centres	8.0	4.8
Succession plans	34.1	30.3
Planned job rotation	28.0	26.3
High flier schemes	14.2	11.4
International experience schemes	19.2	19.3
	N=261	*N=228*

Source: Gunnigle *et al.*, 1997a

The results reveal that a variety of strategies are adopted by organisations in an attempt to develop a strategic orientation to their employee development initiatives. Again there is relative stability between the results presented here, and those recorded in 1992. In particular, succession plans, planned job rotations and formal career plans are favoured most by respondents, while assessment centres are utilised by only a very small minority of organisations. While it is recognised that assessment centres are costly, since they make use of a variety of behaviour predictors, they are particularly useful in taking decisions concerning promotion and career development in general.

SUMMARY OF KEY PROPOSITIONS
- Learning can be defined as the process through which individuals assimilate new knowledge and skills that result in relatively permanent changes in behaviour. This learning can be conscious or unconscious, formal or informal, and requires some element of practice and experience.
- Learning differs from training in that training tends to be more immediate and job-related, while learning focuses on behaviour changes that endure over time.
- Single loop learning is used for routine, repetitive issues (action – outcomes – actions), while double loop learning is more complex and requires that the individual questions why such behaviour is occurring.
- Behaviourist theories of learning suggest that learning is a function of experience. Classical conditioning refers to reflexive or involuntary learning that is a function of the connection between a stimulus and a response. Operant conditioning focuses on the concept of reinforcement and the consequences of particular behavioural responses to a stimulus.
- Cognitive theories set out to describe an individual as a knowing being and suggest

that memory, intuition and perception of the environment all play an important role in explaining how individuals learn.

- Social learning theory suggests that behaviour, and therefore learning, is a function of how individuals perceive each other and that people imitate behaviour that is deemed to result in positive consequences.
- An individual's propensity to learn is determined by a range of variables such as age, education, motivation, learning style, and learning delivery.
- Learning transfer refers to the extent to which skills and abilities acquired during a training session are applied to the actual work situation or to the learning of a new, but related, skill.
- The learning organisation describes a climate which facilitates the learning of all organisational members and is rooted in the notion that innovative organisations should be designed as participative learning systems which place an emphasis on information exchange and being open to enquiry. Learning organisations allow employees to make mistakes and take risks.

DISCUSSION QUESTIONS

1. Define learning. How does it differ from training?
2. Contrast the behavioural and cognitive theories of learning. How have they helped our understanding of human learning?
3. What is learning transfer? How might learning transfer be maximised?
4. To what extent is the learning organisation concept a useful one?
5. How would you characterise the current state of training and development in Ireland?

CHAPTER 6

Communication in Organisations

LEARNING OBJECTIVES

- To introduce and define the concept of communication.
- To outline the communication process.
- To assess listening skills.
- To present a model of how managers communicate and depict information flow in the organisation.
- To outline the barriers to communication and set out the characteristics of effective communication.

INTRODUCTION

Box 6.1 Communications in the future!

The year is 2005: all employees of leading companies take part in policy-making, regularly pass on views to management and receive instant feedback...

So you think that internal communications is all about the provision of information and the management of media? Come on a journey to the year 2005...

The team leaders of WorldComm have gathered at its headquarters in St Petersburg, the world's software capital. They have just been reappointed. However, their power depends on a continuing process of supportive appraisal by those they facilitate. This is based partly on a set of communication competencies which exemplify a style called 'success through others'.

Elsewhere in WorldComm, the communication planning forum has assembled. This negotiates, via satellite, with the architects of the quarterly business-planning process, which new organisational initiatives will be unleashed into the organisation. The new organisational digestion indicator (ODI) has shown that the rate of introduction of process improvements into the business is in the indigestion range. As a result, they agree that the £1 billion customer improvement programme should be delayed by three months.

The ODI is just one of the ways in which employees' views and concerns are assessed and fed into the decision-making process on a 'real-time' basis (i.e., people can feed their views into the computer which collates them and relays the results instantly to management policy meetings). Other measures include an on-line information service and touch-tone telephone questionnaire which measures the extent to which the ethics and values are being lived.

At the policy decision-making meeting which is being held, unusually, around a table, another member of the communication planning team is directly inputting a real-time news report that will be instantly reviewed and delivered to company news stations in offices around the world and direct to home workstations. Stock exchanges and employees now have equal billing.

Meanwhile, in the culture/brand function, a group of academics is hearing how the old departments of human resources, marketing and corporate affairs were brought together to integrate the management of the culture and the presentation of the company to the outside world.

And in the chief executive's office a compendium of the employees' views on their satisfaction with work and organisational ethics is being assessed. WorldComm's record in employee satisfaction now appears in the annual report as a statutory requirement. GlobalComm's record of employee satisfaction is, by comparison, very poor, and its standing in *Fortune* magazine's corporate reputation index has gone into freefall, along with Global's share price.

Source: Smyth, J. (1995), 'Harvesting the Office Grapevine', *People Management*, Sept. 7, Vol. 1, No. 18.

Early discussions of management gave little emphasis to communication. Although it was implicit in the management function of command and the structural principle of hierarchy, Luthans (1992) argues that the early theorists never fully appreciated its significance or fully developed or integrated it into management theory. Traditionally, information has gone up the management hierarchy to where decisions were made and then back down to where they were implemented. Today, everyone knows that communication is vital to the organisation. Indeed, Smythe (1995, p. 31) goes so far as to say that 'the "discipline" of organisational communication has arrived', as the illustration in Box 6.1 demonstrates. However, not everyone is able to create the type of information-rich environment that is necessary in today's competitive world. Communicative interactions in the form of meetings, phone calls, memos, interviews, reports, advertisements etc. make communication a pervasive feature of organisations. Any individual who is to be an effective member of an organisation must be a competent communicator; and, for an organisation to be effective, its communication must be effective. Creating the right communications environment may require a large-scale change in attitudes and approaches of all organisational stakeholders and a climate of trust that encourages the free flow of ideas.

Interest in business communication has seldom been higher than it is today (McClave, 1997), largely because pay-offs are found both in terms of employee satisfaction and organisational performance. According to Ludlow and Panton (1992, p. 3), communication is important in performance terms because it:

- keeps people in the picture;
- gets people involved with the organisation;
- increases motivation to perform well and increases commitment to the organisation;
- makes for better relationships and understanding between boss and subordinate, colleagues and people within the organisation and outside it;
- helps people understand the need for change, how they should manage it and how to reduce resistance to change.

Similarly, in an attempt to highlight the importance and economic values of information and communication systems, Woods (1993, p. 7) assesses the potential of a variety of different communication channels for addressing the broad human and institutional development functions on which growth and success depend.

Table 6.1: Comparative potential of different communications media

	COMMUNICATION MEDIA							
Functions	Press	Books	Radio	TV	Phone	Phone+	Computers	Informatics
Topical information	XXX		XX	XXX	XX	XX	X	XX
Formal education	X	XX	X	X	X	XX	XX	XXX
2-way communication			X		XXX	XXX	X	XXX
Interactive learning		X			X	XX	XX	XXX
Skill development		X		X	X	XX	XX	XXX
Motivation	X	X	X	XX	XX	XX	X	XX
Entertainment	X	X	X	XXX		X	X	XXX
Group decisions	X		X	XX	X	XX	X	XXX
Data supply	X	XX				XX	XX	XXX
Data processing						X	XXX	XXX
Planning		X			XX	XX	XX	XXX
Design		X				X	XX	XXX
Financing					X	X	XX	XXX
Monitoring					X	XX	XX	XXX
Financial control		X			X	XX	XX	XXX

Notes:
1. *'Phone' refers to traditional, voice only telephone services. 'Phone+' (also called 'telematics') is what becomes possible with teleconferencing, and with networks and databases where telephony links remote computers to mainframe computers. 'Informatics' goes beyond telematics reorder by decentralizing substantial memory and processing power to local level, and linking the uses of the whole family of digital technologies.*
2. *Printed and broadcast media have potential in most of the functions other than those for which they are given a rating in Table 6.1, but their relative potential in those functions is small.*
3. *One can argue over the relative potential of one communication medium over another. For example: is TV more entertaining than radio or books? What is their potential in supplying data? A medium able to communicate in sound, pictures, graphics and script has a greater potential in these fields than media able to communicate only with literate people. Broadcast media have the disadvantage that the information and the entertainment they offer is sent at the convenience of the broadcaster, not the viewer or listener. (Video recorders are being used increasingly to overcome this difficulty in relation to TV.) A medium able to provide information and interactive learning and entertainment materials on demand has greater potential than those that cannot.*

Source: Woods, 1993, p. 8.

The table indicates the relative potential of a host of different communication channels for developing what are viewed as critical functions.

By way of tapping into this potential, there is now clear evidence that organisations across Europe are going beyond trite statements about their employees being their major asset, to developing and increasing the amount of communication and consultation in which they involve those employees (Brewster *et al.*, 1994) The considerable moves that have been made by many employers in Europe to expand the degree of information given to the workforce irrespective of legal requirements is clear and it reflects a central theme of standard concepts of modern people management – the requirement to generate significant workforce commitment (Mayrhofer *et al.*, 1997). Kar (1972) estimated that between 40 and 60 per cent of work time in a typical manufacturing plant can involve some phase of communication, while Beach (1970) estimated that top and middle-level executives devote 60 to 80 per cent of their total working lives to communication. Thus for management, as well as organisational theorists, communication is the key element and theoretical construct, respectively, for describing and explaining organisational phenomena. In his classical study, Mintzberg showed that communication in its various forms is one of the key tasks of the job of managers (Mintzberg, 1975). From a different point of view, Weick states that 'interpersonal communication is the essence of organisation because it creates structures that affect what else gets said and done by whom' (Weick, 1989, p. 97). Even more significant is communication in the conceptualisation of organisations made by sociological systems theory. Luhmann argues that communications are the basic elements of social systems; especially the (latent) structures that form and guide communications are relevant if one is interested in the behaviour of organisations (Luhmann, 1987).

In the international realm, communication has a central place, too.

All international business activity involves communication. Within the international and global business environment, activities such as exchanging information and ideas, decision-making, negotiating, motivating and leading are all based on the ability of managers from one culture to communicate successfully with managers and employees from other cultures. (Adler, 1991, p. 64)

Literature on international HRM stresses that cross-border communication happens constantly in multinational companies. This includes communications between expatriates and host country members as well as between employees of various offices in different countries (Briscoe, 1995; Dowling *et al.*, 1994).

DEFINING COMMUNICATION

Communication has many definitions – at least one hundred according to Goldhaber (1990). It may, however, be studied from different perspectives. In this chapter we are concerned about how information is exchanged and shared in the organisational context.

Axley (1996) defines communication as a process of sending and receiving messages with attached meanings, with the ultimate meaning in any communication being created by the receiver or perceiver of the message.

Fisher (1993) suggests that communication may be defined as consisting of two types of actions: those that *create* messages or displays; and those that *interpret* messages or displays. A display consists of information not necessarily intended as a message, but from which an observer can derive meaning. A principle of communication holds that 'a person cannot *not* communicate'. Thus one's clothing, posture or facial expression make a meaningful display, whether or not we intend them as messages.

Organisational communication is similar to other forms of communication in that it involves making and interpreting message displays. But it differs also as it is viewed as an ongoing process that includes patterns of interaction between organisational members that both emerge from and shape the nature and actions of the organisation and the events within it. McClave (1997, p. 20) simply refers to it as internal communication, which is the exchange of information that occurs among people within the organisation which can occur in a formal or informal way. Formal organisational communication generally follows the formal organisation structure and employs methodologies sanctioned by management. Informal organisational communication springs up by virtue of common interests between people in organisations – these interests may be caused by work, social or outside relationships. The most powerful channel is the 'grapevine', which, McClave argues, has several positive features including the fact that it is often the only source of vital information for employees, it acts as a social glue in holding the organisation together and, contrary to popular belief, grapevine information has been found to be mainly accurate (pp. 24–25). It has been estimated that managers receive over half the information they need for planning purposes through the grapevine.

Price (1997, p. 349) conceives of organisational communication simply as the degree to which information is transmitted among members of the organisation. While this transmission assumes many forms (formal discussions between superiors and subordinates, informal conferences among subordinates, publication of various types of newsletters, production of radio and television programmes, posting of announcements on bulletin boards, the use of public address systems and so forth), he notes that four broad dimensions are found in the extant literature. Concurring with many writers, the first and most pervasive distinction is between formal and informal communication. As we have highlighted, the basis of this distinction is whether the transmission is official or unofficial. The second common distinction identified by Price is between vertical and horizontal communication. Vertical communication refers to the transmission of information in superordinate-subordinate relationships, whether from superordinate to subordinate or from subordinate to superordinate. Horizontal communication refers to the transmission of information among peers. A third distinction advanced differentiates between personal and impersonal communication. The basis of this distinction is whether or not the information is transmitted in situations where mutual influence is possible. Personal conversations and telephone calls are examples of personal communication, whereas the mass media is an example of impersonal communication. Fourth, Price distinguishes between instrumental and expressive communication. The transmission of information necessary to do a job is instrumental communication, whereas expressive communication refers to the residual category of non-job information.

Thus to a large extent, an organisation *is* communication; both formal and informal; vertical and horizontal; personal and impersonal; and instrumental and expressive. This, Fisher (1993, p. 3) notes, is more true than ever now, because the information age is upon us. Sophisticated communication technologies bring outside information into organisations faster and in greater volumes than ever before. In this vein, Wilson *et al.* (1986) take a more contingency view of organisational communication, suggesting that it is an evolutionary, culturally dependent process of sharing information and creating relationships in environments designed for manageable, goal-oriented behaviour. The primary purpose in organisational communication is thus to achieve 'co-ordinated action' (Baskin and Aronoff, 1980). Just as the human nervous system responds to stimuli and co-ordinates responses by sending messages to various parts of the body, communication co-ordinates the various parts of the organisation.

THE COMMUNICATION PROCESS

The key elements in the communication process are illustrated in Figure 6.1.

Figure 6.1: The communication process

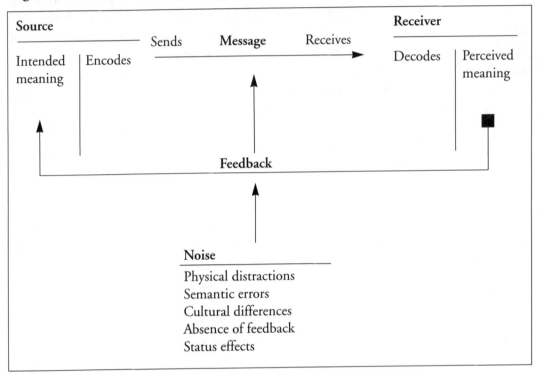

Source: Based on Shannon and Weaver, 1949

Arguably one of the most influential linear models, its earlier iterations did not include a feedback loop. The key elements in the communication process include a source, who encodes the intended meaning into a message; and a receiver, who decodes the message. The receiver may or may not give feedback to the source. Noise is the term used to describe any barriers to or disturbance within the communication process that disrupts it and distorts or interferes with the transfer of messages.

The information source is a person or group trying to communicate with someone else. Reasons for why the source is communicating could include changing the attitudes, knowledge, or behaviour of the receiver. In group or organisational communication, an individual may send a message on behalf of the organisation. The source is responsible for preparing the message, encoding it and entering it into a transmission medium. The next step in the communication process is encoding, the process of translating an idea or thought into meaningful symbols that can be transmitted. The symbols may be words, numbers, pictures, sounds or physical gestures and movements. The source must encode the message in symbols that the receiver can decode properly; the source and the receiver must attach the same meaning to the symbols. When we use the symbols of a common language, we assume that those symbols have the same meaning to everyone who uses them. Yet the inherent ambiguity of symbol systems can lead to decoding errors. The resulting message may be written (letters, memos, reports, manuals, forms), oral (formal speeches, informal conversations, group discussions), non-verbal (including human elements such as facial expressions or body language), or perhaps some combination of these. This message is then translated through various possible channels, or delivery media, which are the path of transmission.

Figure 6.2 presents the results of a European-wide survey on the common methods organisations use to communicate with their employees. It presents the overall averages across Europe of organisations reporting an increase and/or decrease in the use of various methods. Overall one can see a definite increase in the use of various communication fora.

Figure 6.2: Common methods used by organisations to communicate with employees

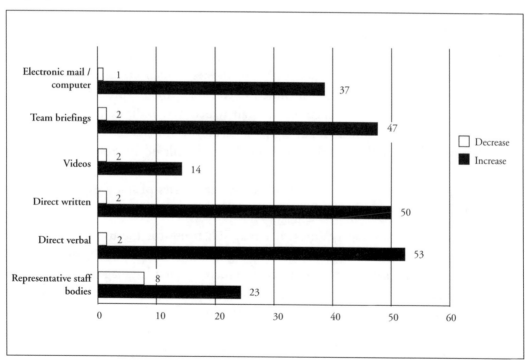

Source: Mayrhofer *et al.*, 1997

Critically, the choice made here relating to the channels can have an important impact on the communication process, as different media have different capacities for carrying information. Some messages are better handled by specific channels, while some individuals are not particularly comfortable with certain channels. Typically organisations produce a great deal of written communication of many kinds. A letter is a typical formal means of communicating with an individual, often someone outside the organisation. Internally, probably the most common form of written communication is the memo. Usually addressed to individuals inside the organisation, they tend to address single topics and, while more impersonal than other modes, they are less formal than letters. Reports are typically used to present the results or progress of specific projects and are often a central aid to decision-making. The most common form of organisational communication is oral. This form of communication is particularly powerful because it includes not only the speaker's words, but also their changes in tone, pitch, volume and speed. Typically, people will draw upon all of these cues associated with oral communication for the purpose of understanding the message. Non-verbal communication includes all of the elements associated with human communication that are not expressed orally or in writing (Moorehead and Griffin, 1995). Human elements include facial expressions and physical movements that may be conscious or unconscious. Among the common facial expressions which have been identified and classified are interest/excitement, enjoyment/joy, surprise/startle, distress/anguish, fear/terror, shame/humiliation, contempt/disgust, and anger/rage. Body language elements (referred to as the study of kinesics) which are often drawn upon during the communication process, include eye contact, which expresses a willingness to communicate; sitting on the edge of the chair which may indicate a nervousness or anxiety; or folded arms, which might signal a certain defensiveness. Drooped shoulders, a furrowed brow, talking with your hands, and the tilt of the head may all prove to be important.

Ekman and Friesen (1969) have identified five categories of body expressions that we commonly draw upon as part of our communication repertoire.

- *Emblems* refer to common gestures that may substitute for the use of words. The conventional wave of the hand as a gesture of goodbye is a classic emblem.
- *Illustrators* serve to accompany and to complement spoken language. They are used for emphasis or directions. On being asked what time it is, when one holds up three fingers while saying it is 3 o'clock, one is making use of an illustrator.
- *Regulators* control verbal interaction, for example when you nod your head while someone is talking to you this signals that they should continue to do so.
- *Affect displays* reveal the emotional state of the communicator, e.g. a frown or a clinched fist indicating anger.
- *Adaptors* are non-verbal habits unique to the individual, for example scratching one's nose or pulling at one's ear.

Thus the possible elements involved in decoding can be complex. Decoding is the process by which the receiver of the message interprets its meaning. The receiver will typically draw upon his/her knowledge and experience to decode the message. The meaning the receiver attaches to the symbols must be the same as the meaning intended by the source for effective communication to have taken place. The receiver of the message may be an individual, a group or an organisation. A critical skill necessary for the proper reception of the message is good active listening. Described as active listening, the receiver has a very definite responsibility, i.e. not passively absorbing the message, but actively trying to grasp the facts and the emotions.

Box 6.2: Listening skills activity

Good listening skills are essential for effective communication and are often overlooked when communication is analysed. This self-assessment questionnaire examines your ability to listen effectively. Work through the following statements, marking 'Yes' or 'No' in the space next to each one. Mark each statement as truthfully as you can in the light of your behaviour in the last few gatherings or meetings you have attended.

	Yes	No
1. I frequently attempt to listen to several conversations at the same time.	—	—
2. I like people to give me the facts and then let me make my own interpretation.	—	—
3. I sometimes pretend to pay attention to people.	—	—
4. I consider myself a good judge of non-verbal communications.	—	—
5. I usually know what another person is going to say before he or she says it.	—	—
6. I usually end conversations that don't interest me by diverting my attention from the speaker.	—	—
7. I frequently nod, frown, or in some other way let the speaker know how I feel about what he or she is saying.	—	—
8. I usually respond immediately when someone has finished talking.	—	—
9. I evaluate what is being said while it is being said.	—	—
10. I usually formulate a response while the other person is still talking.	—	—
11. The speaker's 'delivery' style frequently keeps me from listening to content.	—	—
12. I usually ask people to clarify what they have said rather than guess at the meaning.	—	—

13. I make a concerted effort to understand other people's point of view.
    — —

14. I frequently hear what I expect to hear rather than what is said.
    — —

15. Most people feel that I have understood their point of view when we disagree.
    — —

Scoring: The correct answers according to communication theory are as follows:

No for statements 1, 2, 3, 5, 6, 7, 8, 9, 10, 11, 14.

Yes for statements 4, 12, 13, 15.

If you missed only one or two responses, you strongly approve of your own listening habits, and you are on the right track to becoming an effective listener. If you missed three or four responses, you have uncovered some doubts about your listening effectiveness, and your knowledge of how to listen has some gaps. If you missed five or more responses, you probably are not satisfied with the way you listen, and your friends and co-workers may not feel you are a good listener either. Work on improving your active listening skills.

Source: Glenn and Pond, 1989

There is a final aspect of our communication model/process which Shannon and Weaver originally neglected to consider, namely feedback. When we communicate face to face we get some instant feedback on how our message has been received and interpreted. Our ability to exchange meaning effectively is greatly enhanced by this rich feedback loop (Buchanan and Huczynski, 1997). Feedback allows us to check constantly the accuracy of the coding and decoding processes. With more formal and remote methods, feedback can, at worst, be non-existent; or perhaps, at best, slow and unreliable, and thus we need to take more care in coding the message.

HOW MANAGERS COMMUNICATE

Thornton (1966) summarised a variety of survey results by stating that 'A manager's number one problem can be summed up in one word: communication.' This is rather unsurprising since, for approximately 80 per cent of all managers, much time is spent on verbal communication. Luthans and Larsen (1986) combined the direct observation of managers in their natural setting with self-report measures to try to determine how they actually communicated. The model presented in Figure 6.3 depicts the results.

Figure 6.3: How managers communicate: the managerial communication model

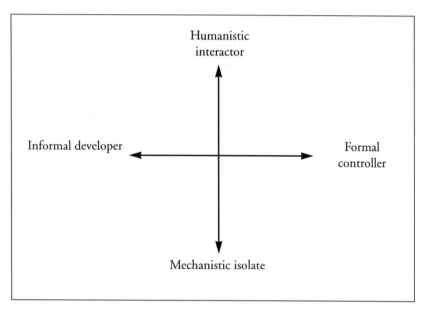

The first dimension of the managerial communication model represents a continuum ranging from the humanistic interactor (who frequently interacts both up and down the organisation hierarchy and exhibits human-oriented activities) to the mechanistic isolate (who communicates very little, except on a formal basis). The other dimension describes a continuum from the informal developer (who communicates spontaneously in all directions and exhibits activities related to developing his or her people) to formal controller (who uses formally scheduled communication interaction and exhibits monitoring/controlling activities). This empirically derived model describes two major dimensions of managerial communication. It provides a framework for how managers communicate on a day-to-day basis and, according to the authors, can be used as a point of departure for formally defining communication and the processes and systems of communication in today's organisations.

As highlighted earlier in this chapter the flow of communication internally through formal channels in the organisation may be in different directions, namely downward, upward and/or lateral.

Figure 6.4: Direction for information flow in organisations

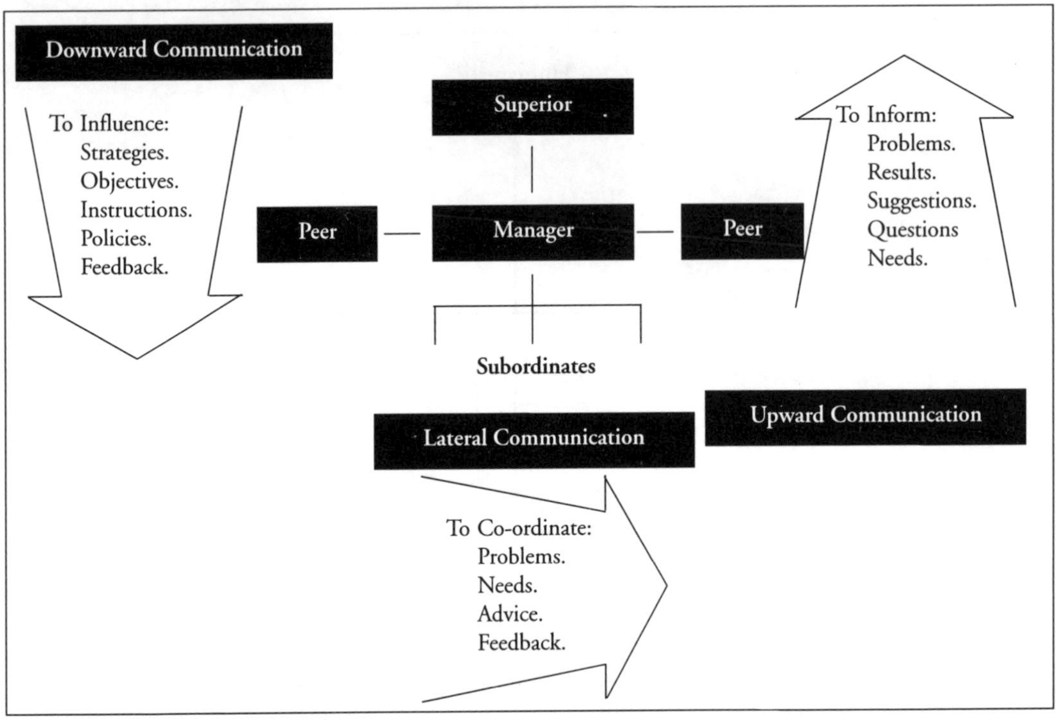

Source: Schermerhorn, 1996

Downward communication follows the chain of command from top to bottom. It 'describes the transfer of information about management decisions, policies and attitudes to those lower in the hierarchy' (McClave, 1997, p. 22). It is typically used for reiterating the nature of key strategic decisions and providing information on business performance results. The downwards messages also consist of information which is necessary for any staff to carry out their work, such as policies and procedures, orders and requests which are passed down to the appropriate level in the hierarchy. Upward communication describes the flow of messages from lower to higher levels in the hierarchy. Upwards messages are reports, requests, opinions and perhaps complaints. Sideways or lateral messages are between different departments, functions or people at the same level in the organisation and serve the important purposes of informing, supporting and co-ordinating activities across internal organisational boundaries.

INDIVIDUAL AND ORGANISATIONAL BARRIERS TO COMMUNICATION

Barriers to communication, often referred to as 'noise', are obstacles that distort or block the flow of needed information, thus interrupting the organisation's performance orientation and preventing people from exchanging ideas and emotions as effectively as they might wish. The barriers may be associated with the individual or the organisation.

- *Message uncertainty.* Often we may be unclear about what exactly it is we want to communicate. It may be lack of understanding on our part, it may be that we are not certain about what message the receiver needs in order to achieve the desired effect, or perhaps it might be that we are uncertain about how much information is necessary.

- *Perceptual selectivity and/or incompatible viewpoints.* The fact that people can take in and understand only a certain amount of information at one time. Perceptual distortions can be caused by having a poor self-concept or self-understanding, or a poor understanding of others. People may fail to communicate because they see the world in very different ways. Shared understanding may be impossible for them.

- *Language differences.* The fact that the same words can mean different things to different people. Semantic problems occur when people use either the same word in different ways, or different words in the same way. Problems of this nature also occur when people use jargon which they expect others to understand, or language which is outside the other's vocabulary.

- *Implicit assumptions.* Beliefs that the communicator holds without being fully aware of them and without having thought them through. Communication will likely fail if the sender and the receiver have different assumptions about some aspect of the message and are unaware that they differ.

- *Status and authority effects.* Social factors within an organisation that lead to mistrust between its members or groups. Effects such as these are particularly common in hierarchical structures. Task differentiation and specialisation at different levels in the organisation results in differences in jargon, training and work focus that may impair organisation members' understanding of each other.

- *Lack of feedback.* Anything that keeps the sender from knowing that the other has received, acknowledged, and understood the message. Although one-way communication is quicker, two-way is more accurate. While it may be difficult, in complex situations it helps both sender and receiver to measure their understanding and may improve their joint commitment to the issues at hand.

- *Lack of consultation/involvement and/or deception.* Tendency to avoid the input of persons who will be affected by, or who are capable of improving a decision. A person may sometimes decide that it is not in his or her best interests to tell other people all they might like to know, so the person refrains from communication; or perhaps the communication is ambiguous, involving messages which it is known will be misinterpreted. Or people may simply tell lies, hoping that they will not be caught out or, if they are, that the receiver will be powerless to do anything about it.

CHARACTERISTICS OF EFFECTIVE COMMUNICATION

Effective communication is a critical organisational process as well as a key skill for managers. Dawson (1996, p. 193) identifies five characteristics of an ideal communication process:

1. *Accuracy:* the message clearly reflects intention and truth as seen by the sender and is received as such.
2. *Reliability:* diverse observers would receive the message in the same way.
3. *Validity:* the message captures reality, is consistent, allows prediction and incorporates established knowledge.
4. *Adequacy:* the message is of sufficient quantity and appropriate timing.
5. *Effectiveness:* the message achieves the intended result from the sender's point of view.

McClave (1997, pp. 14–15), outlines critical principles of effective communication from both the perspective of the communicator/sender and the receiver/perceiver.

Table: 6.2: Principles of effective communication

As communicator:

Think carefully about your objectives before communicating: Ask yourself what are you trying to achieve. Do you want to inform, persuade, advise or consult the receiver? What kind of response do you need?

Put yourself in the receiver's shoes: Remember that the receiver's perception or frame of reference may not be the same as your own.

Choose the right medium, or combination of media: Difficulties can arise if the wrong medium is used. For instance, when giving a talk, you may leave the audience bewildered if you try to describe a complicated process by means of speech alone. A combination of words and graphics may be necessary.

Organise your ideas and express them carefully: Take time to structure your ideas in a logical sequence. In choosing your words, take into consideration the understanding and linguistic ability of the received . . . Use language suited to the context in which communication is taking place . . . Language that is appropriate to the shop floor may be very inappropriate in a committee meeting.

Consider the context: Breakdowns in communication often occur because the receiver is given information at the wrong time or in the wrong place. Even a very important message can be promptly forgotten if the receiver is very busy or preoccupied in thought. In general, always put yourself in the receiver's position and try to anticipate any difficulties or concerns he may have.

Check for feedback: Make sure your message has been received and understood . . . Be prepared to repeat or re-explain if necessary.

As receiver:

Give the message your full attention: Many messages are misunderstood because the receiver is daydreaming or not concentrating. Focus on the message and try to ignore or remove distractions.

Interpret the message correctly: Interpreting the message requires effort. If you are unsure about what is being said, ask for clarification. Check the meaning of unfamiliar words or references. Be alert for non-verbal nuances that may subtly alter the meaning of the communication.

Keep an open mind: You should not allow dislike of the communicator or disagreement with his beliefs to influence your judgement. Try to acknowledge your own prejudices and make an objective assessment of the message, no matter what your relationship with the sender.

Record information you are likely to forget: . . . Listeners in particular should take the time to jot down factual information they are likely to forget.

Respond appropriately: Respond positively to the communicator by providing feedback, following up enquiries or taking whatever other action is necessary.

THE ROLE OF THE COMMUNICATIONS FUNCTION IN LEADING-EDGE COMPANIES

In the high performance organisation, information is a tool, not a privilege. The overarching philosophy is that everyone in the organisation must have access to the maximum amount of information that it is reasonable to be able to assimilate, understand and utilise. In a debate on the role and significance of communication in today's business environment, Smythe (1995) writing in *People Management*, argues that the role of internal communications in an organisation is no longer limited to merely providing information to employees; rather in the present business environment it has a role to play in defining and improving the relationship between employers and employees and in helping in the management of strategic, structural, technological and process changes within the organisation. Of greater significance, Smythe's research identifies eight practical roles which the communication function will likely perform in leading-edge organisations, namely acting as the cultural conscience of the organisation, the communication planner, the communicator of decisions, the facilitator of re-visioning, the provider of the big picture context, the facilitator of real-time listening, the integrator of the internal culture and the external brand, and the facilitator of consultation, involvement and empowerment.

1. *The cultural conscience of the organisation:* Smythe argues that the style of relationships between people in the organisation is one of the most tangible experiences that employees have of the organisation's culture and that relationships are the prime conduit or window through which employees experience, learn and contribute to the organisation's culture. In this respect he suggests that organisation

communication can provide the instruments to measure relationship styles and facilitate debate among the leaders of the organisation on what kind of relationship styles will be most useful.

> Becoming the organisation's conscience is important if, as seems likely, the styles of relationship are critical to retaining customers, employees and productive supplier and partner alliances . . . The communication role is to understand the expectations and ethics that the organisation must be aligned with. Consequently it must facilitate the articulation of values and behaviour that should characterise relationships between employees and between employees and key external groups. (Smythe, 1995, p. 27)

2. *The communication planner:* Traditionally communication and information in the organisation context were rather more scarce than they are today. Smythe notes that the dramatic increase in the volume of communication brings with it the challenge of reconciling the needs and capacity of the audience. This role, he suggests, should fall to a communication planner who acts as negotiator between the suppliers of information on the one hand and the capacity of employees to digest information on the other.

> The communication planner would act in the manner of an air-traffic controller, permitting digestible quantities of information at any one time to be discharged to employees.

3. *Transparency of decisions:* While institutional secrecy was the order of the day in earlier times, such constraints are becoming less and less common. Today, Smythe notes, instant communication is a role born of necessity. Decision-makers require speed of implementation and recipients want clear, quick and honest reporting. The implication of this, he suggests, is the necessity to give communicators access to the decision-making fora of the organisation, and to use modern speedy technologies to distribute information.

4. *Big picture context:* Here Smythe argues that issues need to be dealt with as part of an overall organisational plan and the communications role is to use the channels and media of communication creatively to tell stories about new procedures, processes and products and to put them in the context of the overall vision. People, he suggests, react well to working in the context of a compelling vision.

5. *Facilitator of re-visioning:* The research demonstrates that organisations with vision sparkle with new ideas and take big leaps, often risky ones, to gain competitive advantage. Smythe argues that the quest to build a visioning ethos into organisations has fallen into the barren territory of producing mission statements that inspire no one and, in a compelling fashion, he suggests that 'the real task is to

hijack the often dull planning process to license a period of imagination'. The communication role here is to build inspiring re-visioning into the planning process and to channel the results into the communication and transmission of the 'big picture'.

6. *Real-time listening:* It is argued that the basis of a good relationship is good listening skills. (If you have not already done so, take some time to complete the Listening Skills Activity presented in Box 6.2 earlier in this chapter). In a more macro way there is a need to reflect on how the organisation as a whole listens. Real-time listening is a continuous process and is deemed critical to the on-going psychological health of the organisation. One needs to be continuously versed in what concerns people have, what they want to know more about and what they have heard from the organisation and from each other. Thus, it is suggested that there must be processes in place to listen and to engage management in hearing what has been fed back, so that there is a real connection between communication and listening.

7. *Productive consultation, involvement and empowerment:* This is a theme that we have already visited in this book. The central issue, according to Smythe's reflections, is the attitude that management has about the role of employees in the decision-making process. Are employees there to implement the ideas of the few, without questioning these ideas or influencing them? Or is it worth taking the time to seek and make use of employee input?

8. *Integrator of internal culture and external brand:* Finally, Smythe highlights as an emerging communication role that which aims to reconcile the thinking and the programmes conceived by the inward- and outward-facing disciplines of the organisation so that the promises that organisations make and the experiences of its customers are aligned.

SUMMARY OF KEY PROPOSITIONS

- Communication is involved in all the activities of the organisation and is the process by which two or more parties exchange information and share meaning. The purposes of communication in organisations are to achieve co-ordinated action, share information and express feelings and emotions.
- Organisations depend on complex flows of communication – upward, downward and laterally – to operate effectively.
- People communicate in organisations through written, oral and non-verbal means.
- The communication process involves a source encoding a message into symbols and transmitting it through a medium to a receiver who decodes the message and responds with feedback, as a means of verifying the meaning of the original message.

DISCUSSION QUESTIONS

1. How is communication in organisations an individual as well as an organisational process?
2. What place do informal communication channels have in organisations today?
3. Describe the main barriers to communication you are familiar with and give an example of each.
4. Think of a situation in which you felt there was a communication problem. Outline the things you would do to improve communications in that situation.

CHAPTER 7

Groups and Group Dynamics

LEARNING OBJECTIVES

- To understand the benefits of groups and be aware of the main reasons why people are organised (or organise themselves) into groups at work.
- To trace the different stages that groups go through from the time they form to the time they disband.
- To understand the concept of group cohesiveness, how it develops and what its benefits are.
- To understand the effects of excessive cohesiveness in groups.
- To improve group decision-making by helping people to be more objective and sometimes more critical of group decisions.

INTRODUCTION

This chapter specifically addresses the concept of groups and group dynamics at work. From an organisational behaviour perspective, an understanding of how people behave in groups may be even more important than how they behave on their own. Group influence, group formation, the development of norms in groups and various outcomes of group interaction are central concepts in building an understanding of the ways in which people operate at work. This chapter also explores some of the central theoretical foundations of organisational group dynamics, and explains key concepts associated with group behaviour.

THE NATURE OF GROUPS

The exploration of motivation in Chapter 4 has provided evidence that the need for 'belongingness' is an important motivator as well as a strong human need (Maslow, 1943; Alderfer, 1972). Most people get a lot out of belonging to groups either inside or outside their organisations, to the extent that some people often find it very difficult to function if they do not belong to an identifiable group.

Of course it's not just individuals who get a lot out of groups. Organisations purposely arrange people into work groups in order to deal with large, difficult or complex jobs. Groups can be good for people *and* their organisations (Handy, 1988).

Benefits of groups to individuals

Group membership is, of course, not just an organisational phenomenon: it is an experience that people are exposed to from the moment they are born by joining a family unit, and continues to be part of their experience right through the various stages of their development (Hellriegel *et al.*, 1989). By the time an individual joins an organisation as an employee, he or she will probably have had a wide variety of experiences in group settings and learned to play certain roles and both fulfil and satisfy a range of social needs. People have a tendency to join groups because of the benefits that they derive from group membership. Personal benefits from group membership include the following:

- Groups provide people with friendship and social support – a sense of belonging.
- Groups help people to be more aware of their own identity, i.e. who they are and what they represent in relation to others around them.
- Groups (particularly at work) can help to lighten someone's workload, or make the work process easier by providing extra manpower to complete a difficult or demanding task.
- Groups help people to become involved in a common activity which may further their own development or career. Group involvement can, for example, help people to become more creative, more diverse or even more skilled than they would have been outside the group.

Benefits of groups to organisations

Groups of people can be more useful to organisations than a number of individuals working in isolation. More and more it is being recognised that not only do individuals like to be part of a group at work (for the reasons outlined above), but that bringing people together is also good for the organisation, especially if what has to be done is difficult, complicated, strenuous or time-consuming. Groups are good for organisations because:

- When people get together in groups, there is a combination of skills, ideas and perspectives which help in the completion of difficult tasks.
- When people get together in groups, it may sometimes be easier to solve problems or to make more informed decisions.
- When people get together in groups, it is often more likely that there will be higher levels of commitment and participation among individuals in their work situation. In satisfying individual needs, group membership can encourage continued commitment in work situations. Organisations increasingly recognise the need for their employees to be committed to their organisations, and creating good working groups is one way of achieving this objective.

- When people get together in groups they can often help to resolve conflicts that might never be dealt with if people were kept apart. Organisations bring people together in order to help them to discuss such problems and issues so that unnecessary or dysfunctional conflict does not arise.

However, despite the potential benefits outlined above, groups and group formation do not always create these benefits for their organisations. Groups can also cause difficulties for organisations in ways which will be discussed later in this chapter.

Definition of a group

The concept of a group can be interpreted in any number of ways. It might be argued that a nation of people can be regarded as a group (in the sense that everyone shares a common national identity), or that an organisation is a group (in that all people are members of one specific establishment). However, from a behavioural perspective, there are several factors that need to be considered before a collection of individuals can be defined as a group. A common and often quoted definition of groups comes from Schein:

> A group is any number of people who *interact with each other,* are *psychologically aware of one another* and *perceive themselves to be a group.* (Schein, 1988)

Group members are generally defined by an identifiable membership, 'group consciousness', a sense of shared purpose, interdependence, interaction and an ability to act in a united manner (Mullins, 1996)

Perhaps the most effective definitions are those that are multidimensional, recognising the structural, dynamic and contextual aspects of the idea of 'group'.

From a contextual point of view, prerequisites such as interdependence of tasks and goals (Lewin, 1947), the existence of a common fate (Lewin, 1948; Campbell, 1958) and the psychological perception that the group exists (Schein, 1988) may all provide a rationale for differentiating between groups and non-groups in any social setting. Also, structural issues such as the roles, relationships and status of each member (Sherif and Sherif, 1979) play an important part in differentiating between one type of social group and another, and can be seen as important contextual determinants of group interaction.

In terms of process, such dynamics as interaction (Schein 1988) and face-to-face contact (Bales, 1950; Homans, 1950) also help to refine our understanding of what a social group represents. The content of group dynamics depends on the formal and informal tasks and objectives for which the group exists. The discussions and activities in which group members engage, and the outcomes achieved other than the maintenance of the group, can all be seen to relate to group 'content'.

From a subjectivist point of view, the existence of a group and group membership may depend entirely on the 'self-categorisation' referred to by Turner (1982). From an objectivist perspective, a group is more likely to be defined according to some externally identified assignment, title or arrangement. Brown (1988) augmented existing definitions like the one provided by Schein above and proposed that: 'a group exists when two or more people define themselves as members of it and when its existence is recognised by at least one [non-member]' (Brown, 1988, pp. 2–3).

It is reasonable to argue that unless individuals in the group perceive themselves to be members and define themselves as such, then the existence of that membership is entirely questionable and the sustainability of the group in terms of its processes and outcomes is unlikely to be maintained. Therefore, unless group members see themselves to be somehow connected with, and part of the group, the ability to define a collection of individuals as a group becomes precarious.

THE IMPORTANCE OF GROUPS

Organisational theory once spent relatively little time concerned with questions about how people behaved and how they interacted with one another at work. In the midst of the Industrial Revolution, Frederick Taylor wrote *The Principles of Scientific Management* and his work was symptomatic of the mechanistic, hyper-rational thinking that had become dominant in much of management thought both in the US and here in Europe. Tayloristic thinking did not account for or consider the social dimension of individuals. People were seen as commodities and resources that could be applied to organisational problems in very much the same ways as machines. Of course it can be convincingly argued that this kind of thinking is still alive and well in at least some current organisational contexts today. From a theoretical perspective, research and hypotheses which support the mechanistic application of 'human resources' to the workplace can be seen to have originated from the beginning of the Industrial Revolution.

With the arrival of the Industrial Revolution, new machinery, new technology and new organisational structures became more sophisticated and more complicated than the simpler social and work-orientated structures that had gone before. But formal knowledge about how people were likely to behave in large organisational settings did not progress as fast as the new forms of organisations themselves.

It was not until the 1920s that researchers began to consider the importance of social and inter-group dynamics at work. The now famous Hawthorne studies explored below provided some of the first evidence that social and group dynamics were starting to be seen as important considerations for understanding behaviour at work. The Hawthorne studies gave rise to a new school of thought in the area of organisational theory which came to be known as the human relations school.

Some theorists argue today that while the human relations school gave rise to more enlightened understanding of important behavioural issues at work, the iron fist of industrialism did not disappear; it just became hidden by a velvet glove (Mills and Simmons, 1995). Others argue that the naked exploitation that had characterised employers' approaches to the workforce in the early part of the century was at least somewhat tempered by the arrival of the human relations school (Huczynski and Buchanan, 1996) which started to alert theorists and practitioners to the importance of recognising the individual's social needs and of allowing groups to participate at least in some way in decisions that affected their working lives.

THE HAWTHORNE STUDIES

Between 1924 and 1927 a series of studies were carried out at the Hawthorne works of the Western Electric Company in the state of Illinois in the US. Their initial impetus was driven by a focus on scientific principles of the workplace, and the types of research questions that the investigators were originally interested in addressing related to how the physical surroundings of the organisation could enhance productivity and efficiency. Elton Mayo and his colleagues were interested in answering the following key research question: Would improvements in the physical surroundings, such as better lighting, have any effect on worker productivity?

Results of the Hawthorne studies

After testing different levels of light intensity and other aspects of physical working conditions, measuring changes in productivity and then analysing the results, the researchers were initially disappointed. Even after elaborate adjustments in the physical conditions under which employees were working, they were not able to establish any relationship between characteristics of the work surroundings and productivity of the workers. In some groups, output fluctuated randomly; in others, it appeared to increase. For one group in particular, it seemed that regardless of the alterations made in the environment, productivity increased. Baffled by these results, the researchers began to consider psychological factors that might be responsible for the increased productivity.

Eventually, after a series of different tests with two main groups within the Western Electrical Company, the researchers concluded that, far more important than any physical characteristics of any surroundings, were the human factors associated with the activities that people are asked to do at work. Conditions of the experiment were such that people who had previously never been consulted about or involved in decisions relating to their work, were suddenly being chosen for special treatment, and high levels of interest in every aspect of their behaviour were being demonstrated. Most importantly, according to the reports of the studies, the subjects were given an opportunity to work together in a social group setting and more of an opportunity to get to know each other than had been the case before the studies began (Mayo, 1933; Roethlisberger and Dickson, 1939). The most powerful proposal coming from the Hawthorne studies was that people prefer to work in groups and that people are likely to be more productive when they work together in participative group settings.

Problems with the Hawthorne studies

The Hawthorne studies are still recognised as an important turning point in the development of theory about organisational behaviour and groups operating within organisations. However, there are several legitimate criticisms about the perspectives adopted, the methodologies used and the results reported.

Firstly, while the researchers on the Hawthorne project heralded a fundamental change in the ways in which organisations were to be understood and studied, many people argue that they actually served to reinforce rather than to undermine the original Taylorist assumptions guiding most management thinking of the time. As Mills and Simmons (1995) point out:

> Scientific management . . . is a strand of [organisational theory] which arose out of the needs of employers to increase their employees' efficiency. Similarly, the human relations strand of organisational behaviour developed out of the specific concerns of the Western Electric Company to improve productivity. This led to the development of organisational principles that were managerialist in nature, that is, that take the defined needs of those in charge of organisations as the starting point for the developments of research foci and projects . . . [As a result] managerialist approaches to organisations have developed into a strong and dominant orthodoxy and alternative ways of viewing organisations have been treated as deviant and non-legitimate theories of organisation. (p. 11)

While the managerialist perspective is obviously an important standpoint from the point of view of understanding organisational behaviour, it is not the only one. An excessive emphasis on purely managerial concerns can prevent the consideration of alternative viewpoints, and thus restrict the sound development of knowledge in the area.

Recently, however, attempts have been made to redress this paradigmatic imbalance in the organisational behaviour literature. For example, Gareth Morgan (1986) and Mills and Murgatroyd (1994) encourage us to use perspectives other than purely managerialist ones, to help explain the nature of organisations and organisational group dynamics.

Secondly, the Hawthorne studies have been criticised for failing to recognise the 'sex power differential' (Stead, 1978). Of the two main groups studied, one ('the relay assembly group') was all female and the other ('the bank wiring group') was all male.

As Acker and Van Houten (1974) argue:

> The [male and female groups] were studied in different ways. [The male group was] free to continue their usual work practices, including the autonomy to develop and maintain their own work norms. The [female group] on the other hand [was] carefully recruited, closely supervised and in numerous ways told that they should improve their productivity. (p. 156)

There were strong differences in the findings between the male and female groups studied. Most striking was the fact that the all-female group increased its productivity and the all-male group restricted its outputs. These important results and contingencies were under-emphasised in the reporting of the research, thus disregarding possibly one of the most interesting and important aspects of the study.

Thirdly, the cultural specificities of the study make the results difficult to validate across cultures and over time. There were no studies to which this research could be compared for cultural differences. In Ireland, or in other European countries, similar studies at the time might have suggested different patterns of behaviour according to various cultural dimensions (Hofstede, 1991). Such information is, however, not available.

The Hawthorne effect

The Hawthorne studies gave rise to the expression 'the Hawthorne effect' which refers to the simple principle that when groups of people are aware that they are being observed, their behaviour may be (sometimes dramatically) different from when they are not being observed. While this is a useful principle, it draws to attention one of the methodological problems of studying human behaviour. It is not always easy to find out about people's natural tendencies in groups. In order to study groups we often need to observe their behaviour. But by observing group behaviour, it is possible that we will get a distorted picture of the natural behaviour and tendencies of that group.

Despite these criticisms, the Hawthorne studies represent an important series of studies for our understanding of organisational behaviour. Schermerhorn *et al.* (1996) summarise their contribution as follows:

> It is what the Hawthorne studies led to in terms of future research that counts most, rather than what they actually achieved as research. The studies represent an important historical turning point that allowed the field of management a new way of thinking about people at work. They extended the thinking of researchers beyond the concern for physical and economic considerations alone and clearly established the managerial significance of the psychological and sociological aspects of people as human beings. As a result the Hawthorne studies have had a major impact on what

135

we study as part of organisational behaviour. This legacy includes an interest in the group as an important force in the work setting and the importance of social relationships as a determinant of behaviour at work. (p. 710)

This interest in groups continues to be important in all organisational settings today. The remainder of this chapter examines some of the key concepts relating to groups: group norms, group cohesiveness, group development and group management.

GROUP NORMS

A group norm is an unwritten rule of behaviour shared by all members of the same group.

There are certain codes of behaviour in a group setting to which almost every member of the group is expected to conform. A norm is a rule which people must stick to if they are to continue to be accepted by the rest of the group.

Norms are rules of behaviour which are set down by the group itself, not by anyone outside the group. Group members develop and define acceptable ranges of tolerable behaviour that occurs within that group. It is not the group's managers or supervisors who decide what group norms exist within the group, and sometimes formal structures, systems and rules can do very little to control or to guide the norms that emerge.

Norms are not always under the control of people higher up in the organisation and they may not always encourage behaviour that is good for the organisation either. Small groups inside the organisation can band together and set goals for themselves which can also be either compatible or incompatible with those of the organisation.

Changing group norms can be a very difficult thing to do *because group norms are usually developed for actions and behaviour which is seen to be important for the survival or benefit of the group members* (regardless of whether they are good for the overall organisation).

THE EXPERIENCE OF GROUP PARTICIPATION

It is regularly argued, particularly by social psychologists and sociologists, that people are social animals and that groups are a natural and inevitable part of social and psychological life. Human beings are seen in much of the literature as 'group beings' (Brown, 1988). But participating in any social group, and experiencing the dynamics that emerge, is not always easy. Research has shown that some groups make the process of initiation deliberately unpleasant, often attributed to the group's functional need to de-sensitise new members to some of the inevitable difficulties that are faced as the group achieves its objectives (e.g. van Gennep, 1960). Other groups can develop strategies whereby initiation is a pleasant and rewarding experience, often seen as an attempt to encourage cohesiveness and to ensure that members make an initial commitment that may be robust enough to carry them through more difficult group experiences.

Being part of a group may be accompanied by moderate or serious disadvantages for the individual. Membership may require sacrificing aspects of one's individuality and suppressing personal values or views; it may expose individuals to uncomfortable social arenas; it may force co-operation in situations where there is an urge to compete or withdraw; it may require considerable extra commitment, effort and dedication to particular activities; it may alienate group members from non-members who may be socially or politically important in other contexts. These are some of the examples of the drawbacks that may develop as a result of joining and maintaining membership of social and organisational groups.

On the other hand, group membership may bring special privileges such as recognition, protection or prestige which may be considered valuable or important enough to outweigh some of the associated disadvantages. In many social settings, groups can provide benefits ranging from psychological satisfaction to physical survival. The perception of the relative advantages and disadvantages of group membership often depends (among other things) on whether original joining conditions were voluntary or involuntary, pleasant or unpleasant (Festinger, 1957; Aronson and Mills, 1959) and whether group pressure is moderate or severe (Keisler and Keisler, 1969). However, establishing the level of choice and constraint to which individuals are exposed when joining certain groups is not a straightforward process. Some membership may appear entirely voluntary when in fact subtle pressures are being brought to bear on joining decisions. On the other hand, individuals may claim not to have had a choice in the joining of a particular group even though the decision was mostly attributable to their own preferences with no external pressure. For political, psychological or self-justification reasons, personal freedom of choice is not always revealed. There is a variety of advantages, disadvantages, motives and pressures associated with the decision to join a group in any setting.

Group context

The context within which a group operates can be analysed from several perspectives. Bateman and Zeithaml (1989) refer to the 'psychological context' of groups in strategic settings. Essentially, this concept defines the cognitive, emotional and behavioural frameworks that provide a context for group action and interaction. Generally, group contexts are complex and often difficult to identify, but recognising that there are several dimensions may be extremely useful in the analysis and understanding of group processes.

Initiation and precedent-setting is very much connected with the context within which the group emerges, and initiation ceremonies or rituals can often give important clues as to the basic contextual features of the group. Rituals and ceremonies which often characterise group activation may reflect and illuminate group contexts upon which activities, interactions and outcomes are built (Moreland and Levine, 1982). Whether membership is voluntary or involuntary (or as is more likely, somewhere along a continuum between the two), evidence has repeatedly shown that initiation of a group not only changes the way in which individuals define themselves, but also gives rise to an effort to define and explore the identity, purpose and value of the group itself (Brown, 1988). Important precedents may be set which can have a fundamental effect on the ongoing dynamics which characterise the group.

One of the ways of facilitating an identification of the important aspects of group context is to analyse the dynamics associated with group initiation. This early phase in the group's development is generally charged with high levels of uncertainty and ambiguity (Wilson, 1994). Under such circumstances, members may attempt to reduce uncertainty through the development of a shared language and through the use of symbolism (Prasad, 1993; Poole *et al.*, 1990). Expressing group initiation in some ceremonial or ritualistic way may help to identify where the limits and boundaries of the group are to be drawn in the minds of members. There may be a need to differentiate between 'groupness' and 'non-groupness'. Initiation activities such as introductions, receptions, organisation-wide communications regarding the new group, etc., represent 'transition rites' (Van Maanen, 1976) which acknowledge that there has been a significant change from one state of affairs to another. This may reflect important contextual information about the culture, values, pressures, influences and expectations at play, even before the group begins to address the purposes for which it has been formed. This information may in turn come to define the group more clearly as events unfold.

Group initiation is also a time where the group's context and dynamics may be somewhat blurred. Members can originate from different personal contexts and bring with them a variety of assumptions, perspectives, needs and goals. Depending on how the early stages are managed, this context may be reshaped or manipulated in sometimes very subtle ways in order to facilitate the achievement of the group's goals/activities/functions as defined and understood at a particular point in time. Initiation ceremonies are often seen as one way of facilitating group cohesiveness and the development of a shared purpose, early on in the group's existence. Such characteristics may be important for the subsequent maintenance and ongoing survival of the group. Any effort to define or to differentiate the group may reduce perceptions of uncertainty or fear, allowing for more emotionally and psychologically tolerable group situations.

Interdependence of task and fate as key contextual group factors

Past events are likely to have some impact on the shape of any current group context. For example, 'norms' or 'ranges of acceptable behaviour' (Sherif and Sherif, 1979) arise through members' experience of events and then become contextual 'fixtures' within a group, allowing for the development of clearer ideas about what is socially appropriate and inherently acceptable for the group (Brown, 1988). Group norms may take time to develop, but when they do, they often guide group behaviour in identifiable and powerful ways.

Two contextual fixtures that Brown (1988) identifies as important influencers of dynamics such as cohesiveness and group identity are based on the concept of interdependence. Firstly, 'interdependence of fate' has been found to influence feelings of cohesiveness, group membership and motivation to band together (Jacobsen, 1973; McCarthy, 1979) which can have important effects on the ways in which members perform together to produce effective outcomes.

Secondly, 'interdependence of task' refers to a more specific type of interdependence. When individuals share a common objective, and when each member must play a unique role in the achievement of this objective, task interdependence can be said to be high (Brown, 1988; Saavedra *et al.*, 1993). Such a contextual factor plays a part in the group's definition and identity as defined by members. Task interdependence may, for example, give rise to the emergence of coalitions within organisations (Narayanan and Fahy, 1982) which may further clarify the relationship between one group and another.

Contextual factors relevant to groups and their dynamics include such concepts as interdependence, psychological frameworks and past events which give rise to group norms. The existence of such factors can be identified and clarified through an examination of various sources of evidence such as the differences in group roles as evidenced in group interaction and activity, observations of the ways in which tasks are defined, objectives are set and outcomes are reached. An analysis of the context of a group forms the beginnings of overall group analysis and draws on evidence which demonstrates the dynamics of group initiation and development as well as data which provides background information on events and structures that were a social reality prior to the group's existence.

Group structure

As a concept, group structure can be viewed as part of the group's 'internal context'. Collins (1981) and others would argue that structures are in fact simply repeated patterns of behaviour and that 'the structure is in the repeated actions of communicating, not in the contents of what is said; those contents are frequently ambiguous or erroneous, not always mutually understood or fully explicated' (Collins, 1981, p. 995).

Role differentiation and the extent to which this exists within a group is one of the central dimensions of a group's structure. The functions of this differentiation include such practical issues as division and distribution of activities, coherence and predictability of group operations and such psychological functions as self-definition within the group (Brown, 1988). Status differentiation is a second important structural variable, and the extent to which this exists in a group may serve to provide important explanations of how and why group members behave in the ways that they do.

In any group setting, evidence of role and status differentiation should be sought in order to provide another bank of data which may help to build a meaningful picture of the process, content and outcomes of a particular stream of group activity. The chain of command that exists within and between groups gives rise to an important set of relationships and may serve to clarify the routines or patterns by which groups become characterised (Collins, 1981).

INSTRUMENTAL AND SOCIAL DIMENSIONS OF GROUPS

Task-orientated behaviour can be referred to as 'instrumental activity'. This relates to the processes and dynamics that occur which relate specifically to the task for which the group has been formed (Bales, 1950). Differentiating between this type of activity and other types (social or emotional) is important in that this may provide strong clues as to where the real priorities, needs and influences of group members lie.

In the course of task accomplishment, processes may occur which cause emotional wear and tear (Brown, 1988), which may cost more than they gain in personal terms in favour of group task achievement, or which may be necessary for the emotional or social satisfaction of various members even when not directly focused on group task accomplishment. Bales (1953) was among the first social researchers to point out the potential diversity of major group processes and to trace different types of behaviours that operate simultaneously and may give rise to competing demands being made on the group. Group theorists often point out that dynamics within groups are charac- terised by complexity, ambiguity and often apparent chaos (Janis, 1982). Much of this complexity may be attributable to the emotional and social needs that reach the surface of group activity and may conflict with or delay the completion of formal group tasks.

Activity which, for example, demonstrates individual emotion or shows concern for the feelings of others can be referred to as 'socio-emotional activity' (Bales, 1953). Socio-emotional behaviour has more recently been referred to as 'maintenance behav- iour' (e.g. Marcic, 1992) and rather than conflicting with the requirements of the task, may indirectly support or facilitate the achievement of group goals. Maintenance activ- ities, while fulfilling social and/or emotional needs, may be necessary for group effectiveness rather than superfluous to, or conflicting with it (Schein, 1988; Marcic, 1992). Such behaviours are seen to maintain the working order of the group, create an appropriate climate within which to accomplish tasks and allow for the development of relationships that lead to collaboration and good use of various member resources.

THE STAGES OF GROUP FORMATION

It has long been recognised that groups of individuals brought together for a particular purpose experience different dynamics and behaviours according to their stage of formation. This may loosely relate to the amount of time individual members have spent together either before or during identifiable group membership.

When a group gets together for whatever reason (whether it is to get a job done, to provide friendship and support, to set up a decision-making committee, etc.) the members of the group are likely to go through different stages of development (Tuckman, 1965). A collection of people who have never worked together before will need to spend time getting to know each other, finding out about the needs and goals of each individual, and learning about each other's strengths and weaknesses.

It is natural that it will take some time before the group is up and running and achieving the goals for which they came together. The following describes the kinds of stages that a group can go through before they start to achieve these goals at a level with which most people will be satisfied (Tuckman, 1965).

1. The forming stage

If a collection of individuals first meet in a working situation, it may take some time before they realise that each person is interested in forming an informal or friendly group with whom they can socialise at weekends or play sports in their free time. As soon as this becomes clear, there may be one or two individuals who find that they don't really fit in, or that they don't enjoy the activities that the group has in mind. These individuals may voluntarily leave the group to join a different one, or remain alone. Other individuals may be seen as having hidden motives within such a social group (for example you may find that there are higher-ranking individuals who want to become part of the group to get the 'low down' on what the attitudes are towards management or to find out about work-related issues). If the rest of the group sees that this is the case, such individuals may be 'expelled' from group membership by being made to feel unwelcome, or openly told that they do not belong.

This type of process is an example of what is often called the forming stage of group development where group membership and group goals are clarified. Also, some basic issues may be established which help to give the group its identity, and perhaps in some way sets it apart from the rest of the organisation.

At the forming stage of group development, group members may clarify the following issues:

- Will the group have a name?
- Who will be the leader or organiser of the group?
- Will people from outside work be allowed to participate?

- How many times will the group meet?
- For how long will the group stay together?

It's important for a group to clarify such issues as this process *helps to give group members a clear idea of the purpose and nature of the group.*

The storming stage

Once the basics have been clarified, a group moves on to the second stage of development, known as the storming stage. The kinds of behaviours that are evident at this stage usually include a certain level of conflict. Conflict can be destructive but it can also be positive within the organisational setting. This is true for groups within the organisation as well. At this stage, a deeper level of understanding emerges as people get to know each other better. More individuals may be identified as having hidden motives who may not have been so evident at the beginning. There may be conflict over who occupies the leadership role (for example, an individual who was originally accepted as the leader, may show that they are not completely committed to the goals of the group, and a more suitable candidate for leadership may emerge or be chosen by the others).

Even the goals which seemed clear earlier on, may change (for example a group which originally organised a sporting activity may have done so with the goal of forming friendships or keeping fit. However, as time goes on, the activity becomes more competitive, and people become less interested in friendships, and more interested in winning the games that they play).

This stage is really characterised by a *re-evaluation of the original assumptions that people have made about the reasons for the group's existence, and an elucidation of the part that each person plays within the group.*

The norming stage

This stage is where the group starts to focus on its activities and establishes set norms and ways of doing things. It is often when the talking ends and the 'doing' starts. At this stage, people have usually identified each group member's particular strengths and are learning to use these strengths to their best advantage. Similarly, certain weaknesses may have been identified which are also recognised when the group is together. Using the sports group example, one person may be seen as a particularly skilful goalie, someone else may be identified as an excellent striker etc., so it becomes the norm that they will play in these positions.

The norming stage is, quite simply, when the group norms are established. *Acceptable behaviour is clarified and people very quickly become aware of what they are expected to do, and how they are expected to behave.*

The performing stage

If people have established themselves as a permanent group, this is ideally the final stage of development that the group will reach. Whilst in any group there is usually room for improvement, the performing stage is when people have 'got it right'. *They have resolved any of the confusion and conflict that may have existed at earlier stages, they are happy with the part that each member is playing in the group setting and they are achieving their goals as effectively as possible.* At this stage the group can be seen as having reached maturity, where communication does not break down, where everyone knows what they have to do, usually enjoys it, and achieves personal fulfilment from their membership as well as contributing in an important way to the success of the group. Needless to say, this does not accurately describe the experience of all groups.

These four stages may not always be an accurate description of what really goes on in groups. Groups are not as predictable in their development as might be suggested from this section. It is useful to examine what can and does happen when groups get together and develop, but these stages are only pointers to the potential that groups have to develop successfully.

The stages of group development outlined above assume that all group members join the group at the same time. In reality, this is not always true: in most organisations, group membership changes quite frequently. Individuals come and go, so that the nature of the group and the individuals within it often changes on quite a regular basis. For this reason, the stages of group development may not always be as clear-cut as outlined above.

The stages of forming, storming, norming and performing, really describe the ideal and successful ways in which groups should develop. What *should* happen, is not always what *does* happen. It is often the case that groups get 'stuck' at one of the first three levels, and never actually reach the stage where they are performing effectively together.

SOME COMMON PITFALLS IN THE PROCESS OF GROUP DEVELOPMENT

Some reasons why groups may get stuck at the forming stage of development

People sometimes find that when a group forms, there is an inability on behalf of group members to break the ice and to start communicating about the reason they have formed. If this happens, and if such a problem continues, the reason for forming will become very hard to clarify and the group may break up or fizzle out.

If there is a constant inflow of newcomers at the forming stage, it becomes difficult to set objectives or to agree on who should occupy the leadership role, and so effective group formation may be difficult or impossible.

If for other reasons (such as people being coerced into group membership) there is little or no commitment to the purpose of the group, then formation will be very half-hearted and the group is unlikely to progress successfully on to the next stages of development.

Some reasons why groups can get stuck at the storming stage of development

People often find it very difficult to cope with the storming stage because it is usually the first time when conflict or disagreement occurs. The group is still fragile and can easily come apart if this conflict is not resolved successfully.

Again, if group members do not learn to interact, to cope effectively with conflicts that arise and to operate beyond formal, surface introductions and clarifications, it will be much more difficult for the effective development to progress.

Some reasons why groups can get stuck at the norming stage of development

If people don't recognise their own strengths and weaknesses, or recognise what is expected of them by other members of the group, it can be very difficult for effective norms to be established. Also, if people don't feel comfortable enough to voice their opinions about what they think is good or bad about the group, they won't have a chance to make the most of the skills that do exist and work on developing the skills that don't.

One of the most important things about achieving a good atmosphere for groups to develop successfully is to be able to recognise the above pitfalls and to avoid them or cope with them if they arise.

DEVELOPING COHESIVE GROUPS

The concept of group cohesiveness is an important notion in the theoretical and practical understanding of group behaviour (Hosking and Morley, 1991). Cohesiveness has been described as the cement 'binding together group members and maintaining their relationships with one another' (Schacter, 1951, p. 229). The concept of cohesiveness is not always defined with such certainty. But while it has traditionally been referred to as a complex and ambiguous term (Allport, 1962), the intuitive meaning is generally described as a condition in which group members feel bonded together in ways that reinforce the existence, maintenance and purpose of the group (Budge, 1981). The following are the common determinants of cohesive groups:

High levels of communication

Studies have shown that the more that people talk or communicate with others in the group, the more likely it is that they will become cohesive (Hogg, 1992; Cook, 1978).

Group size

The size of a group (i.e. the number of members) also affects the amount of group cohesiveness that there is. If a group is too large, it is harder for every member to feel that they really belong. Psychologists have suggested that anything above twelve members can significantly reduce the group's ability to become cohesive (Schein, 1988).

Co-operation and competition

Some experimental studies have shown that co-operative group behaviour is more likely to lead to group cohesiveness (Hogg, 1992). Research has concluded that if group members spend more time co-operating with each other, they are more likely to feel that they belong to the group and are more likely to continue to be committed to the group, whereas competition inside the group can cause the group to pull apart rather than to feel cohesive. However, Myers (1962) found that (given certain aspects of the group contexts, cultures and values), team members expressed greater esteem for one another where there were high levels of competition.

A feeling of acceptance

If each group member feels accepted by their group, then there is more likely to be a tendency to stick together, and group cohesiveness is also more likely to be high (Hogg, 1992).

Outside threat

If a group experiences a threat from outside of the group, they will often band more closely together than they did in the past. If conflict arises between one work group and another, these groups may become more internally cohesive, developing a unity of purpose in an effort to strengthen themselves against what they perceive to be an outside threat (Thomas, 1976).

Success and performance

The more successful a group feels, and the more it achieves rewards for what it does, the more likely the group members will enjoy belonging to the group. Group cohesiveness can be created or very much strengthened by the successful achievement of the goals that the group has set (Janis, 1972).

These factors, along with successful development as outlined in the last section, all contribute to the feeling of belongingness and commitment generally referred to as cohesiveness (Budge, 1981).

Cohesiveness usually exists when there are:

- Good levels of communication.
- Acceptance of each group member.

- A commitment to the survival of the group in the face of outside threats.
- An atmosphere and feeling of success.

Intuitive experience, as well as what has been presented in this section, may very much suggest that group cohesiveness often creates an agreeable and favourable feeling within a group. Indeed, evidence does show that cohesive group members usually enjoy group membership and experience good levels of self-esteem by remaining part of the group. In organisational settings, the existence of group cohesiveness can contribute to the morale, the commitment and the performance of each group member.

However, too much group cohesiveness can sometimes make group members unrealistic in their aims and objectives, as well as in their assessment of their strengths. There are some reasons why group cohesiveness sometimes causes groups to make bad decisions.

'GROUPTHINK'

'Groupthink' (Janis, 1972) is another concept which has become associated with the workings of groups in organisations. In this section we investigate what it means and why it can be another important label in helping to understand group behaviour.

In the last section we saw how group cohesiveness can help to create very real benefits for good group performance. Belongingness and commitment are very important features within. They help them to stay together and to work together effectively. However, sometimes groups can become so cohesive that they are unaware of what is going on around them and as a result may ignore, or be less responsive to, the rest of the organisation.

These types of problems can create many difficulties for an organisation, and Irving Janis (1972) suggests that they arise at least in part from 'over cohesiveness' or the 'groupthink phenomenon'.

Groupthink is what happens when people in a group become so close (or cohesive) that any disagreement between people becomes less and less likely to occur. As a result, the group develops a way of thinking which prevents them from being realistic or critical about what they are doing or the ways in which they are doing it. The people in the group are then less likely to question the reasons for their actions.

If this does happen, the group can become blind to their weaknesses or potential weaknesses, because agreeing with each other becomes more important than doing the right things or being effective in achieving their goals. Too much agreement can lead to a false sense of security where everyone feels very cosy in the group, and no one is prepared to rock the boat by pointing out weaknesses or mistakes that are being made.

Here are some of the factors that Janis has identified which together give rise to what he calls the 'groupthink phenomenon':

1. *A feeling of invulnerability.* When groups develop a record for excellent or highly successful performance, they can develop the feeling that they are invincible. The group's success can lead to a false sense of security which prevents members from being realistic in their evaluation of the risks associated with various courses of action.

2. *False logic.* Groups which are very cohesive will often develop a false logic about what they are capable of doing. They try to rationalise their actions even if there is evidence from outside the group that this logic is wrong.

3. *A feeling that the group is morally right.* Groups can start to feel justified in their decisions even if it means that individuals may suffer, that they will incur costs which could have been avoided or that in some way they are in breach of moral or ethical codes of behaviour. There can be a tendency for groups to believe that what they are doing is morally correct, or to ignore the moral implications of their activities.

4. *Shared stereotypes.* Groups that experience 'groupthink' can be very quick to stereotype anyone who criticises or disagrees with what the group is doing.

5. *Pressure.* Individual members who do express reservations or doubts about the group's collective decisions can experience direct pressure from other members not to emphasise their doubts, to agree with the majority or, in some instances, to withdraw or resign from the group.

6. *Self-censorship.* Group members in a highly cohesive group may be likely to be reluctant to communicate anything negative about the group to other people in the organisation. This results in an inadequate exploration and analysis of what the group is doing.

7. *An illusion of agreement or unanimity.* Often groups become convinced that everyone agrees with the decisions of the group. This can prevent members from exploring or even from expressing their doubts about particular courses of action.

These are the kinds of things that can cause a very cohesive group to make the wrong decisions, and taken together, they explain the 'groupthink phenomenon'. In the next section you'll see that managing groups involves helping to prevent this from happening.

This section should have given you a good idea as to what can happen in highly cohesive groups. This is not to say that cohesiveness is always damaging. You have also seen that groups who are close and committed can be excellent. From the point of view of organisational effectiveness, groups are not a straightforward concept. While it is true that people naturally join groups, and that organisations can benefit from this natural tendency, it is also argued that groups need to be managed in the right ways. Managing groups involves recognising the mistakes that they can make, and avoiding such mistakes, or rectifying them if they are made.

MANAGING GROUPS

Managing group norms

Norms are used by groups to regulate and control the behaviour of each member within it. They are useful in that they help the group to survive, they make everyone's behaviour more predictable, and they *express what the group believes in.* People who can't influence the group are unlikely to be able to change norms or have control over such norms.

Because norms emerge within cultural as well as organisational contexts, it is not always possible for managers to ensure that group norms are compatible with the goals of the organisation. Cultural differences between various subgroups in any one organisation can give rise to very different norms arising in different areas and divisions.

- *Stay aware of what the group is doing.* Norms are rules which have not been written down, so the only way to find out what they are is to be observant and to know what's happening within different groups.
- *Develop good interaction patterns within groups.* Sometimes groups develop norms without consciously deciding to do so. Norms can be very similar to habits. Some habits are good, others are bad. In order to uncover bad habits, it is a good idea to talk about them, or question them: asking groups *why* they are committed to certain behaviour can often help them to consider norms which they have never before recognised and to do something about them.
- *Recognise fears and clarify issues.* Groups who are together for some time, develop their own goals of survival. If an organisation asks a group to work harder than they have in the past, there may be fears that one or two people within the group will lose their jobs, if the group as a whole becomes more efficient. It is important when managing groups to recognise the legitimate fears that a group may have and to clarify what may or may not happen if a group changes its norms. Lots of norms emerge in groups due to unvoiced fears. Getting these fears out into the open can help a group to change its perspective and ways of doing things.
- *Provide rewards for compatible group norms.* If organisations build in rewards (recognition, praise, bonuses etc.) for groups whose norms support good performance, this may provide motivation for groups to maintain or to develop group norms which are congruent with the goals of the organisation.

So, while managing groups norms is not an easy process, there are some things organisations can do to make it more likely that norms will be managed well: stay aware, communicate, recognise fears in the group and provide rewards for groups whose norms satisfy the goals of the organisation.

Managing group development

The main issue involved in managing group development is understanding what *should* happen during group development. If, for example, a group has been together for a long time, and members are still fighting about who should do what, there is evidence that they have not effectively negotiated the early stages of group formation. If this can be recognised, it is possible to 'start again' and to try to resolve issues which should have been resolved earlier in their development as a group.

The development process can be significantly facilitated by having a structured checklist which outlines all the issues that should be resolved, and when they should be resolved. Also, it can be very helpful to establish a time frame which identifies when the group should aim to be at the final 'performing' stage of their development. For each group, this time frame will be different, depending on the nature of the tasks they must complete. In setting time frames for group development it is important not to be too rigid – groups sometimes need to resolve certain issues in their own time, and too much pressure from outside can prevent groups from developing their own dynamics and ownership of their activities.

So to recap, some of the keys to managing group development involve the following:

1. *Know about the ideal stages of group development* and how the situation differs from this ideal.
2. *Help the group to resolve important issues at each stage of development* – especially its goals and activities.
3. *Have a checklist of which issues should be resolved when.*
4. *Aim to be up and running* as a group *within a certain specified time frame;* but
5. *Be flexible* where necessary (e.g., if the task is very complicated, or if confidence levels are low).

Managing cohesiveness and 'groupthink'

Preventing groupthink also involves an initial awareness that it can happen, and how it can be damaging for group members and the overall performance of the group.

Key people within the group should be appointed to encourage others to express their doubts; individuals within the group (especially leaders) should be ready to accept criticism as well as praise; make sure that higher-status people (e.g. supervisors or managers within the group) express their opinions last; divide into subgroups when difficult problems or disagreements arise.

It is much easier for people to give honest opinions to a small group (of say three people) than it is for them to 'come clean' with a large group (say twelve people). Steps for managing small 'breakaway' group discussions should include the following: divide into smaller groups of around three or four people, discuss the problem within these small groups, appoint a spokesperson for each group, return to the larger group, have each spokesperson give feedback about the results of their small group discussions. This process is more likely to lead to a wider variety of opinions being given and more options being explored.

Box 7.1: How to deal with 'groupthink'

- Ask each group member to be a critical evaluator of all ideas and suggestions generated by the group.
- Encourage people to voice and explore their doubts.
- Create subgroups with different leaders to work on the same problem.
- Invite outside experts to observe and react to group discussions.
- Have a different member act as 'devil's advocate' at each group meeting.
- Hold 'second chance' meetings once an initial decision is made.

Adapted from Janis, 1982

SUMMARY OF KEY PROPOSITIONS

- This chapter introduced some of the original theoretical foundations of groups and group development in organisational settings. Most of the research about groups and group dynamics is managerialist in its perspective on organisational analysis. Nevertheless, groups can be very useful, not just for organisations but also to fulfil the needs of individual group members.
- A review of the original Hawthorne studies shows that the experiments were flawed in some serious ways, but that they led to the central propositions that people often prefer to operate in groups and that creating organisational groups can enhance organisational effectiveness
- Group norms were discussed, and described as unwritten rules of behaviour to which each member is expected to conform. It was pointed out that some group norms create effective and productive ways of doing things, but that others can be damaging for the organisations to which the group belongs.
- Group development has been described as comprising four key stages (forming, storming, norming and performing). In ideal situations, different issues relating to the group are resolved at different stages, but these stages of group development don't always reflect reality.

- Group cohesiveness is a sense of belongingness and commitment to a group that keeps group members together. It arises as a result of several factors in the course of a group's existence. These factors include: good levels of communication and co-operation, acceptance of all group members, commitment to the survival of the group and a general atmosphere of success. Group cohesiveness, while desirable in a group, can sometimes be damaging due to what has come to be known as the 'groupthink problem'.

- The concept of groupthink was explained and explored. It was described as behaviour that emerges when people become so close that any disagreement is less and less likely to occur. The group is prevented from being realistic or critical about what they are doing and the ways in which they are doing it. The causes of groupthink are: a feeling of invulnerability; false logic in the group; a feeling that the group is morally right; shared (and inaccurate) stereotypes; pressure put on anyone who rocks the boat; self-censorship; an illusion that all group members agree on certain things and mindguards which protect the group from negative information.

DISCUSSION QUESTIONS

1. Think of a group to which you belong. See if you can give any examples of group norms from the description you have just read.
2. Do you think that the stages of group formation outlined in this chapter is an unrealistic picture of what really happens in group situations?
3. Is group cohesiveness always a positive factor which enhances successful performance of the group?

CHAPTER 8

Teams and Team Development

LEARNING OBJECTIVES
- To understand what teamwork is about, and why it is important in the context of organisations.
- To recognise that it is difficult to be unequivocal in attributing team-based activity to organisational success.
- To be able to recognise the different tasks and team processes.
- To recognise some common problems which arise when teams are being developed and be aware of how to avoid these problems.
- To know about the different roles that people can play within their team.
- To recognise important features of a good team and ways in which these features can be introduced into teamwork situations.

INTRODUCTION

The concept of a 'team' is central to organisational life in Ireland and, indeed, throughout the world. The language of teams is used regularly in organisational settings, and many strategists and human resource specialists believe in and champion the benefits and advantages of team-based activity at work. Even the most brief examination of literature on organisational behaviour shows the huge popularity that the concept of teams and team-building has gained. The language of teams has become a central part of the projected identities of large and small organisations. Examples of recent job advertisements in Ireland shows how prevalent the team concept is when organisations project an image of themselves to the outside world, particularly when they are attempting to attract high-calibre employees.

Both theorists and practitioners have often promoted team-based activity at work. There is a wide range of evidence which champions the team concepts both from an individual and an organisational perspective. People who are team members at work, often report higher levels of motivation, of satisfaction and even of self-esteem. Organisations which have successfully implemented team initiatives often report higher levels of productivity and effectiveness overall). However, some perspectives on teams suggest that there is a lot of inaccurate or manipulative hype surrounding the concept. Chris Argyris (1990) for example proposes that teams, in the real sense of the

Figure 8.1: Extracts from some typical appointments advertisements in the Irish context

---

'Seeking a good challenge? Join our **highly motivated team . . .** '
(Procter & Gamble)

'**Team Builder** required.'
(Saville Systems)

'**Our team** can use your consulting skills.'
(Coopers & Lybrand)

'Operations manager: Will require excellent organisational skills, communication skills and the ability to **motivate and lead a team** of managers.'
(HMV Ireland)

'**Team** facilitator: Working as part of the Human Resources **Team**, you will be responsible for the development and co-ordination of all **team-based activities**.'
(Transitions Optical)

'PC Network administrator: Will work in the PC network support **team**.'
(Analog Devices)

'Community development co-ordinator: You will work as part of a small **team**.'
(Dublin Inner City Partnership)

Source: Irish Times, Business Section, 4 April 1997

word, often do not exist in the ways that organisations would like to think that they do (claiming for example that 'the management team is a myth'). Others claim that the team concept is simply a manipulative and exploitative tool, used by managers to get more out of their employees.

Whatever the opinions on the strengths and weaknesses of teams, their importance in organisational settings has certainly gained enormous popularity, particularly over recent decades of organisational behaviour research. In this chapter, we explore some of the reasons why this is the case.

TEAMS: A DEFINITION

There are many potential definitions of teams in organisations. Depending on their perspectives and activities they can be structured in a variety of ways and fulfil a variety of purposes. Despite the potential diversity of the team concept, an organisational team can be broadly defined as 'a small group of people with complementary skills who work together to achieve a common purpose for which they hold themselves collectively accountable' (Schermerhorn *et al.*, 1996). A team can also be defined as a group of people which has fine-tuned its performance, built on its skills and is constantly improving itself, as well as contributing to the improvement and success of its organisation (Katzenbach and Smith, 1993).

Types of organisational teams

Top management teams

The 'top management team' is the leading group in an organisation – the group of people who operate at the strategic apex of the organisation (Mintzberg, 1988). Issues that they are responsible for addressing relate to the long-term direction of the organisation. However, many people who are at the top of their organisations will tell you that the group of people they are accompanied by, do not behave like a team at all. A top management team can only be considered to be a team if they fulfil the broad definitions outlined above. More details about effective top management team functioning are discussed later in this chapter.

Project teams

Project-based teams can be created in organisations in order to investigate and to address certain issues or problems for which a solution is sought. Project teams can be multi-status and multi-disciplinary and yield, as a beneficial by-product, increased levels of cross-functional interaction, allowing individuals from one part of the organisation to gain insights into the problems or concerns of people in other divisions or at other levels. A multi-disciplinary team project is a group of people who have been drawn together from various departments and divisions, often in order to exchange different perspectives on common organisational issues in order to identify and sometimes implement solutions.

Functional teams

Functional teams are made up of groups of people who carry out various tasks within the organisation. Organisations which refer to their 'sales teams', their 'marketing teams', their 'research teams' and so on, are referring to functional groups that may have in some way developed team-like characteristics.

While there are various team labels in organisations, there are both theorists and practitioners who readily admit that so-called teams do not necessarily fit the description in the real sense of the word (see the definitions of teams above). What organisations refer to as teams can often simply be a label for a group of people who may or may not be working well together as a team (e.g. Argyris, 1990). A group of people and a team of people have the same potential for performance. Organisations often devote enormous effort to try to 'build' groups of people into 'teams' in an attempt to realise this potential.

A cautionary note on attributing organisational effectiveness to team-based activity

It is often difficult to be sure exactly what combination of factors leads to organisational effectiveness. For one thing, the concept of effectiveness is difficult to define because different people within the organisation may have different views about what effectiveness means. Marketing people may believe that organisations are effective to the extent that they promote their brands and attract customers to buy their products or services; personnel people may believe that effectiveness depends on the organisation's ability to attract, select, motivate, train and retain good quality people; the finance department may see organisational effectiveness as the ability to keep costs low and revenues high, while research and development may consider organisational effectiveness to be characterised by the organisation's ability to develop new products and to advance innovative ways of doing things.

So, organisational effectiveness is not an objective standard to which all organisations can aspire in any straightforward way. It means different things to different people and, depending on the roles that people play in their organisations, the pursuit of organisational effectiveness can be characterised by a variety of very different perspectives, by conflict and by efforts to pursue goals which are at least sometimes mutually exclusive. The personnel department may be eager to develop new training initiatives that may be seen by the finance department as too costly. Marketing people may put the R&D department under pressure to speed up the product development cycles so that they can get the product to market as fast as possible, while the R&D people claim that they need more time if they are to make any real or substantial breakthroughs in a particular area.

Secondly, organisational effectiveness can be attributed to a variety of different activities, variables and events both inside and outside the organisation. It may be difficult to establish in any really objective way, why some organisations succeed and others fail. Organisations that introduce new initiatives like team activities and team-based structures may also have a variety of qualities and characteristics that make them successful or that contribute to their organisational effectiveness. Sometimes it is difficult to be sure that an organisation is effective because of a team orientation, or that a team orientation exists because an organisation is effective.

Techniques for better management of organisations sit side by side with a myriad of other variables: the economic conditions, the history of the organisations, random or at least unpredictable changes in market demands; earthquakes, hurricanes, assassinations, oil crises, droughts, wars and other global events can impact on organisations and their ability to survive in ways that may override or eliminate the benefits of any of the micro processes introduced by managers within the company. Ireland exists within a small, open economy, which often makes the country all the more vulnerable to the peaks and troughs of bigger economies and worldwide events

Nevertheless, initiatives that involve team creation and team-based activity can and do make a difference in individual companies. It is simplistic to say that team-based organisations will automatically be successful. A more accurate perspective incorporates the idea that organisational productivity can be facilitated by a team orientation, in conjunction with a wide variety of other factors both internal and external to the organisation.

Box 8.1 is an example of a team-based activity.

Box 8.1: The team approach at Aughinish Alumina

In 1993, Aughinish Alumina Ltd in Co. Limerick adopted a partnership ethos between management, workers, customers and unions at its plant. Anna Nolan reports on a source of pride to the company

'Our productivity per person would not be matched by anyone else within the industry', says Sexton Cahill, human resources manager at Aughinish Alumina Ltd (AAL). This is a significant claim, since AAL is operating in a highly competitive industry. As part of the international Alcan group, it produces Alumina from imported Bauxite at its large plant on the County Limerick side of the Shannon Estuary. The alumina is then sent abroad to be smelted into aluminium. Aluminium prices were under pressure all through last year.

Mr Cahill gave much of the credit for this high productivity to the partnership ethos which was introduced into the plant in 1993 and has been steadily developed ever since. 'The company is the preferred supplier for its customers worldwide, its safety record is excellent and its cost-effectiveness has improved,' he says.

'The fact that we continue to survive is a vote of confidence on behalf of Alcan,' he says. 'Our costs are not the lowest, but we are good.'

The AAL workforce currently totals 450 people, and most operate on variable shifts, as the plant is open 365 days a year. The largest group consists of 156 plant operators, most of whom are on 24-hour, four-cycle shifts, and the second largest of 112 craftspeople and fitters.

The workforce, too, is benefiting from partnership since everyone is now on an annual salary, has the same holidays, is on the same pension scheme and shares the same restaurant facilities. Those are tangible benefits. The intangibles include having more say in how the company is run and how changes are introduced, improved manual handling and safety, and an all-round improvement in the grievance and disputes procedures.

The three trade unions in the plant (SIPTU, TEEU and AEEU), have all taken part in the introduction of partnership. Idealistic as it may seem, this is the way partnership is supposed to work. All the stakeholders should have equal involvement. In AAL the stakeholders are the workforce (including management), the parent company, the trade unions, the customers and the local community.

In day-to-day operation, in teamwork mode, a smaller subset of stakeholders is identified and teams of three to a dozen people are set up to take charge. A key part of the partnership is that each team has a facilitator.

'The facilitator is intended to help develop accountability for their own performance for everyone on that team,' says Sexton Cahill.

The ICTU conducted a survey last year of teamwork at AAL, and the outcome was highly supportive. 'This methodology of working now would be the preference of employees,' Cahill says.

Cahill lists the changes that have taken place: from a hierarchical structure to a flat organisation, from supervisory management to facilitative leadership, from an adversarial to a collaborative culture, from a focus on individual tasks to self-managed work teams and from a 'them and us' mindset to 'we'.

Apart from the bottom line advantages such as improved costs and productivity, the company benefits from getting the viewpoint and experience of all its employees, and a better utilisation of everyone's education, skill and knowledge.

Working in partnership is an ongoing process. 'The system is now stable, but it is necessary that we continue to grow the partnership concept' states Cahill.

Source: Irish Times, Business Section, Friday, 7 May 1997

WHEN TEAMWORK IS APPROPRIATE

Not all work situations demand teamwork. However, in today's complex business environments, more and more organisations are adopting team-based activities and philosophies.

When a task requires teamwork, it usually means that the following factors exist:

1. Working together will produce better results than working apart.
2. The task requires a wide mixture of different talents and skills.
3. The job needs constant adjustment in what people do and in how work is co-ordinated.
4. Competition between individuals is likely to be damaging.
5. The pressure of the job creates more stress than one single person could comfortably handle.

TEAM TASKS AND TEAM PROCESSES

In order for a team to perform effectively, there are two different aspects of its functioning which people need to concentrate on. These two things are: *what* the team is doing, and *how* it is doing it. In other words, the team must attempt to perfect the *task* it has to complete, and the *process* by which it goes about achieving the task.

The team process

How the team operates, is just as important as what it does. When people talk about team processes, they refer to the following types of behaviours:

- Activities and discussions which help the team to remain in good working order.
- Maintaining a good work atmosphere.
- Developing and keeping good working relationships.
- Dealing with tension and conflict within the team.
- Keeping communication open between all team members.
- Meeting regularly.
- Sharing information.
- Offering praise and encouragement to one another.
- Accepting one another's points of view.

All of these kinds of behaviours help the team to maintain the qualities that make it a team. However, this is not adequate in itself. No matter how well team members are able to work as a team, they must also be getting the job done. The second pillar of good team behaviour is *task-oriented* activity.

The team task

What the team is aiming to achieve, should also be a primary focus for all members. Keeping the goals in sight helps them to be organised and motivated. Teams are brought together to achieve certain goals. They need to be focused on these goals and to monitor how close they are to achieving them. Task behaviours refer to the following types of activities:

- Proposing tasks or goals.
- Solving problems relating to these tasks or goals.
- Collecting relevant information and facts about the tasks.
- Exploring alternative courses of action and generating ideas.
- Reaching decisions about what needs to be done.
- Sticking to deadlines.
- Concentrating on the quality of the work.

PROBLEMS WITH DEVELOPING TEAMS

The language and rhetoric of teams, team-building and team success has sometimes led to an image of teamwork that at one extreme is unrealistic and at the other is charged with cynicism and mistrust (Carson, 1992). In order to develop a balanced picture of the potential benefits of teams, the following issues should be considered.

Inadequate attention to team characteristics

It is easy to give lip service to team development in organisations by simply using the label 'team' when referring to groups of people that are in reality loosely connected within a structure. Various team characteristics can have a strong effect on the performance of the team.

Recent research carried out on top management teams in the Irish setting demonstrates that top team characteristics are an important consideration where various aspects of the team's performance is concerned, particularly pioneering behaviour (e.g. Moore *et al.*, 1996).

Box 8.2: Top teams and pioneering

Our findings suggested that there are several links between top management team characteristics and pioneering behaviour.

1. Boundary spanning

Firstly, a strong relationship was found between pioneering and 'boundary spanning'. Boundary spanning refers to the extent to which a top management team communicates and interacts across various organisational boundaries. Boundaries between departments and other groups may serve to undermine communication and innovation, unless such boundaries are spanned effectively. Indeed, our study found that the more a team was involved in boundary spanning activity, the more likely it was to be a pioneer. This also reflects previous evidence which suggests that boundary spanning is an effective way of facilitating the recognition of new opportunities. For example, Quinn (1985) argues that not only must organisations have a strong market orientation at the very top of the company, but also that mechanisms must exist which facilitate boundary spanning between technical, marketing and top management functions. Boundary spanning is itself an indicator of a firm's ability to recognise new opportunities. Evidence from our study supports this assertion.

2. Stock options, company shares and risk-taking activity

As mentioned earlier, really creative teams need to operate in environments where risk is tolerated and where experimentation with new ideas includes, at least some allowance for failure.

Our study found a statistically significant relationship between the risk dimension of pioneering behaviour and specific aspects of top management team compensation arrangements. For example, the more stock options offered to top management team members, the more likely the team was to demonstrate pioneering behaviour. It appears that the option to buy stock at some point in the organisation's future encourages risk-taking which leads to innovation and pioneering.

On the other hand, it was also found that top managers of pioneering companies hold relatively *less* company shares. Our findings suggest that stock options have a positive relationship and share ownership has a negative relationship with risk-taking behaviour. It also appears then, that when top managers actually own considerable shares on the organisation, their tendency to take risks may be significantly reduced.

3. Age profile of the top management team

Several studies have in the past suggested that older decision-makers have more cognitive limitations and are less adept at handling information than their younger counterparts (see Kirchner, 1958; Weir, 1964). It has also been proposed that the age profile of the top management team has a significant bearing on the firm's risk orientation (Hambrick and Mason, 1984). Older managers, it is argued, are less likely to take risks when deciding on future strategies and may rely on incremental change processes rather than quantum leaps in product portfolios, strategic options and so on (Johnson, 1990). The stereotype of the older manager is that he/she possesses less physical and mental stamina, has greater psychological commitment to the organisational *status quo* and sees financial and career security as his/her primary goal.

Contrary to these assertions, our research reveals that pioneering organisations are more likely to have older rather than younger top managers at the helm. How do we explain these surprising findings? Perhaps the benefits of experience bestow knowledge and confidence in older managers which facilitate a more risk-tolerant style, and that the stereotypes of older managers have been exaggerated in the past. Another explanation might be found in the *relative* youth of the sample we chose. The average age in our sample is 44 years. Other studies such as those carried out by Wiersema and Bantel (1992), and O'Reilly and Flatt (1989) used samples with considerably higher average ages (56 and 53 years respectively).

Future investigation may reveal an 'inverted U-shaped' relationship between age and risk-taking behaviour. In other words, there may be an optimal age profile associated with risk-taking. If the age profile of a top management team is *above* this optimal level, risk-taking and innovation may be reduced due to the implementation of more conservative strategies. However, if it is *below* a certain age, risk-taking may not occur due to a lack of experience, confidence, knowledge structures and so on.

4. Educational profile of the top management team

We found that pioneering firms have *relatively* less educated top managers. While further research may be necessary to clarify the relationship between educational level and pioneering, this is nevertheless an interesting finding.

While education continues to be one of the primary criteria for selection or promotion within the managerial ranks of organisations, it appears that there is a limit to which education is associated with innovative or risk-taking behaviour. Perhaps this is because more educated managers tend to be more exhaustive in their search for information than their less educated counterparts (Hambrick and Mason, 1984). The search for more information is obviously time-consuming and by its very nature is intrinsically less risk-orientated than the decision which is made more quickly, but with less information. An extensive, comprehensive search for information is more likely to be associated with linear, logical top management team dynamics. This type of orientation may be more likely to appear in teams with extensive educational experience and qualifications. Norburn (1989) says that while educational level does differentiate top managers from other organisational members, their success or failure may be more likely to be associated with factors such as breadth and multiplicity of experience. If pioneering is a contributor to organisational success, our findings suggest that higher levels of education may not be as necessary as previously assumed. In some contexts, educational levels may even hinder the risk tolerance associated with creativity, innovation and pioneering.

5. Team homogeneity and speed of strategic response

Fast strategic adjustment is an important stage in the pioneering process. Part of our study attempted to isolate certain variables that might be associated with a top team's ability to adjust speedily to new strategies, product innovations and so on. We hypothesised that if top team members were all *similar* in certain aspects (age, length of time in the organisation and education level), they would be faster to adjust strategically than those teams which were more *diverse* in terms of age, tenure and education. Our hypothesis was derived again from work by O'Reilly and Flatt (1989) and Wiersema and Bantel (1992) who suggested that homogeneity or similarity of top management teams can lead to less conflict at times when implementation is taking place, and faster more effective communication. It has been suggested on the one hand that the more alike the top management team feels, the stronger the team norms and the better the communication patterns, the faster decision consensus is reached. On the other hand, team member homogeneity may lead to high levels of group cohesiveness which has been shown to be linked with some dysfunctional characteristics. Excessive group conformity is an example of such dysfunctionality, leading to poor decision quality and sometimes excessive risk-taking (e.g. Janis, 1971).

In the light of previous evidence we expected to find some relationships between homogeneity and pioneering. However, our study yielded no evidence of any relationship between top management team homogeneity and pioneering behaviour. Based on our evidence, homogeneity of age, tenure and education are not factors when considering whether a team is likely to be pioneering in its strategic orientation.

Of course we cannot assume that other dimensions of homogeneity such as personality, gender, background and so on, might not demonstrate a relationship with pioneering. Undoubtedly, there is scope for further investigation here.

To summarise, we found that pioneering in organisations was positively related to such factors as TMT boundary spanning behaviour, the existence of stock options and a higher average TMT age profile. We found that it was negatively related to share ownership among TMT members and higher levels of TMT educational qualifications. We found no significant relationship between TMT homogeneity of age, organisational tenure or education.

Our research has identified certain TMT factors that appear to be related to an organisation's ability to pioneer. These findings should be supplemented by further research and investigation, and may provide implications for the selection, compensation and development of top management team members in the future.

Source: Moore et al., 1996

PROBLEMS WITH DEVELOPING TEAMS (continued)
Autonomy versus accountability

As more and more organisations use the methodologies of self-managed teams, autonomous work groups and cross-functional teams, the problem of accountability often becomes an issue (Carson, 1992). Individual accountability is often easier to establish than team accountability – especially because responsibility over tasks and outcomes can become ambiguous. While there is a wide variety of evidence that demonstrates the benefits of teams, the potential of team working can be lost when accountability is not considered. Some researchers and practitioners argue that while teams need to be put in place, the team's energy needs to be harnessed by maintaining the principle of individual accountability.

Too much or too little conflict

Effective teams are made up of individuals who occupy a variety of complementary goals. One of the problems associated with developing teams relates to the difficulty of the negotiation and agreement of the various roles that each individual should take on. There may be struggles over who should become the team leader, who should facilitate activity, and where the real expertise lies. Because teams often demand a wide variety of different types of skills and perspectives, it is common to encounter clashes when priorities are being established (Brown, 1988).

However, teams should also be characterised by healthy levels of conflict. 'You need to surround yourself with able people who argue back'. Confrontation of divergent views is an important principle of effective teams (Thomas, 1976) and unless conflict can be expressed, important and creative ideas in the team may be lost (Harrison, 1972).

Too much or too little control

Ideally, when groups of people become teams, they should start to create results far beyond what would have been possible before. Given the right conditions, teams have the capacity to be very creative and innovative (e.g. Prince, 1970). In cross-functional teams particularly, and because of the ways in which individuals combine to form a team, plenty of new ideas become available and are discussed. This is one of the benefits of teamwork. Teamwork can help people to become more innovative, which is one of the central reasons why efforts to create teams emerge. However, such creativity becomes less likely if too much control is exerted over people. If a team is not given the freedom to explore new ideas and to come up with its own solutions to specific problems, a lot of the benefits of teamwork can be lost. Because teams inevitably exist within a given organisational structure, and because power is distributed in certain ways within that structure, teams are generally subject to a certain level of control and co-ordination.

Some control and co-ordination is of course necessary, otherwise activities become disjointed and confused. Someone (perhaps a team leader) needs to be given a certain amount of controlling power in order to ensure that the team gets its job done in the best way possible. Control is particularly important when there are pressing deadlines which have to be met.

Creating effective teams is accompanied by the difficulty which lots of organisations experience in striking a balance between too much and too little control (Carson, 1992). Too much control smothers a lot of potential creativity, whereas too little results in time wasting and confusion.

Not enough training

If people are not trained for teamwork and for the specific tasks that they are required to complete they will not be able to operate successfully in a team situation. Training is particularly important during those times when an organisation is undergoing a lot of change and where new practices are being introduced. Unless organisations are prepared to invest in training people for the ways in which their jobs are changing and in training them to be a team member, the benefits of teamwork will undoubtedly suffer.

Unsuitable or defensive management philosophy

If top management does not agree with the idea of teamwork, it is much less likely that the reality of teams will ever get off the ground. Teams need the support of top management; and management must support teams through their actions as well as through what they say. Top management is often the rock upon which good teamwork perishes. For teams to work properly, they must operate in an atmosphere of openness and trust. Communication must be as honest and up-front as possible. This is a philosophy which a lot of top managers can find threatening. Creating teams means giving teams the power and authority to make a lot of their own decisions, and this means taking power away from where it traditionally lies. As a result, such managers may work against the principle of teamwork rather than for it, and consequently, people remain divided and the benefits of teamwork may again be lost.

Unfair rewards

Effective teams can help to yield positive results for their individual members and their organisations. If used at appropriate times, and if managed well, their benefits can far outweigh the costs of developing them. Effective teams are usually very aware of their successes as well as their failures, and unless the organisation is prepared to reward the achievements that they produce, dissatisfaction among team members is likely. If a team is not rewarded, its members will begin to feel undervalued within the organisation. As a result, morale and motivation may be lost. This is another way in which teamwork can be damaged.

Teamwork involves people *working together* to produce work of *really high quality* by *pooling their resources* and *maximising the potential* of each individual. It also requires *integrating activity* in a *co-ordinated* and *organised* way.

TEAM ROLES

A team role simply refers to the part that someone plays within their team. Research by Belbin (1981, 1993) suggests that effective teams need to have a variety of participants who play very different roles within the team structure. Belbin's research suggests that it is possible to identify several roles that are important for team effectiveness, and that more effective teams have members who recognise the roles that they play best and who attempt to enhance the strengths of that role.

While one person cannot play the variety of roles necessary to complete difficult tasks, a team can be created by combining different individual roles and building high-functioning groups of people. Table 8.1 shows the different role types that Belbin says are necessary for teams to fulfil their potential. Each role makes a unique and crucial contribution to the work of an effective team; and each role is characterised by some weaknesses, which Belbin refers to as 'Allowable weaknesses' in that other team members, playing other roles, can compensate for them.

PREPARATION FOR TEAM DEVELOPMENT

Selection, training, rewards, and a good management philosophy can go a long way to creating the atmosphere needed for teams to flourish. Teamwork can be developed without solving all of the problems outlined in the last section, but it helps if most of them are being dealt with in some way. There are some more specific ways in which people can be prepared for teamwork.

The following are some helpful guidelines for people interested in developing teams in their organisations.

Don't expect to create a team overnight

Real teams take time. It is important not to be too eager to get teams off the ground. Chapter 7 shows that group development involves a sometimes lengthy process of different stages. Only when group formation has been resolved can effective team principles be developed. Teams cannot be forced to be fully operational within unrealistic time frames. Like any set of relationships, they need time to grow and to flourish.

Clarify the aims of the team

One way to set the scene for good teamwork, is to clarify exactly how you want the group to improve its performance. Laying down vague directives like 'This group needs to perform better' or 'This group needs to become a team' does not serve to focus efforts. People need to know in what ways their performance should improve.

Table 8.1: Belbin's team roles

Role name	Contribution to team	Allowable weaknesses
Plant.	Creative, imaginative, unorthodox, solves difficult problems.	Ignores details. Can be too preoccupied to communicate ideas effectively.
Resource investigator.	Extroverted, enthusiastic, communicative. Explores opportunities and develops contacts.	Overoptimistic. Can lose interest once initial enthusiasm has passed.
Co-ordinator.	Mature, confident, a good chairperson. Clarifies goals, promotes decision-making, delegates well.	Can be seen as manipulative. Delegates personal work.
Shaper.	Challenging, dynamic, thrives on pressure. Has the drive to overcome obstacles.	Can provoke others and hurt people's feelings.
Monitor evaluator.	Sober, strategic and discerning. Sees all options. Judges accurately.	Lacks drive and the ability to inspire others. Overly critical.
Team worker.	Co-operative, mild, perceptive and diplomatic. Listens, builds trust, averts friction, calms the waters.	Indecisive in crunch situations. Can be easily influenced.
Implementer.	Disciplined, reliable, conservative and efficient. Turns ideas into practical actions.	Somewhat inflexible. Slow to respond to new possibilities.
Completer.	Painstaking, conscientious, anxious. Searches out errors and omissions. Delivers on time.	Inclined to worry unduly. Reluctant to delegate. Can be a nit picker.
Specialist.	Single-minded, self-sharing, dedicated. Provides knowledge and skills in rare supply.	Can be narrow in what is contributed to the team. Can dwell on technicalities and overlook the big picture.

Source: Belbin, 1993, p. 23

The best way to do this is to generate and agree on specific aims. As soon as people have been given goals, it becomes a lot easier for them to know where they're going and to organise themselves to achieve these goals.

Resistance to change

If people are not used to being part of a team, there are many reasons why the prospect of team participation may be intimidating. Teamwork places a lot of demands on people, can carry negative associations, and the introduction of teamworking can result in resistance to the concept. Negotiation and agreement of the terms of teamwork initiatives needs to be carried out from the outset.

People need to feel responsible for their own development within the team

People need to be given the authority to make their own unique contribution to the team.

Everyone in the team should be consulted about everything to do with the team

It must be recognised that everyone has an important contribution to make. One way of showing this is to make sure that people communicate their ideas, are asked about any proposals that are being made, and that their contributions are taken seriously. If people get the chance to participate, they will be more likely to be committed to the aims of the team, and believe in what the team is all about.

Be prepared to learn from your mistakes

Teams are brought together for difficult tasks, and difficult tasks are likely to include some mistakes. Team errors can be very useful in the long run because they help people to learn about how to avoid the same ones in the future. Encouraging an atmosphere where people are not afraid to try out new things (and therefore run some risk of failure), is something which helps teams to become more creative.

Teams can also be risky

Sometimes when an excellent team operates in an organisation, other people who are not members of the team can become resentful or dissatisfied. Being on the outside, looking in on a team which works well together, and which has a great sense of direction and high levels of morale, can be somewhat demoralising for others not in the same situation. Also, if a team is created, the people within the team usually develop new skills and abilities which can sometimes cause them to grow out of the work that they are doing inside the team. People's expectations change, and a time may come when certain individuals start to demand more than what the team has to offer.

Laying the groundwork for good team development involves keeping all of the above points in mind, and ensuring that people are clear about the kinds of things that good teamwork can uncover in an organisation. The potential pitfalls associated with creating teams can be avoided if the team members are observant and prepared. The points outlined in this section can help with this preparation for the development of high-performing teams (Woodcock, 1979).

GUIDING PRINCIPLES OF TEAMWORK

A good way of helping team members to commit themselves to the idea of teamwork is to get the team to develop its own general set of rules which will help everyone to stay focused on their teamwork principles.

Examples of the kinds of statements which could be generated in a team discussion are as follows.

All team members will undertake to:

- Treat each other with trust and respect.
- Keep their promises to each other.
- Demand honesty from each other.
- Quickly resolve any issues that interfere with a good team spirit.

Characteristics of effective teams

An effective team should have all or most of the following characteristics (adapted from Woodcock, 1979):

- Clear objectives which have been agreed upon by all team members.
- A relaxed and informal atmosphere where people are allowed to express their opinions and ideas.
- Support and trust.
- Criticism is honest, direct and constructive, but not personal.
- Activities are distributed fairly among group members.
- An accurate awareness of performance levels and capabilities.
- An ability to deal with disagreements.
- Appropriate leadership.

TEAM CREATIVITY

More and more, teams are being brought together in organisations, not just to enhance the conditions for collaboration, but to increase overall levels of organisational creativity. A knowledge of the creative process and how it unfolds in team settings is becoming an important dimension in team development.

Due to predictable problems with construct validity and measurement, the concept of creativity has been defined and gauged in a wide variety of ways. Generally though,

167

creativity can be said to require a multiplicity of attributes including such properties as curiosity, self-confidence, optimism, flexibility, humour, imagination, openness to experience, tolerance of ambiguity, independence, originality, responsiveness, motivation and a freedom from the fear of failure. These attributes are not just a function of individual attributes and personality, but also of the types of organisations within which individuals and groups operate and the climate that is fostered within group settings. Creative thinking is facilitated and constrained by many contextual and organisational variables. The ability for teams to be creative may depend on a combination of any of the following factors.

1. Team composition

The various mix of individual personalities, levels of self-esteem, cognitive styles and abilities, task-relevant knowledge and skill, past reinforcement history and so on, may have a fundamental effect on a group's ability to be creative, to develop vision and to manage the creative process. Traditional managers are often evaluated for competences such as logic, analytical skills, and organising ability. These are typically 'left brain' capabilities. Developing creative energy involves facilitating 'right brain' skills such as imagination, conceptualisation and intuition and ensuring that there is a good mix of both types of ability. Generally, group diversity tends to have a positive effect on creativity, and diversity of individual behaviour and style can have a positive bearing on overall group effectiveness, including the capacity to create a meaningful and worthwhile vision of the future.

2. Leadership style and team atmosphere

Evidence has repeatedly shown that democratic, collaborative leadership styles are positively correlated with creativity in organisations, and that autocratic leadership styles are negatively correlated with effective idea generation and innovative outcomes. The prevalence of status consciousness, rule-bound behaviour and unequal power distribution may inhibit the free exchange of ideas which is (at least to some extent) why it is difficult for traditionally bureaucratic organisations to achieve high levels of creativity. There are a number of ways in which some of the negative effects of bureaucratic behaviour can be overcome. Leaders need to encourage and reward 'devil's advocacy' within organisational groups; be impartial, at least at the early stages of a group process such as vision development and problem-solving; gather as much relevant information from as many sources as possible; check agreement from all group members on an ongoing basis; detect any residual doubts, second thoughts or reservations as well as uncover progressive ideas from those who might be inhibited about or unaccustomed to voicing their views. It is possible to create open and confrontational group atmospheres where members feel free to experiment with ideas, to propose alternatives and to disagree with the majority view in the interests of effective task accomplishment. Leaders can set important precedents by encouraging and rewarding dissenters from the outset and ensuring that all participation is recognised and integrated into either the content or the process of group activity.

3. Knowledge banks and creative use of existing information

Research on organisational innovation and more recently on creativity, has supported the notion that an elaborate variety of available resources is positively associated with high rates of innovative thinking. Evidence strongly suggests for example, that the existence and development of a 'bank' of knowledge to which groups have open access, is a worthwhile resource that can aid the initiation and progress of beneficial creative processes. While existing knowledge often confers the ability to recognise the relative importance of new information, it is also important for groups not to become constrained by current frames of reference. For real benefit to be derived, the acquisition and assimilation of information is not enough. Unless this information is exploited in focused, appropriate and original ways, its benefits may be lost. An organisation's capacity to exploit information effectively does not just depend on its ability to obtain information from external sources. It is also important that information transfer within and between key internal groups occurs frequently and effectively.

Initiating and developing the creative process

Teams that have been charged with the responsibility for complex and non-routine tasks need to spend time agreeing and developing effective processes which will ensure that maximum benefit is gained from their activities. This is especially important in a context where time is precious and resources are scarce. While the creative process is not easy to analyse, it has been suggested by behavioural theorists that it is characterised by four major stages.

Four stages associated with the creative process

1. Preparation

This is an active process whereby information is gathered from both traditional and non-traditional sources. 'Creative decision-makers study the issues surrounding a decision and participate extensively in group meetings where new ideas and alternative points of view abound' (Griffin and Moorhead, 1995, p. 255). It is desirable at this stage, that participants in the creative process are encouraged to be relatively unbridled by practical issues associated with implementation. Of course practical considerations must become part of the emerging plan for action, but if this happens too early on, good ideas and important perspectives may never come to light, and the value of group energy may become caught up in operational rather than strategic issues.

2. Incubation

The incubation stage is characterised by such cognitive processes as reflection and consideration. This is more likely to occur outside formal meetings, during informal discussions where developing ideas are 'thrown around'. It is useful to spend time trying to find different ways of viewing various issues, and involving non-members (i.e. those outside the formally created committees/groups) in in-depth discussions about emerging patterns of thought.

3. Illumination

The illumination stage involves the development of effective insights whereby a set of conceptual breakthroughs paves the way towards the implementation of good ideas. Insight often involves lateral thinking and a sudden mental reorganisation of the elements of a problem that make the solution obvious, or at least clearer than originally was the case. Participants in the creative process need to work on the skills associated with the development of effective insights. Skills which facilitate insight include: selecting information relevant to a problem and ignoring distractions; bringing together apparently unrelated but useful pieces of information; and comparing new problems with the existing base of knowledge and information.

4. Verification

Creative insights and visions must finally be verified and validated. This happens when the gaps between the ideal and the real begin to close. People may start to suggest ways in which visions of the future can be realised given current strengths and weaknesses in the system, and recognising opportunities to be exploited and existing restrictions to be overcome. Practical operational issues must be considered at this stage and first steps towards the realisation of the vision need to be initiated.

SUMMARY OF KEY PROPOSITIONS

- In this chapter, we examined the concept of teams and how good teams are developed. Teamwork was described as people working together to produce work of really high quality by pooling their resources and maximising the potential of each individual. Good teamwork requires the integration and co-ordination of activities.
- Teamwork is particularly appropriate under certain conditions. There are two different sets of behaviours which are useful for teams: task behaviours (i.e. getting the job done), and process behaviours (i.e. keeping the team together).
- There are some common organisational problems which can combine to prevent a group from becoming a team. These problems are: bad recruitment and selection, too much or too little control, inadequate training, unsupportive management and unfair rewards.

- To prepare a group for developing into a team, it is important to recognise that team development takes time, the aims of the team must be clear, people may be afraid to join a team, and they need to be made to feel responsible for their own development. Consulting everyone within the team is important, as well as being prepared to learn from the team's mistakes.
- We examined some of the useful roles that should be played in teams, along with some of the behaviours that can be damaging to team performance; and we looked at some of the main characteristics of effective teams.

DISCUSSION QUESTIONS

1. Is your group a team? Think of a group of people with whom you work or have worked, and ask yourself:
   - Do I achieve results that far exceed what I could do alone?
   - Does the activity I am engaged in involve pooling resources (i.e. skill, effort, commitment and creativity)?
   - Does the work in this group go beyond satisfactory, standard performance and reach levels of really high quality?
   - Am I maximising my potential as a member of the group?

Possible problems

Maybe the group is made up of the wrong people. Perhaps the group does not have the right mix of skills and attitudes to become a team. Is this a problem in the group in which you work? What skills are missing?

Perhaps there are too many unnecessary controls on group members so that they are afraid of or prevented from coming up with their own ideas as to how the work should be done. Ask yourself have you ever had ideas about improving teamwork or other work processes which you did not voice? Are there too many rules which prevent you from being creative? If so, what are these rules and why do you think they exist?

On the other hand, teamwork may not exist because of too little control. Is the work that you do in groups disorganised or disjointed? Are people unsure as to where everyone fits in and what they are expected to do?

Do people have enough training to organise themselves into an effective working team?

The above questions should have helped you to identify some of the problems that may exist which can prevent groups from becoming teams.

2. Discuss the kinds of activities that effective teamwork involves.
3. Outline your views on some of the ways in which team creativity in teams can be enhanced.

CHAPTER 9

Organisation Structure and Culture

LEARNING OBJECTIVES
- To define structure.
- To provide an outline of the components of structure.
- To examine various approaches to organisation structure.
- To define organisational culture and examine its characteristics.
- To examine critical contributions on culture.

INTRODUCTION

Developing a structure that supports the strategic and operational goals of the organisation is a challenging task. The way in which the structure manifests itself will determine how efficiently and effectively its activities are carried out. Knowledge of that structure is a critical first step to understanding the processes which occur within the organisation, and detailing its structure is the most accessible way of describing it; and yet a solely structural analysis is incomplete. Structure seems to provide the basic framework, but an understanding of cultural processes is also necessary in order to get a more meaningful picture of what happens in modern organisations. This chapter concentrates on both of these aspects of organisational life.

STRUCTURE

Structure refers to the relationships among the parts of an organised whole: it is a social creation. Mintzberg (1983) in his acclaimed work, *Structure in Fives*, simply defines it as 'the sum total of the ways in which labour is divided into distinct tasks and then its co-ordination is achieved among these tasks'. Thus, organisations create structure to facilitate the co-ordination of the activities and to control the actions of their members. The structure defines tasks and responsibilities, work roles and relationships, and channels of communication. It creates a framework through which the activities of the organisation can be directed and controlled. The design of an appropriate structure is a critical activity and it involves the development of a framework which is compatible with the needs of the particular business or institution.

THE COMPONENTS OF STRUCTURE

Tiernan *et al.* (1996) highlight that arising from the mainstream literature, the main components of organisational structure can be classified into two critical areas: structural configuration and structural operation.

Figure 9.1: Components of organisational structure

Structural configuration	Structural operation
Division of labour.	Formalisation.
Spans of control.	Decision-making.
Hierarchical levels.	Responsibility.
Departmentalisation.	Authority.

Source: Tiernan *et al.*, 1996

Structural configuration refers to the size and shape of the structure and can be assessed from the organisation chart. Structural operation focuses on the processes and operations of the organisational structure.

Division of labour

The division of labour defines the distribution of responsibilities. It refers to the extent to which the work of the organisation is broken down into different tasks, to be completed by different people. As far back as 1776 Adam Smith illustrated the concept of the division of labour in a pin manufacturing firm:

> One man draws out the wire, another strengthens it, a third cuts it, a fourth points it, a fifth grinds it at the top for receiving the head; to make the head requires two or three distinct operations; to put it on is a peculiar business, to whiten the pins is another; it is even a trade by itself to put them into the paper; and the important business of making a pin is, in this manner, divided into about eighteen distinct operations.

The classical theorists were strong advocates of the division of labour, viewing it as a means of significantly increasing the economic efficiencies of the organisations.

Span of control

Span of control refers to the number of subordinates who report to a single supervisor or manager and for whose work that person is responsible. This concept is related to the notion of hierarchy. Generally, the broader the span of control, the fewer the number of levels in the hierarchy. With wider spans of control, employees tend to have more freedom and discretion. In contrast, narrow spans of control usually lead to high levels of supervision. With effective spans of control, employees can be given a degree of freedom, while at the same time having some form of guidance from a supervisor, should assistance be necessary. Several theorists have attempted to identify what the optimal span of control might be. Mintzberg (1979) concluded that the size of the span depends on a number of factors, not least the degree of specialisation, the similarity of tasks, the type of information available, the need for autonomy, direct access to supervisors, and the abilities and experience of both supervisors and employees.

Hierarchical levels

The number of levels and the extent of hierarchy outlines the reporting relationships within the organisation from top to bottom.

Departmentalisation

The classical theorists argued that activities in an organisation should be specialised and grouped into departments. This element of structural configuration is essentially concerned with the co-ordination of the various activities of the organisation. There are four main forms of departmentalisation which an organisation might adopt, namely functional, divisional, geographic and matrix.

Functional departmentalisation is one of the most frequently occurring modes of co-ordinating and it is one where the activities are grouped together by common function. This form is typically found in small or medium-sized companies or in those companies where only a few products are produced. It is seen to be most effective in a stable environment where the technology used by the organisation is of a routine nature, where there is low interdependence between departments and the organisation is controlled through the vertical hierarchy (i.e. formal authority in the organisation lies with senior managers in the functional department).

Under a *divisional* approach, the organisation uses the products or services, project groups or projects as the basis for differentiating the company. The distinctive feature is that the divisions of the organisation are grouped according to their organisational outputs. Thus, an organisation which manufactures four distinct products may create a sub-division for each product. A product-based structure is an example of divisional departmentalisation.

With *geographical* departmentalisation, the organisation is structured around activities in various geographical locations. This approach is common among organisations which provide goods or services over a wide area. Each region or country may have distinct tastes or needs, and organisations may find it more appropriate to respond to these particular needs by locating in that region.

Functional, product or geographic departmentalisation may be combined to form what is termed a *matrix* approach. Typically, functional and product lines are overlaid to form a grid. It may be required by an organisation whose structure is multifocused, needing to emphasise both product and function at the same time.

Formalisation

Formalisation refers to the degree to which rules and procedures shape the jobs and tasks completed by employees, and consequently the degree to which the jobs within the organisation are standardised. Organisations are said to be highly formalised if their work activities are governed by many rules and procedures. The degree of formalisation can vary widely between organisations and within organisations. The critical purpose of formalisation, according to Mintzberg (1979) is to predict and control how employees behave on the job.

Decision-making

Decision-making may be centralised or decentralised. Centralisation refers to the degree to which decision-making is concentrated at a single point in the organisation. An organisation characterised by centralisation is inherently different from one that is described as decentralised. In a decentralised scenario, action can be taken more quickly to solve problems, more individuals typically provide input into the decision and individuals are less likely to feel alienated or divorced from critical aspects of their working lives.

Responsibility

Responsibility is essentially an obligation to perform. When one is given rights, one also assumes a corresponding obligation to perform. In the organisational setting managers and supervisors are responsible for achieving certain goals and for the conduct of their subordinates.

Authority

Authority refers to rights inherent in a managerial position to give orders and expect those orders to be obeyed. It is power that has been legitimised within a certain social context. In the case of organisational authority, the social context is the organisation and the authority is associated with the position in the hierarchy.

Mintzberg (1983, pp. 4–20) offers a slightly different analysis, arguing that five co-ordinating elements seem to explain the fundamental ways in which organisations co-ordinate their efforts: mutual adjustment, direct supervision, standardisation of work processes, standardisation of work outputs, and standardisation of worker skills. These, he suggests, should be considered the most basic elements of structure, the glue that holds organisations together. Mutual adjustment achieves the co-ordination of work by the simple process of informal communication. The success of the undertaking depends primarily on the ability of the specialists to adapt to each other. Direct supervision achieves co-ordination by having one person take responsibility for the work of others, issuing instructions to them and monitoring their action. In effect, one brain co-ordinates several hands. Mintzberg argues that work may also be co-ordinated without either mutual adjustment or direct supervision *per se,* but rather through standardisation. Co-ordination, he suggests, is achieved on the drawing board before the work is undertaken, There are three basic ways to achieve such standardisation. Work processes are standardised when the contents of the work are specified or programmed. Outputs are standardised when the results of the work are specified or programmed. If neither the work nor the outputs are standardised, the worker who comes to work may be. Skills and knowledge are standardised when the kind of training required to perform the work is specified. These five co-ordinating mechanisms typically occur in a sequence so that as organisational work becomes more complicated, the desired means of co-ordination seems to shift from mutual adjustment to direct supervision to standardisation (often of work processes, but may be outputs or knowledge and skills). However, typically organisations will not rely on any single co-ordinating mechanism, but will mix them. Thus a certain amount of mutual adjustment and supervision will always be evidenced, regardless of the extent of standardisation. This is variously reflected in the major 'Schools of Thought' which have dominated the extant literature.

For Child (1984, p. 7) designing an appropriate structure for an organisation centres around five major issues:

1. Should jobs be broken down into narrow areas of work and responsibility so as to secure the benefits of specialisation? Or should the degree of specialisation be kept to a minimum in order to simplify communication and to offer members of the organisation greater scope and responsibility in their work? Another choice arising in the design of jobs concerns the extent to which the responsibilities and methods attaching to them should be precisely defined.

2. Should the overall structure of an organisation be 'tall' rather than 'flat' in terms of its layers of management and its spans of control? What are the implications for communication, motivation and overhead costs of moving towards one of these alternatives rather than the other?

3. Should jobs and departments be grouped together in a 'functional' way according to the specialist expertise and interests that they share? Or should they be grouped according to the different products and services which are being offered, or the different geographical areas being served?

4. Is it appropriate to aim for an intensive form of integration between different segments of an organisation or not? What kind of integrative mechanisms are there to choose from?

5. What approaches should management take towards maintaining adequate control over work done? Should it centralise or delegate decisions? Should a policy of formalisation be adopted? Should work be subject to close supervision?

Different schools of thought provide rather different answers to these critical questions on how to approach the issue of structuring the primary reporting relationships. Here we review three prominent strands of this literature: classical, contingency and more recent innovations and adaptations.

The classical school of thought

The classical school of thought advocated a universalist approach to organisational structure, arguing that there was one best way to structure the organisation's activities. They offered prescriptions on designing for best fit in all situations. One of the most significant contributions was made by Henri Fayol (1841–1925).

Table 9.1: Fayol's fourteen management principles

1. **Division of labour:** Divide work into specialised tasks and assign responsibility to individuals.
2. **Authority:** Equal delegation of responsibility and authority.
3. **Discipline:** Establish clear expectations and penalties.
4. **Unity of command:** Each employee should report to one supervisor.
5. **Unity of direction:** Employee efforts should be guided to achieve organisational goals.
6. **Subordination of individual interest to general:** Group interests should not precede the general interests of the organisation.
7. **Remuneration:** Equitable rewards for work.
8. **Centralisation:** Decide the importance of superior and subordinate roles.
9. **Scalar chain:** Lines of authority and communications from the highest to the lowest level.
10. **Order:** Order tasks and materials to support organisational direction.
11. **Equity:** Treat employees fairly.
12. **Stability of tenure:** Minimise turnover to ensure loyalty of personnel.
13. **Initiative:** Employees should have freedom and discretion.
14. **Esprit de corps:** Unity of interest between management and workers.

Fayol emphasised that his principles of management should be applied in a flexible way. Tiernan *et al.* (1996) argue that his principles remain important not only because of the influence they have had on succeeding generations of managers, but also because of the continuing validity of the work.

Equally influential in the classic school was the sociologist Max Weber (1864–1920). Weber concentrated in a more specific way than Fayol on how to structure the organisation for success. He advanced the critical elements of 'ideal bureaucracy' as a means of promoting efficiency in organising. It had six critical elements:

1. *Division of labour:* tasks were divided and delegated to specialists so that responsibility and authority were clearly defined.
2. *Hierarchy:* positions were organised in a hierarchy of authority from the top of the organisation to the bottom, with authority centralised at the top.
3. *Selection:* employees were recruited on the basis of technical qualifications rather than favouritism.
4. *Career orientation:* managers were viewed as professionals pursuing careers rather than having ownership in the organisation.
5. *Formalisation:* the organisation was subject to formal rules and procedures in relation to performance.
6. *Impersonality:* rules and procedures were applied uniformly to all employees.

The strength of bureaucracy was in its standardisation. Employee behaviour was controlled and made predictable through adherence to rules and procedures. For Weber, bureaucracy represented the most efficient form of social organisation largely because it was rational and logical and focused on goal attainment. It emphasised a narrow division of labour, narrow spans of control, many levels of hierarchy, limited responsibility and authority, centralised decision-making and high formalisation. Tiernan *et al.* (1996) note that 'the bureaucratic structure was particularly popular in large organisations as it allowed such organisations to perform the various routine activities needed for effective operation. This structure became the dominant form of structure used by the majority of organisations, as it appeared to offer an efficient form of structure and was technically superior to any other form.'

Jackall (1988) argues that large bureaucratic corporations operate on the basis of such values as control, order, elitism, pragmatism, and competition for status.

In fact the bureaucratic context typically brings together men and women who initially have little in common with each other except the impersonal frameworks of their organisation. Indeed the enduring genius of the organisation form is that it allows individuals to retain bewildering diverse private motives and meaning for action as long as they adhere publicly to agreed upon rules.

The contingency school of thought

Contingency approaches to organisational structure became popular in the 1950s and 1960s and were developed to overcome many of the inadequacies associated with the classical school. Essentially, contingency approaches argue that there is no one best way of structuring an organisation.

The most appropriate structure depends on a number of contingencies or structural imperatives. The three most popular contingencies are size, technology and the environment. Contingency theory argues that the most appropriate structure for an organisation depends on its size, technology and environment. Each of these imperatives has been widely researched by different theorists and no single theorist or researcher can be attributed with the formulation of contingency theory. (Tiernan *et al.*, 1996)

The size imperative argues that the most appropriate structure for an organisation is determined by its size. Kimberly (1976) has argued that the measurement of size is important and can include employees, profit, turnover and sales. Larger organisations are generally more complex and bureaucratic (Blau and Schoenherr, 1971). Increased size, therefore, leads to more complexity which in turn leads to more bureaucratic structures to facilitate control (Robey, 1991). Size is an important contingency that determines the most appropriate type of structure. As the organisation increases in size, the original structure is simply unable to handle the complexity. Similarly, a small organisation does not need so many bureaucratic structures and controls to operate effectively.

The most influential work within the technology imperative was completed by Woodward (1965). Woodward sought to examine whether spans of control and hierarchical levels have universal application. She studied the performance and structure of 100 UK manufacturing organisations and concluded that different technologies create different kinds of demands on organisations, which are met by different types of structure. In other words, the most appropriate structure was dependent upon the technology used.

Woodward identified three different types of technology:

1. *Unit production* occurs where one or a small number of finished goods are produced according to a customer specification; for example, tailor-made clothes or specially printed cards or invitations.
2. *Mass production* occurs where large batches of standardised goods are produced on an assembly line by assembling parts in a particular way; for example, car manufacturers.
3. *Continuous process production* occurs where raw materials are transformed into finished goods using a production system whereby the composition of the raw material changes; for example, the manufacture of pharmaceuticals.

Woodward concluded that successful organisations displayed an appropriate fit between the technology used and the structure.

More recent work on an extension of contingency theory has been advanced by Mintzberg (1981). He identified a range of structures and situations in which they are most commonly found. Mintzberg's framework provides guidelines for the choice of an appropriate structure depending on the age of the organisation, its external environment and the nature of its employees. Mintzberg argued that a vitally important consideration in structuring an organisation was to achieve a match or fit between the various parts. In this sense, there must be a fit between the structure, the structural imperatives (size, technology and environment), the organisation's strategy and the various components of the structure (co-ordination, division of labour, formalisation and decision-making). If these various elements do not fit together, then the structure will be ineffective (Mintzberg, 1981).

Mintzberg identified five types of structure, namely *simple, machine bureaucracy, professional bureaucracy, divisionalised* and *adhocracy.*

Box 9.1 Mintzberg's structure types

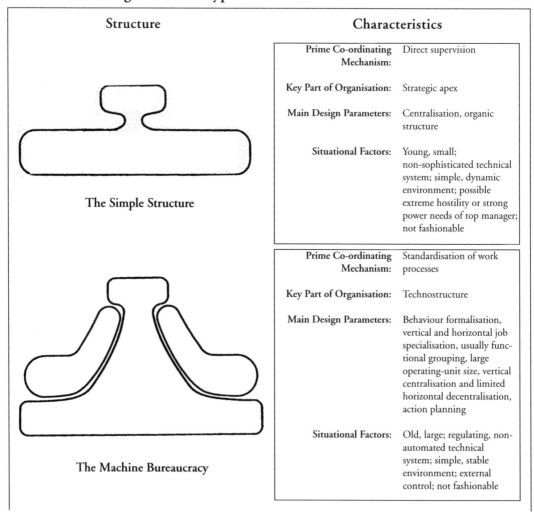

Structure	Characteristics	
The Simple Structure	Prime Co-ordinating Mechanism:	Direct supervision
	Key Part of Organisation:	Strategic apex
	Main Design Parameters:	Centralisation, organic structure
	Situational Factors:	Young, small; non-sophisticated technical system; simple, dynamic environment; possible extreme hostility or strong power needs of top manager; not fashionable
The Machine Bureaucracy	Prime Co-ordinating Mechanism:	Standardisation of work processes
	Key Part of Organisation:	Technostructure
	Main Design Parameters:	Behaviour formalisation, vertical and horizontal job specialisation, usually functional grouping, large operating-unit size, vertical centralisation and limited horizontal decentralisation, action planning
	Situational Factors:	Old, large; regulating, non-automated technical system; simple, stable environment; external control; not fashionable

Structure	Characteristics	
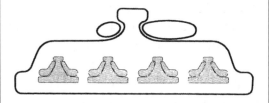

The Professional Bureaucracy | Prime Co-ordinating Mechanism: | Standardisation of skills |
	Key Part of Organisation:	Operating core
	Main Design Parameters:	Training, horizontal job specialisation, vertical and horizontal decentralisation
	Situational Factors:	Complex, stable environment; non-regulating, non-sophisticated technical system; fashionable

The Divisionalized Form | Prime Co-ordinating Mechanism: | Standardisation of outputs |
	Key Part of Organisation:	Middle line
	Main Design Parameters:	Market grouping, performance control system, limited vertical decentralisation
	Situational Factors:	Diversified markets (particularly products or services); old, large; power needs of middle managers; fashionable
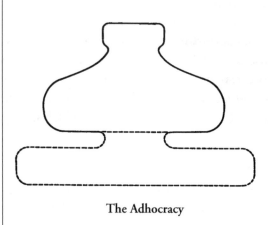

The Adhocracy | Prime Co-ordinating Mechanism: | Mutual adjustment |
	Key Part of Organisation:	Support staff (in the Administrative Adhocracy; together with the operating core in the Operating Adhocracy)
	Main Design Parameters:	Liaison devices, organic structure, selective decentralisation, horizontal job specialisation, training, functional and market grouping concurrently
	Situational Factors:	Complex, dynamic (sometimes disparate) environment; young (especially Operating Adhocracy); sophisticated and often automated technical system (in the Administrative Adhocracy); fashionable

Source: Mintzberg, H. (1983), *Structure in Fives: Designing Effective Organizations,* Englewood Cliffs, Prentice Hall

The *simple* structure is found in small, relatively new organisations that operate in a simple and dynamic environment. Direct supervision is the main co-ordinating mechanism, which means that a supervisor or manager co-ordinates the activities of employees. The structure is quite organic with little specialisation and little formalisation. The CEO holds most of the power and decision-making authority. Due to its simple yet dynamic environment, it must react quickly to changing events.

A *machine* bureaucracy corresponds to a typical bureaucracy and can be found in large, mature organisations operating in a stable and simple environment. Standardisation of work processes is the main co-ordinating mechanism, which means that the methods employees use to transform inputs into outputs are standardised. There is a strong division of labour, high formalisation and centralised decision-making. Due to its stable and simple environment the machine bureaucracy does not have to change or adapt quickly.

Professional bureaucracies are usually professional organisations located in complex and stable environments. The primary co-ordinating mechanism is the standardisation of employee skills which means that the skills or inputs into the various processes are standardised. The division of labour is based on professional expertise, and little formalisation exists. Decision-making is decentralised and occurs where the expertise is based. An example of a professional bureaucracy is a hospital or university.

The *divisionalised* structure is found in old and large organisations operating in simple and stable environments with many distinct markets. It could, in fact, be a machine bureaucracy divided into the different markets that it serves. Decision-making is split between headquarters and the divisions, and standardisation of outputs is the main co-ordinating mechanism used. Due to the fact that control is required by headquarters, a machine bureaucracy tends to develop in each of the divisions.

An *adhocracy* is found in young organisations operating in complex and dynamic environments, normally in a technical area. Co-ordination is achieved by mutual adjustment, which means that employees use informal communication to co-ordinate with each other. Decision-making is spread throughout the organisation, and there is little formalisation. Specialists are placed in project teams to achieve the work of the organisation. This form of structure is designed to encourage innovation, which is very difficult to do with the other structures.

Recent thinking on organisation structure

Tiernan (1996) and Tiernan *et al.* (1996) argue that there have been two major evolutions in organisational structure to date. The first occurred in the early 1900s and involved a recognition of the independent roles and function of management and ownership. The second evolution took place some twenty years later and introduced the command/control organisation (more commonly termed bureaucracy), with which we are so familiar today. Now organisations are coming to terms with the third evolutionary period. The shift this time is from bureaucratic hierarchical forms to more flexible and adaptable forms.

Bureaucracy has been the dominant form of organisation structure used by organisations. The main reason for its dominance is that it is a rational and efficient form of structure when the environment is simple and stable. However, when the external environment becomes complex and dynamic, the rigidity of the bureaucratic structure hampers its ability to be flexible and adaptive. Recent trends in organisational structure have centred on the need to achieve competitive advantage in an increasingly complex, dynamic and competitive environment. (Tiernan *et al.*, 1996)

Many of the developments have built on Mintzberg's conceptualisations of the influence of the business environment on the organisation's structure. Drucker (1992) has argued that, due to the nature of the current business environment, organisations are now undertaking fundamental changes to their structures. To achieve competitive advantage, organisations must be flexible and adaptive, to respond to and anticipate change in the business environment. Many organisations have looked to organisational structure as a means of providing such flexibility and adaptability. As a result of the nature of the business environment and the ineffectiveness of traditional bureaucratic structure, organisations have experimented with four main structural trends (for a detailed discussion see Tiernan, 1993; 1996).

The first trend has been towards flatter, less hierarchical structures. Reducing the layers in the hierarchy is designed to reduce costs, free up information flows, speed up communications and allow more innovative ideas to flourish. Organisations, therefore, are reducing hierarchy to more manageable levels. Organisations, according to Tiernan, have also widened the traditional division of labour. Previously, individuals were boxed into segmented and isolated work tasks with little knowledge or training in other areas. Due to the need to be more flexible, many organisations have now widened job categories and trained employees to be multi-skilled. Changing attitudes among the workforce have led to the creation of new structures which allow individuals more responsibility and authority over their work and a larger role in decision-making. The final trend has been to move away from segmented and isolated work to team-based operations. Organisations are experimenting with task forces for short-term problem-solving exercises and with cross-functional and cross-hierarchical teams to achieve longer-term objectives. Organisations are also introducing team mechanisms for completing tasks. Such team mechanisms have been called *self-managed teams* and autonomous work groups and they complete the work of the organisation with the guidance of a supervisor.

As a result of these trends, the cluster organisation has emerged as a radical and innovative form of organisational structure in which groups of employees are arranged like grapes growing on a common vine. A cluster is a group of employees from different disciplines who work together and are undifferentiated by rank or job title. No direct reporting relationships exist within the clusters, and support areas only have a residual hierarchy.

> The cluster is accountable for its business results and has a customer focus. It develops its own expertise, shares information broadly and pushes decisions towards the point of action. The central element of the cluster organisation is the business unit which is a profit centre. The cluster organisation contains other forms of clusters including project teams, alliance teams, change teams and staff units. In the cluster organisation staff units run their own businesses selling to internal and external customers where possible. (Tiernan *et al.,* 1996)

The cluster organisation has become popular in professional organisations. It is unlikely that the cluster approach would suit all organisations. High volume, low variance activities are poorly suited to clusters since the work cannot be made more challenging and interesting. In such a situation there is little scope for increasing responsibility and discretion. It is also difficult to see how traditional assembly line organisations could adopt such a structure, as it would involve eliminating all hierarchy and job titles. The cluster organisation, therefore, may be the most appropriate structure for professional organisations rather than mass production organisations.

ORGANISATIONAL CULTURE

While the effectiveness and success of an organisation is determined in large measure by a well thought-out structure, it would be unwise to ignore the considerable impact of an organisation's culture on its performance. As Dawson (1996, p. 142) notes:

> there has been a growing realisation on the part of organisational theorists as well as practitioners that structure . . . can only go so far in either providing the social mechanisms for co-ordination and control from a managerial perspective or in explaining human behaviour as work from a theoretical perspective. Structure . . . seems to provide the basic framework, but cannot either determine organisational life, or fully account for the effects of the organisation on people's behaviour.

Throughout human history, cultures have provided much of the additional guidance needed for human beings to collectively survive, adapt, and achieve (Geertz, 1971). Similarly, cultural processes underlie much of what happens in modern organisations. They prescribe some behaviours, and forbid others. They influence the emotional responses that people have. They filter the way people view and interpret their worlds. Consequently, as Trice and Beyer (1993) point out, the relative neglect of cultural processes in the study of organisations is unfortunate, given the central role that they play in channelling human behaviour. Organisational cultural research underwent a major revival in the 1980s with the emergence of the excellence literature (Peters and Waterman, 1982), the high performance literature (Vail, 1982) and the Japanisation thesis (Ouichi, 1981) all of which have been interpreted to mean that attention to culture pays off and can be critical for organisational adaptability, performance and productivity. In a similar vein, and approximately at the zenith of this cultural revival, Deal and Kennedy (1982) persuasively argue that the culture of an organisation could similarly be managed towards achieving greater effectiveness. There was a growing realisation that structural, rational approaches to understanding organisations missed crucial aspects of how organisations function (Pondy and Mitroff, 1979) and a call was made for the establishment of corporate culture as a school of thought within organisational behaviour (Schein, 1985).

DEFINING AND MEASURING ORGANISATIONAL CULTURE

The issue of defining organisational or corporate culture remains contentious. There are probably as many definitions of culture as there are writers who discuss it. Arguably some are unnecessarily complex and academic. Hatch (1997) provides a set of selected definitions that reveals the diversity of views that permeate the literature (Table 9.2).

Table 9.2: Selected definitions of organisational culture

Elliott Jaques (1952: 251) 'The culture of the factory is its customary and traditional way of thinking and doing of things, which is shared to a greater or lesser degree by all its members, and which new members must learn, and at least partially accept, in order to be accepted into service in the firm.'

Andrew Pettigrew (1979: 574) 'Culture is a system of publicly and collectively accepted meanings operating for a given group at a given time. This system of terms, forms, categories, and images interprets a people's own situation to themselves.'

Meryl Reis Louis (1983: 39) 'Organisations [are] culture-bearing milieus, that is, [they are] distinctive social units possessed of a set of common understandings for organising action (e.g., what we're doing together in this particular group, appropriate ways of doing in and among members of the group) and languages and other symbolic vehicles for expressing common understandings.'

Caren Siehl and Joanne Martin (1984: 227) '. . . organisational culture can be thought of as the glue that holds an organisation together through a sharing of patterns of meaning. The culture focuses on the values, beliefs and expectations that members come to share.'

Edgar Schein (1985: 6) 'The pattern of basic assumptions that a given group has invented, discovered, or developed in learning to cope with its problems of external adaptation and internal integration, and that have worked well enough to be considered valid, and, therefore, to be taught to new members as the correct way to perceive, think, and feel in relation to these problems.'

John van Maanen (1988: 3) 'Culture refers to the knowledge members of a given group are thought to more or less share; knowledge of the sort that is said to inform, embed, shape, and account for the routine and not-so-routine activities of the members of the culture. . . . A culture is expressed (or constituted) only through the actions and words of its members and must be interpreted by, not given to, a fieldworker. . . . Culture is not itself visible, but is made visible only through its representation.'

Harrison Trice and Janice Beyer (1993: 2) 'Cultures are collective phenomena that embody people's responses to the uncertainties and chaos that are inevitable in human experience. These responses fall into two major categories. The first is the *substance* of a culture – shared, emotionally charged belief systems that we call ideologies. The second is *cultural forms* – observable entities, including actions, through which members of a culture express, affirm, and communicate the substance of their culture to one another.'

Source: Hatch, 1997

A straightforward definition is advanced by Hellreigel *et al.* (1992). They define organisation culture as the philosophies, ideologies, values, beliefs, assumptions, expectations, attitudes and norms shared by the members of the organisation. It includes the following dimensions:

- observed behaviour and the language commonly used when people interact;
- the norms shared by working groups throughout the organisation;
- the dominant values held by an organisation such as product quality or price leadership;
- the philosophy that guides an organisation's policy towards employees and customers;
- the rules that a newcomer must learn in order to become an accepted member;
- the feeling or climate conveyed in an organisation by the physical layout and the way in which its members interact with customers or other outsiders.

Schein (1985, p. 169) suggests that organisational culture refers to a system of shared meaning held by the members that distinguishes the organisation from other organisations. This system of shared meaning essentially represents a critical set of characteristics that the organisation values.

Hofstede (1991) describes how, from his perspective, people acquire mental programs or the 'software of the mind' which create patterns of thinking, feeling and action. He suggests that culture is about the collective programming of the mind which distinguishes the members of one group or category of people from another.

Through a review of the extant literature, Robbins (1991, p. 573) identifies ten characteristics that 'when mixed and matched, tap the essence of an organisation's culture':

1. *Individual initiative:* the degree of responsibility, freedom and independence that individuals have.
2. *Risk tolerance:* the degree to which employees are encouraged to be aggressive, innovative and risk-seeking.

3. *Direction:* the degree to which the organisation creates clear objectives and performance expectations.
4. *Integration:* the degree to which units within the organisation are encouraged to operate in a co-ordinated manner.
5. *Management support:* the degree to which management provide clear communication, assistance and support to their subordinates.
6. *Control:* the number of rules and regulations, and the amount of direct supervision that is used to oversee and control employee behaviour.
7. *Identity:* the degree to which members identify with the organisation as a whole rather than with their particular work group or field of professional expertise.
8. *Reward system:* the degree to which the reward allocations (that is salary increases, promotions) are based on employee performance criteria in contrast to seniority, favouritism etc.
9. *Conflict tolerance:* the degree to which employees are encouraged to air conflicts and criticisms openly.
10. *Communication patterns:* the degree to which organisational communications are restricted to the formal hierarchy of authority.

Each of these characteristics is seen to exist on a continuum from low to high and, by examining and appraising the organisation on these characteristics, an overall composite picture of the organisation's culture can be gleaned. This picture, however it looks, creates a degree of order, particularly for the members of the organisations, in what is a very uncertain, disorderly business environment. It can prove to be an important coping mechanism.

Culture does not exist in a vacuum but is linked to larger cultural processes within the organisation's environment. Every organisation expresses aspects of the national, regional, industrial, occupational and professional cultures in and through which it operates (Phillips *et al.*, 1992). Hatch (1997, p. 200) argues that:

> Each organisation is formed, in part, through cultural processes established by a variety of environmental actors. However, the most immediate source of outside influence on the organisational culture is found within the organisation – its employees. Before joining an organisation, employees have already been influenced by multiple cultural institutions such as family, community, nation, state, church, educational system and other work organisations, and these associations shape their attitudes, behaviour and identity . . . Because of this it is difficult to separate an organisational culture from the larger cultural processes.

From a research, conceptualisation and measurement perspective, organisational culture can be viewed either as a 'variable' (see, for example, Deal and Kennedy, 1982) or as a 'metaphor' (see, for example, Morgan, 1986). The meaning one attaches to culture will fundamentally influence the likely methodologies employed in researching the phenomenon. Those who argue that culture is a variable believe that culture is an objective reality that can be isolated and measured and is something that can be altered by management for the purpose of achieving organisational objectives. This is what Daft (1989) calls 'culture at the surface level' that is bound up with the slogans, symbols and ceremonies that signify underlying values.

> This dominant perspective holds that corporate culture is 'out there' existing independently of employees and alongside company objectives, technology and structure. It consists of a single set of shared and consistent values and beliefs embedded in stories and symbols, and which are transmitted by company rites and rituals. These act to eliminate ambiguity for members as to how they should think and act. Most importantly corporate culture is capable of being consciously created and managed. (Buchanan and Huczynski, 1997, p. 514)

Those who suggest that it is a metaphor believe that culture is a mental state not easily pinned down, or altered to suit particular ends. Also referred to as the 'subsurface level of culture', the unwritten norms and values are critical for guiding and influencing employee behaviour (Daft, 1989). Culture here exists in and through the social action of the actors, and therefore supports the notion that competing subcultures, affiliated to particular departments in the organisation for example, could exist. As Buchanan and Huczynski (1997) point out, culture is deeper than its simple symbolic manifestations.

> Stories, rituals, material symbols and language within organisations are a means of transmitting culture, but are not culture itself . . . This perspective . . . offers management fewer levers with which to shape it or use it as a tool of control. Although managers might be able to change the outward manifestations of culture to some degree, the basic assumptions of company employees will remain the same. (p. 515)

CULTURAL MANIFESTATIONS AND CHARACTERISTICS

Cultural expression in an organisation has several manifestations which can be observed for the purpose of understanding the dominant values of the culture (Table 9.3).

Williams *et al.* (1989) have identified six elements that characterise organisational culture. Culture is:

- learnt;
- both input and output;
- partly unconscious;
- historically based;
- held rather than shared;
- heterogeneous.

Table 9.3: Manifestations of corporate culture

- *Rite:* relatively elaborate, dramatic, planned set of activities that consolidate various forms of cultural expressions onto one event, which is carried out through social interactions, usually for the benefit of an audience.

- *Ceremonial:* a system of several rites connected with a single occasion or event.

- *Legend:* a handed-down narrative of some wonderful event that is based in history but has been embellished with fictional details.

- *Story:* a narrative based on true events – often a combination of truth and fiction.

- *Symbol:* an object, act, event, quality, or relation that serves as a vehicle for conveying meaning, usually by representing another thing.

- *Language:* a particular form or manner in which members of a group use vocal sounds and written signs to convey meanings to each other.

- *Physical Setting:* things that surround people physically and provide them with immediate sensory stimuli as they carry out culturally expressive activities.

- *Artefact:* material objects manufactured by people to facilitate culturally expressive activities.

Source: Trice and Beyer, 1984

Culture is learnt because individual beliefs, attitudes and values are gained from the individual's environment and therefore culture can be seen to be gained from the environment which is common to all its members, both internal and external environments.

In terms of culture being both an input and an output, the argument is that the culture that people learn (input) affects the way they act in the future (output). The strategies, structures, procedures and behaviours adopted by management affect the work environment of the future. However, the managers, if they are members of the organisation for some time, are themselves a product of the culture and the strategies which they have implemented. Thus, people create a culture by their actions, the way they behave etc. and this culture in turn affects how they behave in future. Arguably therefore, culture is often highly resistant to change.

Culture is seen to be partly unconscious because commonly-held beliefs of individuals in organisations may exist at an unconscious level. This may occur simply because conscious beliefs and underlying attitudes become so commonplace that they are taken for granted and so become the norm over time, or because members unconsciously process information that influences the way they think. Williams *et al.* (1989) suggest that individuals process information at various levels of consciousness, and information processed below the threshold of awareness can critically influence behaviour in organisations.

Culture is seen to be historically based, largely as organisations are developed from the original assumptions, strategies and structures made by their founders. Once the organisation has made a strategic decision, this limits the degree of freedom for succeeding generations. The die has been cast and these assumptions may be present many generations after their foundation. The original culture influences successive generations because decisions affecting the future of the organisation are made within the context of existing culture, e.g. Guinness, Marks & Spencer, and Bewleys.

A key feature of culture in organisations and in society is that mostly it is commonly shared. Generally, individuals discuss and reach consensus on how to think and behave in a given situation, i.e. they agree to hold common values. Individuals within a given organisation will come to adopt similar ways of thinking and behaving even though they may be widely separated geographically or functionally. It is this perhaps which seems to give culture its slightly mystic quality. In reality though, this common thought and behaviour results from common learning, common history and a common environment.

In practice, culture is also likely to be heterogeneous or not completely integrationist. Most organisations are characterised by sub-cultures which form around different roles, functions and levels. Probably very few beliefs, attitudes or values are completely common to all members. Sub-cultures tend to develop in large organisations to reflect common problems, situations, or experiences that members face. Also labelled a 'differentiation perspective on culture', generally sub-cultures comprise the dominant core values of the accepted organisation's culture plus a set of additional values and/or meanings that are specific to the function or group. Most organisations generally comprise an executive culture focusing upon managing and resourcing, and a blue-collar culture focusing upon production. Sub-cultures of a greater or lesser significance exist in any culture. These sub-cultures can often be beneficial if they instil a sense of common purpose and identity within a given department. Equally they can be highly detrimental if they limit co-ordination or cause unhealthy conflict across the organisation.

Trice and Beyer (1993) in their influential treatise on the cultures of work organisations argue that cultures are characterised by being collective, emotionally charged, historically based, dynamic, inherently symbolic and, at the same time, inherently fuzzy. Cultures are not produced by individuals acting on their own. They emerge and are given meaning as individuals interact with one another. 'Cultures are the repositories of what their members agree about and persons who do not endorse and practise prevailing beliefs, values, and norms become marginal and may be punished or expelled. Belonging to a culture involves believing what others believe and doing as they do – at least part of the time! (p. 5).

Cultures are emotionally charged because their substance and forms are infused with emotion as well as meaning, and cultures may assist in directing emotion into socially accepted channels. Cultures develop over time and cannot be completely divorced from their histories. They will be derived from the context in which people have found themselves. Despite this link with the past, cultures are dynamic phenomena continuously sprouting variants, depending on what the preferences of a given generation are. They are inherently symbolic because symbolism itself is important for expressing and communicating the essence of the culture. However, they are also fuzzy because many symbols can be difficult to interpret and can have multiple meanings.

PERSPECTIVES ON CULTURE

The literature abounds with theories and models seeking to clarify the concept of culture, 'many of which are inconsistent with each other and fail to provide clear guidelines for measurement' (Buchanan and Huczynski, 1997, p. 512). Here we review four critical contributions to the literature: Charles Handy's work on culture and structure compatibility, the excellence school and its attempts to link culture and performance, Schein's contribution on what to look for when trying to discover the essence of the culture, and Hofstede's work on larger national cultural systems embracing the notion that the organisation and its culture is largely a manifestation of this larger system.

Handy on organisation culture

Charles Handy, in his work, *Understanding Organisations* (1976), drawing upon earlier research by Harrison (1972), developed a four-way typology of common cultural types, namely *power, role, task* and *people* orientations.

Power orientation (Figure 9.2)

In an organisation that demonstrates a power orientation, the organisation will attempt to dominate its environment, and those who are powerful within the organisation strive to maintain absolute control over subordinates. Work is typically divided by function or product and the organisation structure tends towards a traditional framework, presented as a web structure.

Figure 9.2: Power culture

Culture	Diagrammatic representation	Structure
Power or club		Web

Source: Handy, 1976

The functions or departments are represented by lines radiating out from the centre, but the essential feature is that there are also concentric lines representing communications and power. The further away from the centre one is, the weaker the degree of power and influence that one possesses. The organisation is dominated from the centre. Decisions can be reached quickly, but the quality of the decision depends to a large extent upon the ability of managers in the inner circle who, in turn, are dependent upon their affinity and trust, both within the organisation and within suppliers, customers and other key stakeholders and influencers. Employees are rewarded for effort, success and compliance with essential core values. Change is very much determined by the central power source. While this type of culture places a lot of faith in the individual, the organisation operates with apparent disregard for human values and general welfare, and is highly competitive. It is often seen as tough and/or abusive, and may suffer from low morale and high turnover in the middle layers as individuals fail or opt out of the competitive atmosphere.

Role orientation (Figure 9.3)

An organisation that is role-oriented aspires to be as rational and orderly as possible. In contrast with the wilful autocracy of the power culture, there is a preoccupation with legitimacy, loyalty and responsibility as the culture is built around defined jobs. Rules and procedures dominate, creating many bureaucratic characteristics. People fit into jobs and are recruited for this purpose, hence rationality and logic are at the heart of the culture which is designed to be stable and predictable. The culture is represented by the greater temple design since the strengths of the organisation are designated to be in the pillars which are co-ordinated.

Figure 9.3: Role culture

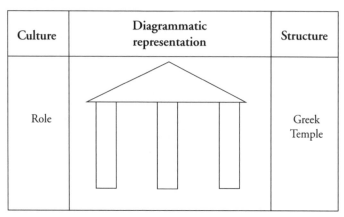

Culture	Diagrammatic representation	Structure
Role		Greek Temple

Source: Handy, 1976

However, although the strength of the organisation is in the pillars, power lies at the top. There remains a strong emphasis upon hierarchy and status, with rights and privileges clearly defined and adhered to. Conflict is regulated by rules and procedures, predictability is high, and stability and respectability are valued almost as much as competence. While high efficiency is possible in stable environments, Handy argues that role culture is less suitable for dynamic environments or situations. Communication goes up and down the organisation, but is less likely across the organisation between departments or sections. Decisions continue to be the reserve of those at the top, which may mean that leader satisfaction is high; but people lower down the organisation may feel frustrated and lacking in status.

Task orientation (Figure 9.4)

In such organisations, functions and activities are all evaluated in terms of their contribution to organisational goals. Management in the task culture is concerned with the continuous and successful solving of problems, and performance is judged by the success of task outcomes. The culture is depicted as a net because, for particular problem situations, people and other resources can be drawn from various parts of the organisation on a temporary basis. Once the problem is dealt with, individuals will move on to different tasks and, as a consequence, discontinuity is a key element.

The attainment of goals is the persuasive ideology in task-oriented organisations. Nothing is allowed to get in the way of task achievement. If individuals do not have necessary technical skills or knowledge, they are retrained or replaced. Emphasis is placed on the development of meaningful flexibility, hence project groups and collaboration between groups is commonplace. Expertise is the major source of individual power and authority. This culture is adaptable and individuals retain a high degree of control over their work; it is common in volatile environments.

Figure 9.4: Task culture

Culture	Diagrammatic representation	Structure
Task	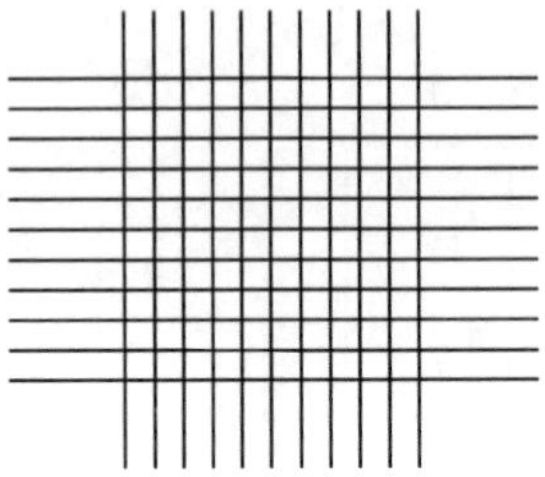	Net

Source: Handy, 1976

People orientation (Figure 9.5)

This type of culture differs from the other three since, in this instance, the organisation exists primarily to serve the needs of its members. The organisation provides a service for individual specialists which they could not provide for themselves. Authority in the environment sense is redundant, although where necessary, it may be assigned on the basis of task competency. In place of formalised authority, individuals are expected to influence each other through example and helpfulness. Consensus methods of decision-making are preferred, as the figure illustrates, and roles are assigned on the basis of personal preferences and the need for learning and growth.

Figure 9.5: People culture

Culture	Diagrammatic representation	Structure
Person or existential	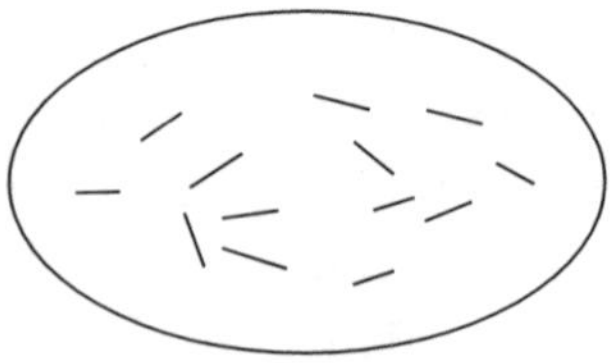	Cluster

Source: Handy, 1976

In a people-oriented culture people are not easy to manage as there is little influence that can be brought to bear on them; being professionals, alternative employment is often easy to obtain. The psychological contract thus stipulates that the organisation is subordinate to the individuals and depends on the individual for its existence. Clearly, many organisations cannot exist with this kind of culture since organisations tend to have objectives above and beyond the collective objectives of those who comprise them. The culture is most often found in clubs, societies and professional bodies.

Excellence in organisation culture

It has been suggested that a strong organisation culture can help an organisation successfully implement new business strategies, and can also help the organisation achieve levels of excellence. For example, studies of Japanese methods of management suggest that the high levels of excellence achieved and the success of their organisations are partly explained by a strong organisation culture which encourages employee participation, job security and open communication. Cultural strength denotes the agreement among members of an organisation about the importance of specific values. If widespread consensus exists about the importance of those values, the culture is said to be cohesive and strong. If little agreement exists, the culture is described as weak (Arogyaswamy and Byles, 1987). Among the most popularised findings on the relationship between culture and excellence are those reported by Peters and Waterman in their book *In Search of Excellence* (1982). They argue that excellent organisations do not insist on sticking to the rules but get on with the job. They identify what their customers want and they ensure that they get it. People within the organisation are encouraged to use their own initiative and to take risks. They view employees as a key resource and encourage harmonious relations. Managers in these organisations are in touch with the workforce and the organisation sticks to what it knows best. From their research in forty-three 'high performing' American companies, the authors identify six main attributes which characterise the cultures of 'successful' organisations. These attributes are:

- *A bias for action, for getting on with it:* these organisations do not feel that they have to stick constantly to the rule book. They believe in 'Do it, try it, fix it.'
- *Close to the customer:* customers are seen as all-important and the organisation can learn from them. Customers are provided with quality, service and reliability.
- *Autonomy and entrepreneurship:* risk-taking and innovation are encouraged in the organisation. People are allowed the freedom to be creative.
- *Productivity through people:* the excellent organisations treat their employees as a key resource. They encourage good management/labour relations and accept that their employees *are* the organisation.
- *Hands-on, value driven:* these organisations feel that their philosophy and values are

tied in to success. Managers at all levels spend a considerable time walking around, assessing what is going on and being seen to do so.

- *Stick to the knitting:* excellent organisations concentrate their energies and resources on running what they know how to run. They do not waste time with other kinds of business where they do not have the same competency.

An emphasis on these values found favour and resonance with top managers, as witnessed by the number of organisations that attempted to transform their culture. The teachings of the 'excellence school' seemed to promise flexibility and innovation, together with employee commitment and loyalty while avoiding the rigidities of bureaucracy. However, as history was to demonstrate, 'Excellent companies could fall from grace' (Dawson, 1996, p. 159). A short two years after the publication of *In Search of Excellence,* many commentaries began appearing about the less-than-excellent fortune of many of the organisations investigated by Peters and Waterman.

> The erstwhile champion of excellence has now moved on from prescribing universal recipes for success, having declared that the era of sustainable excellence is ended and that managers need to learn to thrive on chaos.

Having found one way to excellence they must learn that sticking to that managerial knitting will not necessarily stand them in good stead even in the medium term (Dawson, 1996, p. 160).

Schein on organisation culture

Schein (1984, 1985) developed what arguably has become one of the most influential theories of organisational culture, from a methodological/measurement perspective. He argues that culture exists at three different levels; at the surface level there exists a series of *artifacts,* underneath these artifacts there are a series of held *values* and at the deepest level there are a set of core *assumptions.* Artifacts are the visible, tangible and audible remains of behaviour that are grounded in cultural norms, values and assumptions. Hatch (1997, p. 216) suggests that artifacts might include physical manifestations such as buildings, dress/appearance and/or logos, behavioural manifestations such as rewards/punishments, communication patterns and/or ceremonies, and verbal manifestations such as jokes, jargon, nicknames and/or anecdotes and stories. Values are guarded principles that give definition to the culture. They may not be as visible as artifacts, but they are typically more conscious than assumptions. Assumptions are taken for granted and likely exist outside ordinary awareness.

Figure 9.6: Three levels of organisational culture

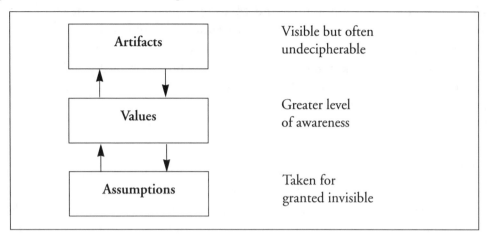

Source: Schein, 1985

According to Schein, culture and its maintenance is driven from the centre out, from the central assumptions, values and norms to the surface artifacts which we can observe. However, once the artifacts appear on the surface, they in turn begin to be interpreted in ways that can again eventually influence the values and assumptions that gave life and meaning to them in the first instance.

Culture and the wider society: the work of Hofstede

We mentioned earlier that culture does not exist in a vacuum and that it is difficult to separate an organisational culture from the larger cultural processes. While the nature of the industry acts as a determinant of the organisation's culture (specific industries have certain cultural characteristics which become manifest in the organisation's culture), there is little disputing the fact that the organisation's culture is more broadly developed by the prevailing national culture within which it operates (see also the discussion on cultural values and perception in Chapter 3). Geert Hofstede carried out a cross-cultural study to identify the similarities and differences among 116,000 employees of the same multinational organisation located in forty countries. His overall aim was to identify broad parameters of differences between national cultures and establish the impact of culture differences on management. From his research he identified four such value dimensions which he claims discriminate between national cultures: *power distance, uncertainty avoidance, individualism/collectivism* and *masculinity/femininity.*

1. *Power distance* refers to the extent to which individuals accept that power is distributed unequally. Thus high power distance implies a high acceptance of power inequalities in that society.

2. *Uncertainty avoidance* refers to the extent to which individuals feel uncomfortable with uncertainty and ambiguity, and as a consequence seek to develop ways of working which limit their exposure to uncertainty and ambiguity.

3. *Individualism/collectivism* refers to the extent to which there is a preference for membership of tightly-knit collectives with strong bonds of loyalty and mutual care, or a preference for a more loosely-knit society in which individuals and their families are rather more independent.

4. *Masculinity/femininity* refers to a preference for achievement and assertiveness rather than a preference for modesty and caring.

Figures 9.7 and 9.8 present the results of Hofstede's cluster analysis in the form of what he himself refers to as a series of cultural maps. While some concern has been voiced that the country differences found in Hofstede's research are not representative due to the single company sample, further research by him and others supports many of these dimensions.

Figure 9.7: Position of forty countries on power distance and individualism

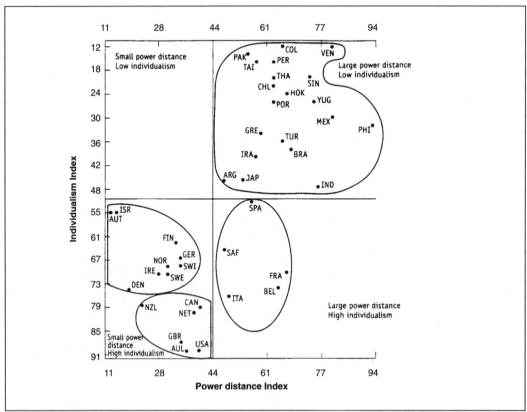

Source: Hofstede, 1980, 1991

Figure 9.8: Position of forty countries on uncertainty avoidance and masculinity dimensions

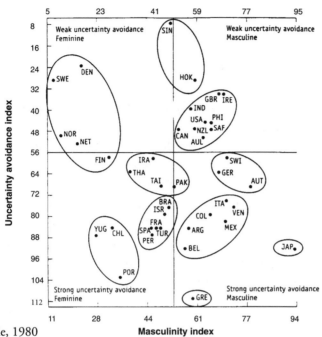

Source: Hofstede, 1980

POWER INDEX KEY			
ARG	Argentina	JAP	Japan
AUL	Australia	MEX	Mexico
AYT	Austria	NET	Netherlands
BEL	Belgium	NOR	Norway
BRA	Brazil	NZL	New Zealand
CAN	Canada	PAK	Pakistan
CHL	Chile	PER	Peru
COL	Columbia	PHI	Philippines
DEN	Denmark	POR	Portugal
FIN	Finland	SAF	South Africa
FRA	France	SIN	Singapore
GBR	Great Britain	SPA	Spain
GER	Germany	SWE	Sweden
GRE	Greece	SWI	Switzerland
HOK	Hong Kong	TAI	Taiwan
IND	India	THA	Thailand
IRA	Iran	TUR	Turkey
IRE	Ireland	USA	United States
ISR	Israel	VEN	Venezuela
ITA	Italy	YUG	Yugoslavia

Hofstede argues that the first two dimensions (power distance and uncertainty avoidance) have the strongest influence on organisations and that the different combinations and permutations of power distance and uncertainty avoidance are suggestive of different perspectives on the process of organising. Organisations in countries with high power distance would tend to have more levels of hierarchy (vertical differentiation), a higher proportion of supervisory personnel (narrow spans of control), and more centralised decision-making. Those countries with high uncertainty avoidance tended to have organisations which are more highly formalised as evidenced by the greater emphasis on proceduralisation and rule-making, and management tended to be more risk averse. Countries that demonstrated high collectivism had a preference for group/collective decision-making and for seeking out co-operation and consensus. Those countries ranked high on masculinity demonstrated a management style less focused on the employee or the development of strong social relationships and more on the execution and completion of the task. More feminine-orientated countries tended to view the managerial role as one which needed to demonstrate a concern for employee well-being. Ireland, according to Hofstede's cluster analysis, ranks with Finland, Norway, Sweden, Denmark and Germany, as a country in which one witnesses small power distance and reasonably high levels of individualism. However, Ireland ranks with Britain, Canada, New Zealand and South Africa in terms of being a largely masculine culture with low uncertainty avoidance. Small power distance combined with low uncertainty avoidance values incline to a view of an adhocracy, or village market! Drawing upon Hofstede's work and upon a broader extant literature, Dineen and Garavan (1994) provide a more socially embedded set of prominent Irish cultural characteristics (with stronger explanatory power) that are important in the context of better understanding Irish business (Table 9.9).

Table 9.9: Prominent cultural characteristics found in Ireland

Cultural characteristic	How it manifests itself in Ireland
Individualism versus collectivism.	Relatively moderate degree of individualism.
Pride in the country.	Moderate to high.
Attitude to time.	Plenty of time, not viewed as tangible commodity.
Attitude to work and achievement.	Reasonable work ethic, but ambivalent towards achievement.
Uncertainty avoidance.	High degree of uncertainty avoidance.
Relationships to nature.	High attachment to nature.
Youth orientation of society.	Considerable extolling of youth values.

Attachment to hierarchy.	Very high attachment.
Attitude to competition.	Competition not overemphasised.
Talent for motivating a workforce.	Moderate ability.
Formality/informality.	Relatively informal in one-to-one relationships.
Reputation for marketing push.	Very poor.
Masculine/feminine values.	Predominantly masculine values.
Creativity and willingness to exploit innovation.	Moderate willingness.
Acceptance of business by the public.	High level of acceptance.
Co-operation/conflict.	High degree of co-operation encouraged.
Attitude towards foreign influences.	Healthy attitude.
Willingness to delegate authority.	Poor.

Source: Dineen and Garavan, 1994

SUMMARY OF KEY PROPOSITIONS

- The structure defines tasks and responsibilities, work roles and relationships and channels of communication. It creates a framework through which the activities of the organisation can be directed and controlled.
- The main components of organisational structure can be classified into two critical areas: structural configuration and structural operation.
- The classical school of thought advocated a universalist approach to organisational structure, arguing that there was one best way to structure the organisation's activities. They offered prescriptions on designing for best fit in all situations.
- Contingency theory argues that the most appropriate structure for an organisation depends on its size, technology and environment.
- Mintzberg's framework provides guidelines for the choice of an appropriate structure depending on the age of the organisation, its external environment and the nature of its employees.
- Under more recent innovations, cluster-based structures have emerged. A cluster is a group of employees from different disciplines who work together and are undifferentiated by rank or job title. No direct reporting relationships exist within the clusters and support areas only have a residual hierarchy.
- Organisation culture can be defined as the philosophies, ideologies, values, beliefs, assumptions, expectations, attitudes and norms shared by the members of the organisation.
- Organisation culture does not exist in a vacuum but is linked to larger cultural processes within the organisation's environment. Every organisation expresses aspects of the national, regional, industrial, occupational and professional cultures in and through which it operates.

- The manifestations of culture include rites, ceremonials, legends, stories, symbols, language, physical setting and artifacts.
- Handy, drawing upon earlier research, developed a four-way typology of common cultural types, namely power, role, task and people orientations.
- The 'excellence' school argued that a strong organisation culture can help an organisation successfully implement new business strategies, and can also help the organisation achieve levels of excellence.
- Schein argues that culture exists at three different levels; at the surface level there exists a series of artifacts, underneath these artifacts there are a series of held values and at the deepest level there are a set of core assumptions.
- Hofstede identified four value dimensions which he claims discriminate between national cultures: power distance, uncertainty avoidance, individualism/collectivism and masculinity/femininity.

DISCUSSION QUESTIONS

1. Distinguish between the 'formal' and the 'informal' organisation. Does the informal organisation reinforce or contradict the formal organisation structure?
2. Examine the different types of departmentalisation an organisation can use. What factors influence the choices that organisations make here?
3. Do different organisational structures make different behavioural demands on employees and management?
4. What are the functions of an organisation's culture?
5. How would you go about measuring an organisation's culture?
6. From your reading of this chapter, what is the evidence to suggest that the formation and development of an organisation's culture is subject to external influences and processes?

CHAPTER 10

Effective Leadership

LEARNING OBJECTIVES

- To describe the nature of leadership.
- To differentiate between leadership and management.
- To summarise the functions of a leader.
- To review trait leadership theory.
- To examine behavioural leadership theory.
- To describe some contingency theories.
- To examine charismatic theories of leadership.

INTRODUCTION

While leadership means different things to different people, it is generally regarded as a critical factor in the success of any kind of social activity (Statt, 1994). The burning cry in all organisations, according to Perrow (1973), is for good leadership, but we have learned that, beyond a threshold level of adequacy, it is extremely difficult to know what good leadership is. Unlike some other aspects of organisational behaviour, there are many studies and a considerable body of knowledge on leadership, but the impetus for this development arguably springs from a dissatisfaction with many theories. Many studies of the concept point to the conclusion that it is a variable, contingent activity influenced by a whole series of external variables. However, despite the fact that there remain many unanswered questions, according to House and Aditya (1997), the various contributions have been cumulative, and a great deal is known about the leadership phenomenon. Leadership may be interpreted in simple terms, such as 'getting others to follow' or interpreted more specifically, for example as 'the use of authority in decision-making'. It may be exercised as an attribute of position, or because of personal knowledge or wisdom (Mullins, 1991). Leadership is a widely talked about subject and at the same time it is somehow puzzling. The ability to provide effective leadership is one of the most important skills that a manager can possess. Manz and Sims (1991, p. 18) argue that:

> When most of us think of leadership, we think of one person doing something to another person. This is 'influence', and a leader is someone who has the capacity to

influence another. Words like 'charismatic' and 'heroic' are sometimes used to describe a leader. The word 'leader' itself conjures up visions of a striking figure on a rearing white horse who is crying 'Follow me!' The leader is the one who has either the power or the authority to command others.

Thus there is little doubt that leadership is a skill that is respected and admired, but it appears rather elusive to many people. Pettinger (1994, p. 31) maintains that:

> Leadership is that part of the management sphere concerned with getting results through people, and all that entails and implies – the organisation of the staff into productive teams, groups, departments; the creation of human structures; their motivation and direction; the resolution of conflicts at the workplace; creating vision and direction for the whole undertaking; and providing resources in support of this.

A slightly narrower interpretation is advanced by Tannenbaum *et al.* (1961) when they suggest that leadership is an interpersonal influence which is exercised in a situation and directed through the communication process towards the attainment of a specified goal.

LEADERSHIP AND MANAGEMENT

In drawing attention to the distinction between leadership and management, Bennis (1989) argues that in order to survive in the twenty-first century,

> we are going to need a new generation of leaders – leaders, not managers. The distinction is an important one. Leaders conquer the context – the volatile, turbulent, ambiguous surroundings that sometimes seem to conspire against us and will surely suffocate us if we let them – while managers surrender to it. (p. 7)

'Managers', according to Bennis and Nanus (1985) 'do things right', while, 'leaders do the right things'. While both leadership and management can be conceived of as being essentially about influence and the use of power, there is a strong argument to be made that leadership is a different concept than management *per se*. Hersey and Blanchard (1983) conceive of management as a special kind of leadership in which the achievement of organisational goals is paramount. The key difference between the concepts, they argue, therefore lies in the word 'organisation'. Leadership occurs any time one attempts to influence the behaviour of an individual or group, regardless of the reason. It may be for one's own goals or for those of others, and they may or may not be congruent with organisational goals. Critically, it is not axiomatic that every leader is a manager, though conversely Mintzberg (1973) argues that leadership behaviour can be an integral part of a manager's job and in his research he identifies ten main roles grouped into three areas (Table 10.1).

Table:10.1: Managerial roles identified by Mintzberg

Interpersonal.	Figurehead.
	Leader.
	Liaison.
Informational.	Monitor.
	Disseminator.
	Spokesman.
Decisional.	Entrepreneur.
	Disturbance handler.
	Resource allocator.
	Negotiator.

According to Statt (1994), chief executives will spend much more of their time on the interpersonal roles than would more junior managers. However, this does not mean that they will be any more effective as leaders. He argues that the job titles and the job descriptions, and the amount of time the job demands for activity defined as leadership simply tells us what is done. It does not tell us how it is done, and that is where leadership ability and effectiveness would come in.

> But in any organisation we tend to look automatically at the apex for evidence of leadership. Indeed the greatest fallacy of leadership is that it always comes from the top down. It most certainly does not. (Statt, 1994, p. 337)

Many believe management and leadership to be more delineated as organisational and/or societal roles.

> Management is more usually viewed as getting things done through other people in order to achieve stated organisational objectives. The manager may react to specific situations and be more concerned with solving short-term problems. Management is regarded as relating to people working within a structured organisation and with prescribed roles. To people outside of the organisation the manager might not be seen in a leadership role. The emphasis of leadership is on interpersonal behaviour in a broader context. It is often associated with the willing and enthusiastic behaviour of followers. Leadership does not necessarily take place within the hierarchical structure of the organisation. Many people operate as leaders without their role ever being clearly established or defined. A leader often has sufficient influence to bring about long-term changes in people's attitudes. Leadership can be seen primarily as an 'inspirational process'. (Mullins, 1991, p. 421)

Table 10.2: Distinguishing between a manager and a leader

Manager	Leader
Motivates people and administers resources to achieve stated organisational goals.	Motivates people to develop new objectives.
Short-range view.	Long-range perspective.
A copy.	An original.
Maintains.	Develops.
Focuses on system and structure.	Focuses on people.
Implements.	Shapes.
Relies on control.	Inspires trust.
Eye on the bottom line.	Eye on the horizon.
Narrows down horizons.	Opens up horizons.
Rational.	Emotional.
Classic good soldier.	Own person.
Accepts the status quo.	Challenges the status quo.
Does things right.	Does right thing.

Source: Adapted from Bennis, 1989

Zaleznik of the Harvard Business School (1977) argues forcefully that there is a difference between leadership and management, and highlights a number of differences associated with their motivation, personal history and how they actually think:

- Managers tend to adopt impersonal or passive attitudes towards goals. Leaders adopt a more personal and active attitude towards goals.
- In order to get people to accept solutions, the manager needs to continually co-ordinate and balance in order to compromise conflicting values. The leader creates excitement in work and develops choices that give substance to images that excite people.
- In their relationships with other people, managers maintain a low level of emotional involvement. Leaders have empathy with other people and give attention to what events and actions mean.
- Managers see themselves more as conservators and regulators of the existing order of affairs with which they identify, and from which they gain rewards. Leaders work in, but do not belong to, the organisation. Their sense of identity does not depend upon membership or work roles and they search out opportunities for change.

While many of the differences cited are not scientifically derived, arguably an individual can be a leader without being a manager, and a manager without being a leader.

LEADERSHIP FUNCTIONS

As far back as 1962, Krech *et al.* identified fourteen leadership functions which demonstrate the complexity of leadership. They saw the leader as:

1. *Executive:* top co-ordinator of the group activities and over-seer of the execution of policies.
2. *Planner:* deciding the ways and means by which the group achieves its ends through both short-term and long-term planning.
3. *Policy-maker:* the establishment of group goals and policies.
4. *Expert:* a source of readily available information and skills.
5. *External group representative:* the official spokesperson for the group, the representative of the group and the clearing house for outgoing and incoming information.
6. *Controller of internal relations:* determines specific aspects of the group's structure.
7. *Purveyor of rewards and punishment:* control over group members by the power to provide rewards and apply punishments.
8. *Arbitrator and mediator:* controls interpersonal conflict within the group.
9. *Exemplar:* a model of behaviour for members of the group, setting an example of what is expected.
10. *Symbol of the group:* enhancing the group unit by providing some kind of cognitive focus and establishing the group as a distinct entity.
11. *Substitute for individual responsibility:* relieves the individual member of the group from the necessity of, and responsibility for, personal decision.
12. *Ideologist:* serving as the source of beliefs, values and standards of behaviour for individual members of the group.
13. *Father figure:* serving as focus for the positive emotional feelings of individual members and the object for identification and transference.
14. *Scapegoat:* serving as a target for aggression and hostility of the group, accepting blame in the case of failure.

More recently, Dawson (1996, p. 218) assembles what she describes as a 'long and incomplete list' of leadership functions. From a review of the extant literature she argues that the list can be classified into five key areas, i.e. task functions, cultural functions, symbolic functions, political functions and relational functions. Task functions are largely concerned with task completion, while cultural functions are associated with creating and sustaining a performance culture and climate in the organisation. Symbolic functions are seen to be important, arguably because leaders are important for what they stand for as much as for what they actually do. Political functions are associated with the leader's role in relation to outsiders, while relational functions deal with the nature of the relationship between the leader and the followers.

Table 10.3: Leadership functions

1. *Task functions*
   Strategist : enunciating policy, objectives, goals.
   Executive : ensuring action to secure objectives.
   Co-ordinator : ensuring all parts and contributions fit together.
   Procurer : procuring important resources including information.
   Monitor/evaluator : checking and evaluating performance.
   Rectifier : putting right or improving performance.
   Problem definer : identifying and conceptualising problems.
   Problem solver : identifying and implementing solutions in an imaginative way.
   Expert : supplying wisdom, skills and knowledge.

2. *Cultural functions*
   Missionary : building a spirit of inquiry and commitment to continuous learning and improvement.
   Role model : setting an example of expected behaviour.
   Ideologist : originating and purveying values and sets of assumptions.
   Consciousness raiser : liberating unconscious thoughts and aspirations of followers.

3. *Symbolic functions*
   Visionary : formulating and communicating a view of the future.
   Interpreter : creating and managing meaning.
   Father or mother figure : providing a focus for identifications, reference and occasional
   Scapegoat   rebellion.
   Moral authority : acting as a target for blame and hostility.
     : legitimating activities.

4. *Political functions*
   Representative : representing the group externally.
   Politician : securing external support.

5. *Relational functions*
   Rewarder/sanctioner : dispensing rewards and punishments.
   Coach : encouraging and supporting others.
   Arbiter and mediator : working between different interest groups.
   Teacher : imparting knowledge and skills.
   Welfare worker : attending to group members' well-being.
   Peacemaker : securing consensus.
   Referee : ensuring fair competition.
   Communicator : ensuring open communications.
   Honest broker : securing trust between parties.

Source: Dawson, 1996

TRAIT THEORIES OF LEADERSHIP

It is almost a truism to suggest that good leadership is essential for business performance; but what makes a good leader? Among the earliest theories of leadership were those which focused on traits (Gibb, 1947; Stogdill, 1948). The earliest trait theories, which can be traced back to the ancient Greeks, concluded that leaders are born, not made. Up to approximately 1950 most studies sought to identify leadership traits, principally because prominent leaders seemed to possess certain 'exceptional characteristics'. Also known as the 'Great Man theory', the assumption was that it is possible to identify a unifying set of characteristics that make all great leaders great, and so psychologists set about looking for the personality characteristics or traits that distinguished leaders from other people. If the concept of traits were to be proved valid, there would have to be specific characteristics in existence that all leaders possess. The trait theories argued that leadership is innate, the product of our parents given at birth. The chosen individuals are born with traits (particularly personality traits, though physical traits possibly had a role to play) which caused them to be self-selected as leaders. The findings emanating from this early work tend to disagree on what sets of traits distinguish leaders from followers. Among the characteristics identified are:

- Intelligence.
- Initiative.
- Dependability.
- Lateral thinker.
- Self-assurance.
- Maturity.
- Visionary.
- Social well-being.
- Need for achievement.
- Need for power.
- Goal-directedness.

The vast amount of research effort expended by psychologists on this topic, up to the middle of the twentieth century, was reviewed in what Statt (1994, p. 326) refers to as 'a very important article' written by Stogdill (1948). Stogdill found that such people did tend to be higher in certain characteristics than other people, for example intelligence, level of activity and social participation, but that this relationship was inconsistent, and even where it was found it was a lot less influential than had generally been assumed. He therefore concluded that, while any useful theory of leadership had to say something about personal characteristics, by themselves they explained very little about leadership behaviour in organisations.

Leadership was much more a matter of context and situation, Stogdill suggested. People who exhibited behaviour in one situation might not do so in another . . . the reason for this was that whatever leadership may be it is always a relationship between people. (Statt, 1994, p. 326)

Overall, the research effort dedicated to the search for universal traits possessed by leaders resulted in little truly convincing evidence. Robbins (1991) goes so far as to say it resulted in 'dead ends'. Certainly, much of the research work has identified lists of traits which tend to be overlapping or contradictory and with few significant correlations between factors. As Luthans (1992) points out, only intelligence seemed to hold up with any degree of consistency, and when these findings were combined with those of studies on physical traits, the overall conclusion was that leaders were more likely to be bigger and brighter than those being led, but not too much so! Despite this, Stogdill argued that it was not entirely appropriate to abandon the study of traits, and that the best way forward was to introduce an interactional element into the equation whereby traits and their significance/universality would be considered in the context of the situational difficulties or demands facing the leader.

However, this view that leaders are born and not made is much less widely held today. There has been an incremental shift away from this thinking for a number of reasons. First, the enormous range of traits potentially affecting leadership ability is problematic and there is a difficulty associated with measuring their existence. This appears a critical weakness according to House and Aditya (1997) largely because there was little empirically substantiated personality theory to guide the search for leadership traits. The lists of traits tend to be exceptionally long and there is not always agreement on how they should be prioritised in terms of their importance. This resulted in an inability to produce many replicative investigations. Second, if we were to rely on birth alone to produce leaders, then potentially we would not have enough leaders to go around. Third, there is a growing body of evidence on the influence of nurturing and life experiences in this area. Fourth, our leadership needs are diverse and are commonly dispersed throughout society with the result that if the specific situational demands of the leader are taken into account, the replication problem once again raises its head. Overall, many psychologists remain unconvinced that there is any link between any specific characteristics and any form of leadership. Finally, from a methodological perspective there is likely going to be some subjective judgment in determining who is regarded as an effective, 'good' leader (see Yetton, 1984).

BEHAVIOURAL THEORIES OF LEADERSHIP

As convincing evidence failed to accumulate through trait-based research, increasingly researchers began to seek out behaviours that specific leaders exhibited. The central hypothesis in this school of thought was that critical specific behaviours differentiate leaders from non-leaders. Extensive research studies on behavioural classifications of leadership were conducted at Ohio State University (Stogdill and Coons, 1957) and the University of Michigan (Likert, 1961).

Ohio State University leadership studies

These studies, which began in the 1940s, sought to identify and classify independent dimensions of leader behaviour. Questionnaires were designed containing a list of items detailing specific aspects of leadership behaviour. From a list of more than 1,000 dimensions, they eventually consistently identified two categories that accounted for most of the leadership behaviour. These two dimensions were labelled *initiating structure style* and *considerate style*. Initiating structure style reflected the extent to which the leader defines and structures his/her role and the roles of the followers in achieving established organisational goals. The considerate style reflected the extent to which the leader focuses on establishing trust, mutual respect and rapport between himself/herself and the followers, and among the group of followers.

Both styles were found to be uncorrelated, thus potentially giving rise to four possible types of leadership behaviour:

1. Low on initiating structure style and low on considerate style.
2. High on initiating structure style and low on considerate style.
3. High on initiating structure style and high on considerate style.
4. Low on initiating structure style and high on considerate style.

Figure 10.1: Four leadership styles

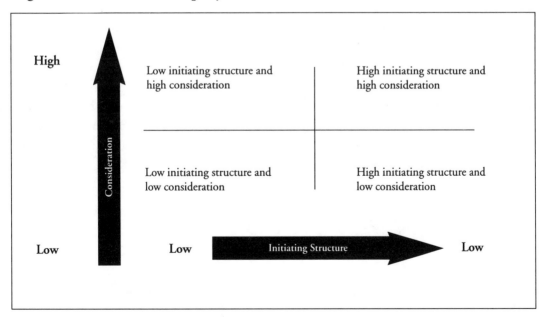

Though criticised on methodological grounds, particularly for their reliance on questionnaires, the research demonstrated that leaders high in initiating structure style and high in considerate style were generally more likely to achieve superior performance among their followers. Followers were also more likely to describe feelings of satisfaction when compared with their counterparts operating under the leadership of those who were low on either style, or both.

University of Michigan studies

Similar to the work being done at Ohio, the Michigan studies, under the direction of Rensis Likert, sought to examine the nature of the relationship between the behavioural characteristics of leaders and performance effectiveness. The research resulted in a two-way classification of leadership, namely employee-oriented and production-oriented styles. The employee-oriented leader was one who emphasised interpersonal relations in the workplace, while the production-oriented leader concentrated on the technical aspects of the work. The results demonstrated that employee-oriented leaders consistently achieved higher productivity and higher job satisfaction among their work groups. Conversely, production-oriented leaders were more likely to be associated with lower group productivity and lower job satisfaction. However, it also emerged that employee-oriented and production-oriented approaches need to be balanced. Employee-oriented leaders who achieved superior results consistently recognised that production was one of the major responsibilities of their work!

The managerial grid (Figure 10.2)

The managerial grid advanced by Blake and Mouton (1962) has been particularly influential as a two-dimensional model of leadership. The grid, which has two axes (concern for people and concern for production) can be taken to represent the initiating structure style and the considerate style of the Ohio research, or the employee-oriented and production-oriented dimensions of the Michigan work. Their writings begin from the assumption that a manager's job is to foster attitudes about behaviour which promote performance, creativity and entrepreneurship. Such managerial competence can be taught and learned. Their managerial grid provides a framework for understanding and applying effective leadership.

Figure 10.2: The Blake and Mouton grid

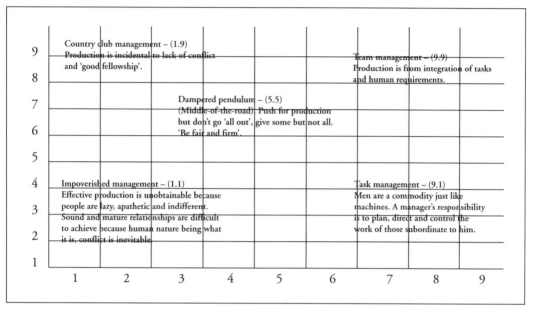

Source: Blake and Mouton, 1962

The grid results from combining two fundamental ingredients of managerial behaviour, namely a concern for production and a concern for people. Any manager's approach to their job will show more or less of each of these two fundamental constituents. They may show a high degree of concern for one or the other of these, or there is the possibility that they might lie in the middle with an equal concern for both. Different positions on the grid represent different typical patterns of behaviour. The grid indicates that all degrees of concern for production and concern for people are possible. Only five key styles are isolated for illustration.

- 9,1 management focuses almost exclusively on production issues. Thus this type is one who expects schedules to be met and has a desire for the smooth running of production operations in a methodical way. Interruptions in this schedule are viewed as someone's mistakes. Disagreement is viewed as being dysfunctional and is seen as insubordination.
- 1,9 management style or 'country club style' almost exclusively emphasises people concerns. People are encouraged and supported in their endeavours as long as they are doing their best. Conflict and disagreement are to be avoided and even constructive criticism is not seen as helpful as it interrupts the harmonious relationship.
- The 1,1 style, also known as impoverished management, signals little concern for either production or people. 1,1 managers avoid responsibility and task commitment. Leaders of this kind avoid contact where possible, and display little commitment to problem-solving.

213

- The 5,5 manager displays the middle-of-the-road style where they push enough to get acceptable levels of production, but in the techniques and skills that they use they also demonstrate a concern for people. They demonstrate a firm but fair attitude and have confidence in their subordinates.
- The 9,9 manager demonstrates a high concern for production and a high concern for people issues. This is a team manager whose goal is one of integration. They aim for the highest possible standard and insist on the best possible result for everyone. There is usually maximum involvement and participation, and the achievement of difficult goals is viewed as a fulfilling challenge. It is accepted that conflict will occur. When it happens it is handled in an open and frank manner and is not treated as a personal attack. This style, Blake and Mouton argue, is always the best style to adopt since it builds on long-term development and trust. This style of leadership, in order to be truly effective, requires an appropriate cultural fit. The value set of the whole organisation must seek to support this style of leadership.

CONTINGENCY LEADERSHIP THEORY

Contingency theories are based on the premise that the predicting of leadership success and effectiveness is more complex than the simple isolation of traits or behaviours. Situational variables, or the context in which leadership is occurring, are also viewed as having strong explanatory power. Both Fiedler's and House's theories are examined here.

Fiedler's Theory

In the 1970s Fred Fiedler conducted a series of studies dedicated to the leadership of work groups. Beginning with the assumption that anyone appointed to a responsible leadership position of this kind will possess the requisite technical expertise, his research question was what is it about leadership behaviour which leads to effective group working, 'effective' meaning how well the group performs the primary task for which it exists. Fiedler's research identifies two main leadership styles, namely 'relationship-motivated leaders' and 'task-motivated leaders'. The former get their satisfaction from having good relationships with others. They usually encourage participation and involvement and are always concerned about what the other team members think of them. Conversely, task-motivated leaders are strongly focused on the task. The emphasis is on proceduralisation and task completion.

Fiedler subsequently developed an instrument to classify these two styles (Box 10.1). The instrument asks leaders to review all people with whom they have ever worked and think of the one with whom they could work least well. They are then asked to rate this 'least preferred co-worker' (LPC) along a number of dimensions. Fiedler has found that relationship-motivated leaders will score relationship issues high in spite of their problems with the LPC. Conversely, task-motivated leaders were found to rate the LPC low on all dimensions. Fiedler emphasises that both these leadership styles can be useful and effective in appropriate situations. He thus argues that it is necessary to have a contingency perspective on leadership, because effective leadership will be contingent on the nature of the tasks to be completed and the context in which this is to be done.

Box 10.1: LPC Activity

Think of the person with whom you work least well. He/she may be someone you work with presently, or may be someone you knew in the past. He/she does not have to be the person you like least well, but should be the person with whom you now have or have had the most difficulty in getting a job done. Describe this person as he/she appears to you by placing an 'x' at the point at which you believe best describes that person. Do this for each pair of adjectives.

Pleasant	8 7 6 5 4 3 2 1	Unpleasant
Friendly	8 7 6 5 4 3 2 1	Unfriendly
Rejecting	8 7 6 5 4 3 2 1	Accepting
Helpful	8 7 6 5 4 3 2 1	Frustrating
Unenthusiastic	8 7 6 5 4 3 2 1	Enthusiastic
Tense	8 7 6 5 4 3 2 1	Relaxed
Distant	8 7 6 5 4 3 2 1	Close
Cold	8 7 6 5 4 3 2 1	Warm
Co-operative	8 7 6 5 4 3 2 1	Unco-operative
Supportive	8 7 6 5 4 3 2 1	Hostile
Boring	8 7 6 5 4 3 2 1	Interesting

Quarrelsome	_	_	_	_	_	_	_	_	Harmonious
	8	7	6	5	4	3	2	1	
Self-assured	_	_	_	_	_	_	_	_	Hesitant
	8	7	6	5	4	3	2	1	
Efficient	_	_	_	_	_	_	_	_	Inefficient
	8	7	6	5	4	3	2	1	
Gloomy	_	_	_	_	_	_	_	_	Cheerful
	8	7	6	5	4	3	2	1	
Open	_	_	_	_	_	_	_	_	Guarded
	8	7	6	5	4	3	2	1	

Scoring:

Your score on the LPC scale is a measure of your leadership style and it indicates your primary motivation in a work setting. To determine your score, add up the points (1 through 8) for each of the sixteen items. If your score is 64 or above, you are a high LPC person or relationship-oriented. If your score is 57 or below, you are a low LPC person or task-oriented. If your score falls between 58 and 63, you will need to determine for yourself in which category you belong.

Source: Fiedler and Chemers, 1974

House's path-goal theory

Advanced by Robert House (1971) as a contingency theory of leadership, path-goal theory extracts critical elements from expectancy theory of work motivation and the Ohio State University research on behavioural aspects of leadership. House argues that leaders are effective if they can help subordinates to identify a goal and then enable them to achieve it. The terminology 'path-goal' is used as a result of the belief that effective leadership is about clarifying the path to help others to get from where they are to the achievement of their work goals and to smooth the journey along the path by reducing and/or eliminating roadblocks and pitfalls. House identifies four leadership styles, namely directive, supportive, participative and achievement-oriented, and two classes of situational variables that influence the leadership behaviour-outcome relationship, namely the personal characteristics of the subordinates and the environment of the subordinates. These situational variables are seen to influence the perceptions and motivations of subordinates, and consequently the leader is advised to adopt the style which, in the given circumstances, is most likely to result in the identification and achievement of appropriate goals. Robbins (1991, p. 370) outlines a number of useful hypotheses that have emerged from path-goal theory research:

• Directive leadership leads to greater satisfaction when tasks are ambiguous or stressful than when they are highly structured and well laid out.

- Supportive leadership results in high employee performance and satisfaction when subordinates are performing structured tasks.
- Directive leadership is likely to be perceived as redundant among subordinates with high perceived ability or with considerable experience.
- The more clear and bureaucratic the formal authority relationships, the more leaders should exhibit supportive behaviour and de-emphasise directive behaviour.
- Directive leadership will lead to higher employee satisfaction when there is substantive conflict within a group.
- Subordinates with an internal locus of control (those who believe they control their own destiny) will be more satisfied with a participative style.
- Subordinates with an external locus of control will be more satisfied with a directive style.
- Achievement-oriented leadership will increase subordinates' expectancies that effort will lead to high performance when tasks are ambiguously structured.

CHARISMATIC LEADERSHIP THEORIES

Like some of the early work associated with trait theory and behavioural theory, studies on charismatic leadership have been directed at identifying behaviours that differentiate charismatic leaders from their non-charismatic counterparts. House (1977) suggests that charismatic leaders are exceptionally self-confident, strongly motivated to attain and assert influence, and have strong conviction in the moral correctness of their beliefs. In the tradition of trait theory, these personality traits are believed to be antecedents to charismatic leadership. Conger and Kanungo (1988) define it in the context of followers making attributions of heroic or extraordinary leadership abilities when they observe certain behaviours. Significant here are transactional, transformational and superleadership.

Transactional and transformational leadership

From the 1970s more research attention was paid to the hypothesis that more successful organisations (using objective performance indicators) have better top management leadership than less successful organisations. Dedicated to identifying 'charismatic' characteristics of leaders, it was viewed as important in the context of organisations attempting to transform traditional systems, methodologies and approaches in an attempt to meet the emerging strategic imperative. Bryman (1993) refers to the work in this area as the 'new leadership theories'. Research work emanating from both the US and the UK lent support to the hypothesis (see Peters and Austin, 1985 and Goldsmith and Clutterbuck, 1984). The single factor that made the crucial difference was what Burns (1978) coined as 'transformational leadership'. Burns identified two types of political leadership, *transactional* and *transformational*.

217

Table 10.4: Approaches of transactional versus transformational leaders

Transactional leaders

1. *Contingent reward:* Contracts exchange of rewards for effort, promises rewards for good performance, recognises accomplishments.
2. *Management by exception (active):* Watches and searches for deviations from rules and standards, takes corrective action.
3. *Management by exception (passive):* Intervenes only if standards are not met.
4. *Laissez-faire:* Abdicates responsibilities, avoids making decisions.

Transformational leaders

1. *Charisma:* Provides vision and sense of mission, instills pride, gains respect and trust.
2. *Inspiration:* Communicates high expectations, uses symbols to focus efforts, expresses important purposes in simple ways.
3. *Intellectual stimulation:* Promotes intelligence, rationality and careful problem-solving.
4. *Individual consideration:* Gives personal attention, treats each employee individually, coaches, advises.

Source: Bass, 1990

The more traditional transactional leadership involves an exchange relationship between leaders and followers, but transformational leadership is more about leaders adjusting the values, beliefs and needs of their followers. Bass suggests that transactional leadership is largely a prescription for mediocrity, while transformational leadership consistently leads to exceptional performance in organisations that really need it. He argues that the development and utilisation of transformational leadership through a sustained focus on the human resource policy areas of recruitment, selection, promotion, training and development will yield dividends in the health, well-being, and effective performance of the modern organisation.

Transformational leadership theory has been criticised on a number of accounts. Statt (1994, p. 339) describes it as the 'Loch Ness monster' of leadership theory. He accepts that while a number of perfectly sober observers claim to have seen it, he has never witnessed it. Furthermore, he suggests that upon close observation, transformational leadership represents a reversion to the much maligned notion of great man theory. Robbins (1991, p. 354) agrees that it does represent a return to traits, but from a different perspective.

> Researchers are now attempting to identify the set of traits that people implicitly refer to when they characterise someone as a leader. This line of thinking proposes that leadership is as much style – projecting the appearance of being a leader – as it is substance.

A more serious criticism questions the methodological foundations of the theory. Most of the research to date has relied on Bass's original questionnaire which has been criticised, or on qualitative research that largely describes leaders through interviews. In relation to the latter, Luthans (1992) cites Tichy and Devanna's (1986) research which, through a series of interviews with top managers in major companies, revealed that transformational leaders share the following characteristics:

- They identify themselves as change agents.
- They believe in people.
- They are courageous.
- They are visionaries.
- They have an ability to tolerate ambiguity, complexity and uncertainty.
- They are value-driven.

From strong man to superleadership

More recently it has been argued that leadership style may be better interpreted as being arranged along a continuum, with leadership approaches ranging from a completely 'strong man' approach dedicated to the issuing of strict instructions and tight supervision to one that is based on the principle of 'superleadership', the objective of which is to lead others to lead themselves. Figure 10.3 presents a perspective on different approaches to leadership.

The authors argue that viewpoints on what constitutes successful leadership in organisations have changed over time. The strong-man view of leadership is the earliest dominant form. Based on the principle of autocracy, the emphasis is on the strength of the leader. The expertise for knowing what should be done rests entirely with the leader, and his/her power stems entirely from his/her position in the organisation. The second view of leadership is based on that of the transactor. The emphasis here is on the rational exchange process (exchange of rewards for work performed) in order to get employees to do their work. The focus here, according to the authors, is on goals and rewards, and the leader's power stems from his ability to provide followers with rewards. The third type of leader they identify is that of the visionary hero. The emphasis here is on the ability of the leader to create highly motivating and absorbing visions. The focus in the relationship is on the leader's vision, and the leader's power is based on the followers' desire to relate to the vision. The final view of the leader is that of the superleader. Rather than using the title to create a larger-than-life type of figure, the authors argue that ironically the emphasis in this relationship is largely on the followers. The objective of the leader is to help the followers to become self-leaders. Power is more evenly shared between the leader and the followers, the objective being to ensure that all followers experience commitment and ownership of their work.

Figure 10.3: Four types of leaders

	Strong man	Transactor	Visionary hero	Super leader
Focus	Commands.	Rewards.	Visions.	Self-leadership.
Type of power	Position/authority.	Rewards.	Relational/ inspirational.	Shared.
Source of leader's wisdom and direction	Leader.	Leader.	Leader.	Mostly followers (self-leaders) and then leaders.
Followers' response	Fear based compliance.	Calculative compliance.	Emotional commitment based on leader's vision.	Commitment based on ownership.
Typical leader behaviours	Direction command.	Interactive goal setting.	Communication of leader's vision.	Becoming an effective self-leader.
	Assigned goals.	Contingent personal rewards.	Emphasis on leader's value.	Modelling self-leadership.
	Intimidation.	Contingent material reward.	Exhortation.	Creating positive through pattern.
	Reprimand.	Contingent reprimand.	Inspirational persuasion.	Developing self-leadership through reward and constructive reprimand.
				Promoting self-leading teams.
				Facilitating a self-leadership culture.

Source: Manz and Sims, 1989

Strategic leadership: the impact of the top management team

So-called strategic leadership (House and Aditya, 1997) is concerned with those executives who have overall responsibility for the organisation. Until relatively recently this aspect of leadership was largely unresearched, but in a concerted effort to move beyond a simple examination of singular leaders at the top of organisations, recent research (Bantel and Jackson, 1989; Hambrick and Mason, 1984) has cast its net wider to focus on the cluster of executives who comprise the 'dominant coalition' in organisations. Thus, according to Hambrick (1994), the expression 'top management team' entered the leadership literature in about 1980 and has been pervasive ever since. Recently popularised organisational forms continually emphasise the concept of the team as a pivotal lever for sustained competitive advantage. The relative neglect of strategic leadership, according to House and Aidya (1997) is ironic since the study of effective organisational policies and strategies has been one of the most important foci of business school education ever since the founding of the earliest such schools. This collective group at the top of the organisational hierarchy will almost invariably have more influence on the course of the firm than any other people in the organisation. Thus Hambrick (1994, p. 174) predicts that 'for those interested in explaining organisational outcomes, analytic attention to the group of executives at the top will not be misplaced'. A comprehensive summary of the literature on strategic leadership in the form of the top management team is presented by Finkelstein and Hambrick (1996) when they debate about whether or not the top management team actually matter. Based on studies of the characteristics of top executives that have been found to be associated with organisational effectiveness, they conclude that top managers do indeed matter, but they are often constrained by factors in their environments, organisational inertia and by their own limitations. Some of the most significant findings concern relationships between the composition and behaviour of the top management teams and important organisational outcomes such as competitiveness and performance. Other prominent research has linked characteristics of top management teams to organisational diversification, innovation, strategic change and decline.

RECENT IRISH EVIDENCE

As part of an international study of leadership, dedicated to developing a cross-national theory of leadership which will redress the US cultural bias of much of the extant literature, Keating *et al.* (1996), employing a pluralist methodology, report new, important data on several Irish leadership behaviours.

Using questionnaire data from a sample of 156 middle managers from the food processing and financial services industries, the authors rank the leadership behaviours in the Irish context (Table 10.5).

Table 10.5: Irish leadership attributes

Leadership attributes	Mean (7-point scale)
Self-centred	1.99
Face-saving	2.48
Autocratic	2.48
Bureaucratic	3.50
Status-conscious	3.62
Individualism	3.95
Humane orientation	5.01
Equanimity	5.11
Charismatic	5.11
Diplomatic	5.44
Collective	5.46
Procedural	5.60
Decisive	6.14
Integrity	6.19
Inspirational	6.29
Visionary	6.33
Performance orientation	6.38

The scale scores reflect the validity of the leadership behaviour and the higher the score the more favourable the behaviour is perceived.

In a qualitative phase of this study, participants were asked to define management and leadership, to identify the behavioural characteristics of an average, above-average manager, and an outstanding leader.

The leadership behaviours given prominence by the groups included vision, charisma, competence, inspiration, persistence and risk-taking. There was great dissent in the groups as to whether successful business persons on both the Irish and international stage were in fact outstanding leaders. None of the participants identified an excellent Irish business leader. Reference to outstanding leaders tended in general to refer to figures outside the Irish context. The participants suggested the inability to give credit to successful business people reflected the Irish culture. Contrasting with their lack of confidence in Irish leadership figures, there was a general belief amongst them that Irish managers are extremely adaptable and perform well abroad. (Keating *et al.*, 1996, p. 6)

Research from the University of Limerick on top management teams provides some Irish evidence on strategic leadership (Flood and Smith, 1994; Flood *et al.*, 1997; Morley *et al.*, 1996). Borrowing from trait and behavioural theories of leadership, the central question addressed was the extent to which the top management team demography and process variables impact (directly and indirectly) on the sales growth performance of thirty international divisions of US multinationals operating in Ireland. The demographic variables of this leadership group used in the research were as follows:

- *Job tenure* referring to the stability of employment of the members of the team.
- *Heterogeneity of experience* referring to the variety of previous industry experience in existence in the top management team.
- *Heterogeneity of education* relating to the dissimilarity of the educational backgrounds of the members of the top management team.
- *Functional heterogeneity* referring to the extent of functional diversity that exists within the top management team.

Team size refers to the number of participants/members in the team. The number of members is a critical element of group structure and composition. The process/behavioural variables used were as follows: social integration refers to the extent to which the members of the top management team experience a sense of belonging and a sense of satisfaction with other members of the group; frequency of communication refers to the amount of interaction between the team members (both formal and informal); and communication informality refers to the extent to which there is a preference among the members of the top management team for informal methods of communication such as spontaneous conversations and chance meetings.

A total of four top management team demography variables and two top management team process variables achieved significance in our analysis, suggesting that both demography and process variables are critical in explaining variation in company performance. Table 10.6 reports the means and the standard deviations of the variables in the study, while Table 10.7 reports the results of the multiple regression with sales growth as the dependent variable.

Job tenure and levels of social integration pertaining in the top management team have no impact on sales growth in the organisations studied. In relation to the remaining variables, demographic and process characteristics are seen to have both a direct and indirect effect on sales growth. Team size and heterogeneity of industrial experience have a direct negative impact on sales growth. Conversely, functional heterogeneity has a direct positive impact. Variation in educational backgrounds has an indirect negative effect on sales growth. Finally, two process variables, namely communication informality and frequency of communication, are seen to be significant. Figure 10.4 graphically presents a path model of the results of our analysis.

Table 10.6: Means and standard deviations

Variable	Mean	Standard deviation
Job tenure	55.83	39.07
Social integration	3.51	.428
Frequency of communication	.026	.472
Heterogeneity of experience (industry)	.448	.212
Communication informality	2.20	.319
Heterogeneity of education	.502	.264
Team size	4.37	1.07
Functional heterogeneity	.555	.182
No. of permanent employees (1991)	171.26	179.75

Table 10.7: Multiple regression

Variable	Beta	SE B
Job tenure	-.030	.001
Social integration	.029	.145
Frequency of communication	.301*	.128
Heterogeneity of experience (industry)	-.763**	.317
Communication informality	.417*	.179
Heterogeneity of education	-.099*	.233
Team size	-1.07**	.083
No. of permanent employees (1991)	.249	.108
Functional heterogeneity	.677*	.526

* P<0.05   **P<0.01   ***P<0.001

Figure 10.4: Impact of top management team demography and process on firm sales growth

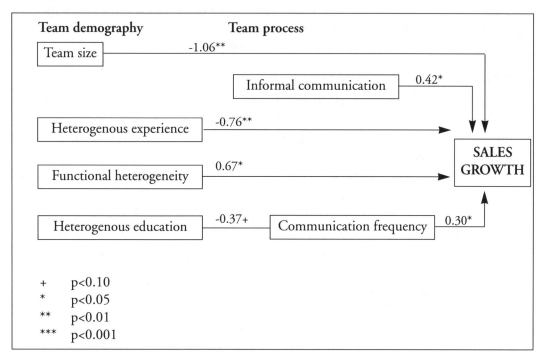

With respect to strategic leadership this research does not support any pure demographic model. In relation to demography variables, team size has a direct negative relationship on sales growth, but the hypothesis that this occurs through negatively impacting on process is not supported. One would have anticipated that larger teams of leaders are arguably less socially integrated and encounter greater difficulties in communicating, which results in poorer performance. Job tenure has no impact on sales growth, or indeed on leadership team processes. One would expect that this demographic variable would be positively related to performance through its impact on team process. The stability and familiarity that tenure should bring would be expected to positively influence social integration and communication and enhance organisational performance. This research suggests that heterogeneity of experience has a direct negative impact on sales growth. An explanation may be that teams with diverse experiential backgrounds encounter difficulties in decision-making which hinders performance. Functional heterogeneity has a direct positive impact on sales growth. Variation in educational backgrounds has a negative impact on frequency of communication, suggesting that the amount of interaction between the members of the TMT is reduced where members of the team have diverse educational backgrounds. Social integration has no impact on sales growth in the Irish context, and our hypothesis that social integration is positively related to organisational performance finds no support. Communication informality and communication frequency have a positive impact on sales growth. As expected, informal communication would appear to facilitate the flow of communication and the number of interactions would appear to be related to performance.

SUMMARY OF KEY PROPOSITIONS

- Leadership may be interpreted in simple terms, such as 'getting others to follow' or interpreted more specifically, for example as 'the use of authority in decision-making'. It may be exercised as an attribute of position, or because of personal knowledge or wisdom.
- Leadership behaviour can be an integral part of a manager's job.
- Leadership activities can be classified into five key areas, i.e. task functions, cultural functions, symbolic functions, political functions and relational functions.
- Leadership trait theory argues that leaders are born and not made. Also known as the 'great man theory', the assumption was that it is possible to identify a unifying set of characteristics that make all great leaders great.
- Behavioural theories argue that specific behaviours differentiate leaders from non-leaders. Critical studies include the Ohio and Michigan studies and the managerial grid.
- Contingency theories are based on the premise that the predicting of leadership success and effectiveness is more complex than the simple isolation of traits or behaviours. Situational variables, or the context in which leadership is occurring, are also viewed as having strong explanatory power.
- Charismatic leadership has been directed at identifying behaviours that differentiate charismatic leaders from their non-charismatic counterparts. Transformational leadership has been influential here.
- Strategic leadership is concerned with those executives who have overall responsibility for the organisation, the top management team, and the impact of their characteristics and behaviours on organisational performance.

DISCUSSION QUESTIONS

1. Leaders are born, not made. Discuss.
2. What are the main problems with trait theory of leadership?
3. What is the managerial grid?
4. What do you understand by contingency theory of leadership?
5. How might an organisation go about adopting the principle of superleadership?
6. What is strategic leadership?

CHAPTER 11

Work Systems and the Impact of Technology

LEARNING OBJECTIVES
- To review schools of thought on work systems.
- To introduce the concept of job design.
- To review Irish and international evidence on job design initiatives.

INTRODUCTION

A critical factor impacting on organisations and organisation behaviour is the work environment within which employees carry out their various tasks and responsibilities. While a complex array of factors impact on the nature of work and work systems in organisations, a critical issue is the nature of the good or service being produced. A production worker in a mass production textile plant clearly encounters a very different work environment from a fashion designer working for an up-market fashion consultancy. Such differences are manifest in a number of areas such as job content, work schedules, nature of supervision and reward systems. A particular and increasingly important influence is the role of technology. Indeed it is almost clichéd to speak of the accelerating rate of technological change and its impact in changing the way work is carried out.

This chapter considers the nature of work systems in organisations and evaluates the impact of technology in impacting on the design of both work systems and individual jobs in organisations.

Our choice of the term 'work systems' is designed to embrace the different components which impact on how work is designed and carried out in organisations. In particular, it incorporates *both* the human and technical aspects of work organisation and job design. All too often one sees these two elements analysed exclusively: the technocratic approach ignoring critical human resource (HR) considerations and the HR approach failing to grasp the impact of technical complexities and realities. The description of work systems provided by Michael Beer and his colleagues (Beer *et al.*, 1985) avoids this pitfall:

> The term work systems . . . refers to a particular combination of job task, technology, skills, management style, and personnel policies and practices. These are seen

as determining how work is organized and managed, how employees will experience work, and how they will perform. (Beer *et al.,* 1985, p. 570)

The work system therefore incorporates the way in which the various tasks in the organisation are structured and impacts on issues such as organisation structure and job design. It reflects the interaction of management style, the technical system, human resources and the organisation's products or services (see Figure 11.1). As noted above, the nature of the goods and services being produced or delivered by an organisation play a key role in determining the characteristics of work systems and job design. For example, organisations whose products require continuous process technology, such as cement production, must operate around-the-clock shift systems and ensure effective ongoing maintenance to prevent a shutdown of the operating technology.

Figure 11.1: Work systems and job design

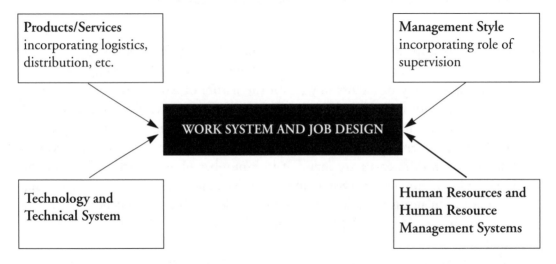

From an employee perspective, a key aspect of work systems is the design of individual jobs which influences job content, autonomy, and the role and extent of supervision. As such, the nature of work systems and, particularly, job design significantly impacts on the extent to which work is intrinsically satisfying for employees. While technical considerations play an important role, decisions on the nature of work systems allow considerable scope for management discretion. Consequently, the particular approaches chosen also provide valuable insights into management beliefs about how employees should be managed, jobs structured and the role of supervision. In this respect it is useful to review different work systems and their implications for organisations and workers.

TRADITIONAL APPROACHES: TASK SPECIALISATION AND THE DIVISION OF LABOUR

While work systems clearly existed in feudal times, it was the effect of technological advancements brought about by the Industrial Revolution which heralded the growth of large-scale organisations concerned with organising labour, capital and technology into effective production systems. In particular, the impact of technology allowed the creation of large-scale production systems (the new factories) which dramatically changed the nature of work. The key changes were that people worked together in much larger numbers and operated technology on a much larger scale than ever before: for example, individual cottage looms were replaced by much larger machines housed in new factory mills. This new technology required a large number of workers to operate effectively. However, change was not confined to issues of scale: the nature of work carried out by these employees also underwent fundamental change. The factory system encouraged a high level of task specialisation: complicated job tasks were broken down into much smaller sub-tasks and technology was used to carry out, or at least aid, many of these sub-tasks. This process is normally referred to as the division of labour, and is at the very core of the emergence of contemporary capitalist society:

> In precapitalist days, most people either directly produced their own subsistence or made some article that could be exchanged for subsistence: peasants grew crops; artisans produced cloth, shoes, implements. But as work became more and more finely divided, the products of work became ever smaller pieces in the total jigsaw puzzle. Individuals did not spin thread or weave cloth but manipulated levers and fed the machinery that did the actual spinning or weaving. A worker in a shoe plant made uppers or lowers or heels, but not shoes. None of these jobs, performed by itself, would have sustained its performer for a single day; and no one of these products could have been exchanged for another product except through the complicated market network. Technology freed men and women from much material want, but it bound them to the workings of the market mechanism. (Heilbroner and Thurow, 1984, p. 22)

The chief exponent of work systems based on the division of labour was Frederick Taylor, the 'father' of scientific management (Taylor, 1947). Taylor's work focused on improving productive efficiency through greater standardisation of work systems and methods. In particular, Taylor encouraged more systematic approaches to the design of jobs and work systems, with specific emphasis on studying the 'best way' of doing particular jobs/tasks and then training workers in the requisite skills, and designing work systems to ensure workers followed this 'one best way'.

Taylor's key principles of scientific management

- Develop a 'science' for every job, based on standardised work rules, motions and equipment/tools.
- Establish a clear division of tasks and responsibilities between management and workers.
- Careful, systematic selection and training of workers.
- Enlist co-operation of workers to operate in line with scientific management principles and provide appropriate economic incentives.

Taylor (1947, p. 109) explained his approach as follows:

First, find, say, ten to fifteen different men who are especially skilled in doing the particular work to be organised; second, study the exact series of elementary operations or motions which each of these men uses in doing the work which is being investigated, as well as the implements each man uses; third, study with a stopwatch the time required to make each of these elementary movements and then select the quickest way of doing each element of the work; fourth, eliminate all false movements, slow movements and useless movements; fifth, after doing away with all unnecessary movements, collect into one series the quickest and best movements, as well as the best implements.

The key characteristics of such 'traditional' approaches to work systems and job design are summarised in Table 11.1. In evaluating the impact of scientific management, one of its important legacies is the notion that work 'planning' (seen as a management task) should be separated from work 'doing' (seen as a worker task). This separation delineated the primary role of management as that of establishing work standards, procedures and methods. Such approaches to work organisation were dominated by the desire to maximise productive efficiency. This efficiency approach, based on Taylorist principles, has been a characteristic of employer approaches to job design since the early years of the twentieth century. Jobs were broken down into simple, repetitive, measurable tasks requiring skills which could be easily acquired through systematic job training. Taylorism helped improve efficiency and promoted a systematic approach to selection, training, work measurement and payment.

While scientific management approaches are often characterised as exclusively a pre-World War Two phenomenon, their widespread application continues today. Huczynski and Buchanan (1991, p. 288) quote the role of an assembly line worker in Toyota, Japan, in the 1980s:

there is only one method of producing goods in the fastest way possible: standardized work. If we don't make the precise motions we're 'taught', it's absolutely impossible to do the required work in the required time. Under such a system, all movements must become mechanical and habitual. (Satosi Kamata, quoted in Huczynski and Buchanan, 1991)

Table 11.1: Key characteristics of traditional approaches to job design

Characteristics	Outcomes
Bureaucratic organisation structure.	Tightly defined jobs.
Top-down management ethos.	Close supervisory control.
Work planning separated from execution.	Minimal employee autonomy or employee participation.
Task fragmentation.	Job specialisation.
Financial incentives based on performance.	Individual payment-by-results payment system.
Focus on 'one best way' of doing jobs.	Rigid training schedule.

An even more recent illustration is provided in the following comment from a recruit in one of the largest chicken processing companies in the United States:

> The scene would have been downright medieval had the technology not been such a marvel. Each bird was hooked by its drumsticks to a shackle line, then carried through a series of precisely engineered turns . . . Each of us was just given one task – a simple, rote, numbingly mechanical motion – and told to do it all day long. (Jesse Katz, quoted in the *Los Angeles Times*, 11 November 1996)

Despite the immense productive efficiencies achieved as a result of the application of scientific management, it is also seen as the source of many of the problems associated with industrial work, such as high levels of labour turnover and absenteeism, and low employee morale and motivation. Steers and Porter (1987, p. 459) offer this analysis:

> Early managerial approaches to job design . . . focused primarily on attempts to simplify an employee's required tasks insofar as possible in order to increase production efficiency. It was felt that, since workers were largely economically motivated, the best way to maximize output was to reduce tasks to their simplest forms and then reward workers with money on the basis of units of output – a piecework incentive plan . . . This approach to simplified job design reached its zenith from a technological standpoint in assembly-line production techniques such as those used by automotive manufacturers . . . On auto assembly lines, in many cases, the average length of 'work cycle' (i.e. the time allowed for an entire 'piece' of work) ranges from 30 seconds to one and a half minutes. This means that workers repeat the same task an average of at least 500 times per day. Such a technique, efficient as it may be, is not without its problems, however. As workers have become better educated and more organized, they are demanding more from their jobs. Not only is

this demand shown in recurrent requests for shorter hours and higher wages, but it is also shown in several undesirable behaviour patterns, such as increased turnover, absenteeism, dissatisfaction and sabotage.

Indeed, one need only reflect on this analysis and the comments of the Toyota and chicken factory workers quoted above to gauge the negative effects of Taylorism. These traditional approaches to work systems and job design reflect a managerial desire to maintain control over the work process and maximise the productive efficiency of the organisation's technical resources. Choices on the organisation of work and the design of jobs were seen as primarily determined by the technical system. Management's role was to ensure that other organisational resources, including employees, were organised in such a way as to facilitate the optimal utilisation of the technical system. This approach often resulted in bureaucratic organisation structures, elaborate procedures and systems, and top-down supervisory control. It also encouraged the fragmentation of jobs into simple, repetitive, measurable tasks which gave post-holders little autonomy. As noted earlier, such approaches to work organisation also reflected managerial assumptions about employees and how they should be managed. Close supervision, detailed work measurement and other types of job control often reflect a managerial belief that employees are inherently lazy and thus need to be coerced to work effectively. Such managerial thinking accords to McGregor's Theory X assumptions on employee motivation. As a result of the negative consequences of scientific management approaches, particularly high employee turnover, absenteeism and monotony, the period since the 1930s has seen extensive experimentation in the area of work systems and job design. Much of this focused on restructuring organisations and jobs to incorporate greater scope for intrinsic motivation and to facilitate greater employee autonomy and involvement. Such approaches reflected more Theory Y assumptions in relation to employee motivation: workers are seen as willing and able to undertake challenging tasks and can do so in a self-directed manner (McGregor, 1960). We now consider these approaches.

THE 'NEW' MODEL: MAKING JOBS MORE INTERESTING

While traditional approaches to work organisation and job design focused on breaking jobs down to improve efficiencies, many of the job re-design initiatives have sought to reconstitute job tasks to larger, 'whole' jobs. This alternative approach was based on the belief that employees gain most satisfaction from the work itself. Two particular themes characterise much of the work on job re-design, namely employee participation and job enrichment.

Let us first consider *employee participation*. We have already seen that scientific management approaches emphasised the separation of work *planning* from *doing*. Planning was seen as a managerial task, while doing was the job of the ordinary worker, whose role was tightly circumscribed to allow little or no scope for employee discretion. Thus,

employee participation was not an issue once the 'one best way' of doing jobs was identified. Their role was to follow, not lead. In contrast, several proponents of job
re-design, identify increased employee participation as a key component of their
approach (see, for example, McGregor, 1960; Beer *et al.*, 1984, 1985). Their rationale
was based on the premise that employees can be motivated by job content and desire
involvement in decisions on their jobs and work systems:

> . . . employees who are involved in decisions about their immediate work will take
> responsibility for reducing costs and improving quality in the same way managers
> are presumed to be able and want to do. (Beer *et al.*, 1985, p. 575)

Increasing employee participation in job-related decisions is a key dimension of
many job re-design initiatives, particularly those based on job enrichment (discussed
below). This type of employee participation differs in extent and orientation from
employee participation in higher-level (e.g. corporate) decision-making. This latter
form of employee participation is often the subject of industrial relations interactions
and may be institutionalised through legislation or collective bargaining arrangements.

Job enrichment is a term which pervades the organisation behaviour literature. It is
concerned with designing jobs in such a way as to provide 'job doers' with the opportunity to gain intrinsic satisfaction from their work:

> Job enrichment is the practice of building motivating factors into job content. This
> job design strategy . . . seeks to expand job content by adding some of the planning
> and evaluating duties normally performed by the manager . . . (Schermerhorn *et al.*,
> 1985, p. 209)

Job enrichment is seen as more comprehensive than other job re-design initiatives
such as job enlargement or job rotation. Job enlargement entails increasing job variety by combining more than one job task so that workers undertake more, different
tasks than previously (Schermerhorn *et al.*, 1985). Job rotation adopts a similar
approach: workers move periodically between different jobs and thus experience a
broader range of job tasks. A criticism of both job enlargement and job rotation
approaches is that they only address task variety rather than level. Workers are
exposed to a greater range of tasks, but the tasks themselves are of a similar level and
require similar skills. Such initiatives are therefore seen as limited in their capacity to
provide greater intrinsic satisfaction: workers may simply find themselves undertaking more boring tasks than previously. Job enrichment is seen as avoiding this pitfall
by increasing job level and challenge to provide greater opportunity for psychological
growth (Gunnigle *et al.*, 1997).

RE-DESIGNING JOBS THROUGH JOB ENRICHMENT

The work of Frederick Herzberg (1968) provides the basis for job re-design initiatives based on job enrichment. This work was considered earlier, in Chapter 4. Herzberg's dual factor theory identified two key sets of factors which impact on employee motivation: 'hygiene' (or maintenance) factors are those associated with job context, such as pay, benefits and working conditions; 'motivator' factors which are more concerned with job content and include issues such as responsibility, achievement and personal growth.

The essence of Herzberg's argument is that hygiene factors of themselves are not an adequate source of employee motivation, although they are very important as a means of reducing dissatisfaction. When this is done, it is the motivator factors which stimulate employee motivation. The job enrichment approach is therefore based on the premise that employees gain most satisfaction from the work itself and that it is the intrinsic outcomes arising from doing meaningful and challenging work that motivates workers to perform well in their jobs.

Given this premise, the challenge for organisations is to develop jobs which increase the capacity for intrinsic satisfaction, challenge and employee involvement. To this end Herzberg established the concept of 'vertical loading', the characteristics of which are outlined in Table 11.2.

Table 11.2: Increasing job challenge through 'vertical loading'

Principle	Motivators involved
A. Removing some controls while retaining accountability.	Responsibility and personal achievement.
B. Increasing the accountability of people for their own work.	Responsibility and recognition.
C. Giving a person complete natural unit of work (module, division, area, etc.)	Responsibility, achievement and recognition.
D. Granting additional authority to an employee in their activity: job freedom.	Responsibility, achievement and recognition.
E. Making periodic reports directly available to the worker rather than to the supervisor.	Internal recognition.
F. Introducing new and more difficult tasks not previously handled.	Growth and learning.
G. Assigning people specific or specialised tasks, enabling them to become experts.	Responsibility, growth and advancement.

Source: Herzberg, 1968

Probably the most comprehensive model of work re-design based on increasing job satisfaction and employee motivation is what has been termed the 'diagnostic approach to job enrichment'. This theory was initially developed by Richard Hackman and Edwin

Lawler in the early 1970s (Hackman and Lawler, 1971), and tested on a sample of telephone company workers. These tests provided favourable results and this work was refined by Hackman and his colleagues throughout the 1970s (see Hackman and Oldham, 1980). This model is summarised in Table 11.3 and comprises four main components:

1. *Critical psychological states:* The key job conditions necessary to promote higher levels of employee satisfaction and motivation.
2. *Core job characteristics:* The key characteristics which need to be built into jobs to allow workers achieve these critical psychological states.
3. *Implementation strategies:* The steps needed to ensure jobs are designed to incorporate the core job characteristics required to adequately enrich jobs.
4. *Personal and work outcomes:* The benefits of such work re-design initiatives for both individual workers and for the organisation.

Table 11.3: Work re-design: the job characteristics model and employee motivation

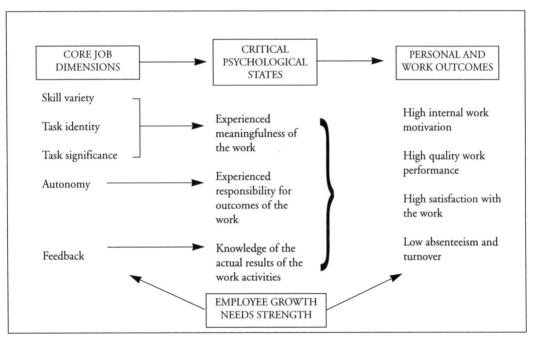

Source: Hackman and Oldham, 1980

At the core of Hackman and Oldham's (1980) approach is the need to design jobs to provide high levels of intrinsic rewards and satisfaction for workers. To this end, three basic conditions (the critical psychological states) were identified as necessary:

1. Work should be meaningful for the 'doer'.
2. 'Doers' should have responsibility for the results.
3. 'Doers' should get feedback on the results.

This approach suggested that it was the design of work and not the characteristics of the employee which had the greatest impact on employee motivation. Hackman and Oldham identified five 'core job characteristics' which needed to be incorporated into job design to increase meaningfulness, responsibility and feedback:

1. *Skill variety:* Extent to which jobs draw on a range of different skills and abilities.
2. *Task identity:* Extent to which a job requires completion of a whole, identifiable piece of work.
3. *Task significance:* Extent to which a job substantially impacts on the work or lives of others either within or outside the organisation.
4. *Autonomy:* Freedom, independence and discretion afforded to the job holder.
5. *Feedback:* Degree to which the job holder receives information on their level of performance, effectiveness, etc.

Having identified the factors necessary to promote satisfaction and intrinsic motivation, the next stage is to incorporate these characteristics into jobs through various job re-design strategies. Hackman and Oldham identify five implementation strategies to increase task variety, significance, identity, and create opportunities for greater autonomy and feedback:

1. *Form natural work groups:* Arrange tasks together to form an identifiable, meaningful cycle of work for employees, e.g. responsibility for single product rather than small components.
2. *Combine tasks:* Group tasks together to form complete jobs.
3. *Establish client relationships:* Establish personal contact between employees and the end user/client.
4. *Vertically load jobs:* Many traditional approaches to job design separate planning and controlling (management functions) from executing (employee's function). Vertically loading jobs means integrating the planning, controlling and executing functions and giving greater responsibility to employees (e.g. responsibility for materials, quality, deadlines and budgetary control).
5. *Open feedback/communication channels:* Ensure maximum communication of job results (e.g. service standards, faults, wastage, market performance, costs).

The espoused advantages of re-designing jobs along the lines of Hackman and Oldham's job enrichment model are summarised thus:

> By re-designing jobs to increase variety, identity, significance, autonomy and feedback, the psychological experience of working is changed . . . individuals experience the work as more meaningful, they feel more responsible for the results, and they

know more about the results of their efforts. These psychological changes lead to many improved work outcomes which have been observed following the re-design of work . . . (Beer *et al.*, 1985, pp. 576–7)

Hackman and Oldham thus argued that these changes have positive long-term benefits for both the organisation and the individual employee, such as increased motivation and improved performance. However, their theory also posits that not all workers are expected to respond favourably to job enrichment initiatives (Hackman *et al.*, 1975). Employee 'growth-need-strength' is considered the most important source of variation in this respect: only those workers with a strong desire for achievement, responsibility and autonomy will be motivated by increased intrinsic satisfaction and hence motivated to perform better. For other workers, these changes may be a source of anxiety and lead to resentment and opposition to job re-design and other changes in the work system.

Table 11.4: Growth needs and worker responses to job enrichment

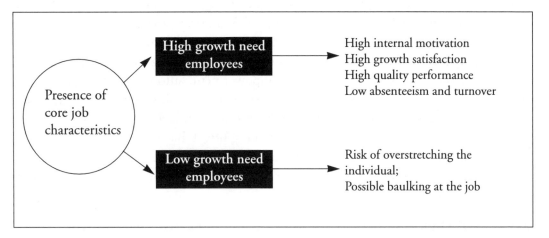

Source: Hackman *et al.*, (1975) 'A new strategy for job enrichment', *California Management Review*, Vol. 7, p. 60

This 'diagnostic approach' to job enrichment has been tested in a variety of work contexts such as banking, medicine and telecommunications. Schermerhorn *et al.* (1985) suggest that while the results have been promising, further research is necessary to refine and support the concept:

At the moment, researchers generally feel that job enrichment is not a universal panacea for job performance and satisfaction problems. They also recognize that job enrichment can fail when job requirements are increased beyond the level of individual capabilities and/or interests. (Schermerhorn *et al.*, 1985, p. 213)

In the Irish context, support for the job enrichment approach is to be found in Blennerhassett's study of motivation among civil service executives (Blennerhassett,

1983). This study found that respondents identified the work itself as the most important potential source of job satisfaction and motivation. However, Blennerhassett also found that respondents rated their jobs very poorly on the core job characteristics of skill variety, identity, significance, etc., and generally felt their jobs allowed little scope for satisfaction, motivation or involvement. Since the study population compared executive and higher executive officers, these findings raise serious questions about the design of jobs in the civil service, and possibly beyond.

IMPROVING THE QUALITY OF WORKING LIFE

While job enrichment clearly has potential to positively impact on how employees experience work, its essential focus on job content has limitations. Numerous factors beyond the particular job and tasks undertaken impact on how employees experience work and working life. These include issues such as working conditions, employee involvement and autonomy, work intensity, and the nature of supervision. The 'quality of working life' (QWL) approach has its origins in developments in the US during the 1960s and 1970s (see, for example, Walton, 1973; Skrovan, 1983). The QWL concept addresses the overall quality of employee experiences in the workplace. While embracing job design as a critical influence on the quality of working life, this approach also addresses broader issues such as employee empowerment, autonomy, participation, justice, working conditions and job security. A particular stimulus for the QWL approach was a desire to improve the quality of work life for employees and avoid what were seen as characteristics of a low quality of working life. Table 11.4 summarises some of the main characteristics of low and high quality work life as identified in the extant literature (see for example Steers and Porter, 1987; Schermerhorn *et al.,* 1985; Schuler and Jackson, 1996).

Table 11.5: High and low quality working life: indicative characteristics

Low quality of working life	High quality of working life
Jobs characterised by low levels of task significance, variety, identity and feedback.	Adequate and fair reward systems.
	Safe and healthy working conditions.
No or little employee involvement.	Opportunity to use personal capabilities
Top-down communications.	Opportunity for personal growth and
Inequitable reward systems.	development.
Inadequate job definition.	Integration into social system of
Poor employment conditions/Hire-and-fire	organisation.
approach.	High labour standards/employee rights.
Discriminatory HR policies.	Pride in relevance and value of work.
Low job security.	Balance between work and non-work roles.

A particular concern of QWL approaches was the desire to increase employee influence and involvement in work organisation and job design. Again this challenges some traditional management assumptions about employees. It involves recognising that employees can and want to make a positive input into organisational decision-making. It assumes that such involvement is valued by employees and results in increased commitment, responsibility and performance. Increased employee influence in work system design also addresses the issue of employee supervision as an aspect of the management role. If employees are to be involved in making decisions about the organisation of work and responsible for the subsequent execution of such decisions, much of the 'control' aspect is removed from the supervisory role. It necessitates a change in attitude to workforce management. Supervisors become less concerned with monitoring and controlling employee performance and more involved in advising and facilitating employees in carrying out their jobs.

This approach requires high levels of commitment and trust from both management and employees. Management must feel confident that employees have the required competence and will use their greater levels of influence positively and to the benefit of the organisation. Employees must be happy that their increased commitment and sense of responsibility will not be abused or exploited by employers.

There are various mechanisms available to encourage increased levels of employee participation in the design and operation of work systems. Possibly the best-known approach is *quality circles*. These are small groups of employees and managers who meet together regularly to consider means of improving quality, productivity or other aspects of work organisation. They are seen as having played an important role in the success of Japanese organisations and have been successfully applied in Western economies, including Ireland.

There are numerous other participative and consultative mechanisms which may be established and can work effectively in an appropriate organisational environment. Creating such an environment has become an important concern for organisations. Past experiences in applying various techniques to improve employee motivation and involvement have demonstrated that these operate best where there is a change in the overall corporate approach. The issue for senior management is how to create a corporate culture whose values, beliefs and practices establish an organisational environment within which employees are highly committed to, and work towards, the achievement of business goals.

THE TREND TOWARDS HIGH PERFORMANCE WORK SYSTEMS
The period since the late 1970s has witnessed dramatic advances in the area of technology and, particularly, information technology. Many of these advances, in both hardware and software, dramatically impact on work systems and the work experience

of employees. Many aspects of these developments also impact directly on our daily work routines: word processing, electronic mail, computerised procurement and stock control, and on-line data access are just some of these developments.

More recent analyses of work organization under such new technologies question the viability of pre-existing theories such as those associated with task specialisation, job enrichment and improving the quality of working life. For example, Buchanan and McCalman (1989) point to the limited impact of job re-design theories and argue that this needs to be remedied:

> It (job design) has tended to be regarded as an isolated management technique aimed at local organisational problems and at individual jobs rather than realising that it must form part of the whole company philosophy, through all levels, if it is to be really successful. (Buchanan and McCalman, 1989)

More specifically, Maccoby (1988) criticises the partial nature job re-design theories and suggests that they provide little insight into how workers can become more involved in 'the management of the business and work independently' (Maccoby, 1988, p. 29; also see Buchanan and Huczynski, 1991). Maccoby points to the significant impact of recent technological developments in altering requisite job skills: increasingly many jobs demand skills such as data processing and retrieval, and increased diagnostic/analytical/problem-solving abilities. These changing job demands impact, in turn, on the training and education requirements in the workforce, often demanding increased levels of education. Maccoby also points to the impact of technology in changing the 'traditional' relationship between management and workers, embracing the potential to increase employee autonomy and teamworking, and also providing opportunities for greater worker interaction with suppliers and customers.

Others point to the impact of heightened competitive pressures in encouraging organisations to continuously improve performance on criteria such as responsiveness, quality, and cost (Kochan *et al.*, 1986; Buchanan, 1994; Roche and Gunnigle, 1995). Currently, a significant source of debate in relation to the nature of work systems and nature of jobs is the increasingly competitive nature of product and service markets. One can point to a number of reasons for this increase in competitive pressures, such as greater trade liberalisation, deregulation in capital, product and service markets, improved communications and transport infrastructures, and greater market penetration by organisations from Asia (see Roche and Gunnigle, 1995). An important aspect of increased competitiveness is the pressure on organisations to increase speed to market, improve quality, and cut costs. Indeed, the period since the 1980s seems to have witnessed some regression in the quality of work life as workers are expected to undertake increased workloads and experience an intensification in the pace of work (see, for example, Delbridge and Turnbull, 1992; Sewell and Wilkinson, 1992). These developments have particularly significant implications for Ireland as a result of its status as a small, open economy which is highly export-oriented and reliant on mobile foreign investment. As a consequence, developments in the world economy have particularly significant implications for Irish organisations, requiring greater responsiveness to competitive pressures in an effort to maintain market share while, at the macro level, efforts are focused on ensuring the business climate remains attractive to foreign investors. Improved human resource utilisation through work systems design is often viewed as an important source of enhanced organisation performance. Of particular significance is the concept of 'high performance work systems' which are viewed as significantly different from preceding innovations in work organisation.

The concept of high performance work systems is very much associated with the new 'high tech' companies of the 1980s, and especially those which located at greenfield sites in attempts to establish a fundamentally different type of organisation and organisation culture (see Lawler, 1978, 1982; Buchanan and McCalman, 1989). The essence of high performance systems appears to lie in the adoption of a culture of continuous improvement and innovation at all levels in the organisation and the implementation of a range of work organisation and human resource systems to sustain and develop this culture, particularly teamworking, quality consciousness, employee autonomy, and flexibility. They are also felt to reflect an increased management emphasis on developing broadly-defined, challenging jobs within more organic, flexible organisation structures:

> The high performance work organisation has a distinctive structure which is designed to provide employees with skills, incentives, information and decision-making responsibilities that will lead to improved organisational performance and facilitate innovation . . . The main aim is to generate high levels of commitment and involvement of employees and managers . . . (Tiernan *et al.*, 1996, p. 113)

High performance work systems are thus seen as embracing much more than a change in the nature of jobs. Rather, they appear to embrace fundamentally different assumptions about organisational structure and orientation, so that all aspects of organisational management are altered to embrace a 'new' culture designed to improve performance and responsiveness through developing a more committed, flexible and skilled workforce. This interpretation is reflected in Buchanan's (1994) conception of high performance work systems:

> The term 'high performance' is used . . . to refer to systemic, integrated developments in the application of autonomous group working, with multiple and related implications beyond the confines of the original technique, invading the domain of supervisory and management structures, and affecting also training and payment systems as well as other aspects of organizational design and working conditions. (Buchanan, 1994, p. 101)

As noted earlier, the primary motive behind the emergence of high performance systems appears to lie in the pressures on organisations to improve the overall competitive position of the organisation. This may explain its prevalence in high tech sectors, especially electronics and software, which tend to be characterised by high levels of market volatility and product innovation. In relating the experience of Digital Equipment Corporation (possibly the most prominent early exemplar of high performance work systems), Perry (1984, p. 191) notes how the company's Connecticut (Enfield) plant sought to respond to increased competition and product change:

> The goal at Enfield was flexibility: the capacity to respond quickly and effectively to an uncertain environment. Traditional ways to handle uncertainty had included the introduction of new procedures, changing the structure, employing more people, and tightening management controls. These strategies simply increased overheads, increased the complexity of the organization and generated more uncertainty. To deal with these issues, management decided to introduce a more participative style of decision-making, multi-skilled operating teams, an innovative rewards system, and systematic career planning and development. The plant manager's review of these changes revealed a 40 per cent reduction in product manufacturing time, a sharp increase in inventory turnover, a reduction of levels of management hierarchy to three, a 38 per cent reduction in standard costs, a 40 per cent reduction in overheads, and equivalent output with half the people and half the space. (Buchanan, 1994, p. 102; summary of more detailed review by Perry, 1984)

High performance work systems are also intimately linked to external standards: the idea that organisational performance should be disaggregated and compared to valid external standards such as cycle time, re-work, labour costs and productivity (Vaill, 1982). The external comparators may be other similar companies or simply other plants within the organisation's portfolio. The growth of total quality management and, particularly, quality accreditation schemes, have been an important catalyst in this regard. For example, companies who trade internationally often seek to achieve ISO 9000 which is a worldwide standard. In Ireland the Quality Mark Scheme, introduced in 1982, is an increasingly important goal. In Ireland the diffusion of a quality orientation is reflected in the fact that by the end of 1993 over 1,000 organisations had been approved to ISO 9000 standard and this number is increasing annually.

The use of external standards is seen as an important factor in differentiating high performance work systems from quality of work life (QWL) and job enrichment approaches. The source of difference lies in the suggestion that QWL and job enrichment approaches stemmed from internal stimuli, primarily related to costs of negative employee behaviours such as absenteeism, turnover and boredom (see Buchanan, 1994). As noted above, the stimulus for high performance work systems related to external pressures to improve competitiveness on dimensions such as lower costs, better quality and greater flexibility. As such, Buchanan (1994) argues that the development of such systems is more strategic than operational reflecting, in particular, managerial desires to improve competitiveness and customer service. Consequently, it is felt that the stimulus for the development of high performance work systems is more enduring than those underpinning previous work re-design initiatives and, thus, more likely to achieve greater practical diffusion and implementation.

KEY HUMAN RESOURCE DIMENSIONS OF HIGH PERFORMANCE WORK SYSTEMS

It is clear from our preceding discussion on high performance work systems that a critical focus of these systems entails the development of new or different approaches to the management of employees as well as in the structure of jobs and systems. These themes pervade both what is termed the high performance literature (Vaill, 1982; Perry, 1984; Lawler, 1986; Buchanan and McCalman, 1989), and, indeed, the 'excellence' literature (Peters and Waterman, 1982; Moss Kanter, 1983; Quinn Mills, 1991). Almost all contributors highlight the need to empower employees in an attempt to make the organisation more effective. While commentators may differ on detail, there is overwhelming support for the use of group or team-based work systems as a means of developing a highly skilled, flexible and motivated workforce within a leaner, flatter, more responsive organisation structure.

This section seeks to identify some of the principal human resource dimensions which appear to characterise high performance work systems.

Some of the most important early work on high performance work systems was undertaken by Ed Lawler in the United States (Lawler, 1978, 1982, 1986). He paid particular attention to newly designed plants which opened on greenfield sites and which were viewed as a new departure in terms of work systems and management style. Lawler sets out a list of organisational design features which, he suggests, significantly increase employee involvement in the workplace and help to improve organisational performance. While Lawler (1982) feels that this list is an ideal and not characteristic of any particular organisation, he argues that it most closely approximates to the configuration of employment practices adopted by companies which located at (or sometimes relocated to) greenfield sites in the United States during the late 1970s and early 1980s. Lawler argued that such new plants were especially likely to embody high employee-involvement work systems and employment practices comprising mutually reinforcing arrangements and practices such as autonomous work groups, quality circles, and gain-sharing plans (Lawler, 1978, 1982, 1986). He describes the all-prevailing nature of changes in work systems and human resource practices in these new plants as follows:

... almost no aspect of the organisation has been left untouched. The reward systems, the structure, the physical layout, the personnel management system and the nature of jobs have all been changed and in significant ways. (Lawler, 1978, pp. 6–7)

Table 11.6: Organisational characteristics of high performance, high involvement work systems

Organisational structure	Flat and lean. Enterprise-oriented. Team-based. Participative structure; councils, fora.
Job design	Job enrichment. Autonomous teams/work groups.
Information system	Open flow. Work/job focus. Decentralised and team/group-based. Participatively established goals/standards.
Career system	Career tracks/ladders/counselling. Open job posting.
Selection	'Realistic' job preview. Team/group-based. Potential- and process-skill oriented.
Training	Strong commitment and investment. Peer training. 'Economic' education. Interpersonal skills.
Reward system	Open. Skill-based. Gain-sharing/share ownership. Flexible benefits. All salary/egalitarian.
Personnel policies	Employment tenure commitments. Participatively established through representative group(s).
Physical layout	Based on organisational structure. Egalitarian. Safe and pleasant.

Source: Adapted from Lawler, 1982

Lawler thus argues that increased employee involvement levels and enhanced organisational performance outcomes are most likely to occur in these new plants because of their capacity to establish a totally 'congruent system' at the outset and to reinforce this desired approach through the selection of people who are 'compatible' with the new system. In the British context, a study of work practices (Income Data Services, 1984) in four greenfield establishments also found evidence of innovation in work practices and identified six common features of greenfield sites:

1. Reduced number of management tiers.
2. Abolition of the roles of traditional supervisors and enhanced status of first-line managers.
3. Minimisation of status differentials between employee grades.
4. Greater devolution of responsibility for execution of work/tasks to employee groups.
5. Greater dissemination of information on work-related matters.
6. Greater emphasis on direct communication with employees through group meetings rather than trade unions

Beaumont and Townley (1985) suggest that the key managerial concern in establishing at a greenfield site is related to the objective of introducing new methods of work organisation or new work practices, and argue that the essential attribute or component of the term 'greenfield site' is innovatory work practices and arrangements. They suggest that such characteristics of greenfield sites reflect a management emphasis which is predominantly concerned with the achievement and maintenance of maximum flexibility in operations.

In evaluating the impact of high performance work systems, it is useful to reflect on the extent to which this development represents a fundamentally new approach to the design of jobs and work systems. Huczynski and Buchanan (1991) address this issue and identify the following distinctions between the high performance work systems (HPWS) approach of the 1990s and the quality of work life (QWL) approach of the 1960s and 1970s:

More strategic focus: it is argued that the HPWS approach seeks to improve organisational competitiveness through increased flexibility and quality, while the QWL approach primarily concentrated on achieving reductions in absenteeism and turnover.

Focus on performance rather than job experience: The HPWS approach has a strong focus on performance criteria: increased employee autonomy is seen as leading to increased employee competence/skills, better decision-making, greater flexibility/adaptability and better use of technology. In contrast, the major rationale of the QWL approach was based on improving the job experience of employees: increased autonomy was seen as leading to increased worker satisfaction and a better job experience.

Major change in management style: The HPWS approach is seen as requiring a fundamental overhaul of management style, requiring major cultural change and redefinition of the role of management, from top management down. The QWL approach appeared to adopt a more limited approach, involving only a re-orientation in the role of first line supervisors.

Long-term comprehensive strategy: The HPWS approach is seen as a major change initiative affecting the whole organisation and involving a long-term commitment by all parties. The QWL approach tended to be more of a quick fix applied to isolated and problematic work groups.

Representative of strategic human resource management: Consistent with the argument that the 1980s and 1990s witnessed a move from reactive/operational personnel management to strategic human resource management (HRM), it is argued that HPWS is a key element of strategic HRM while QWL is more of a personnel administration technique. (Huczynski and Buchanan, 1991, p. 86)

In essence it appears that while the high performance concept has its roots in the individualistic and group approaches to job restructuring of previous decades, there is a shift in orientation away from job enlargement, job enrichment and quality circles towards a more all-inclusive approach, linking individual contributions, group performance and competitive advantage, which, according to Buchanan and McCalman (1989), affords to these traditional strategies a new acceptability. It also appears that high performance work systems reflect a strategic shift in approaches to workforce management, and may serve to encourage a wider understanding of the applications of traditional job restructuring techniques, variations of which have enjoyed a renaissance in recent times.

SOME IRISH EVIDENCE

In Ireland, the first prominent examples of organisations which sought to develop high performance work systems along the lines described above, came from the ranks of firms which had experimented with such systems elsewhere. These were mostly US 'high tech' companies such as Digital, Apple and Amdahl. More recently we have seen greater diversity in the range of companies undertaking such initiatives. One of the mostly widely quoted examples is that of Bord na Mona (see O'Connor, 1995; Magee, 1991). Here we find a semi-state company which, by the 1980s, faced severe competitive problems, particularly in relation to high costs, poor productivity and a pressing need to improve quality, performance and employee relations (Magee, 1991). In an attempt to deal with these issues, the company undertook a number of radical initiatives. First, a new multi-disciplinary and team-based management structure was established. The initial challenge was to reduce costs, which was addressed by a major redundancy programme which saw 2,500 workers (out of approximately 5,000) leave the company. After this, management initiated a more fundamental overhaul:

It was recognised by everyone concerned . . . that cost-cutting through redundancy would not be enough. We had to change our work practices at the same time. We knew that a fundamental restructuring of how we did our business had to be undertaken to create flexibility in adapting to changing markets, to improve productivity and to improve our competitive position. After extensive negotiation, the 'enterprise scheme' was introduced with the full agreement and co-operation of all parties. The Bord na Mona enterprise scheme allows our staff to form their own autonomous enterprise units, which are team based and where the unit's earnings are directly related to performance and productivity. *Our workers have become their own bosses.* (O'Connor, 1995, p. 116)

The introduction of autonomous work groups (AWGs) meant that instead of working in isolation, the workers became team members. Leaders were selected for these AWGs, which then assumed responsibility and authority for the completion of tasks (Tiernan *et al.*, 1996). In addition to the establishment of AWGs, Bord na Mona also reduced the number of levels in the management hierarchy. It seems that the results of these various changes have been extremely positive. Edward O'Connor, then Managing Director of the company, summed up the experience as follows:

The spirit of enterprise this has brought into Bord na Mona has increased productivity per worker in a way that is truly amazing. Our productivity has increased by 75 per cent. Our people now make their own decisions and take their own risks. The series of work groups or enterprise units that have been set up have different structures, but essentially Bord na Mona supplies them with services and they produce quality peat, at a price which is agreed in advance. These are people who, formerly, did what they were told to do, got paid whether or not peat was produced, whether the sun shone all summer or whether it rained all the time . . . The new work practices and systems we have introduced amount to nothing less than a fundamental restructuring of the organisation. (O'Connor, 1995, p. 117)

HIGH PERFORMANCE WORK SYSTEMS AND WORKING LIFE

While much of the organisation behaviour literature on high performance work systems inevitably emphasises its human resource dimensions, it is important to note that these approaches also incorporate technical changes in the work process. In this respect two critical techniques which are commonly used are 'just-in-time' and statistical process control. Just-in-time (JIT) approaches focus on reducing waste, with particular emphasis on eliminating inventories (of materials, work in progress and finished goods). Statistical process control (SPC) approaches seek to apply rigorous statistical analysis of quality and performance levels to improve performance.

In evaluating the impact of high performance work systems which incorporate JIT and SPC, an issue of particular significance is their impact on the work experience of employees. This involves the coupling of initiatives to improve worker participation and autonomy, with particular management techniques designed to improve quality and productivity, particularly just-in-time manufacturing systems and statistical process control. The combination of JIT and SPC approaches with initiatives to increased employee involvement and autonomy are often seen as the essence of moves towards *total quality management* or *world class manufacturing* (see Gunnigle *et al.*, 1995). The introduction of these initiatives is generally based on the premise that increased employee involvement/autonomy is consistent with the use of JIT, SPC or related techniques. Indeed, the argument that employee involvement/autonomy mutually complements the use of SPC and JIT is often a key selling point in encouraging employees to co-operate in the introduction of such approaches.

However, it should be pointed out that this is not necessarily the case (see discussion below on the automobile industry). In her incisive review of the implications of techniques such as JIT and SPC for employees and their work experience, Klein (1989) argues that such changes in production systems do not necessarily make for a more empowered workforce:

In Japan . . . where JIT and SPC have been used most comprehensively, employees are routinely organized into teams, but their involvement in workplace reform is typically restricted to suggestions for process improvement through structured quality control circles or *kaizen* groups. Individual Japanese workers have unprecedented responsibility. Yet it is hard to think of them exercising genuine autonomy, that is, in the sense of independent self-management.

To be sure, managers can – and must – involve workers in workplace decisions. But the attack on waste, it must be understood, inevitably means more and more strictures on a worker's time and action. Our conventional Western notions of worker self-management on the factory floor are often sadly incompatible with the schedules, nature of supervision and reward systems. A particular and increasingly important influence is the role of technology. Indeed it is almost clichéd to speak of the accelerating rate of technological change and its impact in changing the way work is carried out. (Klein, 1989, p. 60)

Using examples from both the US and Japan, Klein argues that increased pressures and constraints on workers is a common by-product of such manufacturing reforms. While allowing for greater employee involvement and autonomy than traditional assembly line systems, they are not conducive to the high levels of employee empowerment often thought to accompany such manufacturing reform and the move to high performance work systems:

True, under JIT and SPC, employees become more self-managing than in a command-and-control factory. They investigate process improvements and monitor quality themselves; they consequently enjoy immediate, impartial feedback regarding their own performance . . . They also gain a better understanding of all elements of the manufacturing process.

On the other hand, the reform process that ushers in JIT and SPC is meant to *eliminate all variations within production* and therefore requires strict adherence to rigid methods and procedures. Within JIT, workers must meet set cycle times; with SPC, they must follow prescribed problem-solving methods. In their pure forms, then, JIT and SPC can turn workers into extensions of a system no less demanding than a busy assembly line. They can push workers to the wall. (Klein, 1989, p. 61)

This analysis thus questions many aspects of the thesis that high performance work systems necessarily contribute to an improved work experience. In particular, Klein (1989) points to important aspects of the work experience which may be lost as a result of recent manufacturing reforms using SPC and JIT, namely:

1. *individual autonomy:* which may be reduced due to the elimination of inventories under JIT, resulting in less slack or idle time which in turn lessens the opportunity for workers to discuss issues, evaluate changes and make suggestions;
2. *team autonomy:* may be reduced because of the greater interdependency between groups, due to the absence of buffer inventories with resulting work pressures reducing the time available to consider broader changes in the work process or system;
3. *ability to influence work methods:* may be reduced because SPC sets strict guidelines for working methods and procedures.

However, this analysis does not necessarily mean that the adoption of high performance work systems which adopt techniques such as JIT and SPC do not positively impact on the job experience of workers. Rather, it points to the fact that these techniques and systems may be applied in differing ways. Thus, the issue of management choice is important. Klein (1989) argues that the key to improving employee involvement and autonomy while instigating high performance work systems is to provide for greater collaboration between teams and to allow greater opportunity for teams and individuals to propose and evaluate suggestions for changes in the work process and in the conduct of different jobs. Klein offers other suggestions to mitigate some of the more unfavourable effects of JIT and SPC:

1. Rethink zero inventory: it is argued that the maintenance of some inventory is more sensible for a number of reasons, such as reduced employee stress, increased individual and team involvement, better quality of work life and as an insurance against system breakdown.
2. Emphasise work flow rather than pace: here Klein suggests that while JIT reduces worker ability to control work pace, the adoption of a kanban system will help improve individual initiative and individual and team communications by allowing

workers to answer to each other rather than to the output of the system or to supervisors.

3. Focus on task design not execution: based on the argument that task design allows greater opportunity for team involvement (once designed, there may be little capacity for changes to the mode of operation).

4. Give workers the right to move and choose (within limits): allow greater autonomy to workers to move between tasks, and to teams in making decisions on issues such as inter-changeability and working time (including breaks).

5. Allow for workplace management of quality and resources: give teams greater discretion (within budget) in making decisions on resource procurement and allocation, personnel selection and training, use of support services, rejection of defective materials and capacity to stop output of poor quality goods.

A final and critical issue for organisations considering the adoption of high performance work systems, is the issue of employee expectations. It is important to avoid the common pitfall of promising more than can be delivered in terms of employee involvement and autonomy, which can quickly lead to widespread disillusionment among employees. One approach, suggested by Klein, is to introduce SPC or JIT approaches before worker participation programmes. It felt that this may remove confusion and reduce the likelihood of unrealised worker expectations:

> If, for example, worker participation programs are implemented after JIT, there will be less confusion: workers will then not be invited to imagine greater freedom just when the new process takes freedom away. Even if some workers participate in the design of the system, this doesn't necessarily mean the plant will be operated by worker teams from the start. Besides, it is the task of managers, as always, to prepare the ground. They ought not to promise workers autonomy when they mean them to deliver an unprecedented degree of co-operation. (Klein, 1989, p. 66)

A LONGITUDINAL PERSPECTIVE ON WORK SYSTEMS AND TECHNOLOGY IN THE AUTOMOBILE INDUSTRY

So far in this chapter we have considered different approaches to the design of jobs and work systems, notably those associated with scientific management, job enrichment, quality of work life and high performance work systems. In so doing we have noted the impact of technological changes in critically impacting on work systems and job content. However, our perspective has primarily focused on micro level developments at the level of the enterprise. It is therefore useful to conclude our analysis with a broader macro level analysis which considers developments in the technological environment and their impact on work systems. In so doing, particular emphasis is placed on contemporary developments, particularly the growth of 'lean production' techniques and quality improvement.

Fordism: the zenith of mass production

We have seen earlier in this chapter how developments in technology heralded what is often termed the Industrial Revolution, beginning in late eighteenth-century Britain. Heilbroner and Thurow (1984) point out that this phase actually entailed a series of 'technological revolutions' whereby the means of production of different items underwent fundamental change. The industries affected were, firstly, spinning and weaving (late 1700s to early 1800s), then rail, shipping, steel, agricultural machinery and chemicals (mid-1800s) and, finally, automobiles, electricity, and consumer durables (early 1900s).

The move towards mass production represented a fundamental change from earlier craft-based methods of production. No industry typified the growth of mass production better than automobiles, and the chief exponent of this approach was Henry Ford and the Ford motor company. It is suggested that the automobile industry was *the* mass production industry (Sweeney, 1997). It was based predominantly on scientific management principles, producing a limited range of models in very large volumes, in massive assembly plants, using rigid production methods whereby workers performed a series of highly specialised repetitive tasks at high speed. In a study by Womack *et al.* (1990), the main characteristics of Fordism are set out as follows:

- The complete and consistent interchangeability of parts and the simplicity of attaching them to each other.
- The fragmentation of production with 'interchangeable' workers performing work cycles of one to two minutes.
- The extreme horizontal division of labour, both in production work and indirect functions such as preparation, quality control, maintenance and repair.
- The use of dedicated machinery that can only do one task at a time and which embodies skills formerly carried out by craft workers.
- The vertical integration of production, with parts and components being manufactured in-house and the manufacture of standardised products with minimum variation.

This same study suggests that mass production in the United States had reached its heyday by the mid-1950s: three corporations (Ford, General Motors and Chrysler) and six models accounted for the overwhelming majority of all car sales. The demise of Fordism appears to stem from two sources. First, the growth of greater diversity in consumer demand (and also in supply by European manufacturers) lessened the demand for 'standard' products. However, another reason for the demise of mass-produced automobiles was related to human resource considerations. Workers were becoming increasingly disillusioned with the jobs they were asked to carry out and this was often manifested in industrial conflict. These labour pressures led to increased pay levels and reduced working hours. However, discontent associated with auto assembly often continued (Womack *et al.*, 1990; *European Industrial Relations Review*, 1992). A good example was the UK where motor company strikes were an important characteristic of industrial relations during the 1960s and 1970s.

Lean production and the impact of Toyotism

In 1990 researchers at the Massachusetts Institute of Technology (MIT) published the results of one of the largest studies undertaken in the automobile or any other industry (Womack *et al.*, 1990). The study looked at ninety assembly plants in seventeen countries. This study concluded that the industrial world is experiencing the most revolutionary change since the growth of mass production as Japanese-inspired 'lean production techniques begin to replace conventional means of mass production' (*European Industrial Relations Review*, 1992, p. 13).

The focus on Japanese 'advantage' in the auto sector began in the 1960s and was largely attributed to lower labour costs which gave a low-cost advantage to Japanese cars. However, the significant impact of Japanese competitors in the auto industry has been their ability to develop and sustain cost and quality advantages over time and, most particularly, in foreign plants in countries such as the US and UK. The fact that these Japanese plants are located in the same regions as European and US auto manufacturers has served to focus attention on Japanese production methods and work systems, such as just-in-time and *kaizen* (continuous improvement).

In their attempt to discern the source of Japanese advantage, the MIT study concluded that their success was due primarily to what they termed 'lean production'. This term was used to indicate that it involved using less of almost everything when compared to mass production: half the human effort, half the manufacturing space, half the investment in tools and half the engineering effort (Womack *et al.,* 1990). Additional advantages noted in the study included the need to carry lower inventory (less than half of that associated with conventional mass production), a lower level of defects and greater product variety. The development of lean production is attributed to Eiji Toyota. It is reported that after a visit to a Ford assembly plant in Detroit, Eiji concluded that the methods used were excessively wasteful and that none of the indirect workers added value to the product. Together with his chief engineer, Taiichi Ohno, they set about developing the system which became known as lean production. The MIT study identified the main characteristics of lean production or Toyotism as follows:

- Workers are organised into teams with a leader who, unlike the mass production foreman, undertakes assembly work and fills in for absent workers. Teams are given responsibility for the functions previously carried out by indirect workers such as simple machine maintenance, quality control, materials ordering and clearing up the work area.

- There is a 'zero defect' approach to production involving an effective system for immediately detecting defects and problems, and tracing them to their root cause to make sure they do not recur. As the process is perfected almost no 'rework' is necessary.
- 'Lean' product development techniques, involving strong design team leadership, personnel continuity of development teams, and an emphasis on communications and 'simultaneous development', drastically reduce the time and effort involved in manufacturing.
- Production in small batches in order to eliminate the costs of high inventories of finished parts required by mass production systems. Cars are built to specific order, with the assistance of flexible machinery, and parts are delivered on a just-in-time basis.
- An absence of vertical integration. Instead, production of parts and components is rationalised through a hierarchy of suppliers. Thus, 'first tier' suppliers are responsible for working as an integral part of the development team, while 'second tier' suppliers are responsible for making the components required for the first tier supplier.

Lean production: a positive work experience?

In evaluating the job experience of workers under lean production, we find some divided opinions. The MIT study suggests that while lean production requires very high effort levels from workers, it represents a more positive work experience than conventional mass production. The essence of the MIT argument is that lean production contrasts the mind-numbing stress of mass production by providing workers with the skills to exercise greater control over their work environment. This, they argue, leads to 'creative tension' at work which requires high effort levels but also gives workers numerous ways to deal with work problems and challenges (Womack *et al.*, 1990; *European Industrial Relations Review*, 1992). The MIT study also compares lean production to what they term the 'neocraftmanship' model associated with some Swedish assembly plants. Again, they find that lean production systems provide a more rewarding and challenging work experience than that found in plants such as Volvo's Uddevalla facility which the MIT study categorises as a very limited form of job rotation. In the Irish context, Mooney (1988) argues that work systems modelled around lean production principles represent a jettisoning of traditional approaches towards a more positive perspective on employees as 'human assets'.

Not everyone agrees with this benign analysis of the work experience under lean production. Earlier in this chapter we quoted an assembly line worker in Toyota (Japan) who emphasised the high pace and repetitive nature of the work undertaken (Kamata, 1984). Similarly, Delbridge and Turnbull (1992), in investigating one of the cornerstones of lean production, namely just-in-time (JIT) manufacturing systems, suggest that such systems can negatively impact on the job experience of employees:

> Evidence from both Britain and America suggests that the experience of work under a JIT system involves work intensification, very little autonomy for the individual, a more complete system of management control and a concomitant decline in trade union (and worker) bargaining power. Team working, job rotation and flexibility are not the means of releasing the untapped reserves of human resourcefulness by increasing employee commitment, participation and involvement . . . Rather they are the tools of work intensification and heightened management control. The emphasis is almost exclusively on the management, or more precisely the maximization, of human resources, involving an instrumental approach which is coherently integrated into corporate business strategy . . . this is not so much a question of choice as necessity, since the JIT system increases the dependency of management on the workforce by removing all elements of slack or waste in the system. (Delbridge and Turnbull, 1992, p. 58)

In a review based on the experiences of the Swedish automobile industry, Berggren (1990) questions the MIT argument that lean production is fundamentally different from mass production. This study compares Japanese lean production systems with Swedish 'whole car' manufacturing systems. Berggren argues that lean production essentially represents another stage in the evolution of mass production since it entails many of the core characteristics of that system: pre-defined work processes, short job-cycles, repetitive tasks and intense supervision. He also points to the intense demands which lean production places on workers in areas such as working time, flexibility, effort levels and attendance. Berggren concludes that the further one moves away from assembly line work systems, the greater the improvements in terms of the job experience of workers (on dimensions such as job satisfaction, challenge, stress and employee involvement). Clearly such 'whole job' systems are very different from assembly line systems in their rejection of task fragmentation and job specialisation.

This latter argument in relation to whole job systems versus assembly systems brings us to a traditional dilemma in the area of job and work system design, namely that concerning cost and profits. We have earlier noted that the 1990s have been characterised by increased competitive pressures on organisations, such as the need to concurrently reduce costs and improve quality and service, the need to reduce cycle times and speed to market, and the need to be more responsive to market trends. All these pressures combine to encourage management to seek improvements in their internal operating systems on dimensions such as costs, speed, quality and flexibility. While on occasion these pressures may serve to improve the job experience of workers in areas such as job content and employee involvement, it is probably more likely to lead to greater job pressures on workers. This is particularly the case in highly competitive sectors where labour costs represent a high proportion of total production costs. In Berggren's study of the automobile industry, he concedes that the long-term viability of the Swedish 'whole car' manufacturing system is dependent not on the quality of the job experience but rather on the extent to which it can be reconciled with profitability. If lean production systems can provide cars at lower cost and equal or better quality then 'whole car' systems cannot compete with assembly line systems.

THE CHOICE FACING ORGANISATIONS

This chapter has considered the nature of work systems in organisations and the impact of technological developments on the design of work systems and individual jobs. Decisions on the nature of work systems are related to both broader environmental factors impacting on the organisation (such as technology and market trends) and to corporate choices about the nature and role of the organisation. Decisions on work systems represent a critical aspect of human resource management in organisations. It influences key areas such as organisational structure, management style, employee motivation and reward systems. While environmental factors exercise a key influence, top management still retain considerable discretion in making choices on the nature of work systems. Indeed, the growth in sophistication and flexibility of information technology may allow employers greater scope to introduce changes in work organisation.

SUMMARY OF KEY PROPOSITIONS

- An organisation's work system incorporates the way in which various tasks are organised and carried out. It encompasses both human and technical aspects and critically impacts on the nature of the work environment, job content and management style.
- From a worker perspective, a key dimension of the work system is the design of individual jobs which determines issues such as job content, skill level, extent of autonomy and involvement and the role of supervision.
- The Industrial Revolution witnessed a change from craft-based production systems to larger scale mass production systems through what became termed the factory system. This system was based on a division of labour based on task specialisation: jobs were broken down into small sub-tasks which were comparatively easy to learn.
- Taylor developed the concept of scientific management which embraced a high division of labour. Scientific management emphasised the achievement of high levels of productive efficiency through the standardization of work methods. It emphasised the identification of the best way of doing jobs and then the careful selection, training and reward of workers who followed this 'one best way'.
- A critical characteristic of scientific management was the separation of work *planning* (a management task) from work *doing* (an employee task).

- While scientific management led to significant improvements in performance, it was also identified as a source of workforce problems, particularly high levels of labour turnover and absenteeism and low employee morale and motivation. These problems were felt to stem from the repetitive and monotonous nature of highly specialised jobs under scientific management.
- The negative effects associated with scientific management led researchers and practitioners to search for ways to make jobs more satisfying and challenging for workers. Such approaches were generally termed 'job re-design' and invariably embraced attempts to reconstitute different jobs tasks into larger 'whole' jobs.
- The most notable job re-design initiative was termed the 'diagnostic approach to job enrichment'. This model, developed by Richard Hackman and Edwin Lawler and based on Frederick Herzberg's work on employee motivation, was grounded on the premise that workers gain most satisfaction from work itself: it was therefore the intrinsic outcomes which arise from undertaking meaningful and challenging jobs which were seen as motivating workers to perform well.
- Using this premise, the researchers Richard Hackman and Greg Oldham developed their widely influential 'job characteristics model' which had four main components: critical psychological states, that is the key job conditions necessary to promote higher levels of employee satisfaction and motivation; core job characteristics, which must be built in to jobs to allow workers achieve the 'critical psychological states'; implementation strategies necessary to ensure jobs are designed to incorporate the 'core job characteristics'; and the personal and work outcomes felt to accrue to individual workers and to organisations as a result of undertaking such job re-design initiatives.
- Three fundamental principles underpin the job characteristics model, namely that work should be meaningful for employees and they should have responsibility for the results of their work and also get feedback on these results.
- A criticism of the job characteristics model was its predominant focus on job content. Many commentators argued that broader organisational considerations should be taken into account in determining the 'total work experience'. This was the basis for what became know as the quality of work life (QWL) movement which sought to improve the quality of work life for employees on dimensions such as autonomy and participation, working conditions, job security and social justice.
- More recently the predominant research focus has switched to the development of what is termed high performance work systems (HPWS). The HPWS approach is seen as more all-embracing than either job enrichment or QWL approaches. Its development appears to stem from two key sources: the increased competitive pressures faced by organisations, and the impact of technological developments, particularly information technology, in changing the nature of organisations and jobs.

- The essence of HPWS appears to lie in the adoption of a culture of continuous improvement and innovation at all levels in the organisation and the implementation of a range of work organisation and human resource systems to sustain and develop this culture, particularly teamworking, quality enhancement, employee autonomy, and flexibility. This approach was initially associated with the new 'high tech' companies of the 1980s, particularly those which located at greenfield sites in attempts to establish a fundamentally different type of organisation and organisation culture.

- HPWS are therefore seen as embracing much more than a change in the nature of jobs. Rather, they are seen as incorporating fundamentally different assumptions about organisational structure and orientation, so that all aspects of organisational management are altered to embrace a new culture designed to improve performance and responsiveness through developing a more committed, flexible and skilled workforce.

- HPWS approaches commonly involve the application of specific management techniques designed to improve performance, quality and cost-effectiveness. The two most commonly used techniques are just-in-time (JIT), designed to eliminate inventories, and statistical process control (SPC), designed to improve quality and performance.

- A common criticism of the HPWS literature is the assumption that adoption of techniques such as JIT and SPC are invariably conducive to increased employee involvement and autonomy. There is considerable research evidence which indicates that this is not necessarily the case. In some ways JIT and SPC can act to limit or reduce employee involvement and discretion. If such techniques are to facilitate an improved work experience for employees, management must carefully consider how these systems are implemented and encourage greater individual and team collaboration in the work process.

- In evaluating alternative work systems, a useful example is the automobile industry. Often termed the first mass production industry, it has in recent decades undergone immense transformation. Companies in this sector appear to be moving away from conventional mass production assembly for both market and human resource reasons. However, different trends are discernible in this change. Of particular note is the emergence of Japanese lean production systems which a recent study has labelled 'the most revolutionary change since Henry Ford's assembly line'. An alternative development in the industry has been a move away from assembly line approaches to 'whole car' systems using autonomous or partially autonomous work teams, an approach pioneered largely by Volvo in Sweden.

- The research evidence on the implications of these new developments for employees is mixed. Some commentators argue that while these approaches are more demand-

257

ing in terms of worker effort they also provide greater opportunity and challenge for workers in influencing the work system. Others are not so sure and point to the negative implications of new work systems such as those based on just-in-time manufacturing and statistical process control. In particular they point to the increased pace and intensity of work, the greater stress on individual workers and the greater surveillance of work performance.

- These different perspectives highlight a traditional dilemma in the choice of work systems, namely the often contrasting pressures for low costs and high output on the one hand, and the desire to create a positive work system and working environment on the other hand. In an era of increasing competitiveness and global competition, it is difficult to see a fruitful reconciliation of these conflicting pressures, particularly in industrial sectors which are exposed to high levels of market competition and volatility.

DISCUSSION QUESTIONS

1. 'Management choices concerning work systems design will have a strong effect on worker satisfaction and performance'. Discuss.
2. Critically evaluate the impact of the Industrial Revolution on the development of work systems.
3a. What do we mean by scientific management?
3b. How has scientific management affected the design of work systems in organisations?
4. Compare and contrast high performance work systems and job enrichment.
5a. Indicate what you see as the main characteristics of so-called high performance work systems (HPWS).
5b. What do you feel have been the main factors which stimulated the development of HPWS?

CHAPTER 12

Conflict in Organisations

LEARNING OBJECTIVES
- To consider the types of conflict that take place in organisational settings.
- To identify some of the key sources of conflict in organisations.
- To explain four key perspectives on organisational conflict.
- To explore strike activity in Ireland in the context of organisational conflict.
- To consider some of the ways in which conflict at work can be managed and resolved.

INTRODUCTION

Conflict is one of the most emotive aspects of organisational behaviour. It is a demanding area for managers to deal with, requiring considerable understanding and inter-personal skills. Conflict occurs whenever disagreement exists in a social situation over issues of substance or emotional discord (Schermerhorn *et al.*, 1985). Conflict is therefore a social process involving more than one person. In this text we are concerned primarily with 'structurally derived conflict' (Huczynski and Buchanan, 1991): that is, conflict that arises as a result of the operation and structure of organisations. When individual or group interests clash, as they inevitably will, given the range and diversity of individual and group interests in organisations, it is likely that conflict will occur on occasion. The most visible organisational manifestation is probably industrial relations conflict, such as a strike or 'go-slow'. However, conflict can take numerous other forms including conflicts between departments or work-groups; or individual, inter-personal conflict. Many managers tend to regard conflict as negative. However, conflict can have strong positive dimensions; such as providing a means to articulate grievances and stimulate changes in areas such as work practices or management regulation.

A DEFINITION OF CONFLICT

There are many different ways that we can view conflict. Conflict can be evaluated positively or negatively, seen as rational or irrational, worthwhile or fruitless. Whatever the perspective adopted, it is possible to identify overall definitions of organisational conflict that will help to clarify the terms of reference relating to conflict. From certain psychological perspectives, conflict can be defined as either intrapersonal or inter-personal. These definitions imply that there are certain inner conflicts that an individual can experience which do not involve other individuals or groups. Inner conflicts can give rise to other types of conflict, but in themselves are not interactive in nature. Inner conflict can result in stress, uncertainty, anxiety or with positive decisions and effective individual development. This chapter focuses on inter-personal conflict which defines a process that involves two or more people or groups. This type of conflict can be described as a process which begins when one party perceives that another party has frustrated (or is about to frustrate) some concern of theirs (e.g. Thomas, 1976).

Conflict can occur in organisations, then, for a wide variety of different reasons. For example, conflict is more likely to arise when one individual feels that someone else is creating obstacles against the achievement of his or her objectives; when managers pursue different goals than the employees for whom they are responsible; when two departments get involved in a competition over scarce resources; when various agreements are violated; or when basic rights within organisational systems are not taken into account. In analysing conflict in organisations, it is important to be aware of the potential sources which give rise to conflict situations.

SOURCES OF CONFLICT IN ORGANISATIONS

In studying the nature of conflict in organisations, it is important that we attempt to identify possible sources of conflict. It is also important to acknowledge that conflict is 'normal' in organisations, although, of course, excessive levels of conflict are undesirable. Huczynski and Buchanan (1991) identify five major sources of conflict in organisations:

- The employment relationship.
- Competition over scarce resources.
- Ambiguity over responsibility or authority.
- Interdependence.
- Differentiation.

Commentators such as Allen (1971) argue that the structure of the *employment relationship*, which emphasises employer needs for productivity, cost-effectiveness and change, is often at odds with employee needs for security, adequate rewards and opportunity for personal growth. It is therefore to be expected that in this 'labour for pay' exchange, interests will clash and result in conflict on occasion (e.g. pay disputes). However, the potential conflict is not simply confined to the 'financial exchange' dimension. The employment relationship also requires the ongoing exercise of employer/managerial authority over employees in the workplace on issues such as working time, work flow and task allocation (Reed, 1989). Again, some degree of conflict here is inevitable as differing interests clash and seek to establish their positions (e.g. disputes over demarcation or work loads).

Another obvious and significant source of conflict in organisations is that which may occur in relation to *resource allocation* decisions. Examples of such decisions include those relating to product development, financial investment, and deployment of human resources. It is clear that some element of both inter-individual, inter-group and intra-group conflict is inevitable in relation to decisions on the allocation of financial, technical and human resources.

Role ambiguity occurs when a person in a role is uncertain about his/her role and/or the role expectations of other members of his/her role set (see, for example, Schermerhorn *et al.*, 1985). Individual workers may often be unclear as to their particular job responsibilities or of the precise roles of other workers and managers. For example, there may be ambiguity in relation to lines of authority in areas such as reporting relationships and financial expenditure. Such ambiguity can lead to conflicts between individuals and groups in relation to divisions of responsibility and the exercise of authority.

The existence of some level of *interdependence* between individuals and work groups may also be a source of conflict in organisations. This is particularly pertinent where, for example, work flow or quality among one group of workers is contingent on the performance of other groups or individuals. If a group is unhappy about the performance of another group, some level of conflict is likely to emerge.

A final source of conflict is *differentiation,* which Huczynski and Buchanan (1991, p. 550) define as 'the degree to which tasks and work of individuals or groups is divided'. It is suggested that such differentiation in organisations leads to the establishment of distinct work groups or *cliques* who establish their own 'norms, values and practices'. As a result those outside such groups may view such *cliques* with suspicion. In turn these distinct groups may themselves view 'outsiders' as 'lesser mortals'. Such perceptions will inevitably lead to some conflicts between individuals and groups. A common example where such conflicts can occur in the industrial relations sphere is in conflicts between skilled and unskilled work groups.

FUNCTIONAL AND DYSFUNCTIONAL CONFLICT

Earlier we suggested that conflict is 'normal' in organisations. In spite of this reality, however, it is still commonplace for conflict to be viewed as an 'abnormal' or 'unnatural' phenomenon. Reasons for this are both numerous and complex. For example, Rollinson (1993) points to the effects of social institutions, such as the Church and some of the more traditional conceptions of the family as significant factors in shaping attitudes to conflict and particularly so in promoting the view that unity and harmony are the 'natural state' for organizations: 'Many of the important institutions in our society – the home, the Church, and so on – are founded on the premise that harmony is a natural state of affairs, and this has a powerful effect on the way conflict is regarded' (Rollinson, 1993, p. 251).

Rollinson also points out that the influence of the classical management theorists such as Taylor (1911) and Fayol (1949) succeeded in establishing the perception that conflict was abnormal in organizations. The contribution of the classical management theorists further led to a vision of the 'ideal' organization as a smoothly run entity where management designed plans in a systematic fashion and all the consituent parts gelled to execute these plans. Unity and harmony were the bywords, whereas the existence of conflict was generally regarded as an unnatural state which wasted scarce resources by consuming management time and channelling employee energies in inappropriate directions. This perspective assumed goal congruity between all the parties in the organisation. Clearly, such assumptions run contrary to evidence on the actual practice of organisational management. There is much evidence to suggest that different groups in any organisational setting are likely to have different goals and motives for behaving in the ways that they do. Organisational strategies, for example, may on the surface tell a story of cohesion and consensus, but in actual fact, any plan for the future of the organisation usually requires addressing and accepting that there is often a wide diversity of different explicit and implicit goals within any one organisation. Usually the functioning of that organisation will depend on recognising and managing the conflicting interests which are bound to lead to at least some levels of conflict.

So, a more realistic view is that conflict cannot be eradicated but rather is to be expected and is indeed a normal phenomenon in organisations. It is equally important to acknowledge that conflict can take differing forms which can have either positive or negative effects. From a management perspective it is therefore necessary that conflict be managed as effectively, constructively and productively as possible. It was noted earlier that there are positive dimensions of organisational conflict. Thomas (1976) argues that unless organisational members recognise the potentially positive effects of conflict, the opportunity to learn and to gain from situations of conflict can be lost. Conflict can motivate by energising the environment and the people who operate within it. Conflict can allow people to become clearer about their own positions, helping them to analyse and confront divergent views within the system. And, as Thomas has argued, the confrontation of divergent views can often lead to ideas of superior quality, ideas that may not have been considered at all, if conflict had not arisen in the first place. Conflict can also act as a catalyst for change and innovation in organisations as well as serving as a 'pressure release' mechanism: allowing parties to vent opinions and positions which are a source of frustration and anxiety. It is therefore useful to consider both functional and dysfunctional forms of conflict in organisations (see, for example, Robbins, 1974). Automatically assuming that conflict is an entirely negative force in an organisation closes people off to the possibilities and opportunities that conflict episodes can unlock. On the other hand, assuming that conflict is always an opportunity for achieving positive outcomes is naive and unrealistic. The extent to which conflict is functional or dysfunctional often depends on how the various parties involved manage the part that they play in conflict situations. In addition, and more recently, descriptions of functional and dysfunctional conflict are normally based on their differing effects on the organisation (Gibson *et al.*, 1994).

Functional conflict then, is that which leads to benefits for the organisation, while *dysfunctional conflict* encompasses that which damages the organisation, through, for example, impeding the achievement of production targets, or any action which threatens the survival or in some way damages the competitiveness of the organisation.

PERSPECTIVES ON CONFLICT IN ORGANISATIONS

The preceding discussion has served to focus our attention on the acceptability of conflict as a feature of organisational life. Management attentions in this sphere may be more appropriately focused on ensuring conflict is functional and does not have an unduly disruptive effect on the organisation. The extent to which this managerialist approach is seen as legitimate may be traced to management perspectives on the normality, desirability and legitimacy of conflict in organisations (see Dunford, 1992). There are schools of thought which legitimise and even encourage the disruptive effects of conflict in organisational settings. Conflict is seen from some perspectives as a rational response to oppressive or unjust management systems, or at least an inevitable feature of organisational life. There are different perspectives on conflict. A widely accepted framework for evaluating differing viewpoints is that which identifies four alternative perspectives on conflict in organisations (see Fox, 1966, 1973; Edwards, 1986; Huczynski and Buchanan, 1991):

1. unitarist perspective;
2. pluralist perspective;
3. interactionist perspective;
4. radical perspective.

The unitarist perspective

The unitarist perspective on conflict in organisations views conflict as an aberration which occurs because 'something has gone wrong'. Harmony and unity are seen as the natural state, with conflict an abnormal phenomenon which occurs as a result of some failure in the normal functioning of the organisation, such as poor communications, poor management or the work of 'trouble-makers'. While viewing conflict as abnormal, the unitarist perspective also sees conflict as essentially negative and damaging to the normal harmonious, productive state of the organisation. Thus conflict is viewed as something which can and should be avoided. Where it does occur, management should take appropriate steps to eradicate it, most probably by addressing the source;

i.e., improve communications or organisation design, train managers or get rid of trouble-makers.

The pluralist perspective

In contrast, the pluralist perspective views conflict as a naturally occurring phenomenon in organisations. It is accepted as an inherent characteristic of organisations arising from the differing perspectives and interests of all the groups and individuals who make up the organisation. Since conflict is seen as inevitable, management should therefore expect it to occur and should plan for this eventuality so that it can be handled success-fully and not endanger the achievement of the organisation's primary objectives. This pluralist perspective is consistent with the view that conflict is not necessarily negative but can have beneficial effects. Efforts should therefore be concentrated on channelling functional conflict to realise such organisational benefits. The emphasis is therefore on the *management* of conflict as opposed to its elimination.

The interactionist perspective

While the pluralist perspective accepts the inevitability of conflict, the interactionist perspective goes further by actually stimulating conflict and also instigating means for its resolution. This approach is based on the view that harmony and unity may serve to dull initiative and innovation. It is therefore seen as appropriate to maintain a certain level of conflict to stimulate creativity and innovation. Thus an 'acceptable' level of conflict is seen as both positive and necessary, particularly in creating a work environ-ment which stimulates change and 'new' thinking.

The radical perspective

The radical perspective is essentially grounded in Marxist theory of capitalist society and social change. Conflict in capitalist societies is seen as a symptom of the structural enmity which exists between capital and labour, employer and employee. Such enmity arises from the organisation of work in capitalist societies and the unequal distribution of power between the dominant establishment group which owns the means of pro-duction (employers, shareholders) and those whose labour is required to produce goods and services (workers). Therefore conflict in organisations is simply a manifestation of broader class conflict in relation to the distribution of power in society. Organisations are simply a microcosm of a broader class conflict between the 'bourgeoisie' (who con-trol economic resources and political power) and the 'proletariat', with managers representing the interests of capital. In the radical perspective, conflict is seen as a means of instigating revolutionary change designed to dismantle the capitalist system, re-distribute power in favour of workers and the working class, and ultimately achieve a classless society.

CONFLICT PERSPECTIVES AND MANAGEMENT BEHAVIOUR

The different perspectives on conflict outlined in the preceding section are more than analytical categories. They play a critically significant role in influencing the reactions and behaviour of individuals and groups who are involved in conflict situations. Of particular interest, from our perspective, is the impact of differing conflict perspectives on the behaviour of managers in dealing with organisational conflict.

Because line managers play a key role in handling many conflict situations in organisations, it is important to consider how differing conflict perspectives can help explain managerial behaviour and, particularly, why managers may approach and behave differently in broadly similar conflict situations. This is probably most apparent in the area of employee relations. The contrast most often used to illustrate this point is that between the unitarist and pluralist manager (Fox, 1966).

The *unitarist manager* tends to conceive of the organisation in terms of a unified team. Within this perspective everybody in the organisation is expected to work assiduously for the overall good of the organisation. Management are seen as the single legitimate source of authority and must command full loyalty and commitment from all members of the organisation. Differing interests or sources of loyalty are not accommodated. Anyone who does not share these common interests and does not accept managerial authority is viewed as an agitator or trouble-maker. Since conflict is seen as an 'unnatural' state, such dissenters are seen as endangering organisational success. Consequently, they must either fall into line, accept managerial authority and demonstrate company loyalty, or risk elimination from the organisation.

In contrast, the *pluralist manager* conceives of the organisation in terms of an aggregation of different interest groups with different objectives but linked together instrumentally by their common association with the organisation. As a consequence part of the managerial role is necessarily concerned with achieving some equilibrium in terms of satisfying the various interest groups, dealing with functional conflict, eliminating/reducing dysfunctional conflict and thus helping achieve the organisation's goals. As the pluralist manager sees conflict as a 'natural state', a certain amount of conflict is accepted as inevitable since the objectives of the parties will clash on occasion. The managers must therefore expect and plan for conflict so that it can be handled successfully and not become dysfunctional. Within this perspective the management role is not to suppress conflicting interests, but rather to aim to reconcile them in the organisation's interests.

In practice, therefore, individuals and groups will have different viewpoints on the organisation and organisation conflict. Depending on their particular conflict perspective, managers will adopt particular approaches and behaviour in conflict situations. Conflict perspectives represent dominant orientations which may be present in particular managerial approaches, and offer a useful framework for evaluating management behaviour in conflict situations. In the employee relations sphere, a number of commentators have focused on how management behaviours differ depending on whether managers adopt a unitarist, pluralist, interactionist or radical perspective on conflict (see, for example, Fox, 1966; Marchington, 1982; Edwards, 1986; Robbins, 1986). In the employee relations sphere, Marchington (1982) provides one commonly used critique. Referring only to the contrast between unitarist and pluralist perspectives, Marchington suggests that managers will adopt particular approaches to the following three key areas:

1. the role of trade unions;
2. managerial prerogative;
3. industrial conflict (see Box 12.1).

Box 12.1: The unitarist and pluralist manager

Contrasting approaches in employee relations

1. *The role of trade unions:* The *Unitarist Manager* sees no role for trade unions in organisations. Unions are viewed as an externally-imposed force which introduces conflict into the organisation and prohibits the development of good employee relations. The unitarist manager feels that management is best positioned to make decisions in the interest of everyone in the organisation. Employees associated with the introduction of trade unionism are seen as disloyal or trouble-makers. The *Pluralist Manager* accepts the legitimacy of trade unions in the organisation. Unions help represent and articulate divergent employee viewpoints.

2. *Management prerogative:* Management prerogative refers to areas of decision-making where managements have absolute decision-making authority. The *Unitarist Manager* is unwilling to accept any diminution in management prerogative. Management is seen as the legitimate decision-making authority and it is its job to take decisions in the best interests of both the organisation and its employees, deciding which issues to discuss with employees and those in which management alone should decide. The *Pluralist Manager* recognises other sources of leadership and loyalty in the organisation and accepts that management should share some of its decision-making authority with other legitimate interest groups, such as trade unions or other representative staff bodies.

3. *Industrial conflict:* The *Unitarist Manager* views the organisation in a unified 'team' or 'family', with everyone working together to achieve company objectives. Industrial conflict is not seen as inherent in workplace employee relations, but rather a symptom of a breakdown in the employee relations framework (e.g. due to a misunderstanding) or introduced by people who do not have the company's interests at heart. The unitarist manager feels that such conflict can be eradicated: for example, by clarifying misunderstandings or dismissing trouble-makers. The *Pluralist Manager* sees a certain degree of industrial conflict as inevitable because of the differing objectives held by different inter-

est groups in the organisation. Since pluralist managers view industrial conflict as inevitable they tend to focus on developing institutional arrangements (such as collective bargaining) to ensure that such conflict is handled in a functional reasonable fashion and does not have a detrimental impact on the overall employee relations fabric.

Source: Adapted from Marchington (1982); see also Gunnigle *et al.* (1995)

In Ireland there is some evidence to suggest the dominance of a unitary perspective among owner/managers in small firms (Gunnigle and Brady, 1984; McMahon, 1996). The unitarist perspective is also considered characteristic of the value system of many American managers (see, for example, Bendix, 1956; Kochan *et al.*, 1986). It is argued that this explains the considerable managerial opposition to trade unions in many US companies and also their preference for more individualist management approaches which emphasise direct communications, regular appraisals and merit-based rewards. This interpretation is very significant in Ireland where the economy is heavily dependent on foreign investment and where the bulk of such investment is American-owned.

TYPES OF CONFLICT

Our most common image of conflict in organisations is probably that of collective conflict, involving some form of dispute between workers and management such as a strike or 'go-slow' (employee relations conflict). However, such employee relations conflict is only one form of conflict in organisations. Conflict may take numerous other forms such as conflict between individuals (interpersonal conflict), conflict between differing groups (intergroup conflict); and conflict between organizations (inter-organisational conflict).

Interpersonal conflict is conflict which occurs between two or more individuals. Almost everyone who has worked in an organisation will have experienced some degree of interpersonal conflict. It may occur between an employee and his/her manager or between two or more employees or managers. *Intergroup conflict* involves conflict between two or more groups within the organisation. Organisations have tremendous potential for intergroup conflict. The fact that organizations are often designed so that people work in comparatively discrete units means that intergroup discord and rivalries inevitably arise. Common sources of intergroup conflict are those relating to resource allocation, interdependence and differentiation. *Employee relations conflict* is a particular form of intergroup conflict stemming from differences between management (employers) and labour (employees) in relation to the terms and regulation of the employment relationship. This is often the most visible form of conflict in organisations, involving issues such as pay, benefits, and working conditions. An important dimension of employee relations conflict is that employees may often be organised into trade unions or other representative associations. *Inter-organisational conflict* involves conflict between two or more organisations. Such conflict may often occur as a result of competition for customers, market share or disputes in relation to patent or copyright. However, other sources are also important such as disputes between organisations and regulatory agencies, such as planning authorities (county councils or corporations) or, for example, the Factory Inspectorate.

Most of these conflict types are detailed here. However, as this chapter focuses on conflict within organisations, it does not address inter-organisational conflict. Before dealing with the issue of conflict resolution, it is useful to consider the area of employee relations conflict a little further since it is one of the most visible and emotive forms of conflict in organisations.

Employee relations conflict

The basis for employee relations conflict is felt to be rooted in the structure of the employment relationship in capitalist economies (see, for example, Blyton and Turnbull, 1994). It is argued that this creates a fundamental antagonism between employers and workers which becomes manifest in differences over issues such as working conditions and terms of employment. Although academics tend to view employee relations conflict as 'natural' in organisations, it is more commonly perceived as extremely negative and damaging for organisations. Rollinson (1993) identifies three principal reasons why employee relations conflict is seen as a particularly objectionable conflict form:

1. Employee relations conflict is vertical in nature and therefore challenges the legitimacy of management authority/prerogative in decision-making.
2. Employee relations conflict is highly visible, both within and outside the organisation. While many interpersonal and other inter-group conflicts take place in a less visible or covert manner, employee relations conflicts tend to be quite overt, often mobilising large numbers of workers.
3. The objective of employee relations conflict tends to be misunderstood. Rollinson argues that employee relations conflict is commonly seen as 'irrational' and, indeed, dysfunctional since such conflicts 'should be capable of being solved by negotiation and compromise' (Rollinson, 1993, p. 252). Rollinson argues that this view is flawed: whilst negotiation is generally capable of resolving much employee relations conflict, it is inevitable that at some stage and in some organizations, either party may not modify its position and use some form of industrial conflict to achieve its aims. As Rollinson comments: industrial action is 'simply a rational extension of the negotiation process' (Rollinson, 1993, p. 252).

In practice, therefore, employee relations conflict seems an inherent feature of organisational life and some degree of industrial conflict is inevitable. One can identify two broad forms of employee relations conflict: unorganized, individual conflict; and organised, collective conflict (Salamon, 1992). *Unorganized, individual conflict* tends to represent spontaneous, reactive and random responses which do not form part of a conscious strategy on behalf of the proponents. Common types of unorganized conflict include absenteeism, turnover, theft and many forms of industrial sabotage. *Organised, collective conflict*, on the other hand, encompasses more systematic, collective efforts in pursuing a conscious strategy through co-ordinated action designed to achieve specified objectives. The most common examples of organised employee relations conflict are strikes, go slows, overtime bans and the withdrawal of co-operation. Of course, this distinction is often more clouded in practice and particularly so in relation to the randomness and spontaneity of unorganized conflict. Blyton and Turnbull (1994) illustrate the difficulty in differentiating between organised and unorganized conflict by citing the 'blue flu' phenomenon in the New York Police Department, whereby all police officers report in sick on the same day. Such co-ordinated forms of traditionally 'unorganized' conflict are likely to become increasingly common as increased competitiveness and job insecurity renders more organised methods, especially strikes, less attractive to workers due to loss of income and possibility of dismissal. It is also clear that certain forms of apparently organised conflict can be quite reactive and spontaneous in nature. For example, so-called 'wildcat' strikes can occur when workers walk off the job in reaction to a particular incident but do not possess any overall strategy.

Box 12.2 summarises the main forms of conflict which may occur in organisations.

Box 12.2: Forms of conflict in organisations

- *Strike:* Collective in nature, involving temporary withdrawal of labour. Strike action can take different forms: *official strikes* are defined as those which have been fully sanctioned by the union executive and normally occur after negotiations have failed to resolve the issue and when all due procedures have been exhausted; *unofficial* strikes are those which have not been sanctioned by the trade union and tend to be quite reactive in nature, often sparked off by a particular event or incident at workplace level such as the dismissal or suspension of a worker.
- *Withdrawal of co-operation:* Collective in nature, involving the withdrawal of representatives from joint institutions, strict interpretation of, and rigorous adherence to, procedure, absence of flexibility.
- *Work to rule:* Collective in nature, involving working only in accordance with the strict interpretation of written terms and conditions of employment, job description or other rules such as those concerning safety or hygiene.

- *Overtime ban:* Collective in nature, involving refusal to work outside normal contractual hours of work.
- *Go slow:* Collective in nature, involving working at a lower than average level of performance.
- *Sabotage:* Individual in nature, involving conscious action to damage goods, equipment or other aspects of the work environment.
- *Pilfering and theft:* Individual in nature, involving stealing items owned by the organisation.
- *Absenteeism:* Absenteeism has been generically defined as 'all absences from work other than paid holidays'. As such it is reckoned that only a small proportion of absenteeism may represent a form of conflict. Where it does, it tends to represent individual response to perceived problems in the workplace.
- *Labour turnover:* Labour turnover refers to the rate at which people leave the organisation. As with absenteeism, only a proportion of labour turnover in organisations is representative of conflict in organisations.
- *Lock-out:* In the employee relations sphere in particular, it is important to acknowledge that employers may also instigate a lock-out. This involves preventing the workforce from attending at work and is the equivalent of strike action by employees.

Source: Salamon, 1992; Gunnigle *et al.*, 1995

CONFLICT HANDLING AND RESOLUTION

A key theme in the preceding discussion is that some degree of conflict is inevitable in organisations. As such, a particular onus falls on management to develop effective strategies to deal with such conflict. Within the organisation, all levels of management have particular and important roles to play in conflict handling and resolution. Line managers and team leaders play a key role in dealing with individual conflicts and grievances which arise at 'shopfloor' level. Senior management have overall responsibility for the development of effective strategies and policies to both limit the extent of conflict (particularly dysfunctional conflict), and to handle any more serious conflicts which arise. As discussed earlier, conflict in organisations should not necessarily be viewed in negative terms and, that properly handled, conflict can have many positive effects, allowing individuals or groups to highlight and pursue issues of concern. While conflict often involves difficult and fraught interactions between individuals and groups, it may ultimately facilitate constructive change and development in organisations.

In evaluating alternative approaches to handling conflict, Schermerhorn (1985) suggests that managers can react in the following ways:

1. Non-attention: whereby no deliberate attempt is made to deal with the conflict.
2. Suppression: whereby an attempt is made quell the conflict (for example by disci-

plining the individual(s) involved). However, suppression does not address the source of the conflict or seek viable long-term solutions.

3. Resolution: involving the search for long-term solutions to the source of conflict.

Using terminology traditionally used in relation to negotiations between two or more parties, Schermerhorn also argues that attempts to manage conflict can result in lose-lose, win-lose and win-win outcomes. *Lose-lose* outcomes involve those where all parties to the conflict are unhappy with the outcome. *Win-lose* outcomes involve one party achieving its desired aims to the detriment of the other party. Win-lose outcomes often result from conflict suppression. *Win-win* outcomes involve all parties to the conflict gaining a satisfactory outcome. Such win-win outcomes ideally involve the elimination of the source of conflict and thus prevent it arising again at some future stage.

Conflict-handling strategies

While the three possible outcomes described above (win-win, win-lose, lose-lose) provide a convenient categorization of conflict outcomes, a more pressing concern for managers confronted with conflict situations is what strategies might optimally be adopted to help resolve such conflicts. One of the most widely quoted models of conflict-handling strategies is that developed by Ken Thomas (Thomas, 1976). This model is summarised in Figure 12.1 and is based on two conflict-handling dimensions:

1. Extent to which a party seeks to satisfy its own concerns/needs *(assertiveness)*.
2. Extent to which a party seeks to satisfy the concerns/needs of the other party *(co-operativeness)*.

The interplay of these two dimensions produces five different conflict-handling orientations:

1. Competition.
2. Collaboration.
3. Compromise.
4. Avoidance.
5. Accommodation.

Each different orientation reflects the preferred approach to conflict handling given the relative extent of assertiveness and co-operativeness.

Figure 12.1: Conflict-handling orientations

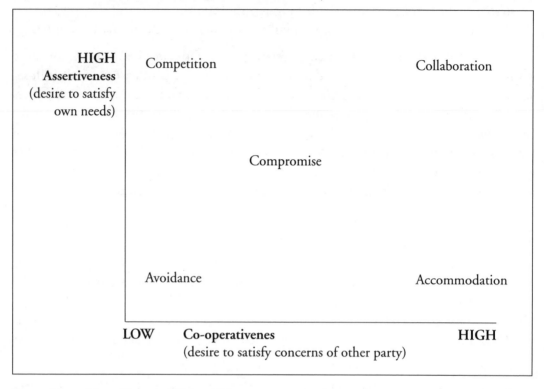

Source: Adapted from Thomas, 1976, p. 900.

In a particular conflict situation, the selection of a specific conflict-handling orientation will be influenced by the extent to which there is a perceived conflict of interest between the parties and also by an assessment of the power and level of commitment of each party (see Dunford, 1992). Such factors facilitate the identification of appropriate contexts for the adoption of particular conflict-handling orientations. Using empirical data, Thomas (1977) positioned each conflict-handling orientation within an 'appropriate' situation or context. The following section briefly describes each of Thomas's conflict-handling orientations and his conclusions in relation to their appropriate operational context (see Thomas, 1976, 1977).

The *competition orientation* is characterised by a desire to win (dominate) at the other party's expense. It entails a highly assertive win-lose approach, involving the use of one particular power base and competitive strength to achieve their objectives regardless of the implications for the other party. This orientation is considered most appropriate in the following situations:

1. When quick, decisive action is required, such as crisis situations.
2. On critical issues where unpopular action is required, such as cost-cutting, re-struc-

turing, enforcing unpopular rules or taking disciplinary action.

3. In dealing with people or parties who are persistently competitive in the face of other non-competitive types of behaviour.

The *collaborative orientation* is characterised by a desire to achieve a mutually acceptable outcome which satisfies the interests of both parties. It requires a problem-solving orientation by both parties, i.e. a willingness to work through issues of conflict, confronting and dealing with problems so that each party benefits from the results. This orientation is considered most appropriate in the following situations:

1. Where each party's concerns are too important to be compromised and thus some integrative solution is required.
2. Where learning is the objective.
3. When it is desirable to merge insights from parties holding different perspectives.
4. When it is desirable to build consensus by taking account of the concerns of all parties in order to achieve commitment of the parties involved.
5. To effectively address feelings of each party which may have interfered with relationships.

It is also argued that groups who are likely to have to work together after a conflict episode, are well advised to search for collaborative solutions to the conflict issues that they face.

The *compromise orientation* is characterised by a desire to seek solutions which partially satisfy the needs of each party. Certain trade-offs are used as keys to conflict resolution, with each party gaining something but also making concessions in relation to their own position so that satisfactory rather than ideal solutions are achieved. This orientation is considered most appropriate in the following situations:

1. Where each party's goals are important but not to the extent which would merit the effort or potential disruption associated with more assertive approaches.
2. Where parties committed to mutually exclusive goals operate from a similar power base.
3. To achieve temporary settlements in relation to complex issues.
4. Where time constraints require that expedient solutions are achieved.
5. As a backup orientation when competition or collaboration approaches are unsuccessful.

The *avoidance orientation* is characterised by withdrawal from the particular conflict situation. It may involve ignoring the conflict, often in the hope that it will go away, and is often used as a result of one or both parties' inability to face up to the conflict and address it adequately. An avoidance orientation, entailing as it does a desire to dodge any manifestation of conflict, may lead to an effective withdrawal of a party from the conflict. Alternatively, a party may attempt to suppress the conflict by disguising or withholding any manifestation of that conflict. This approach may be particularly common where close personal relations exist between the parties and either party may choose to avoid confrontation. The avoidance orientation is considered most appropriate in the following situations:

1. Where the issue is of minor importance or more important issues are pressing.
2. When a party feels there is no chance of satisfying their concerns.
3. Where the issues at hand have a potential for disruption which exceeds the potential benefits of resolution.
4. To allow a 'cooling off' period.
5. Where the collection of adequate information is of greater priority than reaching an immediate decision.
6. Where others can resolve the conflict more effectively.
7. When the issue at hand seems 'tangential or symptomatic of other issues' (Thomas, 1977, p. 487).

The *accommodation orientation* is characterised by a desire to satisfy the concerns of the other party at the expense of one's own interests. It involves allowing the other party's wishes to rule and is often motivated by a stronger wish to maintain the working relationship between parties, than to pursue one's other interests. This orientation is considered most appropriate in the following situations:

1. Where a party finds they are wrong.
2. When the issue at hand is more important to the other party than yourself – to satisfy others and to maintain co-operation/working relationships.
3. To build 'credits' for dealing with subsequent issues.
4. To minimise loss when faced with a losing situation.
5. Where the maintenance of harmony and stability take priority.
6. To allow subordinates to develop and learn as a result of their mistakes.

In evaluating approaches to conflict handling, it is important to note that conflict situations are dynamic in nature. Thus, the parties may start out with a particular conflict-handling orientation. However, as the situation evolves, the parties may alter their position as they gain insights into the other party's position or as power is exercised. Conflict handling is therefore an interactive process (Huczynski and Buchanan, 1991) whereby the actions of one party impact on the behaviour of others involved. Such reactions and modifications are inherent to the conflict handling process. It is often argued that collaboration which scores high on both co-operativeness and assertiveness is the 'ideal' strategy in conflict handling, because it represents an explicit attempt to address the conflict head-on and treat the sources of such conflict. However, it important to acknowledge the reality that many conflicts in organisations are, more often than not, resolved through some form of compromise. In no area is this more pertinent than in employee relations conflict. Indeed, perhaps the most widespread response to industrial conflict in the workplace has been the development of joint mechanisms to discuss and resolve issues of difference through negotiation (Gunnigle *et al.*, 1995). Such institutionalisation of conflict is primarily characterised by the development of agreed procedures to facilitate conflict resolution. This reflects an implicit acceptance that issues of conflict will arise and is characteristic of the pluralist approach to employee relations discussed earlier. In creating institutions (such as negotiating structures) and procedures for handling employee relations and industrial conflict, the parties involved seek to create a framework through which the parties can interact, argue, disagree and agree while allowing for the ongoing operation of the business. Grievance, disputes and disciplinary procedures are a characteristic feature of Irish organisations and represent an important means of dealing with employee relations conflict at the level of the enterprise.

WORKPLACE GRIEVANCES

Individual or small-group grievances are one of the most common sources of conflict in organisations. The term 'grievance' is most commonly used to describe a formal expression of employee dissatisfaction. Given the nature of industrial organisations, it is inevitable that employees, either individually or in groups, will have grievances which they want management to address. The great majority of such grievances normally involve minor complaints related to the immediate work environment. As such, these grievances can normally be handled at shopfloor level by line management and employees and/or employee representatives. It is suggested that managers should pay particular attention to effective grievance handling and its contribution to the promotion of good employee relations in the workplace. It is also suggested that management should handle employee grievances promptly since the non-handling of grievances may give rise to frustration which can permeate through to other employees and promote an uneasy working environment in which disputes and poor employee relations can arise (Gunnigle *et al.*, 1995). Some summary guidelines for managers involved in grievance handling are outlined in Box 12.3.

Box 12.3: Guidelines on handling workplace grievances

- Management should make every effort to understand the nature of, and the reasons for, employee grievances.
- Management should establish a policy which sets out an orderly and effective framework for handling disputes/grievances.
- All levels of management should be aware of the key influences which grievance handling have on the work environment and on organisation performance and of their key role in effective grievance handling.

As noted earlier, workplace grievances or disputes may arise from issues involving either an individual employee or a group of employees. Humphrey (1979) suggests that individual employee grievances at work fall into two categories: personal and work-related. Personal problems may primarily concern the organisation where they influence work performance. For example, a domestic problem might detrimentally affect that employee's performance or attendance. In such situations the organisation should be both supportive and concerned. All employees will, at some time, have issues which cause them concern at work. Should employees have problems which they wish to raise with management these should be handled as expeditiously as possible. Line managers must be aware of the importance of this task and be prepared to listen to and act on employee grievances.

An initial step is for management to try and understand the nature of disputes and grievances. This facilitates an appreciation of the wide variety of issues which can cause grievances and highlights the importance of prevention. A useful approach is to analyse the conditions which are most likely to give rise to serious disputes/grievances. These might include poor working conditions, unsafe work practices, discrimination, job insecurity, inadequate wages, and unrealistic rules and regulations. Of course the list is endless and is particular to the organisation concerned. However, the prime concern of management should be to develop policies and procedures which eliminate the conditions leading to disputes or grievances. Management approaches to handling workplace conflicts will be influenced by the overall organisational approach to human resource management. Differences in approach will result in varying organisational policies and practices. A example of one company's policy is outlined in Box 12.4.

Box 12.4: Sample company policy on workplace grievances (Pharmaceutical Sector)

1. The company recognises that employees have a legitimate interest in the affairs of the enterprise and thus have a right to be concerned and informed about issues which affect them.
2. Employees have a right to bring matters which concern them to the attention of management.
3. Management and employee opinions may be at variance on occasion. In such instances management will strive to understand the employees' viewpoint, explain the management position and seek a mutually acceptable solution.
4. Management will give consideration to matters brought to their attention by employees and action these matters in an appropriate, effective and equitable manner.

CONFLICT OUTCOMES

At the end of a conflict episode, some result will emerge: the conflict may be resolved or, alternatively, it may be suppressed, or simply deferred, to emerge again at some future stage. Such an outcome will have various implications for the participants. Where some solution is found, the parties may have particular responsibilities to execute to ensure that whatever agreement reached is put into practice. The outcome will also affect the perceptions, feelings and future conflict-handling orientations of the parties involved. For example, the parties may feel disappointed or happy with the outcome. This may in turn affect their future relationships and also cause them to adopt differing strategies in their future interactions.

An important theme in our earlier discussion on conflict perspectives, is that conflict in organisations can be functional; that is, it can have positive outcomes for the organisation and for participants. For example, Dunford (1992, p. 229) identifies the following functional outcomes of organisational conflict:

- In conflict situations, differing viewpoints on an issue tend to be proffered: this can lead to the exploration of an array of different solutions and to the identification of 'superior' solutions.
- Conflict situations may lead the parties involved to reflect on their perspectives and commitment to particular issues leading to potentially positive changes in their beliefs and approaches.
- It is likely that the tensions and interaction involved in conflict situations may lead to greater creativity in terms of approaches, solutions, and future working arrangements.
- Conflict can serve to identify fundamental problems in the organisations which need to be addressed. The absence of any manifestation of such conflict may lead to such problems being suppressed and thus continuing to impair the functioning of the organisations.

This latter point illustrates the dangers of passivity for organisations. The absence of conflict may lead to both excessive complacency about the extent of harmony in the organisation and to an organisational climate which is excessively rigid and overly committed to the *status quo*. This phenomenon led Robbins (1978) to suggest that organisations can suffer from a 'lack of conflict' and he identified a number of pointers to this 'condition', as illustrated in Box 12.5.

Box 12.5: Indicators of insufficient conflict in organisations

- Managers who are surrounded by subordinates who always agree with their ideas.
- Subordinates who are afraid to admit to lack of knowledge or uncertainty.
- Excessive emphasis on reaching decisions through compromise so that decision-makers lose sight of values, long-term objectives and organisational well-being.
- A managerial value system based on ensuring an impression of harmony and co-operation in their domains.
- Decision-makers who are excessively concerned with the feelings of others.
- A managerial value system which views popularity as more important than competence or performance in gaining organisational rewards.
- Excessive managerial concern with achieving decisions through consensus.
- Employees who demonstrate an unusually high resistance to change.
- Lack of new ideas being generated.
- Unusually low level of employee turnover.

It is important to note that these are simply indicators that an organisation may be suffering from a lack of conflict. Clearly, many of the phenomena in Box 12.5 above may occur for extraneous reasons: for example, low labour turnover may be due to economic recession and high unemployment. Nevertheless, conflict stimulation may be used in organisations to achieve some of the positive outcomes mentioned earlier.

NATIONAL CULTURE AND ORGANISATIONAL CONFLICT

In Chapter 2, the discussion on cultural values and perception identified the importance of considering national culture as an important potential influence on how people perceive their environment. Since perception is itself a central influencer on how people handle conflict, the impact of national culture needs to be considered here also. Conflict may be managed quite differently depending on the cultural backgrounds and contexts of the participants involved.

Impact of national culture on approaches to conflict and conflict handling

There are clear differences in national cultures and their impact on organisations. In evaluating the impact of differences in national culture on organisations and organisational behaviour, it seems that the effects are quite wide ranging: culture is seen as impacting on issues such as organisation structure, reward systems, management behaviour, manager-subordinate relations, and attitudes to employment and careers (see, for example, Sparrow and Hiltrop, 1994).

In considering the impact of differences in national culture on conflict and conflict handling in organisations, a number of issues emerge. Firstly, culture has an impact on conflict perspectives, particularly the extent to which conflict is seen as legitimate or 'natural' in organisations. Culture also influences the reactions and behaviour of individuals and groups who are involved in conflict situations. An illustration of the impact of national culture on approaches to conflict handling is provided by Tang and Kirkbridge's (1986, summarised in Huczynski and Buchanan, 1991, p. 571) study which compared the conflict-handling approaches of Chinese and British managers. This study concluded that Chinese managers adopted less assertive *compromise* and *avoidance* approaches while their British counterparts tended to adopt more assertive *collaboration* and *competition* styles (see our earlier review of conflict-handling strategies and Figure 12.1). Tang and Kirkbridge attributed the adoption of less assertive compromise and avoidance styles by Chinese managers to the influence of three particular aspects of Confucian and Taoist ideology and values, as follows:

1. *Conformity:* a person is seen as existing as part of a larger family or clan, and interpersonal relations are structured on the basis of respect for hierarchical relationships, with a strong emphasis on duty and obedience. It is suggested that these values lead the Chinese to be socially oriented, submissive to authority and non-aggressive and, consequently, to adopt conflict handling approaches which stress conformity in their interactions with superiors.
2. *Harmony:* which encourages the adoption of a 'middle course' through life between the extremes of action and inaction and which also lead the Chinese to control many of their emotions such a joy, sorrow and anger.
3. *Face:* which encourages the maintenance of composure, even in the most difficult situations – a factor which is felt to explain why Chinese managers tend to avoid extremes or any actions likely to lead to embarrassment either to themselves or others (i.e. loss of face).

Research by King and Bond (1985) also found that Confucian values and beliefs exerted an important influence, particularly in the extent to which national cultures adopt a long-term or short-term orientation in their decision-making. This work found that countries in Eastern Asia tended to adopt long-term orientation and a concern with the future while those in Western Europe and North America adopted a more short-term orientation.

An area of conflict handling where the impact of difference in national cultures seems to have a significant influence is that of negotiations. As noted earlier, negotiations is one of the most important means of addressing conflicts between individuals or groups. The impact of differences in national cultures on approaches to negotiations may become manifest in a variety of ways, such as the following:

- *Preliminaries:* it is suggested that social 'banter' plays an important role in the prelude to negotiations in some countries (e.g. Southern Europe, Africa), whereas in others the tendency is to keep preliminaries to a minimum and 'cut to the meat' immediately (e.g. US, Germany).

- *Interpersonal relations:* In some cultures, the primary emphasis is on the nature of interpersonal relations (e.g. Middle East) rather than the issue at hand. Thus, establishing a good ongoing working relationship is critical: something which might change this, for example changing negotiators, may detrimentally affect negotiations, even if the substance of what is being said remains the same.
- *Win-win versus win-lose:* Some cultures appear to place a greater emphasis on the long term (see above discussion) so that establishing a stable working relationship and achieving a consensus acceptable to all parties involved (e.g. Japan) often takes precedence over achieving a winning 'result' in relation to the issue at hand (e.g. US).

Of course differences in national cultures may, of themselves, become a source of conflict in organisations. This is particularly important in multinational corporations (MNCs) which contain people from diverse cultural groupings. An immediate issue for senior management in MNCs is the extent to which they seek to apply home country (corporate) or host country policies and practices in areas such as recruitment, rewards, supervision and employee relations. Indeed employee relations is an area where national cultures seem to have both a significant impact and potential for conflict. It is widely suggested that managerial values associated with differences in national culture impact on 'preferred' management approaches to employee relations (Rothenberg and Silverman, 1973; Poole, 1986). For example, it is argued that managerial opposition to organised labour is characteristic of the value system of American managers, whereas *human resource management* approaches which emphasise a more individualist orientation, direct communications and merit-based rewards, are very much in line with this value system (Bendix, 1956; Kochan *et al.*, 1986). This interpretation is very significant in Ireland where trade unions have achieved high levels of penetration and legitimacy but where, increasingly, US multinationals seek to avoid trade union recognition (McGovern, 1989; Gunnigle, 1995).

With the increasing internationalisation of business, it is important that organisations address the issue of cultural differences so that any harmful conflicts are minimised. Indeed, managing cultural diversity has become an important theme in international business (Sparrow and Hiltrop, 1994). Adler (1983) identifies three approaches to managing cultural diversity as follows:

1. *Parochial:* this approach does not recognise or acknowledge the existence of cultural differences. As a consequence senior management tend to view home country (corporate) approaches as the 'one best way' and impose these in their international operations. While this approach clearly has tremendous potential for conflict, it is a common strategy in many organisations.

2. *Ethnocentric:* this approach acknowledges cultural diversity but only as a source of problems. However, the 'other approach' is seen as inherently inferior so that senior management still believe in their 'one best way'. This is also seen as a common strategy which results in a considerable degree of conflict.

3. *Synergistic:* this approach acknowledges the existence and legitimacy of differences in cultural approaches and attaches equal importance to all approaches so that none is seen as either superior or inferior. While this approach is seen as a preferred strategy having many advantages for organisations, it is apparently the least-used approach to managing cultural diversity.

In evaluating the impact of national culture on approaches to conflict handling, it is clear that managers need to develop an acute awareness of cultural differences. They must also learn to set aside traditional biases and stereotypes which tend to underpin 'superiority' or 'inferiority' perceptions and lead to conflict. Sparrow and Hiltrop (1994) identify two important sources of information on the extent of cultural awareness:

1. *Intercultural understanding* (based on information from the World Competitiveness Reports).

2. *Foreign language capacity.*

The findings on intercultural understanding together with the World Competitiveness Rankings on the extent of *internationalization* of OECD countries is summarised in Table 12.1 while study findings on language capacity in twelve European Union countries are outlined in Table 12.2.

These findings indicate that Ireland achieves a high ranking on internationalization, a factor most probably related to the economy's strong export orientation and to the high presence of foreign multinational companies. However, Ireland achieves quite low scores on both inter-cultural awareness and foreign language capacity.

Table 12.1: Inter-cultural awareness and internationalization in OECD countries

	Inter-cultural awareness	Internationalization
	Rank	*Rank*
Australia	20	20
Austria	8	11
Belgium/Luxembourg	1	5
Canada	12	12
Denmark	4	9
Finland	13	10
France	17	4
Germany	7	3

Greece	9	21
Ireland	**18**	**8**
Italy	11	16
Japan	14	7
Netherlands	3	2
New Zealand	15	17
Norway	19	19
Portugal	10	18
Spain	16	15
Sweden	5	13
Switzerland	2	14
Turkey	6	22
UK	21	6
USA	22	1

Source: World Economic Forum: 1993 World Competitiveness Report (Intercultural awareness); 1995 World Competitiveness Report (Internationalisation).

Table 12.2: Language capacity in twelve EU countries

	Rank
Luxembourg	1
Netherlands	2
Denmark	3
Belgium	4
Germany (W)	5
Greece	6
France	7
Spain	8
Portugal	9
UK	10
Italy	11
Ireland	**12**

Source: Adapted from Sparrow and Hiltrop, 1994, p. 82

CONCLUSIONS

A pervasive theme in our consideration of conflict in organisations is the issue of legitimacy: the extent to which conflict is seen as a natural phenomenon or, alternatively, the extent to which conflict is seen as abnormal. Where conflict is seen as a natural state, it is likely that managers will focus on addressing the sources rather than the symptoms of conflict. It is also likely that various mechanisms will be established to facilitate conflict handling. Where conflict is seen as abnormal, management will often focus on eliminating conflict altogether. Open communications and high trust are often seen as the answer in this respect. Our conclusion is that some degree of conflict will inevitably occur in all organisations. Such conflict is inevitable because of the range and diversity of individual and group interests in organisations. However, such conflict is not necessarily negative and can, indeed, have many positive benefits for organisations, particularly in facilitating grievance handling and changes in work practices. Because of the inevitability of conflict, the area of conflict handling is an important concern for organisations, and especially so for managers who are often in the front line of conflict situations, particularly in respect of employee relations conflicts.

SUMMARY OF KEY PROPOSITIONS

- This chapter introduced the area of conflict in organisations. Conflict was defined as a process which begins when one party perceives that another party has frustrated (or is about to frustrate) some central concern of theirs.
- Conflict occurs whenever disagreement exists in a social situation over issues of substance or emotional discord. Our focus is on 'structurally derived conflict' which arises as a result of operation and structure of organisations.
- While traditional views of conflict held that any organisational conflict was negative and to be avoided, emerging views recognise that conflict is 'normal' and can have both negative and positive dimensions. The positive effects of conflict include its potential to energise and to motivate people, to identify real problems that need to be changed, and to allow people to express their feelings about issues which are causing stress and anxiety. The negative effects of conflict include its potential to entrench people into positions which cause damage to themselves and others.
- There are five main sources of conflict in organisations: the employment relationship; competition over scarce resources; ambiguity over responsibility or authority; interdependence; and differentiation.
- This chapter also explored four key perspectives on organisational conflict: unitarist, pluralist, interactionist and radical. Each of these perspectives represents different views about the functionality and legitimacy of conflict in organisations.
- Employee relations conflict is a particular form of intergroup conflict stemming from differences between management (employers) and labour (normally organised in trade unions or similar bodies) in relation to the terms and regulation of the employment relationship.
- Senior management in organizations have responsibility for the development of effective strategies and policies to deal with organisational conflict.

- There are a number of different approaches to conflict handling which vary in their approach and effectiveness, namely non-attention, suppression and resolution. These differing approaches can result in either lose-lose (non-attention), win-lose (suppression) or win-win (resolution) outcomes for the participants.

- A key issue for organisations and, particularly, managers is the identification of effective strategies to deal with organizational conflict. Thomas (1976) provides us with a model based on the dominant orientations of the parties involved in a particular conflict situation. This model identifies five such orientations (competition; collaboration; compromise; avoidance; and accommodation) based on the relative extent of *assertiveness* and *co-operativeness* of each party.

- Some organisations may suffer from a lack of conflict which may lead to complacency about the extent of harmony in the organization and to an organisational climate which is excessively rigid and resistant to change and development.

- As business becomes increasingly global it is important that organisations address the issue of cultural diversity so as to both manage 'culturally derived' conflict effectively and to ensure that conflict-handling approaches are appropriate to the national cultures in which they are implemented.

DISCUSSION QUESTIONS

1. Define conflict. Give examples of different types of organisational conflict with which you are familiar.

2. Having explored four key perspectives on organisational conflict (unitarist, pluralist, interactionist and radical), which perspective appeals most to you? Identify a conflict situation with which you are familiar and identify the different accounts that might be given of this situation depending on what perspective on conflict is adopted.

3. Explain and explore the difference between functional and dysfunctional conflict at work.

4. As a class, split into small groups and assign one of five different behavioural approaches to conflict to each of your discussion groups (i.e. avoiding, accommodating, compromising, competing, collaborating). Identify examples of the behavioural approach that you have been assigned, and generate two lists with the following headings: 'When [avoiding] should be used as an approach to conflict' and 'When [avoiding] should not be used as an approach to conflict'. After your subgroup discussions, regroup and exchange the results of your discussion with the groups that tackled different approaches.

CHAPTER 13

Power, Politics and Ethics

LEARNING OBJECTIVES
- To introduce the concepts of power, politics and ethics.
- To outline the key sources of power available.
- To examine the uses of power.
- To highlight critical political tactics useful for influencing targets.
- To examine the sources of personal ethics.
- To review critical issues in social responsibility.

INTRODUCTION

Though traditionally neglected in the extant literature, power, politics and ethics are important concepts for explaining behaviour in organisations. Analyses of power, politics and ethics cast light on the nature of the relationship between organisational stakeholders, and they are dimensions of every organisation. According to Finchman and Rhodes (1988), the study of power and political activity in organisations has some very positive things to recommend it. Firstly, they argue that the stress on 'real' organisational activity is fruitful, when compared with the overly prescriptive approach of many managerial theorists. Secondly, they highlight the fact that this side of the management role has been played down until quite recently encourages a far greater interest in power and any new approach which has the potential to take our understanding forward is wholeheartedly welcome. Thus Pfeffer (1981, p. ix) notes that recent years have brought with them an increasing interest in a political perspective on organisational behaviour: 'This growing concern encompasses . . . topics as diverse as bargaining and influence strategies and the political aspects of organisation development and is at once welcome and long overdue.'

Power may be defined as the ability to engage in action, i.e. the extent to which individuals or stakeholders are able to pursue or convince others to take a certain course of action. The essence of power is control over the behaviour of others. *Politics,* on the other hand, can be viewed as power in action and consists of strategies and tactics drawn upon for the purpose of influencing individuals and groups. Indeed, as early as 1936, Lasswell defined politics as the study of who gets what, when and how. *Ethics* can be conceived of as an individual's personal beliefs regarding right and wrong behaviour. Management ethics are the standards of behaviour that guide individual managers in their work. Thus, what constitutes ethical behaviour can vary from one person to another, and while ethics is relative and not absolute when people talk about ethical behaviour, they do usually mean behaviour that conforms to generally accepted social norms. Importantly though, from an organisational behaviour perspective, ethics is defined in the context of the individual which means that people have ethics, organisations *per se* do not. This chapter focuses on each of these three important dimensions of organisational life.

POWER

According to Statt (1994) one of the most striking aspects of our everyday experience of organisations is that some people seem to have more influence over what happens than other people. The exercise of this influence is often referred to as having power. Power is an element in almost all social relationships. The concept of power is 'as ancient and ubiquitous as any that social theory can boast' (Dahl, 1957, p. 201). Tyson and Jackson (1992) argue that the concept of power is central to understanding organisational life, because people devote much of their energies at work to trying to accomplish tasks either for themselves or on behalf of other people. Power does not operate in a vacuum, but is context- or relationship-specific.

Box 13.1: Illustrating power

> Dawson (1996, pp. 167–8) presents a series of mini-case studies as a means of describing power relationships in which the desires, requests and interests of individuals or groups are frustrated either by the decisions or actions of other people or by characteristics of the technical and administrative system that has been created and developed.
>
> In the *post office* a mother tries to obtain her child benefit and is told by the clerk: 'It's not my fault that you can't get your child benefit this week, it's just that your book has run out and your new book hasn't arrived yet. Probably that's because of the train drivers' strike delaying the post, but whatever the reason, I can't do anything about it; I've no authority to pay your benefit without a book.'
>
> The manager of a *purchasing department* of an electrical assembly factory complains to the sales representative of one of their suppliers about late deliveries. 'I'll see what I can do', says the rep. 'The problem is that we are retooling one of our production lines and production are in difficulties. I'll do what I can about your order, but I can't promise anything in the immediate future. You see, production never consult us when they make changes and we have no power to insist. They should produce a lot of stock before shutting down, but they don't want to increase their stock levels.'

In the post office scenario the claimant is less powerful than the officer, who is less powerful than the administrative system when it comes to determining whether or not a mother gets her child benefit.

In the purchasing department scenario, the sales representative of the components factory is less powerful than the production manager over issues of inventory and production schedules. The purchasing manager of the assembly plant may have to bow to the suppliers in the short term, but in the long term he may well discover other suppliers and hence shift his power relationship with the components firms in a fairly dramatic way.

Source: Dawson, 1996

As noted above, power may be defined as the ability to engage in action, i.e. the extent to which individuals or stakeholders are able to pursue or convince others to take a certain course of action. Dahl (1957) defined power as a relation among social actors in which one social actor, A, can get another social actor, B, to do something that B would not otherwise have done. Thus Pfeffer (1981) notes that power is about force, a force sufficient to change the probability of B's behaviour from what it would have been in the absence of the application of that force. Concomitantly, it is about resistance, i.e. the amount of resistance that B can advance because his/her wishes are being overridden. It is also about the likely conflict that will ensue. For Dahl and many other contributors, the acid test of a power relationship was the existence of this conflict of interests between persons or groups.

Generally, definitions of power are synonymous with the concepts of authority and influence. Indeed, one of the earliest writers, Bernard (1938) defined power in terms of 'informal authority'. However, Luthans (1992, p. 427) draws important distinctions between the interconnected, though separate concepts of power and authority, and influence. Like many other contributors to the extant literature, he identifies power as the ability to get an individual or group to do something – to get the person or the group to change in some way. Authority, he argues, legitimises and is a source of power. Authority is the right to manipulate or change others. Power need not be legitimate. Influence, he suggests, is usually conceived of as being broader in scope than power. It involves the ability to alter others in general ways, such as by changing their satisfaction and performance. While both influence and power are involved in the leadership process, influence is more closely associated with leadership. Thus, he suggests that authority is different from power because of its legitimacy and acceptance, and influence is broader than power.

Broadly speaking, the impetus for the study of power in organisations came from two rather different directions (see Hardy and Clegg, 1996). One stream of research can be traced back to the early work of Max Weber. This body of work has focused on the existence of conflicting, competing interests and has examined power from the

287

perspective of domination. The pioneering sociologist Weber defined power as 'the probability that one actor within a social relationship will be in a position to carry out his own will despite resistance' (Weber, 1947, p. 152). In this respect, Hardy and Clegg note that it has largely focused on how power becomes embedded in organisational structures and systems in a way that serves certain, but not all interest groups in the organisation. Weber acknowledged that power was derived from having ownership of and controlling the means of production. However, it could not all be explained on the basis of ownership and non-ownership. Weber argued that power was also derived from knowledge of operations as much as from ownership. Most studies of power in organisations have focused on this type of power, what Pfeffer (1981) refers to as 'vertical or hierarchical power', or the power of supervisors over subordinates, or bosses over employees.

The second major research root associated with power, according to Hardy and Clegg (1996) examined how groups acquire power and wield power not granted to them under official arrangements. This line of research was more closely associated with management theorists who defined power as those actions that fell outside the legitimated structures, and which threatened organisational goals.

> One consequence of the widespread, if implicit, acceptance of the hierarchical nature of power has been that social scientists have rarely felt it necessary to explain why it is that power should be hierarchical. In other words, in this stream of research, the power embedded in the hierarchy has been viewed as normal and inevitable following from the formal design of the organisation. As such, it has been largely excluded from analyses which have, instead, focused on 'illegitimate' power i.e. power exercised outside formal hierarchical structures and the channels that they sanction. (Hardy and Clegg, 1996, p. 624)

Finchman and Rhodes (1988) suggest that by considering the amount of resistance offered by those under power, and also the strength of the sanctions brought to bear by those in power, the different types of power can be seen to fall within a continuum. This, they suggest, represents the extent of conflict between the interests of the 'in-power' group and the 'under-power' group.

It is evident then from this interpretation that power covers a very broad range of behaviours, from almost pure agreement to the resort to violence. In addition, the concept of authority overlaps with that of power, but they do differ. Garavan *et al.* (1993) suggest that power differs from authority in four key ways, as follows:

1. While authority usually operates in vertical directions down the organisational hierarchy, power typically operates in any direction.
2. While authority is often accepted by subordinates, power may not be accepted by those it is exercised upon.

3. In the organisational context, authority is vested in specific roles or position in the organisation, whereas power may arise from different.

4. While authority can be identified from the organisation chart, power is less observable in this concrete way and consequently it is more difficult to identify and label.

Figure 13.1: Types of power

Explaining the sources of power

French and Raven (1959) advance several bases of power which reflect the different bases or resources that power holders might rely upon. The sources they identify are reward, coercive, legitimate, referent, and expert power. Most discussions of power refer to these categories and they are considered a necessary foundation for understanding the multi-dimensional nature of the concept.

Reward power derives from the individual's control over resources and is dependent upon the ability of the power wielder to confer valued material rewards such as pay increases or promotions. In addition, the target of this power must value these rewards. Luthans (1992) argues that to understand this source of power more completely, it must be remembered that the recipient holds the key. If managers offer subordinates what they perceive to be a reward, but subordinates do not value it, then managers do not really have reward power. By the same token, there are instances where managers might not think that they are giving a reward to subordinates, but if subordinates perceive this to be rewarding, the managers nevertheless have reward power. Furthermore, there are instances where managers do not really have the rewards to distribute, but as long as their targets think they have, they continue in the targets' eyes to have reward power.

Coercive power refers to the power to punish or withhold reward, the power to threaten and to use one's position to force others to take action. In both cases it is the desire for valued rewards or the fear of having them withheld that ensure the obedience of those under power (Finchman and Rhodes, 1988). A coercive power source often relies on fear. This form of power has contributed substantially to the negative connotations that power has for many people. Managers generally have coercive power in that they can punish employees, or they can threaten punishment. Some psychologists maintain that much organisational behaviour can be more accurately explained in terms of coercive power rather than on the basis of reward power.

Legitimate power is that which is exercised in accordance with organisational rules and with the authority of the organisation. Finchman and Rhodes go so far as to say that it is identical with authority, and depends upon the belief of individuals in the right of senior people to hold their positions, and their consequent willingness to accept the power holder. Thus, according to Luthans (1992) legitimate power stems from the internalised values of the other persons which give the legitimate right to the agent to influence them. The individual with legitimacy is also in a position to reward or punish. As a source of power, it is dependent upon the position or role the person holds. Luthans (1992) outlines three major sources of legitimate power. Firstly, the prevailing cultural values of a society, organisation or group determine what is legitimate. Certain groups such as managers, or males as opposed to females, or the Church, may possess high levels of legitimate power in a society. Secondly, people may obtain legitimate power from the accepted social structure. Thus, arguably, when manual employees accept employment from a company, they are in effect accepting an established hierarchical structure and granting legitimate power to their supervisors. A third accepted source of legitimate power comes from being designated as the agent or representative of a powerful person, group or establishment. T.Ds, priests, members of the board of directors of a company, or shop stewards would be examples here.

Referent power is contingent upon the charisma, inter-personal skill and/or personal attraction of the individual. Typically here the person under power desires to identify with these personal qualities, and gains some satisfaction from being an accepted follower. It thus comes from the desire on the part of the other persons to identify with the individual wielding the power. They may wish to identify with the powerful person, regardless of the outcomes. In an organisational setting, referent power is arguably different from other types of power. Managers with referent power must be attractive to subordinates such that subordinates will want to identify with them, regardless of whether managers have the ability to reward or punish or whether they have legitimacy. Managers who depend on referent power must be personally attractive characters. Advertisers take advantage of this type of power when they use celebrities such as sports stars to do personal recommendation testimonial advertising.

Expert power, as the name suggests, derives from know-how or expertise which sets the individual apart from others. This source of power is determined by the extent to which others attribute knowledge and expertise to the power seeker. While all the major sources of power depend on the target's perceptions of the power holder, this is especially the case with expert power. The power holder must be seen to be convincing, trustworthy, honest and relevant before expert power is granted.

Finchman and Rhodes (1988) have identified a number of defects in French and Raven's classification. They argue that the reward and coercive forms of power identified are not in fact power sources in themselves – they merely describe the actions of people who have other power resources. In addition, they note that their legitimate and referent forms of power are taken from Weber's typology of authority, although without the addition of his third type, namely traditional authority. However, they do acknowledge that French and Raven's typology does serve to emphasise the fact that within organisations people can draw upon a broad range of different bases of power.

In a similar vein, Garavan *et al.* (1993) identify a range of power sources available to both internal and external organisational stakeholders.

- *Exchange power.* An internal stakeholder will have a lot of exchange power if he/she has control of a specific resource, a technical skill, specific information or a body of knowledge that is essential to the functioning of the organisation. In order for a stakeholder to have exchange power, the particular resource must be concentrated and non-substitutable, which means that it is not available in other places.
- *Position in the hierarchy.* An individual's position in the hierarchy provides them with formal power over others in the hierarchy. This can be conceived as authority.
- *Personal qualities/influence.* Some individuals may have specific personality characteristics which allow them to exercise influence. Influence might also arise because there is a high level of consensus within a particular department. An example here might include the existence of a persuasive personality, charisma, high energy levels.
- *The power of being there.* Individuals who have access to decision-making machinery and decision-makers are said to have power. Stakeholders who may not have strong exchange power may have considerable influence because they are participating in the decision-making process. Access to those who have power is also a source of power in itself.
- *Ability to give rewards or to punish.* Individuals or stakeholders who can distribute rewards to those who carry out their wishes or who can distribute sanctions will have power. In the case of the former, people obey because they believe they will be rewarded in some financial or psychological way and, in the latter case, compliance is secured through fear of punishment or removal of rewards.
- *Perceived power.* A power situation can arise because the decision-maker perceives the stakeholder to possess power. Managers who build up their power base can maintain their image long after their particular skills are no longer relevant to particular

problems or environmental conditions. Managers can make others believe that they possess power.

- *Boundary management functions.* Individuals and stakeholder groups who help the organisation manage its external environment tend to have power. This power arises because of their ability to reduce, control or absorb environmental uncertainty.
- *Control of strategic resources.* Stakeholders who control fundamental resources such as money, product design or human resources tend to have significant power.

The main sources of power for external stakeholders identified by Garavan *et al.* (1993) are as follows:

- *Creating dependency relationships.* External stakeholders such as financial institutions, key suppliers, have considerable capacity to create dependency relationships. Porter (1985) argues that the capacity of a supplier to create a dependency relationship is contingent upon five major factors: the concentration of the suppliers *vis-à-vis* the industry they sell to; the degree of substitutability between the products of different suppliers and the amount of product differentiation; the amount of and the potential for vertical integration; the importance of the supplier to the buyer; and the existence of switching costs if buyers want to switch suppliers.
- *Specialist knowledge and skills.* External stakeholders who possess specialist knowledge and skills critical to company success tend to have power. The extent of this power is contingent on the type of knowledge and expertise involved, how it impacts on the value chain, the supply of it in the external environment, and the extent to which the organisation can create the knowledge or skill itself.
- *Links with internal stakeholders.* External stakeholders who have access to key internal stakeholders can generate significant power. This arises from the realisation that they develop relationships and are influenced also by the power of the internal stakeholder involved.
- *Concentration of external stakeholders.* The power of suppliers, buyers or distribution companies can be significantly influenced by their concentration. The greater the degree of concentration, the greater their potential to set their own terms and to negotiate favourable agreements and contracts.
- *Involvement in the strategy implementation process.* External stakeholders who support key linkages in the value chain can generate power. The knowledge which this involvement generates can be used to the advantage of the external stakeholder and can allow them to dictate terms to the organisation.

Influencing the targets of power

Luthans (1992, p. 433) notes that while most discussions of power imply a unilateral process of influence from the agent to the target, the power relationship can be better understood by examining some of the characteristics of the target. Drawing upon the work of Reitz (1987) he outlines a set of characteristics which have been identified as being especially important to the influenceability of targets:

1. *Dependency.* The greater the target's dependency on their relationship to agents (for example, when a target cannot escape a relationship, perceives no alternatives, or values the agent's rewards as unique), the more targets are influenced.
2. *Uncertainty.* Experiments have shown that the more uncertain that people are about the appropriateness of a behaviour, the more likely they are to be influenced to change that behaviour.
3. *Personality.* There have been a number of research studies showing the relationship between personality characteristics and 'influenceability'. Some of these findings are obvious (for example, people who cannot tolerate ambiguity or who are highly anxious are more susceptible to influence, and those with high needs for affiliation are more susceptible to group influence), but some are not (for example, both positive and negative relationships have been found between self-esteem and influenceability).
4. *Intelligence.* There is no simple relationship between intelligence and influenceability. For example, highly intelligent people may be more willing to listen, but, because they also tend to be held in high esteem, they also may be more resistant to influence.
5. *Sex.* Although traditionally it was acknowledged that women were more likely to conform to influence attempts than men because of the way they were raised, there is now evidence that this has changed. As women's and society's views of the role of women are changing, there is less of a distinction by sex of influenceability.
6. *Age.* Social psychologists have generally concluded that susceptability to influence increases in young children up to about age eight or nine, and then decreases with age until adolescence, when it levels off.
7. *Culture.* Obviously, the cultural values of a society have a tremendous impact on the influenceability of its people. For example, Western cultures emphasise individuality, dissent and diversity, and tend to decrease influenceability, while others, such as many in the Far East, emphasise cohesiveness, agreement and uniformity, which tend to promote influenceability.

Use of power

Power can be a fundamental part of the management process. Many commentators argue that introducing and effectively implementing strategic change requires the use of power and influence. Dawson (1996, p. 175) identifies three main sources of constraint which limit attempts to exercise power in pursuit of interest:

1. *Technological:* the parameters set by the plant, machinery and equipment.
2. *Administrative:* the parameters set by rules, procedures and formal structure.
3. *Ideological:* the views of those who are already in strong positions of power concerning what is feasible and desirable.

Table 13.1: Personal power and political tactics

Expertise	Particularly significant where the skill is in scarce supply. It is possible to use mobility, and the threat of leaving, to gain support for certain changes of strategy – again dependent upon the manager's personal importance to the firm.
Assured stature	A reputation for being a 'winner' or a manager who can obtain results. Recent successes are most relevant.
Credibility	Particularly credibility with external power sources, such as suppliers or customers.
Control over information	Internal and external sources. Information can be used openly and honestly or withheld and used selectively – consequently it is crucial to know the reliability of the source.
Group support	In managing and implementing change it is essential to have the support of colleagues and fellow managers.
Political tactics to obtain results	
Develop liaisons	As mentioned above, it is important to develop and maintain both formal and informal contact with other managers, functions and divisions. Again it is important it includes those managers who are most powerful.
Present conservative image	It can be disadvantageous to be seen as too radical an agent of change.
Diffuse opposition	Conflicts need to brought out into the open and differences of opinion aired rather than kept hidden. Divide and rule can be a useful strategy.
Trade-off and compromise	In any proposal or suggestion for change it is important to consider the needs of other people whose support is required.
'Strike while the iron is hot'	Successful managers should build on successes and reputation quickly.

Research	Information is always vital to justify and support proposals.
Use a neutral cover	Radical changes, or those which other people might perceive as a threat to them, can sometimes be usefully disguised and initiated as minor changes. This is linked to the next point.
Limit communication	A useful tactic can be to unravel change gradually in order to contain possible opposition.
Withdraw strategically	If things are going wrong, and especially if the changes are not crucial, it can be a wise tactic on occasion to withdraw at least temporarily.

Politically successful managers understand organisational processes and they are sensitive to the needs of others.
Effective political action brings about desirable and successful changes in organisations – it is functional.
Negative political action is dysfunctional, and can enable manipulative managers to pursue their personal objectives against the better interests of the organisation.
The strategic leader needs to be an effective politician.

Sources: Alen *et al.*, 1979; Dixon, 1982; Garavan *et al.*, 1993

MacMillan (1978) suggests that there are two basic options open to the strategist who wishes to bring about change. He can either structure the situation so that others comply with his wishes, or he can communicate with people and seek to change their perceptions so that they see things differently and decide to do as he suggests. Arguably, in the former situation the strategist is using power bases as enabling resources, while in the latter situation he is seeking to use influence.

Table 13.2: Some common strategies for developing and using power within an organisation

Develop power by:

Creating dependence in others –

- work in areas of high uncertainty;
- cultivate centrality by working in critical areas;
- develop non-substitutable skills.

Coping with uncertainty on behalf of others –

- prevention;
- forecasting;
- absorption.

Developing personal networks.
Developing and constantly augmenting your expertise.

Use power to:
Control information flows to others.
Control agendas –

- issue definition;
- order of issues;
- issue exclusion.

Control decision-making criteria –

- long versus short-term considerations;
- return versus risk;
- choose criteria that favour your abilities and contributions.

Co-optation and coalition building –

- external alliances (e.g. supplier or customer relationships, interlocking boards of directors);
- internal alliances;
- promote loyal subordinates;
- appoint committees;
- gain representation on important committees.

Bring in outside experts (consultants) to bolster your position.

Source: Hatch, 1997

Distributing power: the empowerment environment

The extent to which employees have a sense of personal power and control has become recognised as central to their performance and well-being. Employee empowerment is a central feature of the new organisation scenario, but conditions must be right for empowerment to thrive. In many organisations, empowerment has become a buzz word, and although often used, the term is often not understood. Where does empowerment begin? What must organisations be like in order for empowerment to occur? As highlighted earlier in Chapter 1 in our discussion on the new environment of organisation, there is often agreement about the way an empowered employee should behave, but much less so on which conditions are necessary for fostering enough empowerment to change a traditionally hierarchical organisation into a more participative one. Dobbs (1993) advances four necessary conditions to encourage empowerment: participation; innovation; access to information; and accountability. These factors combined produce an organisational feeling and tone that can have a dramatic, positive effect on employees.

- *Participation*. People must be actively and willingly engaged in their jobs. They must care about improving their daily work processes and work relationships. Such involvement does not come about simply: it has to be fostered.

- *Innovation*. It is almost impossible for empowerment to exist in environments in which innovation is ignored, or stifled. Empowerment cannot exist in an organisation that expects employees to do their jobs the way they have always done them. Employees need to be given permission to innovate. As Shepard (1967) suggests:

> the most successful corporate innovation systems aren't systems at all. They are environments that are hospitable to interesting people with innovative ideas – environments that encourage people to explore new paths and take meaningful risks at reasonable costs . . . Innovation is as much a core value as is an acceptable return on investment.

- *Access to information*. In many organisations information can be a source of power. In traditional organisations, the senior managers decide who receives what kind of information. In organisations in which employees are empowered, people at every level make decisions about what kind of information they need for performing their jobs.

- *Accountability*. Traditionally, too many workplaces have stifled enterprise, initiative and entrepreneurship, and have failed to create a climate where individuals perceive a sense of personal power. The result is that individuals go elsewhere to engage in activities that provide them with the stimulus to innovate, where they demonstrate far more skill than most employers encourage them to show at work. Many managers still hold the mistaken belief that to empower subordinates is to undermine or indeed lose one's own power. Hollander and Offermann (1990) suggest that an effective way of overcoming such a perception is to ensure that those managers who do empower their employees are not blamed for their people's mistakes and/or failures, nor ignored when their people succeed.

POLITICS

Politics is about access to power and mobilising power. When reviewing how power is utilised in organisations, one inevitably must address the issue of organisational politics, or what Tyson and Jackson (1992, p. 94) term those 'strategies individuals and groups adopt in order to maintain their power, to prevent others from taking their power, or to enlarge their power'. Politics in organisations involves 'those activities taken within the company to acquire, develop and use power and other resources to obtain one's preferred outcomes in a situation in which there is uncertainty or dissension about choices' (Pfeffer, 1981, p. 7). Bacharach and Lawler (1980, pp. 1–2) in their observations on politics note that:

Organizations are neither the rational, harmonious entities celebrated in managerial theory, nor the arenas of apocalyptic class conflict projected by Marxists. Rather, it may be argued, a more suitable notion lies somewhere between these two – a concept of organizations as politically negotiated orders. Adopting this view, we can observe organizational actors in their daily transactions, perpetually bargaining, repeatedly forming and reforming coalitions, and constantly availing themselves of influence tactics . . . politics in organisations involve the tactical use of power to retain or obtain control of real or symbolic resources. In describing the processes of organizations as political acts, we are not making a moral judgement; we are simply making an observation about a process.

Politics permeates organisations because organisations are collections of people who have differing past experiences, differing current circumstances and therefore potentially differing interests (Hickson, 1990). If there was no opposition within an organisation to what a manager wanted to do, then it would be largely unnecessary for them to engage in political activity. The central issue here then is influence, exercised according to the power source one is drawing from (reward, coercive, legitimate, referent and/or expert). The task of accommodating everyone's interests when something is being decided is largely a political one, based on influence. In this respect, four general political tactics can be identified, namely *inducement, coercion, persuasion*, and *obligation*. Inducement implies the ability to control the situation and the outcome is perceived as beneficial by others involved. This is a positive situation. During coercion, the situation is again controlled but the outcome is perceived in negative terms. Specific acts of coercion might include the threat of dismissal, no further promotions or the withdrawal of privileges. Using the tactics of persuasion requires the strategist to sell the benefits of acting in a certain way. This could be the promise of rewards, promotions, greater job security, more authority and responsibility. The outcome in this case should be positive. Obligation, on the other hand, is an intentional tactic where people are persuaded to behave and act in a particular way by appealing to obligation. The obligation could be something that they are said to owe the company, that they owe particular favours or have obligations towards a particular group of people. The outcome in this case is negative.

Table 13.3: Advantages and disadvantages of specific political tactics in a change scenario

Inducement

Advantages

- Break down resistance to change.
- Employees can see some benefits of the change.
- Individual managers have positive feelings about the change.
- The situation is under control.

Disadvantages

- Will incur additional costs for the organisation.
- Must deliver on the inducements offered.
- Change may still be resisted.
- Its success depends on previous initiatives.

Coercion

Advantages

- Management are in control of the situation.
- Suitable in situations where quick decisions have to be made for survival.
- Management are exerting management prerogative.

Disadvantages
- The coercion will have dysfunctional consequences.
- Employees will usually find ways of resisting the change.
- Makes future changes very difficult because it creates negative precedent.

Persuasion

Advantages

- The need for change is communicated.
- There are attempts to educate the organisation on the need for change.
- The change has a better chance of being implemented.
- It is a way of getting undesirable changes implemented.

Disadvantages

- Employees may not believe in the promises made.
- Management credibility may be low
- Can be costly for the organisation.
- Slows down the pace of strategic change

Obligation

Advantages

- Does not involve additional costs to the organisation.
- Suitable tactic where there is high commitment to the organisation.
- Change can be introduced quickly.

Disadvantages

- The outcome will most likely be negative.
- Employees may see the tactic for what it is.
- Employees may expect rewards in return for their commitment.

Source: Garavan *et al.*, 1993

In his examination of the influence process between specialist and executives in organisations, Pettigrew (1974) details a series of political ploys frequently drawn upon as part of their political repertoire (Box 13.2).

Box 13.2: Strategies used by executives

- *Strategic rejection.* If executive is self-assured and powerful, rejects the report.
- *Bottom drawer it.* Executive sends a memo praising the specialist's technicality, and then puts it away and forgets it.
- *Mobilising political support.* Executive calls in the credits from colleagues.
- *Nitty-gritty tactic.* Minor details are questioned, and mistakes in details are raised to try to discredit the whole report.
- *Emotional tactic.* Relies on appeals to emotional states – such as personal consequences of action.
- *But in the future.* Argument that data may be historically accurate but does not consider future changes.
- *Invisible man.* Avoidance, often with the support of a secretary, so no discussion can take place.
- *Further investigation required.* Specialist is sent away to collect more information, either because terms of reference are changed, or to follow up the more interesting issues in the report.
- *Scapegoat.* A suitable scapegoat, who is raised as a threat to any change proposed.
- *Deflection.* Discussion is deflected away from the main areas by concentrating the attention on less crucial matters.

The most political processes

Hickson (1990) argues that the making of particular strategic decisions in organisations may be a highly political affair, or may involve very little political activity, depending on the exact nature of the decision.

The overall character of the processes differ a great deal. The making of one strategic decision may be a most political affair, the next much less so, a third least political of all. This does not denote their importance. All will be strategic with costly and far-reaching consequences, yet some will be more political than others. (Hickson, 1990, p. 178)

The processes that are likely to be politically charged he labels *'sporadic processes'*. Those less politically charged are termed *'constricted processes'*, while those that are least politically prone he describes as *'fluid processes'*.

Sporadic processes are likely to be highly politically charged as they deal with particularly weighty and controversial matters. According to Hickson, these are matters with potentially serious consequences, drawing in a multiplicity of information and views from numerous departments and external sources. 'Many of those involved have interests which come from differing objectives. In short, such a matter is diversely involving, contentious, with external influences, from which come its political nature. Typical examples would be decisions on novel new products and on take-overs' (p. 179).

Constricted processes are likely to be less politically loaded than sporadic ones. A constricted process typically refers to a relatively normal and recurrent matter that has some familiarity about it, e.g. a business plan or a budget. Matters of this nature have been dealt with previously, and the way it will be dealt with is largely understood and accepted. Hickson (1990) notes that its consequences will not likely concern everyone and 'in particular they do not implicate external interests. If strong interests have to be reckoned with they will be from inside the organisation . . . Such a matter is comparatively well known, with consequences that are more limited, influenced by internal interests only' (p. 179).

Fluid processes are least likely to encounter controversy, and consequently, according to Hickson, they are least politically prone. They most especially focus on usual, but non-controversial matters, and while the consequences will likely be felt more broadly, they are not likely to be as serious as those described as constricted or sporadic. Typically fewer interests are involved and their interests are generally highly compatible. Influence is generally evenly spread among the stakeholders. 'Though such a matter can be quite novel and have diffuse consequences, it is not excessively serious nor contentious so it is likely to be dealt with in a relatively smooth, steadily paced, formally channelled, speedy way' (p. 180).

ETHICS

Many people find it hard to take seriously the concept of business ethics, and according to Green (1994) they view it as an oxymoron much like 'jumbo shrimp' or 'military intelligence', because business misconduct has fostered the view that businessmen and businesswomen are unconcerned with ethics and are even prepared to break the law if they can get away with it. Despite this, or perhaps in response to it, over the past twenty years or so, the field of business ethics and social responsibility has achieved a recognised place in business education. Management ethics are those standards of behaviour that guide individual managers in their work, while social responsibility can be viewed as that set of obligations an organisation has to protect and enhance the society in which it functions (Garavan *et al.*, 1993).

Box 13.3: Shouldn't employees already know the difference between right and wrong?

A belief is that any individual of good character should already know right from wrong and should be able to be ethical without special training. You probably think of yourself as an individual of good character. So think about the following real dilemma.

You are the VP of a medium-sized organisation that uses chemicals in its production processes. In good faith you have hired a highly competent person to ensure that your company complies with all environmental laws and safety regulations. This individual informs you that a chemical that the company now uses in some quantity is not yet on the approved Environmental Protection Agency list, although it is undergoing review and is scheduled to be placed on the approved list in about three months because it has been found to be safe. You can't produce your product without this chemical, yet you are not supposed to use the chemical until it is approved. Waiting for approval would require shutting the plant for three months, putting many people out of work, and threatening the company's very survival. What should you do?

Source: Trevino and Nelson, 1995

What kind of factors determine an individual's ethics? Individuals begin to form ethical standards as children during the formative period, in response to their perceptions of the behaviour of their parents and the behaviour that parents allow them to enact. Similarly, individuals are influenced by peers with whom they interact on a continuous basis. Clearly, if these peers have high ethical standards and reject certain behaviours, then the individual is more likely to adopt similar high standards. Clearly also, important events may shape individuals' lives and contribute to their ethical beliefs and behaviour. They may be both positive and negative. Situational factors may also determine ethical behaviour. Individuals may find themselves in unexpected situations which cause them to act against their better judgment. Furthermore, a person's values and morals also contribute to ethical standards. For example, an individual who places financial gain and personal advancement as high priorities will adopt a personal code of ethics that promotes the pursuit of wealth. However, good solid character arguably does not completely prepare one to deal with the many ethical dilemmas that they will face in their working lives. Rest (1988) argues that to assume that any twenty-year-old of good character can function ethically in professional situations, is no more warranted than assuming that any logical twenty-year-old can function as a lawyer without any special education. This raises the question about whether ethics can actually be taught. Many dissenters take the view that educational institutions can do little, if students have not already learned ethics from their parents and families, friends, schools and significant others (Levin, 1990; Hanson, 1988). However, the critical point here relates to the notion of learning. If ethical codes and standards are learned, and clearly they are, then they can be unlearned and new standards can be acquired to replace them with.

Management researchers began to study business ethics and social responsibility during the 1960s by conducting surveys of managers' attitudes towards business ethics (Baumhart, 1961). Since then, Trevino and Nelson (1995) note that interest in the area has grown substantially in the last thirty years to the point where articles and books proliferate the academic and professional press. Management ethics are the standards of behaviour that guide individual managers in their work. However, it is important to note that ethical or unethical actions do not occur in a vacuum. The actions of peer managers, top management combined with the organisation's culture, all contribute to the ethical context of the organisation. That said, the starting-point for understanding the ethical context of management is the individual's own ethical standards. Garavan *et al.* (1993) identify three areas where managerial ethics, the standards of behaviour that guide managers in their work, are most significant:

1. *Relationships of the firm to its employees.* The behaviour of individual managers defines the ethical standards according to which the company treats its employees. Examples of such areas include hiring and firing, wages and working conditions, employee privacy, support for religious beliefs, etc.
2. *Relationship of employees to the firm.* Issues which arise here include conflicts of interest, secrecy, honesty in keeping expense accounts, not making secret profits, accepting gifts from potential clients, etc.
3. *Relationship of the firm to others.* This would include relationships with customers, suppliers, behaviour towards competitors, dealing with stockholders, unions and the local community.

Carr (1968) argues that business has an ethics of its own, different from that which governs our ordinary personal relationships. For the sake of profits and economic success, this ethic permits conscious mis-statements, concealment of pertinent facts, and exaggeration. He likens business ethics to a game of poker governed by an acceptable set of formal rules.

No one expects poker to be played on the ethical principles preached in churches. In poker it is right and proper to bluff a friend out of the rewards of being dealt a good hand. A player feels no more than a slight twinge of sympathy, if that, when – with nothing better than a single ace in his hand – he strips a heavy loser who holds a pair, of the rest of his chips. It was up to the other fellow to protect himself . . . Poker's own brand of ethics is different from the ethical ideals of civilised human relationships . . . No one thinks any worse of poker on that account. And no one should think any the worse of the game of business because its standards of right and wrong differ from the prevailing traditions of morality in our society. (Carr, 1968, p. 145)

This view, according to Green (1994), while holding some truth, also distorts the reality of managerial ethical responsibility. 'Managers are sometimes validly thought of as game players. But game ethics must be replaced by more familiar moral standards when managers' actions seriously impact on persons not playing the business game' (p. 9).

Managing ethical behaviour

Recent years have witnessed many ethical scandals with the result that many organisations have begun to place more emphasis on the ethical behaviour of employees. Significant here are attempts by management to:

- set a good example and act as role models in relation to ethical behaviour;
- establish and manage an organisation's culture so that it clearly delineates what is acceptable and unacceptable behaviour;
- offer employees training and development on how to cope with ethical dilemmas;
- establish an ethics committee that reports directly to the board of directors;
- prepare guidelines that detail how employees are to treat suppliers, customers, competitors and other stakeholders;
- develop codes of ethics which are written statements of the values and ethical standards that guide a company's actions.

Box 13.4: Business ethics and Irish management

Introduction
Do ethical considerations influence the key business dialogues or will the next generation of up and coming top Irish management similarly slip having learnt little from the recent exposés? In effect, what do Irish managers really think about ethics, morality, and business practice?

The study
930 senior managers were surveyed – 530 UK, 100 Republic of Ireland, and 300 US. The sample only involved senior managers, the managerial roles varying from general managers to executive directors and main or subsidiary board members. Differences in sample size reflect the challenge of gaining access to senior level managers and the range and number of medium to large sized organizations in

each of these countries. Questionnaires were distributed to named individuals invited to participate in the study, with the result that an over 70 per cent response rate ensued. 83 per cent of the total sample are between the ages of 36 to 55 years.

Findings

- Irish managers are significantly more convinced than UK, but less than US managers, that every company and every industry should have a code of ethics.
- Irish managers give significantly greater importance than UK or US managers to the influence which increasing public concern about ethical standards has on behaviour in business.
- UK managers agree significantly less strongly than Irish or US managers in three areas, namely that business schools should include more ethics training for students, or with the capacity of public opinion to influence a businessperson's ethical behaviour, or with every company and every industry having a code of ethics.
- US managers are significantly more in favour than UK or Irish managers of consultancy intervention in helping managers to deal with ethical issues.
- Irish managers agree significantly more strongly than UK or US managers that ethical beliefs should be a consideration in the selection of managers.

Ethical standards in Irish business today

Managers were asked whether they believed ethical standards in business have fallen, stayed the same or risen over the last ten years. 37 per cent believe they had fallen, 42 per cent believe they have stayed the same, and 11 per cent believe they have risen. For those who say standards have fallen, greed, self-centredness, increased competition, and social tendency towards a 'me first' mentality, are the chief reasons put forward. Some argue that standards are the same, and that it is merely our awareness of malpractices that has been increased.

The duality of the Irish

These findings are representative of a major duality in the ethical stance of Irish management. On the one hand, the study reveals a generally high awareness of ethical issues and issues surrounding the implementation of ethics in business, but on the other, reveals what is essentially a preparedness to place as highest priority the interest of corporate stockholders. Essentially, the situation is one in which Irish managers may espouse ethical intentions until the need arises to satisfy stockholder needs. A narrow view of corporate responsibility, confined only or mainly to stockholder interests is evidence of profoundly short-term thinking.

Considerations towards enhancing ethical behaviour

Based on the findings of the research, there are a number of practical suggestions which can be made to Irish managers to increase awareness of ethics in business, and enhance the potential for ethical behaviour in organizations.

Shareholder impact

Of prime importance is highlighting to Irish managers the inherent dangers of attributing so great a corporate responsibility solely to stockholders, the most significant of which is the likelihood of creating an organizational culture at senior level which is built around the principle of satisfying stockholder interests at any costs. Such cultures are inevitable breeding grounds of potentially unethical behaviour both among management and staff. There is evidence from the research that Irish managers do indeed recognize the need for a broader concept of organization stakeholders and consequently of corporate responsibilities. This broader concept should be encouraged through reinforcement, education, and training at all levels.

Training and education

Inclusion of business ethics teaching within Irish business schools and university business-oriented courses is considered desirable. Ethics education and training is shown by previous research (Delaney and Sockell, 1992), to have a positive effect on sensitivity to and awareness of potential influences on behaviour, ethical issues, and ethical conflicts, yet few Irish managers have received any ethics education at all.

The role of top management

Enhancing awareness of the crucial role which top management plays in the creation of a culture of ethical behaviour within organizations is equally desirable. Alongside emphasis on the role of top management competence in visioning, communication, and creation of mission and culture outside the ethical dimension in management development, the importance of competence in the ethical dimension should also be highlighted.

Source: Extracts from Alderson, S. and Kakabadse, A. (1994), 'Business Ethics and Irish Management: A Cross Cultural Study', *European Journal of Management*, Vol. 12, No. 4, pp. 432–441

Box 13.5: Advantages and limitations of written codes of ethics

Advantages

1. They are a concrete indication of the organisation's commitment to high standards of ethical behaviour
2. They clearly establish parameters within which individuals must behave.
3. They give employees a commitment that no one will be called upon to do anything in the line of duty that is morally, ethically or legally wrong.
4. It provides employees with a legitimate basis to inform top management of unethical behaviour and have it dealt with.
5. The code may help employees to resolve actual or potential ethical dilemmas.

Limitations

1. They may prescribe what people should do, but they often fail to help people understand and live with the consequences of their choices.
2. The code may be ignored by key people in the organisation, thus openly undermining its effectiveness.
3. Managers may not be prepared to make ethical choices because of the possibility of

unpleasant outcomes such as firing, rejection by colleagues, and the loss of monetary gain.

4. Individual managers must be prepared to confront the consequences of their own decisions and weigh up the options available when making difficult ethical decisions. A code will not do this for them.
5. The code may not cover all possible situations which may arise.
6. The code may be unsuccessfully communicated and may not support appropriate procedures, i.e. discipline procedures and avenues to inform on unethical behaviour.

Source: Garavan *et al.*, 1993.

In relation to broader social responsibility, organisations relate to their environment in ways that may often involve ethical dilemmas and decisions. Garavan *et al.* (1993) argue that organisations exercise social responsibility towards three primary interests, namely organisational constituents, the natural environment, and the wider society.

Organisational constituents are defined as people and other organisations who are directly affected by the behaviour of the organisation and who have a stake in its performance. These include customers, creditors, suppliers, employees, owners/investors, local government, etc. To maintain a social responsibility to investors, for example, requires financial managers to follow proper accounting procedures, provide appropriate information to stakeholders about the financial performance of the company, and manage the organisation to profit shareholders' rights and interests. Insider trading, illegal stock manipulation and withholding financial data are examples of unethical behaviour in this area.

In relation to the natural environment, there has been an increasing awareness of its importance in recent years. Examples of issues which are emerging here include:

- developing feasible ways to avoid contributing to acid rain and global warming;
- developing alternative methods of handling sewage, hazardous wastes and ordinary wastage;
- developing safety policies that cut down on accidents with potentially disastrous environmental results;
- initiating crisis management plans to deal with disasters such as the *Exxon* oil tanker, *Valdez;*
- using recycled materials.

Promoting the general welfare of society is believed by many to be a central aspect of business social responsibility. Examples here of positive activity in this area include:

- making contributions to charities, philanthropic organisations and not-for-profit foundations and associations;

- supporting culturally enriching activities;
- taking an active role in public health and education;
- acting to combat the political inequalities that exist in the world.

Box 13.6: Arguments for and against social responsibility

Arguments for
- Business creates problems and should therefore help to solve them.
- Corporations are citizens in our society.
- Business often has the resources necessary to solve problems.
- Business is a partner in our society, along with the government and the general population.

Arguments against
- The purpose of business is to generate profit for owners.
- Investment in social programmes gives business too much power.
- There is potential for conflicts of interest.
- Business lacks the expertise to manage social programmes.

Source: Garavan *et al.*, 1993

Activity 13.1: The human relationships questionnaire

Developed by Richard Christie, the test attempts to predict whether a person becomes emotionally involved with other people, or simply uses them for his/her own ends. Also known as the Machiavelli Test, it is used to measure machiavellian tendencies. A high score on the test will give you a high machiavellian tendency.

The following questions ask you about how you behave at work, what you believe about human relationships, and what value you place on them.

Each question is presented as a statement: you are asked to choose one of five possible responses:

Strongly agree / Agree / Don't know / Disagree / Strongly disagree.

There are no right answers and no wrong answers; so please be as honest as you can.

(See below for the scoring key).

		STRONGLY AGREE	AGREE	DON'T KNOW	DISAGREE	STRONGLY DISAGREE
1.	You should only tell someone the real reason for doing something if it serves as a successful purpose.	☐	☐	☐	☐	☐
2.	People who lead upright and respectable lives will get on in the world.	☐	☐	☐	☐	☐
3.	Bravery is inherent in most people.	☐	☐	☐	☐	☐

	STRONGLY AGREE	AGREE	DON'T KNOW	DISAGREE	STRONGLY DISAGREE
4. You should always assume that people can be villainous and that this will appeal if given a chance.	☐	☐	☐	☐	☐
5. Telling people what they want to hear is the best way to deal with them.	☐	☐	☐	☐	☐
6. The old saying that 'there's one born every minute' is not true.	☐	☐	☐	☐	☐
7. Lying to other people cannot be forgiven.					
8. Giving the actual reason rather than ones which may carry more weight is the way to behave when asking someone to do something for you.	☐	☐	☐	☐	☐
9. It is sensible to pander to important people.	☐	☐	☐	☐	☐
10. It is hard to be successful in an organisation without cutting corners.	☐	☐	☐	☐	☐
11. What differentiates criminals from other people is that they are foolish enough to get caught.	☐	☐	☐	☐	☐
12. Euthanasia should be a choice for those having an incurable disease.	☐	☐	☐	☐	☐
13. In the final analysis, most people are good and well meaning.	☐	☐	☐	☐	☐
14. You should only act when it is morally defensible.	☐	☐	☐	☐	☐
15. Humility coupled with honesty is a better combination than dishonesty and self importance.	☐	☐	☐	☐	☐
16. Unless forced to work hard, most people will stretch themselves.	☐	☐	☐	☐	☐
17. Being good in all respects is quite possible.	☐	☐	☐	☐	☐
18. The death of a parent is more easily forgotten by most people than the loss of a piece of property.	☐	☐	☐	☐	☐
19. It is simply asking for trouble to trust someone else completely.	☐	☐	☐	☐	☐
20. It is best always to be honest.	☐	☐	☐	☐	☐

Scoring key for human relationships questionnaire					
Question No.	STRONGLY AGREE	AGREE	DON'T KNOW	DISAGREE	STRONGLY DISAGREE
1	5	4	3	2	1
2	1	2	3	4	5
3	1	2	3	4	5
4	5	4	3	2	1
5	5	4	3	2	1
6	1	2	3	4	5
7	1	2	3	4	5
8	1	2	3	4	5
9	5	4	3	2	1
10	5	4	3	2	1
11	5	4	3	2	1
12	5	4	3	2	1
13	1	2	3	4	5
14	1	2	3	4	5
15	1	2	3	4	5
16	5	4	3	2	1
17	1	2	3	4	5
18	5	4	3	2	1
19	5	4	3	2	1
20	1	2	3	4	5

Calculate your overall score. Score =

Score	Comment
20–38	Goodness shines through you. How do you survive?
39–54	No is not an impossible word to say – you only think it is.
55–69	An honest cynic: at least relatively honest.
70–84	Congratulations – you could be an honorary member of the Borgia family.
85–100	You might even be able to teach Machiavelli something. ('Never give a sucker an even break' – W. C. Fields).

Source: Tyson and Jackson, 1992

SUMMARY OF KEY PROPOSITIONS

- Power, politics and ethics are important concepts for explaining behaviour in organisations.
- Power relates to the extent to which individuals or stakeholders are able to pursue or convince others to take a certain course of action. Politics can be viewed as power in action and consists of strategies and tactics drawn upon for the purpose of influencing individuals and groups. Management ethics are the standards of behaviour that guide individual managers in their work. Social responsibility refers to the set of obligations an organisation has to protect and enhance the society in which it functions.

- Authority is the right to manipulate or change others. Power need not be legitimate. Influence is usually conceived of as being broader in scope than power. It involves the ability to alter others in general ways, such as by changing their satisfaction and performance.
- The impetus for the study of power in organisations came from two rather different directions. One stream of research focused on the existence of conflicting, competing interests and has examined power from the perspective of domination. The second major research root associated with power examined how groups acquire power and wield power not granted to them under official arrangements.
- Several bases of power exist reflecting the different bases or resources that power holders might rely upon. The sources identified are reward, coercive, legitimate, referent and expert power.
- Employee empowerment, referring to the extent to which employees have a sense of personal power and control, has become recognised as a central feature of the new organisation scenario.
- Four general political tactics can be identified, namely inducement, coercion, persuasion and obligation.
- Processes that are likely to be highly politically charged are described as sporadic. Those less politically charged are termed constricted processes, while those that are least politically prone are labelled fluid processes.
- Organisations exercise social responsibility towards three primary interests, namely organisational constituents, the natural environment and the wider society.

DISCUSSION QUESTIONS

1. What do you think are the main sources of power within an organisation?
2. What political tactics might you employ to bring about large-scale speedy change in an organisation?
3. Is the use of power in an organisational context ethical?
4. Identify key factors that determine individual ethics
5. Describe five types of unethical behaviour.
6. Think of some examples of firms that are making attempts to be socially responsible. Identify exactly what courses of action they are taking to be so.

CHAPTER 14

Organisation Change and Development

LEARNING OBJECTIVES

- Describe what is meant by organisation change.
- Understand the process of change management in organisations.
- Differentiate between various models of managing change.
- Understand why individuals resist change.
- Outline the various techniques of organisation development.

INTRODUCTION

In recent years, a considerable literature has grown up on organisational change and change management, with the central message of many of the 'change gurus' being that change is the only constant in life. Vaill (1989) argues that organisational environments are characterised by chaotic change, while Peters (1987) suggests that general uncertainty pervades contemporary environments. Change is indeed a pervasive feature of everyday life, and there has never been an age where change did not take place. History presents a story of change through the centuries, *viz* the development of human society. The development of the wheel; the age of renaissance and reformation; the Industrial Revolution; the invention of automotive transport; the discovery of electricity – imagine what life would be like if all of these changes had not occurred. Organisations, like everyday life, are not static. Hussey (1995) argues that change is one of the most critical aspects of effective management and that the turbulent business environment in which most organisations operate means that not only is change becoming more frequent, but that the nature of change may be increasingly complex, and the impact of change is often more extensive. Tersine *et al.* (1997, p. 45) suggest that:

> Change has joined death and taxes as life certainties. Some businesses have been quick to accept and adopt changes, others are struggling to cope with it. Specialists and individualism have been replaced by teams and co-operation. People are being asked to do more with less on a regular basis from a litany of change, innovate, re-engineer, continuously improve, and then change again.

In this chapter we examine the origins of change management from a theoretical perspective; we discuss a number of pertinent models of organisation change and explore a number of key variables that lead to resistance to change initiatives; finally we focus on organisation development as an independent technique in managing successful change.

UNDERSTANDING CHANGE

In general, change can be characterised as either radical or innovative. Radical change relates to large-scale organisation-wide transformation programmes involving the rapid and wholesale overturning of old ways and old ideas and their replacement by new and unique ones. Such change represents a conscious and decisive break with the past and so is often referred to as revolutionary change. Incremental change, on the other hand, refers to relatively small-scale projects that are localised and designed to solve a particular problem, or enhance the performance of a sub-section or part of the organisation. This type of change is sometimes referred to as evolutionary since it can often be incremental, unco-ordinated and indeed piecemeal. This is not to suggest, however, that it is unimportant. In fact, more often it is the incremental changes that keep the organisation on an even keel and so are essential for organisational survival from day to day. Tersine *et al.* (1997) provide an interesting characterisation of change which details that the magnitude and the rate of change can be measured from normal to severe relative to technical/economic and human/social issues. They argue that while severe change might be absorbed on one or the other dimension, it may not be integrated in both at the same time.

Figure 14.1: Taxonomy of change

Technical/Economic	
• New product introduction. • Opening new facilities. • Fluctuation in stock value. • Open new market. • New competitor enters market.	• Introduction of revolutionary new technology by competitor. • Economic depression. • Hostile takeover of company. • Significant change in regulatory environment.
Normal Change	**Severe Change**
• Acquisition. • Hiring new personnel. • Relocation of personnel. • Reorganisation.	• Radical downsizing. • Re-engineering. • Significant legal action taken against organisation. • Facility closing. • Entering international marketplace • Establishing virtual organisation.
Human/Social	

Source: Tersine *et al.*, 1997

Managing change is not unproblematic. Both Blacker and Brown (1986) and Burnes (1996a) suggest that the introduction of initiatives such as total quality management often fail because companies lack ability in terms of planning and managing change, motivating and involving employees, and designing and implementing suitable job and work structures. Wilson (1993) cautions that change of any kind is threatening, for not only is there the uncertainty of the new but also the loss of a trusted friend – 'the way we have always done things around here'.

Burnes (1996b) argues that change management is not a distinct discipline with rigid and clearly defined boundaries. Rather, the theory and practice of change management draws upon a number of social science disciplines and traditions. In particular, three distinct schools of thought are evident.

The individual perspective school

Advocates of the individual perspective suggest that the focus of change should centre around the individual and his/her behaviour. Drawing upon the behaviourist theories of human learning (see Chapter 5 for detailed treatise) this school of thought argues that strong individual incentives are required in order to ensure individuals behave in a manner desired by the organisation. This school of thought also draws upon many of the principles of effective employee motivation in order to reinforce new behavioural outcomes.

The group dynamics school

Lewin (1958) propounded the notion that, since organisations represent collections of individuals who are organized as groups (formal/informal), the most effective means of achieving permanent organisational change is through the changing of group norms, roles and values. (See chapters 7 & 8)

The open systems school

The open systems perspective views organisations as organic entities that are comprised of a number of interconnected sub-systems such as cultural systems, managerial systems, technical systems, and social systems. Scott (1987) suggests that any change in one of these sub-systems will necessarily impact on all of the others and so have repercussions for overall performance.

THEORIES AND MODELS OF CHANGE MANAGEMENT

Approaches to change and change management vary considerably from organisation to organisation, and indeed from country to country. Handy (1986) argues that there is a strong link between culture and managerial practices and so, in different countries, managers' approach to a change initiative will be inherently influenced by the prevailing culture of their situation. In an attempt to describe the underlying concepts of organisational change, a number of models of change management have been developed over the years. Some of the most commonly referenced models are reviewed here.

Action research model

The term 'action research' (or action learning) was coined in the late 1950s and is based on the premise that an effective approach to solving organisational problems must involve a rational, systematic analysis of the issues in question. Burnes (1996) argues that it must be an approach which secures information, hypotheses and action from all parties involved, as well as evaluating the action taken towards the solution of the problem. French and Bell (1984, pp. 98–9) describe action research in the following terms:

> Action refers to programs and interventions designed to solve a problem or improve a condition . . . action research is the process of systematically collecting research data about an ongoing system relative to some objective, goal or need of that system; feeding these data back into that system; taking action by altering selected variables within the system based both on the data and on hypotheses; and evaluating the results of action by collecting more data.

In essence, therefore, action research advocates a dual/collective approach to managing change: first managers, workers and a change agent get together to identify a problem and agree a plan of action to eliminate this problem. This stage requires the frank exchange of information and is open to inquiry. However, action research also recognises that successful action/change is predicated upon the correct diagnosis of the situation and so it requires that those involved in the change initiative formulate a number of alternative scenarios delineating the nature of the problem under review, coupled with action plans for each scenario. Only through a process of elimination, based on critical analysis of each action plan, will a final solution be agreed on, and this forms the basis for the change to be implemented. While this sounds complicated, it really advocates that decision-makers, through a process of consultation and participation, take cognisance of the range of possible alternatives before deciding on a particular course of action. In this way organisations learn from past decisions and individuals are more likely to be committed to the outcomes. Cummings and Huse (1989) argue that, despite its long history, action research remains a highly regarded approach to managing change.

Three-step change model

Lewin (1958) suggested that behaviour in organisation is a combination of two particular forces – those that are intent on maintaining the *status quo*, and those that are pushing for change. Where both sets of behaviours are about equal, then equilibrium is maintained. If the organisation wishes to effect this state of equilibrium then it must either decrease the forces maintaining the *status quo,* or increase those forces pushing for change. Lewin suggests that change is more acceptable if the organisation can manage to decrease or modify the strength of the forces maintaining the *status quo,* rather than imposing change.

Box 14.1: Behavioural change

The level of performance of a workgroup might be stable because group norms maintaining that level are equivalent to the supervisor's pressures for change to higher levels. This level of performance can be increased either by changing the group norms to support higher levels of performance or by increasing supervisor pressures to produce at higher levels.

Source: Cummings and Huse, 1989

Lewin proposed that, in order to ensure that the desired change becomes a permanent feature of organisational life and that new behaviour is successfully adopted, the old behaviour has to be discarded. In developing his model of organisational change, he identified three stages in the change process:

1. *Unfreezing.* Here the organisation must first reduce those forces that are maintaining the organisation's behaviour at its present level. Typically, an organisation might introduce an information/education/communication strategy in an attempt to persuade individuals/groups to modify their behaviour.
2. *Change.* At this stage the organisation is active in developing new behaviours, values and attitudes that are consistent with its desired behavioural outcomes. This is usually achieved through structural and process changes.
3. *Refreezing.* Once the change has occurred the organisation is concerned to ensure it remains in what is now a new state of equilibrium. To this end, it focuses on developing systems, values, norms and a culture that facilitate and reinforce this changed behaviour.

The three-stage model of organisational change was, and is, perceived to be relatively broad and so successive theorists have sought to develop and extend Lewin's work.

Planned change model

In an effort to expand on Lewin's three-step model, a number of writers (i.e. Lippitt *et al.,* 1958; Cummings and Huse, 1989; Bullock and Batten, 1985) have developed various models that are based on a planned set of successive steps or phases that must be followed in order to bring about organisational change. Cummings and Huse (1989) suggest that, in itself, the concept of planned change implies that organisations exist in different states, at different times, and so it is possible to follow a pre-designed plan to move from one phase to another. Organisations therefore must appreciate not only the process of change, but also the various sequential stages that must be gone through to ensure this change. Illustrative of this planned change thesis, Lippitt *et al.*'s (1958) model provides for the introduction of a change agent to oversee and manage a planned change programme. While a varying number of steps have been attributed to this model it essentially involves four main phases. First, the change agent explores the current stage of play in terms of meeting various internal actors and collecting required information. He/she then develops a systematic plan of the required behaviour change, taking into account organisational processes and systems and bearing in mind possible resistance that might be encountered. The third stage involves implementing the change. The fourth and final stage is integration whereby the change is evaluated to ensure consistency with existing systems and processes, and adjustments are made as required. This final stage also represents closure. Once the change is implemented and integrated with the organisation system, the change project is closed.

Burnes (1996b) cites a number of criticisms that have been levelled at the planned change models which are worth noting here:

- They are based on the assumption that organisations operate under stable conditions and can move from one stable state to another in a pre-planned manner. However, both Garvin (1993) and Stacey (1993) argue that such assumptions are increasingly tenuous and that organisational change is more a continuous and open-ended process than a set of discrete and self-contained events.
- The planned change models emphasise incremental or small-scale change and so are not applicable in situations that require rapid radical and/or transformational change.
- They are based on the premise that common agreements can be reached, and that all parties involved in the change process are interested in and support the change initiative. The planned change models largely ignore the realities of organisational conflict and politics.

Emergent change model

The emergent approach to change management, as advocated by both Dawson (1996) and Wilson (1992), is based on the premise that the planned model of change management has limited application in a turbulent business environment that is characterised by uncertainty and complexity. Burnes (1996b) describes the emergent model as an approach to change that views it as a process that unfolds through the interplay of multiple variables (context, political processes and consultation) within the organisation. The model is perceived to be less prescriptive and more analytical than the planned change models, and allows for a more comprehensive understanding of managing change in a complex environment. Dawson (1996) argues that change can best be perceived as a period of organisational transition that is characterised by disruption, confusion and unforeseen events that emerge over long time-frames. Perceived this way, organisational change becomes a process that is continuous and one that requires considerable learning and adaptability on the part of organisational members. Benjamin and Mabey (1993, p. 181) argue that: '. . . while the primary stimulus for change remains with those forces in the external environment, the primary motivator for how change is accomplished resides with the people inside the organisation'.

Burnes (1996b) in a review of the major proponents of the emergent change model identifies some of the main tenets of the emergent change thesis:

- Organisational change is perceived as a continuous process of experimentation and adaptation aimed at matching an organisation's capabilities to the needs and dictates of a dynamic and uncertain environment.
- While comprised of many small and incremental changes, over time the change process can constitute major organisational transformation.
- The key role of managers in this change scenario is to create and/or foster an organisational structure and climate which encourages and sustains experimentation and risk-taking, and to develop a workforce that will take responsibility for change and implementing it.
- Managers are also charged with creating and sustaining a vision of what the changed organisational scenario might be so that successive change initiatives can be judged against this vision.
- Central to this change initiative are the organisational activities of information gathering, communication and learning.

A cursory examination of much of this emergent change management literature might lead one to the conclusion that this emergent change model is based less on change management principles and more on the burgeoning 'learning organisation' literature (see Chapter 5 for discussion on the learning organisation concept) – or indeed vice versa – since both sets of literature depict an organisation that is environmentally driven to adopting a continuous process of transformation and development.

A contingency approach to change management has been proposed by, among others, Dunphy and Stace (1993) who argue that since organisations operate under different circumstances, there must be more than one approach to change management. The choice then facing managers is to adopt the change approach that best suits their particular circumstances.

To review, then, it would appear that both the planned and emergent models of organisational change advocate different approaches to change management. The planned model has greater application in an environment that is relatively stable and predictable and where change can be driven from the top down. The emergent model, on the other hand, is geared towards dynamic, complex environments that are characterised by high risk and unpredictability and so, in such situations, it is not possible to successfully effect change from the top. Having said this, however, it is clear that both models suggest that internal practices must be changed in order to meet the demands of the situational environment, and thus assume that managers do not have any discretion in terms of the choices available to them. The strategic management literature, however, (see, for example, Pettigrew and Whipp, 1993; Montgomery and Porter, 1991; Child, 1972), would suggest that managers have considerable discretion and room for manoeuvre in terms of the strategic choices they make concerning the environment within which they operate, and so not only can they influence the nature of their situational environment (choices made concerning the product/service markets they decide to compete in) but they may also determine their approach to change management (related to their preferred management style, workforce characteristics, and so forth).

MANAGING THE CHANGE PROCESS

As indicated earlier, change can occur at any level within the organisation and can represent incremental or fundamental changes to individuals' lifestyles. Baron and Greenberg (1992) suggest that reactions to change can be categorised along a continuum:

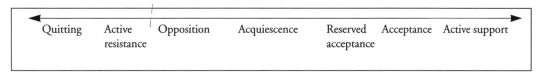

The most extreme reaction is to leave the job because the change is perceived to be intolerable. Active resistance involves personal defiance and encouraging others to resist the change initiative. Opposition essentially involves lack of co-operation and trying to delay proceedings. Acquiescence occurs where individuals may be unhappy about the change but feel powerless to prevent it, so they put up with it as best they can. Reserved acceptance occurs where the main thrust of the change is accepted but individuals may bargain over details. Acceptance is characterised by passive co-operation with the change but no overt wish to participate in it. Finally, at the other extreme there is active support where individuals welcome change and actively engage in behaviours that increase the chances of that change becoming a permanent feature of organisational life.

In view of the myriad of likely responses to change, and the breadth of scope of many change initiatives, it is recommended that a number of key stages be involved in managing the change process (see Figure 14.2).

Figure 14.2: Activities contributing to effective change management

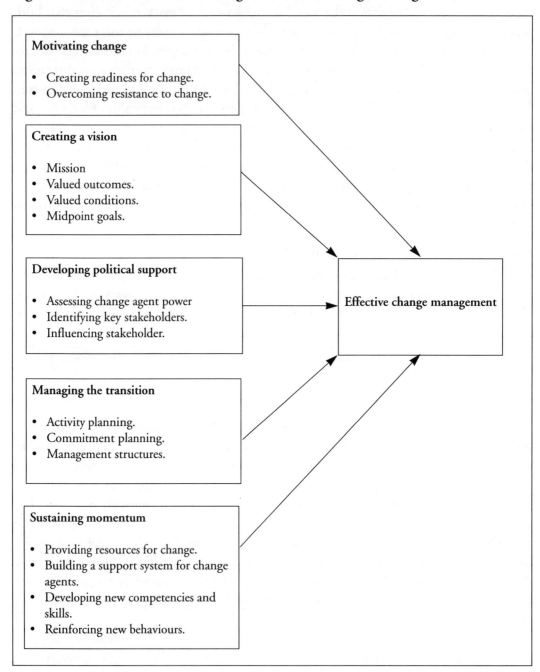

Source: Cummings and Huse, 1989

A number of the stages highlighted in Figure 14.2 are worthy of further elaboration here. The first concerns creating readiness for change by demonstrating the necessity for change in terms of the organisation's desired goals and current practice. It will also involve considerable discussion on the value of change and the positive impact such change will have on organisational members. The second step is more complex and involves overcoming likely resistance to change.

Resistance to change

It is probably fair to say that, while humans are amazingly adaptable beings, individuals are often wary of change since it invariably disturbs the *status quo* and carries with it some degree of uncertainty. Hussey (1995) identifies a range of factors that might explain the root causes of resistance:

- *Actual threats.* Changes that are perceived as having an impact on the value of an individual's job generally tend to raise fears and uncertainties. In particular, individuals may fear loss of employment or resist change that requires them to develop new knowledge and skills – often it is less the fear of change as fear of personal failure or inability to cope that results in much resistance.
- *Imposed change.* In many cases individuals do not understand why changes are being imposed on them and resist them as a result. In other situations anything that is imposed, rather than discussed, can often 'get people's backs up' simply because they had no voice or say in the matter.
- *Lack of faith in those making the change.* This is largely dependent on past experiences and how previous changes were managed. Unsuccessful or uncomfortable transitions can leave individuals feeling 'hard done by' and thus more likely to avoid future changes.
- *The head and the heart.* Here, while individuals appear to agree that change is required, they may be happier to retain the *status quo* – they like the continuity of things staying as they are.

Reducing resistance to change

At least three generic strategies for overcoming resistance to change have been identified:

- *Participation and involvement.* Here organisational members are given ownership of the change process by being involved in its inception and development. From an organisational perspective, a strategy of participation allows for a vast array of opinions to be taken into account and it is likely that problem diagnosis will be more effective as a result. From the individual perspective, organisational members are allowed a say in decisions that affect them and, as a result of being involved, are more likely to understand the change and the rationale for it, thereby reducing fears and resistance.

- *Communication.* Since one of the primary reasons for resisting change concerns uncertainty and lack of information, often all that is required is an effective communications exercise that is designed to eliminate misinformation and misinterpretation of information. Employees can be encouraged to ask questions and share their concerns and thus gain a better understanding of the necessity for change.

- *Training and education.* This strategy is particularly useful where the change initiative involves restructuring jobs and processes. Fear of being unable to function in a new structure can cause unnecessary stress and can lead to decreased productivity even before the change is introduced. It is necessary therefore to adopt a strategic approach to managing the change process so that the necessary training and education programmes and systems can be put in place long before the change is introduced.

Kotter and Schlesinger (1979) outline the particular strengths of these and other methods of reducing resistance to change (Table 14.1).

Table 14.1: Methods of reducing resistance to change

Approach	Situational use	Advantages	Drawbacks
Education and communication	Where there is lack of information or inaccurate information about the change.	Once persuaded, people often will help with the implementation of the change.	Can be very time-consuming if many people are involved.
Participation and involvement	Where the initiators do not have all the information they need to design the change, and where others have considerable power to resist.	People who participate will be committed to implementing change, and any relevant information they have will be integrated into the change plan.	Can be very time-consuming if participants design an inappropriate change.
Facilitation and support	Where people are resisting because of adjustment problems.	No other approach works as well with adjustment problems.	Can be time-consuming, expensive and still fail.
Negotiation and agreement	Where someone or some group will clearly lose out in a change and where that person/group has considerable power to resist.	Sometimes it is a relatively easy way to avoid major resistance.	Can be too expensive for others to negotiate for compliance.

Manipulation and co-optation	Where other tactics will not work or are too expensive.	It can be a relatively quick and inexpensive solution to resistance problems.	Can lead to future problems if people feel manipulated.
Explicit and implicit coercion	Where speed is essential, and the change initiators possess considerable power.	It is speedy, and can overcome any kind of resistance.	Can be risky if it leaves initiators discredited.

Figure 14.2 further highlights that the creation of a vision that can be shared by organisational members is a significant aspect of ensuring the smooth introduction of a change initiative. This will involve developing an organisation mission that employees can identify with and outlining a range of strategies to achieve this mission. Organisations are political entities and thus support from the key stakeholders plays a vital role in ensuring the smooth transition from old to new. Finally, the evaluation of the organisation environment in terms of its culture, policies, systems and procedures is required to ensure that that change becomes a permanent feature of organisational life. It is evident that effective change management involves considerable strategic planning and communication at all levels of organisational life. How is this achievable? In the following section we explore the various dimensions of organisation development as one particular mechanism for managing change.

ORGANISATION DEVELOPMENT

Over the years, it has been common to use the term 'organisation development' (OD) more or less synonymously with organisation change or, in fact, to combine the two terms into one label – organisation change and development. The term OD has been criticised from a number of perspectives. Bennis (1969) argued that OD was undifferentiated; Nord (1974) criticised its value-free supposition; while Lundberg (1991) proposed that the paradigms of OD are unduly restricted and is atheoretical. Notwithstanding these criticisms, the extant OD literature continues to attract a considerable following, although there is evidence of some attempts to reconceptualise the term. To illustrate this reconceptualisation, Lundberg (1991, pp. 9–11) differentiates OD with reference to the critical tasks of most modern organisations:

1. *Organisations have to manage their internal affairs.* Here the focus is on making continuous internal adjustments to ensure that goals are achieved and plans and standards are followed. This internal adjustment constitutes organisation change and will include those activities and processes designed and activated to overcome internal problems and bring performance into line with goals, standards and the like.

2. *Organisations have to survive in their external environments.* As environments become more complex and uncertain, organisations will have to continuously realign themselves with portions of their environment. Lundberg suggests that this lies at the heart of organisation development which focuses on those activities and processes designed to achieve a more appropriate alignment between an organisation and its relevant environment. Enhanced alignment, he suggests, will include those activities and processes which modify the basic character or culture of the organisation; redesigning an organisation's structures, strategies, systems, membership etc. so they become more appropriate for future functioning.

3. *Organisations have to anticipate and prepare for their probable future.* Essentially this third task requires that organisations be capable of dealing with the unknown and so exist in a state of readiness or be 'anticipatively aligned' with their operating environment. Lundberg suggests that dealing with anticipation can be labelled 'organisation transformation' and that transformation almost always requires both organisation change and development.

Lundberg's characterisation of organisation development, as illustrated here, is supported in much of the extant change literature. Luthans (1992) suggests that organisation development is the modern approach to the management of change and so refers to an applied macro-level approach to planned change and development of complex organisations. It is aimed at the development of individuals, groups and the organisation as a total system. Burke (1982, p. 10) defines OD as a planned process of change in an organisation's culture through the utilisation of behavioural science technology, research and theory, while French and Bell (1984, p. 15), in their seminal work describe organisation development thus:

> Organisation development is a top management-supported long-range effort to improve an organisation's problem-solving and renewal processes, particularly through a more effective and collaborative management of organisation culture . . . with the assistance of a change agent or catalyst, and the use of theory and technology of applied behavioural sciences, including action research.

It can be said, therefore, that OD is planned and adopts a systems approach – that is, it operates at all levels within the organisation. It is designed to improve organisational functioning, both in the short term and long term, by focusing on problem-solving and human interaction and socialisation. It is concerned with ensuring that the organisation operates at its most effective and has the capacity to adapt to future change requirements. Warrick (1984) suggests a number of positive benefits of OD (see Box 14.2).

Box 14.2: Ten positive results from OD

1. Improved organisational effectiveness (increased productivity and morals: more effective goal setting, planning and organising: clearer goals and responsibilities: better utilisation of human resources: and bottom-line improvements).
2. Better management from top to bottom.
3. Greater commitment and involvement from organisational members in making the organisation successful.
4. Improved teamwork within and between groups.
5. A better understanding of an organisation and its strengths and weaknesses.
6. Improvement in communications, problem solving, and conflict resolution skills, resulting in increased effectiveness and less wasted time from communications breakdowns, game playing, and win-lose confrontations.
7. Efforts to develop a work climate that encourages creativity and openness, provides opportunities for personal growth and development, and rewards responsible and healthy behaviour.
8. A significant decrease in dysfunctional behaviour.
9. Increased personal and organisational awareness that improves the organisation's ability to adapt to a continuously changing environment and to continue to grow, learn, and stay competitive.
10. The ability to attract and keep healthy and productive people.

Source: Warrick. D (1984), *Mudman: Managing Organisational Change and Development*, NJ: Science Research Associates Inc.

Robbins (1991) suggests that OD is comprised of a number of change techniques – from organisational-wide changes in structures and systems, to psychotherapeutic counselling sessions with groups and individuals, undertaken in response to changes in the external environment that seek to improve organisational efficiency and employee well-being. He identifies a number of principles of OD that are worth highlighting here:

1. *Respect for people.* Individuals are perceived as being responsible, conscientious and caring. They should be treated with dignity and respect.
2. *Trust and support.* The effective and healthy organisation is characterised by trust, authenticity, openness and a supportive climate.
3. *Power equalisation.* Effective organisations de-emphasise hierarchical authority and control.
4. *Confrontation.* Problems shouldn't be swept under the carpet. They should be openly confronted.
5. *Participation.* The more that people who will be affected by a change are involved in the decisions surrounding that change, the more they will be committed to implementing those decisions.

OD is more compatible with organic structures, yet those organisations that might best benefit from OD are probably those that are most likely to resist it – bureaucratic, mechanistic, highly formalised organisations.

IMPLEMENTING ORGANISATION DEVELOPMENT

The implementation of organisation development interventions can be broadly classified as follows: structural interventions; task/technology interventions; and people focused interventions.

Structural interventions

These are designed to make the organisation more organic and responsive to changing environmental demands. Robbins (1991) highlights three common structural interventions:

1. *Structural re-organisation.* This type of OD intervention is highly disruptive since it involves a systems change that impacts on all organisational members. Such change is characteristic of the move from a hierarchical structure to a more decentralised flatter one in order to respond faster to change. The move towards organisational delayering often occurs in tandem with a push for greater flexibility and the adoption of a team approach to organisation design, which requires employees to take responsibility for their work and, often, to learn new skills. Such change is fundamental since it primarily represents a change in what has essentially become a way of life, and so its successful implementation is highly dependent on full consultation and participation.

2. *New reward systems.* Here, the purpose typically is to reinforce a particular type of behaviour (operant conditioning – see Chapter 5) and so organisations might seek to link individuals' pay with performance. This may be organisation-wide, or limited to particular sections or groups of workers; but again, this type of intervention can meet with considerable opposition, particularly in unionised environments. The purpose with this form of OD, as with many others, is to ensure greater operational efficiency and so it seeks to provide a motivating environment where increased effort and greater output are rewarded.

3. *Changing culture.* It has long been argued that culture is a fluid concept that is virtually impossible to interpret, never mind manage or change. However, cultures can become obsolete and so inhibit organisation growth and renewal in a dynamic environment. Cultural change interventions are concerned with developing values, beliefs and norms that are appropriate to an organisation's strategic direction and environmental conditions. The case of Team Aer Lingus is illustrated in Box 14.3.

Box 14.3: Structure and culture change process at Team Aer Lingus

Most forms of planned change are as a direct result of a recent development in either the internal or external environment facing the organisation. In the case of Team Aer Lingus, both internal and external factors began to force change. Firstly the Maintenance and Engineering Division (M and E) had serious industrial relations problems and in 1986 had suffered from a prolonged strike which produced mistrust and bitterness on both sides. It became evident that something different was required to propel M and E into the future. In addition, a new management team took over in 1986 emphasising a more consensual approach. Externally, M and E was faced with the loss of much of its traditional business, a worldwide increase in maintenance capacity and intense competition. As a result M and E was faced with a stark choice to either scale down and cater solely for Aer Lingus, or to expand operations to meet projected demands.

A number of key changes were introduced, the first of which was a trade integration deal which amalgamated the previous eleven into two. A productivity deal soon followed which gave employees monetary compensation for increased productivity. In 1990 M and E was established as a stand-alone subsidiary now called Team. In 1991 a productivity maximisation programme and a quality programme were both introduced to enhance the respective areas. In introducing the various changes, different management styles were used with differing effects. Education, communication, participation, negotiation and agreement were used at different stages. Given that it took four ballots to secure workforce agreement on the establishment of Team, education and communication could have been used to far greater effect.

The changes introduced from the mid-1980s onwards were designed to produce a network form of organisation with a new integrative structure and culture which would allow Team to compete more effectively in the marketplace. There is little doubt about the extent of structural change. The division of labour was considerably widened as a result of integration, which meant that employees completed wider, more varied tasks. The levels in the hierarchy were reduced from ten to seven and the spans of control widened to 6:7:1 compared to 3:5:1 for M and E . . . Formalisation was reduced and there were attempts to decentralise decision-making, responsibility and authority by introducing team-based work and participation in various productivity and quality teams . . . The extent of cultural change, however, was less emphatic. The majority of respondents agree that the focus has shifted to customer, cost and quality awareness and that employees now co-operate to a greater extent. However, employees were largely sceptical about any cultural change in relation to how they were treated and valued by Team and the extent of any empowerment on their behalf.

Source: Extracts from Tiernan, 1996

Task technology interventions

Task technology interventions emphasise changing the jobs that people do and/or the technological processes involved in performing them. Three particular approaches have been developed, namely job redesign, socio-technical systems approach and the quality of working life (QWL) movement. Since these approaches have been discussed earlier in this book, please refer back to Chapter 11 for full details.

People-focused interventions

This approach to OD focuses on changing the attitudes and behaviours of individuals within the organisation through communication, decision-making and problem-solving. A number of specific techniques have been developed to achieve these changes:

1. *Sensitivity training.* Often termed T-group training, sensitivity training requires that small, unstructured groups of individuals are set up. These groups meet on a regular basis without a planned agenda. This is designed to provide members with experiential learning about group dynamics, leadership and inter-personal relations. Over time, as members of the group interact with each other, they begin to learn more about themselves, each other, and how others might perceive their behaviour. The objective of this form of OD is to heighten sensitivity to emotional reactions and thus facilitate improved decision-making, communication and conflict resolution.

2. *Survey research and feedback.* In essence, this form of OD involves conducting an attitude survey of all organisational members to determine views on various organisational processes and systems. A survey questionnaire is developed and administered to all employees. In some organisations, focus groups are set up comprising employees from various sectors and departments to discuss many aspects of work in that organisation. The data from the surveys are then collated and interpreted and generally presented to the management team. The results are fed back to employees through meetings that are set up to discuss the results and matters arising. This form of OD is becoming increasingly popular in Ireland and, in particular, many organisations are commissioning third-level educational institutions to conduct such research on their behalf. The purpose of this is twofold: firstly, the organisation buys in expertise in the form of an experienced researcher who is adept at designing, administering and interpreting such surveys; and secondly, the use of an independent consultant can often reassure employees about responding in a frank manner to the questions posed.

3. *Process consultation.* Here the organisation buys in external expertise in the guise of an OD consultant whose role is to observe how individuals interact with each other. His/her role is to review organisational systems and processes in terms of their effect on organisational communication, individual interaction and work behaviour. In practice the aim of this type of OD may be to diagnose the solution to such problems as dysfunctional conflict, poor communications and ineffective norms. The idea is that, over time, group members can learn to deal with such problems themselves.

4. *Team building.* This form of OD focuses on team dynamics within the organisation. In particular it examines task allocation and the patterns of human behaviour within the work group. Based on Lewin's (1958) approach, it assumes that organisational effectiveness is dependent on the effectiveness of teams; therefore, improvements in how the team operates will likely result in greater organisational efficiency. It goes beyond merely examining group processes, but looks also at tasks to be achieved and role allocation within the team.

Walton (1975) and Guest (1990) both argue that OD, as a change mechanism, is often limited and rarely diffuses throughout the organisation. Guest in particular suggests that much of the innovation is piecemeal and lacks the critical ingredient of strategic integration and that, as a result, it is unlikely to have a positive impact on organisational performance.

Burnes (1996b) provides a classification of change management approaches that encapsulate many of the OD interventions described here.

Table 14.2: A classification of change management approaches

Focus	Approach	Techniques	Involvement
Individual	Behaviourist or Gestalt-Field	Life- and career-planning activities. Role analysis technique. Coaching and counselling. T-group (sensitivity training). Education and training to increase skills, knowledge in the areas of technical task needs, relationship skills, decision-making, problem-solving, planning, goal-setting skills. Grid OD phase 1. Job re-design.	High
Teams and groups	Group dynamics	Team building. Process consultation. Third-party peacemaking. Grid OK phases 1, 2. Quality circles. Survey feedback. Role analysis. Education in decision-making, problem-solving, planning, goal-setting in group settings.	Medium – High

Focus	Approach	Techniques	Involvement
Inter-group relations	Group dynamics	Inter-group activities – process-directed – Task-directed. Organisational mirroring. Techno-structural interventions. Process consultation. Third-party peacemaking at group level. Grid OD phase 3. Survey feedback.	Medium – Low
Total organisation	Open systems	Techno-structural activities. Confrontation meetings. Strategic planning activities. Grid OD phase 4, 5, 6. Culture change. Survey feedback.	Low

Source: Burnes, B. (1991), *Managing Change.* London: Pitman, pp. 176–177

Furnham (1997) cautions that the generation, implementation and diffusion of new ideas and processes in an organisation are particularly difficult, and stresses that organisations must take cognisance of their range of support structures and systems to ensure close coherence with defined goals and objectives. Given the inherent problems associated with generating behavioural changes, and the perceived difficulties of maintaining meaningful change, organisations must have a carefully constructed and clearly articulated means of introducing and sustaining a change initiative.

SUMMARY OF KEY PROPOSITIONS

- Organisation change is one of the most critical aspects of effective management, and the turbulent business environment in which most organisations operate means that, not only is change becoming more frequent, but the nature of change may be increasingly complex, and the impact of change is often more extensive.
- Change can be either incremental and localised or fundamental and organisation-wide.
- Resistance to change can occur at many levels, but primarily is as a result of fear of the unknown, inadequate knowledge, or loss of status. Strategies for overcoming resistance include participation and involvement, training and education, and communication.
- Every work organisation is concerned with being effective. OD is concerned with the diagnosis of organisational health and performance, and adaptability to change.

- OD is action-oriented and tailored to suit individual needs.
- OD intervention can be classified as structural interventions, task technology interventions and people-focused interventions.

DISCUSSION QUESTIONS

1. Define organisation change. Why is change necessary?
2. Outline the various models of change management. Which model has greatest applicability in modern organisations?
3. Why do individuals resist change? How can organisations overcome resistance to change?
4. Define organisation development. Why is OD more applicable in flat organisations?
5. What is sensitivity training? Can you identify any potential problems with this OD approach?

References

Chapter 1

Atkinson, J. (1984), 'Manpower strategies for flexible organisations', *Personnel Management*, August, 28–31.

Block, P. (1992), *The Empowered Manager – Positive Political Skills at Work*, San Francisco: Jossey Bass.

Brewster, C., Hegewisch, A. and Mayne, L. (1994), *Flexible Working Practices: The Controversy and the Evidence*, in Brewster, C. and Hegewisch, A. (eds), *Policy and Practice in European Human Resource Management*, London: Routledge.

Briggs, P. (1991), 'Organisational commitment – the key to Japanese success?', in Brewster, C. and Tyson, S. (eds), *International Comparisons in Human Resource Management*, London: Pitman.

Buchanan, D. and McCalman, J. (1989), *High Performance Work Systems: The Digital Experience*, London: Routledge.

Clutterbuck, D. (1985), *New Patterns of Work*, London: Pitman.

Collard, R. (1989), *Total Quality: Success Through People*, London: Institute of Personnel Management.

Curson, C. (1986), *Flexible Patterns of Work*, London: Institute of Personnel Management.

Dawson, S. (1996), *Analysing Organisations*, London: Macmillan.

Diesing, P. (1972), *Patterns of Discovery in the Social Sciences*, London: RKP.

Dobbs, J. (1993), 'The empowerment environment', *Training and Development*, February.

Feigenbaum, A. (1983), *Total Quality Control*, New York: McGraw-Hill.

Fox, A. (1974), *Man Management*, London: Hutchinson.

Furnham, A. (1997), *The Psychology of Behaviour at Work*, London: Psychology Press.

Geertz, C. (1970), 'The impact of the concept of culture on the concept of man', in Hammel, E. and Simmons, W. (eds), *Man Makes Sense*, Boston: Little Brown.

Gill, J. and Johnson, P. (1991), *Research Methods for Managers*, London: PCP Ltd.

Gunnigle, P. and Morley, M. (1993), 'Something old, something new: a perspective on industrial relations in the Republic of Ireland', *Review of Employment Topics*, Vol. 1 No. 1.

Hardscombe, R. S. and Norman, P. A. (1989), *Strategic Leadership: The Missing Link*, New York: McGraw-Hill.

Hardy, C. and Clegg, S. (1996), 'Some dare call it power', in Clegg, S., Hardy, C. and Nord, W. (eds), *Handbook of Organisation Studies*, London: Sage.

Harrison, R. (1992), *Employee Development*, London: Institute of Personnel Management.

Huczynski, A. and Buchanan, D. (1991), *Organisational Behaviour: An Introductory Text*, Hemel Hempstead: Prentice Hall.

Kotter, J., Schlesinger, L. and Sathe, V. (1979), *Organisation: Text, Cases and Readings on the Management of Organisational Design and Change*, Illinois: Irwin.

Lawler, E. (1986), *High Involvement Management: Participative Strategies for Organisational Performance*, San Francisco: Jossey Bass.

Lincoln, Y. and Guba, E. (1985), *Naturalistic Enquiry*, Beverley Hills: Sage.

McNeill, P. (1990), *Research Methods*, London: Routledge.

Marchington, M. (1982), *Managing Industrial Relations*, London: McGraw-Hill.

Mooney, M. (1989), *From Industrial Relations to Employee Relations in Ireland*, unpublished PhD, Trinity College, Dublin.

Moss-Kanter, R. (1983), *The Change Masters: Corporate Entrepreneurs at Work*, London and Boston: Unwin.

Offe, C. (1976), *Industry and Inequality*, London: Edward Arnold.

Perrow, C. (1967), *Organizational Analysis: A Sociological View*, London: Tavistock.

Perry, B. (1984), *Einfield: A High Performance System*, Massachusetts: DEC Educational Services Development and Publishing.

Purcell, J. (1991), 'The impact of corporate strategy on human resource management', in Sloney, J. (ed.), *New Perspectives on Human Resource Management*, London: Routledge.

Quinn-Mills, D. (1991), *The Rebirth of the Corporation*, New York: Wiley.

Reed, M. (1992), *The Sociology of Organisations: Themes, Perspectives & Prospects*, Hemel Hempstead: Harvester Wheatsheaf.

Robson, C. (1997), *Real World Research*, Oxford: Blackwell.

Salamon, M. (1992), *Industrial Relations: Theory and Practice*, London: Prentice Hall.

Tiernan, S. (1996), *Organisational Transformation: The Case of Team Aer Lingus*, unpublished PhD, University of Limerick: Department of Management.

Vaill, P. (1982), 'The purposing of high performing systems', *Organisational Dynamics*, Autumn, 23–39.

Williams, A., Dobson, P. and Walters, M. (1989), *Changing Cultures: New Organisational Approaches*, London: Institute of Personnel Management.

Chapter 2

Allinson, S. (1990), 'Personality and bureaucracy', in Wilson, R. and Rosenfeld, S. (eds), *Managing Organisations: Experiences, Texts and Cases*, New York: McGraw-Hill.

Aronoff, J. and Wilson, J. P. (1985), *Personality in the Social Process*, New York: Laurence Erlbaum.

Block, J. (1977), 'Advancing the psychology of personality: paradigmatic shift or improving the quality of research?', in Magnusson, D. and Endler, N. (eds), *Personality at the Crossroads*, Hillsdale, New Jersey: Erlbaum, 37–64.

Coopersmith, S. (1967), *The Antecedents of Self Esteem*, San Francisco: Freeman.

Costa, P. T. and McCrae, R. R. (1980), 'Influence of extraversion and neuroticism on subjective well-being', *Journal of Personality and Social Psychology*, No. 38, 36–51.

Dixon, N. F. (1976), *On the Psychology of Military Incompetence,* London: Jonathan Cape.

Dunn, J. and Plomin, R. (1990), *Separate Lives: Why Siblings Are So Different,* New York: Basic Books.

Epstein, S. (1983), 'The stability of behaviour: on predicting most of the people most of the time', *Journal of Personality and Social Psychology*, No. 37, 91–154.

Eysenck, H. (1967), *Dimensions of Personality*, London: RKP.

Forer, B. R. (1949), 'The fallacy of personal validation: a classroom demonstration of gullibility', *Journal of Abnormal and Social Psychology*, No. 44, 118–23.

Gleitman, H. (1991), *Psychology*, 3rd edition, New York: Norton.

Gottesman, I. I. (1963), 'Heritability of personality: a demonstration', *Psychological monographs*, Vol. 9 No. 77.

Haney, C. and Zimbardo, P. G. (1977), 'The socialisation into criminality: on becoming a prisoner and a guard', in Tapp, J. L. and Levine, F. L. (eds), *Law, Justice and the Individual in Society: Psychological and Legal Issues*, New York: Holt, Reinhart and Winston, 198–223.

Hosking, D. M. and Morley, I. E. (1991), *The Social Psychology of Organising: People, Processes and Contexts*, London: Harvester Wheatsheaf.

Milgram, S. (1963), 'A behavioural study of obedience', *Journal of Abnormal Psychology*, No. 67, 371–8.

Mischel, W. (1968), *Personality and Assessment*, New York: Wiley.

Nowicki, S. and Strickland, B. (1981), 'Locus of control', in Aero, R. and Weiner, E., *The Mind Test*, New York: William Morrow, 20–3.

Pervin, L. A. (1990), *Personality: Theory and Research*, 6th edition, New York: Wiley.

Phares, E. J. (1976), *Locus of Control in Personality*, Morrison, New Jersey: General Learning Press.

Pomice, E. (1995), 'Personality attributions and the work environment', *Working Woman*, Vol. 6, 68–75.

Rose, M. (1975), *Industrial Behaviour*, Harmondsworth: Penguin.

Rotter, J. B. (1966), 'Generalised expectancies for internal versus external control of reinforcement', *Psychological Monographs*, Vol. 80 No. 609.

Rotter, J. B. (1982), *The Development and Application of Social Learning Theory*, New York: Praeger.

Steers, R. M. and Mowday, R. T. (1977), 'The motivational properties of tasks', *Academy of Management Review*, October, 645–58.

Thomas, K. (1976), 'Conflict and conflict management', in *Handbook of Organisational Behaviour*, Chicago: Rand McNally.

Wegscheider-Cruise, S. (1987), 'Choicemaking', *Health Communications*, Vol. 2 No. 4.

Chapter 3

Atkinson, R. L., Atkinson, R. C., Smith, E. E. and Bem, D. J. (1993), *Introduction to Psychology*, 11th edition, New York: Harcourt Brace.

Bird, C. P. and Fisher, T. D. (1986), 'Thirty years later: attitudes toward the employment of older workers', *Journal of Applied Psychology*, August, 515–7.

Bruner, J. S. and Minturn, A. L. (1955), 'Perceptual identification and perceptual organisation', *Journal of General Psychology*, No. 53, 21–8.

Bruner, J. S. and Postman, L. J. (1949), 'On the perception of incongruity: a paradigm', *Journal of Personality*, No. 18, 206–23.

Festinger, L. (1957), *A Theory of Cognitive Dissonance*, Illinois: Row Peterson.

Heider, F. (1958), *The Psychology of Interpersonal Relations*, New York: Wiley.

Hofstede, G. (1983), 'Dimensions of national cultures in fifty countries and three regions', in Deregowski, J., Dzuirawiec, S. and Annis, R. (eds), *Explications in Cross Cultural Psychology*, Lisse: Swets and Zeitlinger.

Hofstede, G. (1991), *Culture and Organisations: Software of the Mind*, London: McGraw-Hill.

Kakabadse, A. (1997), 'The billion-dollar manager: global leadership for the next millennium', paper delivered at the Annual John Lovett Memorial Lecture, University of Limerick, Limerick.

Katz, D. (1960), 'The functional approach to the study of attitudes', *Public Opinion Quarterly*, No. 24, 163–204.

Kelley, H. H. (1967), 'Attribution theory in social psychology', in Levine, D. (ed.), *Nebraska Symposium on Motivation*, Lincoln: University of Nebraska Press.

Kelley, H. H. (1973), 'The processes of causal attribution', *American Psychologist*, No. 28, 107–28

McGregor, D. (1960), *The Human Side of Enterprise*, New York: McGraw-Hill.

Mohan, M. (1995). 'The influence of marital roles in consumer decision making', *Irish Marketing Review*, Vol. 8, 97–106.

Osherson, H., Kosslyn, P. and Hollerbach, J. (1990), *Invitation to Cognitive Science; Visual Cognition and Action*, Vol. 2, Cambridge MA: Blackwell.

Pettigrew, A. and Whipp, R. (1991), *Managing Change for Competitive Success*, Oxford: Blackwell.

Plous, S. (1993), *The Psychology of Judgement and Decision Making*, New York: McGraw-Hill.

Posner, E. (1989), *Foundations of Cognitive Science*, Hillsdale, New Jersey: Erlbaum.

Rock, I. (1983), *The Logic of Perception*, Cambridge MA: Bradfors Books/MIT Press.

Ross, L. (1977), 'The intuitive psychologist and his shortcomings: distortions in the attribution process', in Berkowitz, L. (ed.), *Advances in Experimental Social Psychology*, New York: Academic Press.

Rumelhart, D. E. (1984), 'Schemata and the cognitive system', in Wyer, R. S. and Scrull, T. K. (eds), *Handbook of Social Cognition*, Vol. 1, New Jersey: Erlbaum.

Rumelhart, D. E. (1980), 'Schemata: the building blocks of cognition', in Spiro, R. J. *et al.* (eds), *Theoretical Issues in Reading Comprehension*, New Jersey: Erlbaum.

Schermerhorn, J. R., Hunt, J. G. and Osborn, R. N. (1994), *Managing Organizational Behavior*, 5th edition, New York: Wiley.

Smith, P. B. and Harris Bond, M. (1993), '*Social psychology across cultures: analysis and perspectives*', Hertfordshire: Harvester Wheatsheaf.

Stranks, K. (1994), 'Perception and behaviour: impact, influence and outcomes', *Management Review*. Vol. 84 No. 3, 21–31.

Thomas, K. (1976), 'Conflict and conflict Management', in Dunnette, M. D. (ed.), *Handbook of Industrial & Organisational Psychology*, Chicago: Rand McNally.

Weick, K. (1983) 'Managerial thought in the context of action', in Srivastiva, S. and associates (eds), *The Executive Mind*, San Francisco: Jossey Bass.

Chapter 4

Adams, J. S. (1963), 'Towards an understanding of inequity', *Journal of Abnormal and Social Psychology*, November, 422–36.

Alderfer, C. P. (1972), *Existence, Relatedness and Growth*, New York: Free Press.

Cooper, C., Sloan, S. and Williams, S. (1988), *The Occupational Stress Indicator*, Oxford: NFER-Nelson.

Crosier, R. and Dalton, K. (1989), 'Equity theory examined', in Smith, D. (ed.), *Motivation and control in organisations*, New York: Baron Press.

De Vellis, R. F., De Vellis, B. M. and McCauley, C. (1978), 'Vicarious acquisition of learned helplessness', *Journal of Personality and Social Psychology*, No. 36, 894–9.

Eysenck, M. (1996), *Simply Psychology*, Sussex: Psychology Press.

Greenberg, J. and Baron, R. A. (1997), *Behaviour in Organisations*, 6th edition, New Jersey: Prentice Hall.

Hall, D. T. and Nougaim, K. E. (1968), 'An examination of Maslow's need hierarchy in an organisational setting', *Organisational Behaviour and Human Performance*, No. 3, February, 12–35.

Handy, C. (1990), *The Age of Unreason*, London: Arrow.

Hayes, N. (1994), *Foundations of Psychology*, London: Routledge.

Latham, G. P. and Locke, E. A. (1979), 'Goal setting – a motivational technique that works', *Organisational Dynamics*, Autumn, 68–80.

McClelland, D. C. (1961), *The Achieving Society*, Princeton, New Jersey: Van Nostrand.

Maslow, A. H. (1943), 'A theory of human motivation', *Psychological Review*, No. 50, July, 370–96.

Maslow, A. H. (1954), *Motivation and Personality*, New York: Harper.

Maslow, A. H. (1970), *Motivation and Personality*, revised edition, New York: Harper and Row.

Meelad, T., Seanai, A. and Seanai, E. (1953), 'Thoughts on learned helplessness', *Psychology Today*, Vol. 6, 39–54

Miles, E. W., Hatfield, J. D. and Huseman, R. C. (1994), 'Equity, sensivity and outcome importance', *Journal of Organisational Behaviour*, Vol. 15, No. 7, 585–96.

Murray, H. A. (1975), *Explorations in Personality*, New York: Oxford University Press.

Ribeaux, P. and Poppleton, S. E. (1978), *Psychology and work: an introduction*, London: MacMillan. Business Management and Administration Series.

Seligman, M. E. P. (1973), 'Fall into helplessness', *Psychology Today*, No. 7, 43–8

Shenkar, O. and von Glinow, M. A. (1994), 'Paradoxes of organisational theory and research: using the case of China to illustrate national contingency', *Management Science*, Vol. 40, No. 56–71.

Vroom, V. (1964), *Work and Motivation*, New York: Wiley.

Warr, P. (1984), *Work, Jobs and Unemployment*, London: MacMillan.

White, R. W. (1959), 'Motivation reconsidered. The concept of competence', *Psychological Review*, No. 66, 297–333.

Chapter 5

Argyris, C. (1992), *On Organisational Learning*, Cambridge, MA: Blackwell.

Argyris, C. and Schon, D. (1978), *Organisational Learning: A Theory-in-Action Perspective*, Reading-Ma: Addison Wesley.

Arment, L. (1990), 'Learning and training: a matter of style', *Industrial and Commercial Training*, Vol. 22 No. 3.

Bandura, A. (1986), *Social Foundations of Thought and Action*, Englewood Cliffs, New Jersey: Prentice Hall.

Barrow, M. and Loughlin, H. (1992), 'Towards a learning organisation, 1: the rationale', *Industrial and Commercial Training*, Vol. 24 No. 1, 3–7.

Boydell, T. H. (1976), *A Guide to the Identification of Training Needs*, 2nd edition, London: British Association for Commercial and Industrial Education.

Buchanan and Huczynski (1997), *Organizational Behaviour: An Introductory Text*, Hemel Hempstead: Prentice Hall.

Buchanan, D. and McCalman, J. (1989), *High Performance Work Systems: The Digital Experience*, London: Routledge

Buckley, R. and Caple, J. (1990), *The Theory and Practice of Training*, London: Kogan Page.

Burgoyne, J. (1988), 'Management development for the individual and the organisation', *Personnel Management*, June.

Calvert, G., Mobley, S. and Marshall, L. (1994), 'Grasping the learning organisation', *Training and Development*, June.

Daft, R. (1995), *Organisation Theory and Design*, 5th edition, New York: West Publishing Company.

Department of Enterprise and Employment (1997), White Paper on Human Resource Development, Dublin: Government Publications Office.

Garavan, T., Costine, P. and Heraty, N. (1995), *Training and Development in Ireland: Context, Policy and Practice*, Dublin: Oak Tree Press.

Gunnigle, P., Heraty, N. and Morley, M. (1997a), *Personnel and Human Resource Management: Theory and Practice in Ireland*, Dublin: Gill & Macmillan.

Gunnigle, P., Morley, M., Clifford, N. and Turner, T. (1997b), *Human Resource Management in Irish Organisations: Practice in Perspective*, Dublin: Oak Tree Press.

Hatch, M. J. (1997), *Organisational Theory*, New York: Oxford University Press.

Heraty, N. and Morley, M. (1995), 'A review of issues in conducting organisation level research with reference to the learning organisation', *The Learning Organisation*, Vol. 2 No. 4, 27–36.

Hodgetts, R., Luthans, F. and Lee, S. (1994), 'New paradigm organisations: from total quality to learning to world class', *Organisation Dynamics*, Winter, No. 22, 3.

Iles, P. (1994), 'Developing learning environments: challenges for theory, research and practice', *Journal of European Industrial Training*, Vol. 18 No. 3.

Kolb, D. A. (1984), *Experiential Learning – Experience as a Source of Learning and Development*, New Jersey: Prentice Hall.

Latham, G. P. and Crandall, S. R. (1991), 'Organisational and social influences affecting training effectiveness', in Morrision, J. E. (ed.), *Training for Performance*, Chichester: Wiley.

Law, C. (1986), *Helping People Learn*, Cambridge: Industrial Research Unit.

Leavitt, B. and March, J. (1988), 'Organisational learning', *Annual Review of Sociology*, No. 14, 319–40.

Luthans, F. (1992), *Organisational Behaviour*, New York: McGraw-Hill.

McGehee, W. (1958), 'Are we using what we know about training? – Learning theory and training', *Personnel Psychology*, Spring, 2.

McGill, M., Slocum, J. and Lei, D. (1992), 'Management practices in learning organisations', *Organisation Dynamics*, Spring.

Mumford, A. (1989), *Management Development Strategies for Action*, London: Kogan Page.

Pearn, M. and Honey, P. (1997), 'From error terror to wonder blunder', *People Management*, 6 March, 42–45.

Pedler, M., Boydell, T. and Burgoyne, J. (1989), 'Towards the learning company', *Management Education and Development*, Vol. 20 Part 1.

Perry, B. (1984), *Enfield: A High Performance System*, Massachusetts: Digital Equipment Corporation, Educational Services Development and Publishing.

Pont, T. (1991), *Developing Effective Training Skills*, Maidenhead: McGraw-Hill.

Reid, M, Barrington, H. and Kenney, T. (1992), *Training Interventions*, 2nd edition, London: IMP.

Revans, R. (1982), 'Action learning: the skills of diagnosis', *Management Decision*, Vol. 21 No. 2, 46–52.

Rogers, C. R. (1969), *Freedom to Learn*, Columbus: Free Press.

Senge, P. (1990), *The Fifth Discipline*, New York: Doubleday.

Skinner, B. L. (1938), *The Behaviour of Organisation*, New York: Appleton-Century-Crosts.

Stata, R. (1989), 'Organisational learning – the key to management innovation', *Sloan Management Review*, Vol. 30 No. 3, Spring.

West, P. (1994), 'The learning organisation: losing the luggage in transit?', *Journal of European Industrial Training*, Vol. 18 No. 11.

Wexley, K. and Latham, G. (1991), *Developing and Training Human Resources in Organisations*, New York: Harper-Collins.

Chapter 6

Adler, N. (1991), *International Dimensions of Organizational Behavior*, 2nd edition, Boston: Kent.

Axley, S. (1996), *Communication at Work: Management and the Communication Intensive Organisation*, Westport: Quorum Books.

Baskin, O. and Aronoff, C. (1980), *Interpersonal Communication in Organizations*, Santa Monica: Goodyear.

Beach, D. (1970), *Personnel: The Management of People at Work*, New York: Macmillan.

Brewster, C., Hegewisch, A., Mayne, L. and Tregaskis, O. (1994), 'Employee communication and participation', in Brewster, C. and Hegewisch, A. (eds), *Policy and Practice in European Human Resource Management*, London: Routledge.

Briscoe, D. R. (1995), *International Human Resource Management*, Englewood Cliffs: Prentice Hall.

Buchanan, D. and Huczynski, A. (1997), *Organisational Behaviour: An Introductory Text*, Hemel Hempstead: Prentice Hall.

Dawson, S. (1996), *Analysing Organisations*, London: Macmillan.

Dowling, P. J., Schuler, R. S. and Welch, D. E. (1994), *International Dimensions of Human Resource Management*, Belmont: Wadsworth.

Ekman, P. and Friesen, W. (1969), 'The repertoire of non-verbal behaviour: categories, origins, usage and coding', *Semiotics*, Vol. 1, 63–92.

Fisher, D. (1993), *Communication in Organisations*, Minneapolis: West Publishing Company.

Glenn, E. and Pond, E. (1989), 'Listening self-inventory', *Supervisory Management*, January, 12–5.

Goldhaber, G. (1990), *Organisational Communication*, Dubuque: W. C. Brown Press.

Kar, L. (1972), *Business Communication: Theory and Practice*, Homewood: Irwin.

Ludlow, R. and Panton, F. (1992), *The Essence of Effective Communication*, Hemel Hempstead: Prentice Hall.

Luhmann, N. (1987), *Soziale Systeme*, Frankfurt: Suhrkamp.

Luthans, F. (1992), *Organizational Behaviour*, New York: McGraw-Hill.

Luthans, F. and Larsen, J. (1986), 'How managers really communicate', *Human Relations*, Vol. 39 No. 2.

McClave, H. (1997), *Communication for Business*, Dublin: Gill & Macmillan.

Mayrhofer, W., Brewster, C. and Morley, M. (1997), *Communication and Consultation in European Organisations*, Paper presented to the workshop on the 'Impact of Strategy, Job Design and Organisational Structure on HRM', Cádiz, Spain, 25–28 May.

Mintzberg, H. (1975), 'The managers' job: folklore and fact', *Harvard Business Review*, July–August, 49–61.

Moorehead, G. and Griffin, R. (1995), *Organizational Behaviour: Managing People and Organisations*, Boston: Houghton Mifflin Company.

Price, J. (1997), 'Handbook of Organisational Measurement', *International Journal of Manpower*, Vol. 18 Nos. 4, 5 & 6.

Schermerhorn, J. (1996), *Management*, New York: John Wiley and Sons.

Shannon, C. and Weaver, W. (1949), *The Mathematical Theory of Communication*, Urbana: University of Illinois Press.

Smythe, J. (1995), 'Harvesting the office grapevine', *People Management*, Vol. 1 No. 18, 24–31.

Weick, K. E. (1989), 'Theorizing about organizational communication', in Jablin, F., Putnam, L. and Roberts, K., *Handbook of Organisational Communication. An Interdisciplinary Perspective*, Newsbury Park: Sage, 97–122.

Wilson, G., Goodhall, H. and Waagan, C. (1986), *Organisational Communication*, New York: Harper and Row.

Woods, B. (1993), *Communication, Technology & the Development of People*, London: Routledge.

Chapter 7

Acker, L. and van Houten, D. R. (1974), 'Differential Recruitment and Control: the structuring of organisations', *Administrative Science Quarterly*, Vol. 9 No. 2, 152–63.

Alderfer, C. P. (1972), *Existence, Relatedness and Growth*, New York: Collier MacMillan.

Allport, F. H. (1962), 'A structuronomic conception of behaviour: individual and collective', *Journal of Abnormal and Social Psychology*, No. 64, 3–30.

Aronson, E. and Mills, J. (1959), 'The effect of severity of initiation on liking for a group', *Journal of Abnormal and Social Psychology*, No. 67, 31–6.

Bales, R. F. (1950), *Interaction Process Analysis: A Method for the Study of Small Groups*, Reading, MA: Addison-Wesley.

Bales, R. F. (1953), *Task Roles and Social Roles in Problem-Solving Groups*, New York: Holt, Reinhart and Winston.

Bateman, T. S. and Zeithaml, C. P. (1989), 'The psychological context of strategic decisions: a model and convergent experimental findings', *Strategic Management Journal*, Vol. 10 No. 1, 59–74.

Brown, R. (1988), *Group Process*, London: Blackwell.

Budge, S. (1981), 'Group cohesiveness re-examined', *Group*, No. 5, 10–18.

Campbell, D. T. (1958), 'Common fate, similarity and other indices of the status of aggregates of persons as social entities', *Behavioural Science*, No. 3, 14–25.

Collins, R. (1981), 'On the microfoundations of macrosociology', *American Journal of Sociology*, No. 15, 984–1013.

Cook, S. W. (1978), 'Interpersonal and attitudinal outcomes in co-operating interracial groups', *Journal of Research and Development in Education*, Vol. 12, 97–113.

Festinger, L. (1957), *A Theory of Cognitive Dissonance*, Illinois: Evanston.

Handy, C. (1988), *Understanding Organisations*, London: Penguin.

Hellriegel, D., Slocum, J. W. and Woodman, R. W. (1989), *Organisational Behaviour*, 5th edition, Minneapolis: West Publishing.

Hofstede, G. (1991), *Cultures and Organisations: Software of the Mind*, London: McGraw-Hill.

Hogg, M. A. (1992), *The Social Psychology of Group Cohesiveness: From Attraction to Social Identity*, Reading, MA: Addison-Wesley.

Holden, L. P. (1988), 'The team manager as visionary and servant', *Managers Magazine*, Vol. 63 No. 11, 6–9.

Homans, G. C. (1950), *The Human Group*, New York: Harcourt Brace Jovanovich.

Hosking, D. M. and Morley I. E. (1991), *A Social Psychology of Organising*, Hemel Hempstead: Harvester Wheatsheaf.

Huczynski, A. and Buchanan, D. (1996), *Organisational Behaviour: An Introductory Text*, 2nd edition, Hemel Hempstead: Prentice Hall.

341

Jacobsen, S. R. (1973), 'Individual and group responses to confinement in a skyjacked plane' *American Journal of Orthopsychiatry*, Vol. 43, 459–69.

Janis, I. L. (1972), *Victims of Groupthink*, New York: Houghton Mifflin.

Janis, I. L. (1982), *Groupthink*, 2nd edition, New York: Houghton Mifflin.

Kiesler, C. A. and Kiesler, S. B. (1969), *Conformity*, Reading, MA: Addison-Wesley.

Lewin, K. (1947), 'Group decision and social change', in Newcomb, T. N. and Hartley, E. L. (eds), *Readings in Social Psychology*, New York: Holt, Reinhart and Winston.

Lewin, K. (1948), *Resolving Social Conflicts*, New York: Harper.

McCarthy, M. (1979), *Missionaries and Cannibals*, New York: Hodder & Stoughton.

Marcic, D. (1992), *Organisational Behaviour: Experiences and Cases*, New York: West Publishers.

Maslow, A. H. (1943), 'A theory of human motivation', *Psychological Review*, July.

Mayo, E. (1933), *The Human Problems of an Industrial Civilisation*, New York: Macmillan.

Mills, A. and Murgatroyd, J. (1994), 'Organisational rules: a framework for understanding', *Organisational Action*, New York: Houghton Mifflin.

Mills, A. J. and Simmons, T. (1995), *Reading Organisational Theory: A Critical Approach*, New York: Garamond.

Moorhead, G. and Griffin, R. W. (1995), *Organisational Behaviour: Managing People and Organisations*, 4th edition, Boston: Houghton Mifflin.

Moreland, R. L. and Levine, J. M. (1982), 'Socialistion in small groups: temporal changes in individual-group relations', *Advances in Experimental Social Psychology*, No. 15, 137–92.

Morgan, G. (1986), *Images of Organisation*, London: Sage.

Mullins, L. (1996), *Management and Organisational Behaviour*, 4th edition, London: Pitman Publishing.

Myers, A. (1962), 'Team competition, success and the adjustment of group members', *Journal of Abnormal and Social Psychology*, No. 65, 325–32.

Narayanan, V. K. and Fahy, L. (1982), 'The micro-politics of strategy formulation', *Academy of Management Review*, Vol. 17 No. 1, 25–34.

Poole, P. P., Gioia, D. A. and Gray, B. (1990), 'Influence modes, schema change and organisational transformation', *Journal of Applied Behavioural Science*, No. 4, 23–40.

Prasad, P. (1993), 'Symbolic processes in the implementation of technological change: a symbolic interactionist study of work computerisation', *Academy of Management Journal*, Vol. 36 No. 6, 1400–29.

Roethlisberger, F. J. and Dickson, W. J. (1939), *Management and the Worker*, Cambridge, MA: Harvard University Press.

Saavedra, R., Earley, P. and Van Dyne, L. (1993), 'Complex interdependence in task performing groups', *Journal of Applied Psychology*, Vol. 78 No. 1, 61–72.

Schacter, S. (1951), 'Deviation, rejection and communication', *Journal of Abnormal and Social Psychology*, Vol. 46, 190–207.

Schein, E. H. (1988), *Organisational Psychology*, 3rd edition, New York: Prentice Hall.

Schermerhorn, J. R., Osborn, R. N. and Hunt, J. G. (1996), *Managing Organisational Behaviour*, New York: Wiley.

Sherif, M. and Sherif, C. W. (1979), 'Research on intergroup relations', in Austin, W. G. and Worchel, S. (eds), *The Social Psychology of Intergroup Relations*, Monterey, CA: Brooks/Cole, 7–18.

Stead, B. A. (1978), *Women in Management*, New York: Prentice Hall.

Taylor, F. W. (1947), *The Principles of Scientific Management*, New York: Harper and Row.

Thomas, K. (1976), 'Conflict and conflict management', in Dunnette, M. D. (ed.), *Handbook of Industrial and Organisational Psychology*, Chicago: Rand McNally.

Tuckman, B. W. (1965), 'Development sequence in small groups', *Psychological Bulletin*, Vol. 63, 384–99.

Turner, J. C. (1982), 'Towards a cogntive redefinition of the social group', in Tajfel, H. (ed.), *Social Identity and Intergroup Relations*, Cambridge: Cambridge University Press, 15–40.

Van Gennep, A. (1960), *The Rites of Passage*, Chicago: University of Chicago Press.

Van Maanen, J. (1976), 'Breaking in: Socialisation to work' in Dubin, J. (ed), *Handbook of Work, Organisation and Society*, Chicago: Rand McNally.

Wilson, I. (1994), 'Strategic Planning isn't dead – it changed' *Long Range Planning*, Vol. 27 No. 4, 12–24.

Chapter 8

Adair, J. (1986), *Teams and Team Development*, London: Ashridge Press.

Argyris, C. (1990), *Overcoming Organisational Defences*, Needham Heights, MA: Allyn and Bacon.

Belbin, R. M. (1981), *Management Teams: Why They Succeed or Fail*, London: Heineman.

Belbin, R. M. (1993), *Team Roles at Work*, Oxford: Butterworth-Heinemann, 23.

Brown, R. (1988), *Group Process*, London: Blackwell.

Carson, N. (1992), 'The trouble with teams', *Training*, Vol. 29 No. 8, 38–40.

Griffin, R. and Moorhead, G. (1995), *Organizational Behaviour: Managing People and Organisations*, Boston: Houghton Mifflin.

Hambrick, D. and Mason, P. (1984), 'Upper echelons: the organization as a reflection of its top manager', *Academy of Management Review*, No. 9, 193–206.

Harrison, R. (1972), 'When power conflicts trigger team spirit', *European Business*, Spring, 57–65.

Janis, I. (1971), 'Groupthink', *Psychology Today*, 43.

Johnson, M. (1990), 'Age differences in decision making: a process methodology for examining strategic information processes', *Journal of Gerontology, Psychological Sciences*, No. 45, March, 75–8.

Katzenbach, J. R. and Smith D. K. (1993), *The Wisdom of Teams: Creating the High Performance Organisation*, Boston: Harvard Business School Press.

Kirchner, W. (1958), 'Age differences in short term retention of rapidly changing information', *Journal of Experimental Psychology*, No. 55, 352–8.

Moore, S., Morley, M., Fong, C., Flood, P., O'Regan, P. and Smith, K. (1996), 'Taking the lead: an investigation into the process of top management team pioneering', in Leavy, B. and Walsh, J. (eds), *Strategy and General Management: An Irish Reader*, Dublin: Oak Tree Press.

Norburn, D. (1989), 'The chief executive: a breed apart', *Strategic Management Journal*, January/February, 1–15.

O'Reilly, C. and Flatt, S. (1989).'Executive team demography, organizational innovation and firm performance', working paper, Berkeley: University of California.

Prince, G. (1970), *The Practice of Creativity*, New York: Harper and Row.

Quinn, J. (1985), 'Managing innovation: controlled chaos', *Harvard Business Review*, May–June, 73–84.

Schermerhorn, J. R., Osborn, R. N. and Hunt, J. G. (1996), *Managing Organisational Behaviour*, New York: Wiley.

Thomas, K. (1976), 'Conflict and conflict management', in Dunnette, M. D. (ed.), *Handbook of Industrial and Organisational Psychology*, Chicago: Rand McNally, 889–935.

Weick, K. (1977) 'Organisations as loosely coupled systems', *Administrative Science Quarterly*, Vol. 4 No. 2, 132–51.

Weir, M. (1964), 'Developmental changes in problem solving strategies', *Psychological Review*, No. 71, 473–90.

Wiersema, M. and Bantel, K. (1992), 'Top management team demography and corporate strategic change', *Academy of Management Journal*, No. 35, 91–121.

Woodcock, M. (1979), *Team Development Manual*, Aldershot: Gower.

Chapter 9

Arogyaswamy, B. and Byles, C. (1987), 'Organizational culture: internal and external fits', *Journal of Management*, No. 13, 647–59.

Blau, P. and Schoenherr, R. (1971), *The Structure of Organisations.* New York: Basic Books.

Buchanan, D. and Huczynski, A. (1997), *Organizational Behaviour: An Introductory Text*, 3rd edition, Hemel Hempstead: Prentice-Hall.

Child, J. (1984), *Organization: A Guide to Problems and Practice*, London: Harper and Row.

Daft, R. (1989), *Organization Theory and Design*, 3rd edition, St Paul, MN: West Publishing Company.

Dawson, S. (1996), *Analysing Organisations*, London: Macmillan.

Deal, T. and Kennedy, A. (1982), *Corporate Cultures: The Rites and Rituals of Corporate Life*, Reading, MA: Addison Wesley.

Dineen, D. and Garavan, T. (1994), 'Ireland: the emerald isle: management research in a changing European context', *International Studies of Management and Organisation*, Vol. 24 Nos 1 and 2.

Drucker, P. (1992), 'The coming of the new organisation', *Harvard Business Review*, No. 66, 33–5.

Geertz, C. (1971), 'The impact of the concept of culture on the concept of man', in Hammel, E. and Simmons, W. (eds), *Man Makes Sense*, Boston: Little Brown.

Handy, C. (1976), *Understanding Organisations*, London: Penguin.

Harrison, R. (1972), 'How to describe your organisation', *Harvard Business Review*, Sept–Oct.

Hatch, M. (1997), *Organization Theory: Modern, Symbolic and Post Modern Perspectives*, Oxford: University Press.

Hellreigel, D., Slocum, J. and Woodman, R. (1992), *Organisational Behaviour*, New York: West Publishing Company.

Hofstede, G. (1991), *Cultures and Organisations: Software of the Mind*, London: McGraw-Hill.

Hofstede, G. (1980), *Culture's Consequences: International Differences in Work Related Values*, Beverley Hills, Calif.: Sage.

Jackall, R. (1988), *Moral Mazes*, New York: Oxford University Press.

Jaques, E. (1952), *The Changing Culture of a Factory*, New York: Dryden Press.

Kimberly, R. (1976), 'Organisational size and the structuralism perspective: a review, critique and proposal'. *Administrative Science Quarterly*, Vol, 21 No. 2, 571–97.

Louis, M. (1983), 'Organisations as culture bearing milieux', in Pondy, L., Frost, P., Morgan, G. and Dandridge, T. (eds), *Organizational Culture*, Greenwich, Conn.: JAI Press.

Mintzberg, H. (1979), *The Structuring of Organisations: A Synthesis of Research*, New York: Prentice Hall.

Mintzberg, H. (1981), 'Organisational design: fashion or fit', *Harvard Business Review*, No, 59, 103–16.

Mintzberg, H. (1983), *Structure in Fives: Designing Effective Organisations*, New York: Prentice Hall.

Morgan, G. (1986), *Images of Organisations*, London: Sage.

Ouichi, W. (1981), *Theory Z: How American Business can Meet the Japanese Challenge*, Reading, Mass.: Addison-Wesley

Peters, T. and Waterman, R. (1982), *In Search of Excellence: Lessons from America's Best Run Companies*, New York: Harper and Row.

Pettigrew, A. (1979), 'On studying organisational culture', *Administrative Science Quarterly*, No. 24, 570–81.

Phillips, M., Goodman, R. and Sackmann, S. (1992), 'Exploring the complex cultural milieu of project teams', *Pmnetwork*, Vol. 7 No. 8, 20–6.

Pondy L. and Mitroff, I (1979), 'Beyond open system models of organization', *Research in Organizational Behaviour*, Vol. 1 No. 1, 3–39.

Robbins, S. (1991), *Organizational Behaviour: Concepts, Controversies, and Applications*, New York: Prentice Hall.

Robey, D. (1991), *Designing Organisations*. Illinois: Irwin.

Schein, E. (1985), 'Organisational culture and leadership', San Francisco: Jossey-Bass.

Schein, E. (1984), 'Coming to a new awareness of organisational culture', *Sloan Management Review*, Vol. 25, 3–16.

Siehl, C. and Martin, J. (1984), 'The role of symbolic management: how can managers effectively transmit organisational culture?', in Hunt, J., Hosking, D., Schriesheim, C. and Steward, R. (eds), *Leaders and Managers: International Perspectives on Managerial Behaviour and Leadership*, New York: Pergamon.

Tiernan, S. (1993), 'Innovations in organisational structure', *IBAR*, Vol. 14 No. 2, 57–69.

Tiernan, S. (1996), 'The Management of Change in Team Aer Lingus', in *Proceedings of the First Irish Academy of Management Conference, Management Research in Ireland: The Way Forward*, Cork: University College, September.

Tiernan, S., Morley. M. and Foley. E. (1996), *Modern Management*, Dublin: Gill & Macmillan.

Trice, H. and Beyer, J. (1993), *The Cultures of Work Organisations*, Englewood Cliffs, New Jersey: Prentice Hall.

Trice, H. and Beyer, J. (1984), 'Studying organizational cultures through rites and ceremonials', *Academy of Management Review*, No. 9, 653–59.

Vail, P. (1982), 'The purposing of high performing systems', *Organizational Dynamics*, Autumn.

Van Maanen, J. (1988), *Tales of the Field: On Writing Ethnography*, Chicago: University of Chicago Press.

Williams, A. Dobson, P. and Walters, M. (1989), *Changing Culture*, London: Institute of Personnel Management.

Woodward, J. (1965), *Industrial Organisations: Theory and Practice*. London: Oxford University Press.

Chapter 10

Bantel, K. and Jackson, S. (1989), 'Top management and innovations in banking: does the composition of the top team make a difference?', *Strategic Management Journal*, No. 10, 107–24.

Bass, B. (1990), 'From transactional to transformational leadership: learning to share the vision', *Organizational Dynamics*, Winter, 22.

Blake, R. and Mouton, J. (1962), 'The managerial grid', *Advanced Management Office Executive*, Vol. 1 No. 9.

Bennis, W. (1989), 'Managing the dream: leadership in the 21st century', *Journal of Organisational Change Management*, Vol. 2 No. 1, 7.

Bennis, W. and Nanus, B. (1985), *Leaders: The Strategies for Taking Charge*, New York: Harper and Row.

Bryman, A. (1993), 'Charismatic leadership in business organisations: some neglected issues', *Leadership Quarterly*, Vol. 4, 289–304.

Burns, J. (1978), *Leadership*, New York: Harper and Row.

Conger, J. and Kanungo, R. (1988), *Charismatic Leadership*, San Fransisco: Jossey Bass.

Dawson, S. (1996), *Analysing Organisations*, London: Macmillan.

Fiedler, F. (1967), *A Theory of Leadership Effectiveness*, New York: McGraw-Hill.

Fiedler, F. and Chemers, M. (1974), *Leadership and Effective Management*, Scott, Foresman and Co.

Finkelstein, S. and Hambrick, D. (1996), *Strategic Leadership: Top Executives and their Effects on Organisations*, St Paul: West Publishing Company.

Flood, P., Min Fong, C., Smith, K., O'Regan, P., Moore, S. and Morley, M. (1997), 'Top management teams and pioneering: a resource-based view', *International Journal of Human Resource Management*, Vol. 8 No. 3.

Flood, P. and Smith, K. (1994), *Top Management Team Cohesiveness: Impact on Company Performance*, Paper presented to College of Business Conference, Building and Effective and Cohesive Top Management Team, University of Limerick, May.

Gibb, C. (1947), 'The principles and traits of leadership', *Journal of Abnormal and Social Psychology*, Vol. 42, 267–84.

Goldsmith, W. and Clutterbuck, D. (1984), *The Winning Streak*, London: Weidenfeld and Nicolson.

Hambrick, D. (1994), 'Top management groups: a conceptual integration and reconsideration of the "team" label', *Research in Organizational Behaviour*, Vol. 16, 171–213.

Hambrick, D. and Mason, P. (1984), 'Upper echelons: the organization as a reflection of its top managers', *Academy of Management Review*, Vol. 9, 193–206.

Hersey, P. and Blanchard, K. (1993), *Management of Organizational Behaviour: Utilizing Human Resources*, New York: Prentice Hall.

House, R. (1971), 'A path-goal theory of leader effectiveness', *Administrative Science Quarterly*, Vol. 16, September, 321–38.

House, R. (1977), 'A 1976 theory of charismatic leadership', in Hunt, J. and Larson, L. (eds), *Leadership: The Cutting Edge*, Carbondale Il.: Southern Illinois University Press.

House, R. and Aditya, R. (1997), 'The social scientific study of leadership: quo vadis?', *Journal of Management*, Vol. 23 No. 3, 409–73.

Keating, M., Martin, G. and Donnelly-Cox, G. (1996), 'The GLOBE Project: A Case for Interdisciplinary and Intercultural Research', in *Proceedings of the 1st Irish Academy of Management Conference, Management Research in Ireland: The Way Forward*, University College Cork, 12–13 September.

Krech, D., Crutchfield, R. and Ballachey, E. (1962), *Individual in Society*, New York: McGraw-Hill.

Likert, R. (1961), *New Patterns of Management*, New York: McGraw-Hill.

Luthans, F. (1992), *Organizational Behaviour*, New York: McGraw-Hill.

Manz, C. and Sims, H. (1989), *SuperLeadership: Leading Others to Lead Themselves*, New York: Prentice-Hall.

Manz, C. and Sims, H. (1991), 'SuperLeadership: beyond the myth of heroic leadership', *Organisational Dynamics*, Summer, 56–78.

Mintzberg, H. (1973), *The Nature of Managerial Work*, New York: Harper and Row.

Moore, S., Morley, M., Fong, C., O'Regan, P. and Smith, K. (1996), 'Taking the lead: an investigation into the process of top management pioneering', in Leavy, B. and Walsh, J. (eds), *Strategy and General Management: An Irish Reader*, Dublin: Oak Tree Press.

Morley, M., Moore, S. and O'Regan, P. (1996), 'The impact of the top management team on the sales growth performance of international divisions of US multinational enterprises operating in the Republic of Ireland', *Journal of Irish Business and Administrative Research*, Vol. 17 No. 1.

Mullins, L. (1991), *Management and Organisational Behaviour*, London: Pitman.

Perrow, C. (1973), *Organizational Dynamics*, Summer, 2–15.

Peters, T. and Austin, N. (1985), *A Passion for Excellence: The Leadership Difference*, New York: Random House.

Pettinger, R. (1994), *Introduction to Management*, London: Macmillan.

Robbins, S. (1991), *Organizational Behavior: Concepts, Controversies, and Applications*, Englewood Cliffs, New Jersey: Prentice-Hall.

Statt, D. (1994), *Psychology and the World of Work*, London: Macmillan.

Stogdill, R. (1948), 'Personal factors associated with leadership: a survey of the literature', *Journal of Psychology*, Vol. 25, 35–71.

Stogdill, R. and Coons, A. (1957), *Leader Behaviour: Its Description and Measurement*, Columbus OH: Ohio State University Press of Bureau for Business Research.

Tannenbaum, R., Weschler, I. and Masserik, F. (1961), *Leadership and Organization*, New York: McGraw-Hill.

Tichy, N. and Devanna, M. (1986), 'The transformational leader', *Training and Development Journal*, July, 30–2.

Yetton, P. (1984), 'Leadership and supervision', in Gruneberg, M. and Wall, T. (eds), *Social Psychology and Organizational Behaviour*, Chichester: Wiley.

Zaleznik, A. (1977), 'Managers and leaders: are they different?', *Harvard Business Review*, May–June, 67–78.

Chapter 11

Beaumont, P. B. and Townley, B. (1985), 'Greenfield sites, new plants and work practices', in Hammond, V. (ed.), *Current Research in Management*, London: Frances Pinter.

Beer, M., Spector, B., Lawrence, P. R., Quinn-Mills, D. and Walton, R. E. (1984), *Managing Human Assets: The Groundbreaking Harvard Business School Program*, New York: The Free Press: Macmillan.

Beer, M., Spector, B., Lawrence, P., Mills, D. and Walton, R. (1985), *Human Resource Management: A General Manager's Perspective*, New York: The Free Press.

Berggren, C. (1990), 'Det nya bilarbetet' ['The new automobile employment'], PhD dissertation, University of Lund, Sweden.

Blennerhassett, E. (1983), *Work Motivation and Personnel Practices: A Study of Civil Services Executive Staff*, Dublin: Institute of Public Administration.

Buchanan, D. (1994), 'Principles and practice of job design', in Sisson, K. (ed.), *Personnel Management: A Comprehensive Guide to Theory and Practice in Britain*, Oxford: Blackwell.

Buchanan, D. and Hucznyski A. (1991), *Organizational Behaviour: An Introductory Text*, Hemel Hempstead: Prentice Hall.

Buchanan, D. and McCalman, J. (1989), *High Performance Work Systems: The Digital Experience*, London: Routledge.

Delbridge, R. and Turnbull, P. (1992), 'Human resource maximization: the management of labour under just-in-time manufacturing systems' in Blyton, P. and Turnbull, P. (eds), *Reassessing Human Resource Management*, London: Sage.

European Industrial Relations Review (1992), 'Lean production – more of the same or revolution', *European Industrial Relations Review*, No. 223, August.

Gunnigle, P., Heraty, N. and Morley, M. (1997), *Personnel and Human Resource Management: Theory and Practice in Ireland*, Dublin: Gill & Macmillan.

Gunnigle, P., McMahon, G. and Fitzgerald, G. (1995), *Industrial Relations in Ireland: Theory and Practice*, Dublin: Gill & Macmillan.

Hackman, J. R. and Lawler, E. E. (1971), 'Employee reactions to job characteristics', *Journal of Applied Psychology Monograph*, Vol. 55, 259–286.

Hackman, J. and Oldham, G. (1980), *Work Redesign*, New York: Addison Wesley.

Hackman, J. R., Oldham, G., Janson, R. and Purdy, K. (1975), 'A new strategy for job enrichment', *California Management Review*, Vol. 17, 51–71.

Heilbroner, R. L. and Thurow, L. C. (1984), *The Economic Problem*, Englewood Cliffs, New Jersey: Prentice Hall.

Herzberg, F. (1968), 'One more time: how do you motivate employees?', *Harvard Business Review*, January/February, 115–25.

Income Data Services (1984), *Group Working and Greenfield Sites*, London: Incomes Data Services.

Kamata, S. (1984), *Japan in the Passing Lane*, London: Allen and Unwin.

Katz, J. (1996), 'The chicken trail: how Latino workers put food on America's tables', series in *Los Angeles Times*, Vols 10, 11 and 12, November.

Klein, J. A. (1989), 'The human costs of manufacturing reform', *Harvard Business Review*, March–April, 60–6.

Kochan, T., Katz, H. and McKersie (1986), *The Transformation of American Industrial Relations*, New York: Basic Books.

Lawler, E. E. (1978), 'The new plant revolution', *Organisational Dynamics*, Winter, 3–12.

Lawler, E. E. (1982), 'Increasing worker involvement to enhance organisational effectiveness', in Goodman, P. S. (ed.), *Change in Organisations*, San Francisco: Jossey Bass.

Lawler, E. E. (1986), *High Involvement Management: Participative Strategies for Improving Organizational Performance*, San Francisco: Jossey Bass.

Maccoby, M. (1988), *Why Work?: Motivating and Leading in the New Generation*, New York: Simon and Schuster.

Magee, C. (1991), 'A typical work forms and organisational flexibility', paper presented to the Institute of Public Administration Personnel Management Conference, Dublin, 6 March.

McGregor, D. (1960), *The Human Side of Enterprise*, New York: McGraw-Hill.

Mooney, P. (1988), 'From industrial relations to employee relations in Ireland', unpublished PhD thesis, Trinity College, Dublin.

Moss Kanter, R. (1983), *The Change Masters*, London: Unwin Hyman.

O'Connor, E. (1995), 'World class manufacturing in a semi-state environment: the case of Bord na Mona' in Gunnigle, P. and Roche, W. K. (eds), *New Challenges to Irish Industrial Relations*, Dublin: Oak Tree Press.

Perry, B. (1984), *Enfield: A High Performance System*, Bedford, Massachusetts: Digital Equipment Corporation, Educational Services Development and Publishing.

Peters, T. and Waterman, R. (1982), *In Search of Excellence: Lessons from America's Best-run Companies*, New York: Harper and Row.

Quinn Mills, D. (1991), *Rebirth of the Corporation*, New York: John Wiles and Sons.

Roche, W. K. and Gunnigle, P. (1995), 'Competition and the new industrial relations agenda' in Gunnigle, P. and Roche, W. K. (eds), *New Challenges to Irish Industrial Relations*, Dublin: Oak Tree Press.

Schermerhorn, J. R., Hunt, J. G. and Osborn, R. N. (1985), *Managing Organizational Behavior*, New York: Wiley.

Sewell, G. and Wilkinson, B. (1992), 'Empowerment or emasculation? Shopfloor surveillance in a total quality organisation' in Blyton, P. and Turnbull, P. (eds), *Reassessing Human Resource Management*, London: Sage.

Schuler, R. S. and Jackson, S. E., (1996), *Human Resource Management: Positioning for the 21st Century*, St Paul, Minneapolis: West.

Skrovan, D. J. (1983), *Quality of Work Life*, Reading, Mass: Addison-Wesley.

Steers, R. M. and Porter, L. W. (1987), *Motivation and Work Behavior*, New York: McGraw-Hill.

Sweeney, P. (1997), 'Structure, strategy and new product development in the automotive supply industry', unpublished MBS thesis, University of Limerick.

Taylor, F. W. (1947), *Scientific Management*, New York: Harper and Bros.

Tiernan, S. D., Morley, M. J. and Foley, E. (1996), *Modern Management: Theory and Practice for Irish Students*, Dublin: Gill & Macmillan.

Vaill, P. B. (1982), 'The purposing of high-performing systems', *Organizational Dynamics*, Autumn, 23–39.

Walton, R. E. (1973), 'Quality of working life: what is it?', *Sloan Management Review*, Vol. 15, Fall, 11–21.

Womack, J. P., Jones, D. T. and Roos, D. (1990), *The Machine that Changed the World*, New York: Rawson Associates.

Chapter 12

Adler, N. J. (1983), 'Cross-cultural management research: The ostrich and the trend', *Academy of Management Review*, Vol. 6, 65–83.

Allen, V. (1971), *The Sociology of Industrial Relations*, London: Longman.

Bendix, R. (1956), *Work and Authority in Industry*, New York: Wiley.

Blyton, P. and Turnbull, P. (1994), *The Dynamics of Employee Relations*, London: Macmillan.

Dunford, R. W. (1992), *Organisational Behaviour*, Wokingham, England: Addison-Wesley.

Edwards, P. K. (1986), *Conflict at Work*, Oxford: Blackwell.

Fayol, H. (1949), *General and Industrial Management*, London: Pitman.

Fox, A., (1966), 'Industrial Sociology and Industrial Relations', Research Paper No. 3 to the Royal Commission on Trade Unions and Employers' Associations, London: HMSO.

Fox, A. (1973), 'Industrial Relations: A Critique of Pluralist Ideology' in Child, J. (ed.), *Man and Organisation*, New York: Halstead Press.

Gibson, J. L., Ivancevich, J. M. and Donnelly, J. H. (1994), *Organizations: Behavior, Structure, Process*, Burr Ridge, Illinois: Irwin.

Gunnigle, P. (1995), 'Collectivism and the management of industrial relations in greenfield sites', *Human Resource Management Journal*, Vol. 5 No. 3, 24–40.

Gunnigle, P., McMahon, G.V., and Fitzgerald, G. (1995), *Industrial Relations in Ireland: Theory and Practice*, Dublin: Gill & Macmillan.

Gunnigle, P. and Brady, T. (1984), 'The Management of Industrial Relations in the Small Firm', *Employee Relations*, Vol. 6 No. 5.

Gunnigle, P., McMahon, G.V. and Fitzgerald, G. (1995), *Industrial Relations in Ireland: Theory and Practice*, Dublin: Gill & Macmillan.

Hofstede, G. (1980), *Culture's Consequences: International Differences in Work Related Values*, Beverley Hills: Sage.

Hofstede, G. (1991), *Cultures and Organizations: Software of the Mind*, London: McGraw-Hill.

Huczynski, A. A. and Buchanan, D. A. (1991), *Organizational Behaviour: An Introductory Text*, London: Prentice Hall.

Humphrey, P. (1979), *How To Be Your Own Personnel Manager*, London: Institute of Personnel Management.

King, A. Y. C. and Bond, M. H. (1985), 'The Confucian paradigm of man: A sociological view', in Tseng, W. and Wu, D. (eds), *Chinese Culture and Mental Health: An Overview*, New York: Academic Press.

Kochan, T. A., Katz, H. C. and McKersie, R. B. (1986), *The Transformation of American Industrial Relations*, New York: Basic Books.

McGovern, P. (1989), 'Union Recognition and Union Avoidance in the 1980s', in *Industrial Relations in Ireland: Contemporary Issues and Developments*, Dublin: University College, Dublin.

McMahon, J. (1996), 'Employee Relations in Small Firms in Ireland: An Exploratory Study of Small Manufacturing Firms', *Employee Relations*, Vol. 18 No. 5, 66–80.

Marchington, M. (1982), *Managing Industrial Relations*, London: McGraw-Hill.

Mintzberg, H. (1978), 'Patterns in Strategy Formulation', *Management Science*, Vol. 24, May. 934–48.

Mintzberg, H. (1988), 'Opening up the Definition of Strategy', in Quinn, J., Mintzberg, H. and Rames, R. (eds), *The Strategy Process: Concepts, Contexts and Cases*, Englewood Cliffs, New Jersey: Prentice-Hall.

Open University, (1985), 'International Perspectives', Unit 16, Block 5, *Managing in Organizations*, Milton Keynes: Open University Press.

Poole, M., (1986), 'Managerial Strategies and Styles in Industrial Relations: A Comparative Analysis', *Journal of General Management*, Vol. 12 No. 1, 40–53.

Reed, M. (1989), *The Sociology of Management*, Hemel Hempstead, England: Harvester Wheatsheaf.

Robbins, S. P. (1974), *Managing Organizational Conflict*, Englewood Cliffs, New Jersey: Prentice Hall.

Robbins, S. P. (1978), '"Conflict management" and "conflict resolution" are not synonymous terms', *California Management Review*, 21, 67–75.

Robbins, S. P. (1986), *Organizational Behaviour, Concepts, Controversies, and Applications*, Englewood Cliffs, New Jersey: Prentice Hall.

Rollinson, D. (1993), *Understanding Employee Relations*, Wokingham, England: Addison-Wesley.

Rothenberg, H. I. and Silverman, S. B. (1973), *Labor Unions: How To Avert Them, Beat Them, Out-Negotiate Them, Live With Them, Unload Them*, Elkins Park, Penn: Management Relations Inc.

Salaman, M. (1992), *Industrial Relations: Theory and Practice*, London: Prentice Hall.

Schermerhorn, J. R., Hunt, J. G. and Osborn, R. N. (1985), *Managing Organizational Behavior*, New York: Wiley.

Sparrow, P. and Hiltrop, J. M. (1994), *European Human Resource Management in Transition*, Hemel Hempstead, UK: Prentice Hall.

Tang, S. F. Y. and Kirkbridge, P. S. (1986), 'Developing conflict management in Hong Kong: An analysis of some cross cultural implications', *Management Education and Development*, Vol.17, Part 3, 287–301.

Taylor, F. (1911), *The Principles of Scientific Management*, New York: Harper.

Thomas, K. (1976), 'Conflict and Conflict Management', in Dunnette, M. D. (ed.), *Handbook of Industrial and Organisational Psychology*, Chicago: Rand McNally.

Thomas, K. (1977), 'Towards a multi-dimensional values in teaching: the example of conflict behaviors', *Academy of Management Review*, 2, July 1977, 484–90.

Chapter 13

Alderson, S. and Kakabodse, A. (1994), 'Business Ethics and Irish Management: A Cross Cultural Study', *European Management Journal*, Vol. 12 No. 4, 432–41.

Alen, R., Madison, D., Portor, L., Renwick, P. and Mayers, B. (1979), 'Organisational politics: tactics and characteristics of its actors', *California Management Review*, Vol. 22, Fall.

Bacharach, S. and Lawler, E. (1980), *Power and Politics in Organizations*, London: Jossey-Bass.

Baumhart, R. (1961), 'How ethical are business men?', *Harvard Business Review*, Vol. 39 No. 4, 6–8.

Bernard, C. (1938), *The Function of the Executive*, Cambridge, Mass.: Harvard University Press.

Carr, A. (1968), 'Is business bluffing ethical?', *Harvard Business Review*, Vol. 46 No. 1, 145.

Cyert, R. and March, T. (1963), *A Behavioural Theory of the Firm*, Englewood Cliffs, New Jersey: Prentice Hall.

Dahl, R. (1957), 'The concept of power', *Behavioural Science*, Vol. 2 No. 1, 201–15.

Dawson, S. (1996), *Analysing Organisations*, 3rd edition, London: Macmillan.

Dixon, M. (1982), 'The world of office politics', *Financial Times*, 10 November.

Dobbs, J. (1993), 'The empowerment environment', *Training and Development*, February, 55–7.

Finchman, R. and Rhodes, P. (1988), *The Individual, Work and Organization: Behavioural Studies for Business and Management Students*, London: Weidenfeld and Nicolson.

French, J. and Raven, B. (1959), 'The bases of social power', in Cartwright, L. and Zander, A. (eds), *Group Dynamics: Research and Theory*, London: Tavistock.

Garavan, T., Fitzgerald, G. and Morley, M. (1993), *Business Analysis: Books I and II*, London: Certified Accountants Educational Trust.

Green, R. (1994), *The Ethical Manager: A New Method for Business Ethics*, New York: Macmillan College Publishing.

Hanson, K. (1988), 'Why we teach ethics in business school', *Stanford Business School Magazine*, February, 14–6.

Hardy, C. and Clegg, S. (1996), 'Some dare call it power', in Clegg, S., Hardy, C. and Nord, W. (eds), *Handbook of Organization Studies*, London: Sage.

Hatch, M. J. (1997), *Organization Theory: Modern Symbolic and Postmodern Perspectives*, Oxford: University Press.

Hickson, D. (1990), 'Politics permeate,' in Wilson, D. and Rosenfeld, R., *Managing Organizations: Text, Readings and Cases*, London: McGraw-Hill, 175–81.

Hickson, D., Hinings, C., Lee, C., Schneck, R. and Pennings, J. (1971), 'A strategic contingencies theory of intraorganisational power', *Administrative Science Quarterly*, Vol. 16 No. 2, 216–29.

Hollander, E. and Offermann, L. (1990), 'Power and leadership in organizations', *American Psychologist*, February, 184.

Lasswell, H. (1936), *Politics: Who Gets What, When, How*, New York: McGraw-Hill.

Levin, M. (1990), 'Ethics courses: useless', *New York Times*, 25 November.

Luthans, F. (1992), *Organizational Behaviour*, 6th edition, New York: McGraw-Hill.

Pettigrew, A. (1973), *The Politics of Organisational Decision-Making*, London: Tavistock.

Pettigrew, A. (1974), 'The influence process between specialists and executives', *Personnel Review*, Vol. 3 No. 1, 24–30.

Pfeffer, J. (1981), *Power in Organisations*, London: Pitman.

Porter, M. (1985), *Competitive Advantage: Creating and Sustaining Superior Performance*, New York: The Free Press.

Reitz, H. (1987), *Behaviour in Organisations*, 3rd edition, Homewood, Ill.: Irwin.

Rest, J. (1988), 'Can ethics be taught in professional schools? The psychological research', *Easier Said Than Done*, Winter.

Shepard, H. (1967), 'Innovation resisting and innovation producing organisation', *Journal of Business*, Vol. 40, 470–7.

Statt, D. (1994), *Psychology and the World of Work*, London: Macmillan.

Tyson, S. and Jackson, T. (1992), *The Essence of Organizational Behaviour*, Hemel Hempstead: Prentice Hall International.

Trevino, L. and Nelson, K. (1995), *Managing Business Ethics: Straight Talk About How To Do It Right*, New York: Wiley.

Weber, M. (1947), *The Theory of Social and Economic Organisation*, New York: Free Press.

Chapter 14

Baron, R. and Greenberg, J. (1992), *Behaviour in Organisations*, Boston: Allyn and Bacon.

Benjamin, G. and Mabey, C. (1993), 'Facilitating radical change', in Mabey, C. and Mayon-White, B. (eds), *Managing Change*, 2nd edition, London: The Open University/Paul Chapman.

Bennis, W. (1969), *Organisational Development: Its Nature, Origins and Prospects*, Reading, MA: Addison-Wesley.

Blacker, F. and Brown, C. (1986), 'Alternative models to guide the design and implementation of the new information technologies into work organisation', *Journal of Occupational Psychology*, No. 59, 287–313.

Bullock, R. J. and Batten, D. (1985), 'It's just a phase we're going through: a review and synthesis of OD phase analysis', *Group and Organisational Studies*, Vol. 10, December, 383–412.

Burke, W. (1982), *Organisational Development*, Boston: Little Brown, 10.

Burnes, B. (1996), *Managing Change*, 2nd edition, London: Pitman.

Burnes, B. (1996), 'No such thing as . . . a "one best way" to manage organisational change', *Management Decision*, Vol. 34 No. 10, 11–8.

Child, J. (1972), 'Organisational structure, environment and performance: the role of strategic choice', *Sociology*, Vol. 6 No. 1, 1–22.

Cummings, T. and Huse, E. (1989), *Organisation development and Change*, St. Paul Minneapolis: West Publishing.

Dawson, P. (1996), *Organisational Change: A Processual Approach*, London: Paul Chapman.

Dawson, S. (1996), *Analysing Organisations*, London: Macmillan.

Dunphy, D. and Stace, D. (1993), 'The strategic management of corporate change', *Human Relations*, Vol. 46 No. 8, 905–18.

French, W. and Bell, C. (1984), *Organisational Development*, Englewood Cliffs, New Jersey: Prentice Hall.

Furnham, A. (1997), *The Psychology of Behaviour at Work*, London: Psychological Press.

Garvin, D. A. (1993), 'Building a learning organisation', *Harvard Business Review*, July/August, 78–91.

Guest, D. (1990), 'HRM and the American Dream', *Journal of Management Studies*, July, 388.

Handy, C. (1986), *Understanding Organisations*, Harmondsworth: Penguin.

Hussey, D. E. (1995), *How to Manage Change*, London: Kogan Page.

Kotter, J. and Schlesinger, L. (1979), 'Choosing strategies for change', *Harvard Business Review*, March/April, 106–14.

Lewin, K. (1958), 'Group decisions and social change', in Swanson, G. E., Newcomb, T. M., and Hartley, E. L. (eds), *Readings in Social Psychology*, New York: Holt, Rhinehart and Winston.

Lippitt, R., Watson, J. and Westley, B. (1958), *The Dynamics of Planned Change*, New York: Harcourt, Brace and World.

Lundberg, C. (1991), 'Towards a conceptual understanding of organisation development', *Journal of Organisational Change Management*, Vol. 4 No. 4, 6–15.

Luthans, F. (1992), *Organisational Behaviour*, New York: McGraw-Hill.

Mabey, C. and Mayon-White, B. (1993), *Managing Change*, 2nd edition, London: The Open University/Paul Chapman.

March, J. (1981), 'Footnotes on organisation change', *Administrative Science Quarterly*, Vol. 26 No. 4, 563–72.

Montgomery, C. A. and Porter, M. (1991), 'Strategy: seeking and securing competitive advantage', *Harvard Business Review*, Boston, MA.

Mullins, L. (1991), *Management and Organisation Behaviour*, London: Pitman.

Nord, W. (1974), 'The failure of current applied behaviour science: a Marxian perspective', *The Journal of Applied Behavioural Science*, No. 10, 557–78.

Robbins, R. (1991), *Organisational Behaviour: Concepts, Controversies and Applications*, Englewood Cliffs, New Jersey: Prentice Hall.

Peters, T. (1987), *Thriving on Chaos*, New York: Knopf.

Pettigrew, A. and Whipp, R. (1993), *Managing Change for Competitive Success*, London, Blackwell.

Schein, E. (1990), 'Organisational culture', *American Psychologist*, February, 117.

Scott, W. R. (1987), *Organisations: Rational, Natural and Open Systems*, Englewood Cliffs, New Jersey: Prentice Hall.

Stacey, R. (1993), *Strategic Management and Organisational Dynamics*, London: Pitman.

Tersine, T., Harvey, M. and Buckley, M. (1997), 'Shifting organisational paradigms: transitional management', *European Management Journal*, Vol. 15 No. 1, 45–57.

Tiernan, S. (1996), 'From bureaucratic to network organisation: the management of change and the outcomes at Team Aer Lingus' in *Proceedings of The First Irish Academy of Management Conference, Management Research in Ireland: The Way Forward*, Cork, University College, September.

Vaill, P. B. (1989), *Managing as a Performing Art*, San Francisco: Jossey-Bass.

Walton, R. (1975), 'The diffusion of New Work structures: explaining why success didn't take', *Organisational Dynamics*, Winter, 3–22.

Warrick, D. D. (1984), *MODMAN: Managing Organisational Change and Development*, New Jersey: Science Research Associates Inc.

Wilson, D. C. (1992), *A Strategy of Change*, London: Routledge.

Wilson, G. (1993), *Making Change Happen*, London: Pitman.

Index

learning organisation paradigm, 96-102
    characteristics of, 99, 101
learning theory
    application of, 92-102
    learning organisation paradigm, 96-102
    transfer of learning, 95-6
Leavitt, B. and March, J., 84
legitimate power, 290
Levin, M., 303
Lewin, K., 131, 314, 315-16, 329
life experiences
    and personality, 22
Likert, Rensis, 211, 212
Lippitt, R. *et al.*, 316-17
listening skills, 119-20, 127
lock-out, 270
locus of control, 23-5
Louis, Meryl Reis, 185
Ludlow, R. and Panton, F., 112
Luhmann, N., 113
Lundberg, C., 323-4
Luthans, F., 88, 90, 111, 210, 219, 287
    OD, 324
    power, 289, 290, 292-3
Luthans, F. and Larsen, J., 120-21

McCarthy, M., 139
McClave, H., 111, 114, 122, 124
McClelland, David
    achievement motivation theory, 63-5
Maccoby, M., 240
McGehee, W., 84
McGill, M. *et al.*, 98
McGovern, P., 280
McGrath, A., 76
McGregor, D., 41-2, 233
    Theory X, Theory Y, 232
Machiavelli Test, 308-10
McMahon, J., 267
McNeill, P., 5
Magee, C., 246
management. *see also* conflict
    change management, 313-31
    classical theories, 177-8, 262
    communication problems, 120-22
    competitive cultures, 13-15
    contingency theories, 178-82

ethics, 302-10
Fayol's principles, 177
of groups, 148-50
and leadership, 204-7
and 'new' workforce, 11-12
and teamwork, 163
total quality management, 12
managerial grid, 212-14
Manz, C. and Sims, H., 203-4
Marchington, M., 13, 266, 267
Marcic, D., 140
Marxism, 264, 298
masculinity/femininity, 48, 198-200
Maslow, A.H., 55, 56, 129
    critique of theory, 62-3
    hierarchy of needs theory, 61-3
mass production, 179
Massachusetts Institute of Technology, 252-3
Mayo, Elton, 133-4
Mayrhofer, W. *et al.*, 113
Miles, E.W. *et al.*, 73
Milgram, S., 27
Mills, A.J. and Simmons, T., 133, 134
Mills, A. and Murgatroyd, J., 134
Mintzberg, H., 113, 172, 183
    contingency theory, 179-82
    leadership, 204-5
    organisation structure, 175-6
Mischel, W., 27
money
    as motivator, 66-7
Montgomery, C.A. and Porter, M., 319
Mooney, M., 11-12, 253
Moore, S. and Punnett, B., 49
Moore, S. *et al.*, 159
Moreland, R.L. and Levine, J.M., 138
Morgan, G., 134, 187
Morley, M. *et al.*, 223
Moss-Kanter, R., 11, 243
motivation
    defining, 56-60
    guiding behaviour, 57
    need/content theories, 57, 60-67
    process theories, 57, 67-76
    stimulating behaviour, 56-7
motivation *continued*
    and stress, 55, 76-8